MW00975290

\

GNAT User's Guide

GNAT, The GNU Ada Compiler
For GCC version 4.3.3

(GCC)

AdaCore

ISBN 1441437266

Printed in America

Published & distributed under the terms of the GNU Free Documentation Licence by SoHoBooks

http://www.gnu.org
http://gcc.gnu.org/onlinedocs/

About This Guide

This guide describes the use of GNAT, a compiler and software development toolset for the full Ada programming language. It documents the features of the compiler and tools, and explains how to use them to build Ada applications.

GNAT implements Ada 95 and Ada 2005, and it may also be invoked in Ada 83 compatibility mode. By default, GNAT assumes Ada 2005, but you can override with a compiler switch (see Section 3.2.9 [Compiling Different Versions of Ada], page 66) to explicitly specify the language version. Throughout this manual, references to "Ada" without a year suffix apply to both the Ada 95 and Ada 2005 versions of the language.

What This Guide Contains

This guide contains the following chapters:

- Chapter 1 [Getting Started with GNAT], page 5, describes how to get started compiling and running Ada programs with the GNAT Ada programming environment.
- Chapter 2 [The GNAT Compilation Model], page 13, describes the compilation model used by GNAT.
- Chapter 3 [Compiling Using gcc], page 37, describes how to compile Ada programs with gcc, the Ada compiler.
- Chapter 4 [Binding Using gnatbind], page 79, describes how to perform binding of Ada programs with gnatbind, the GNAT binding utility.
- Chapter 5 [Linking Using gnatlink], page 89, describes gnatlink, a program that provides for linking using the GNAT run-time library to construct a program. gnatlink can also incorporate foreign language object units into the executable.
- Chapter 6 [The GNAT Make Program gnatmake], page 93, describes gnatmake, a utility that automatically determines the set of sources needed by an Ada compilation unit, and executes the necessary compilations binding and link.
- Chapter 7 [Improving Performance], page 103, shows various techniques for making your Ada program run faster or take less space. It discusses the effect of the compiler's optimization switch and also describes the gnatelim tool and unused subprogram/data elimination.
- Chapter 8 [Renaming Files Using gnatchop], page 115, describes gnatchop, a utility that allows you to preprocess a file that contains Ada source code, and split it into one or more new files, one for each compilation unit.
- Chapter 9 [Configuration Pragmas], page 119, describes the configuration pragmas handled by GNAT.
- Chapter 10 [Handling Arbitrary File Naming Conventions Using gnatname], page 121, shows how to override the default GNAT file naming conventions, either for an individual unit or globally.
- Chapter 11 [GNAT Project Manager], page 125, describes how to use project files to organize large projects.
- Chapter 12 [The Cross-Referencing Tools gnatxref and gnatfind], page 165, discusses gnatxref and gnatfind, two tools that provide an easy way to navigate through sources.

- Chapter 13 [The GNAT Pretty-Printer gnatpp], page 175, shows how to produce a reformatted version of an Ada source file with control over casing, indentation, comment placement, and other elements of program presentation style.
- Chapter 14 [The GNAT Metric Tool gnatmetric], page 187, shows how to compute various metrics for an Ada source file, such as the number of types and subprograms, and assorted complexity measures.
- Chapter 15 [File Name Krunching Using gnatkr], page 195, describes the `gnatkr` file name krunching utility, used to handle shortened file names on operating systems with a limit on the length of names.
- Chapter 16 [Preprocessing Using gnatprep], page 199, describes `gnatprep`, a preprocessor utility that allows a single source file to be used to generate multiple or parameterized source files by means of macro substitution.
- Chapter 17 [The GNAT Library Browser gnatls], page 203, describes `gnatls`, a utility that displays information about compiled units, including dependences on the corresponding sources files, and consistency of compilations.
- Chapter 18 [Cleaning Up Using gnatclean], page 207, describes `gnatclean`, a utility to delete files that are produced by the compiler, binder and linker.
- Chapter 19 [GNAT and Libraries], page 209, describes the process of creating and using Libraries with GNAT. It also describes how to recompile the GNAT run-time library.
- Chapter 20 [Using the GNU make Utility], page 217, describes some techniques for using the GNAT toolset in Makefiles.
- Chapter 21 [Memory Management Issues], page 223, describes some useful predefined storage pools and in particular the GNAT Debug Pool facility, which helps detect incorrect memory references. It also describes `gnatmem`, a utility that monitors dynamic allocation and deallocation and helps detect "memory leaks".
- Chapter 22 [Stack Related Facilities], page 231, describes some useful tools associated with stack checking and analysis.
- Chapter 23 [Verifying Properties Using gnatcheck], page 233, discusses `gnatcheck`, a utility that checks Ada code against a set of rules.
- Chapter 24 [Creating Sample Bodies Using gnatstub], page 251, discusses `gnatstub`, a utility that generates empty but compilable bodies for library units.
- Chapter 25 [Other Utility Programs], page 253, discusses several other GNAT utilities, including `gnathtml`.
- Chapter 26 [Running and Debugging Ada Programs], page 257, describes how to run and debug Ada programs.
- Appendix A [Platform-Specific Information for the Run-Time Libraries], page 271, describes the various run-time libraries supported by GNAT on various platforms and explains how to choose a particular library.
- Appendix B [Example of Binder Output File], page 277, shows the source code for the binder output file for a sample program.
- Appendix C [Elaboration Order Handling in GNAT], page 291, describes how GNAT helps you deal with elaboration order issues.
- Appendix D [Conditional Compilation], page 317, describes how to model conditional compilation, both with Ada in general and with GNAT facilities in particular.

- Appendix E [Inline Assembler], page 323, shows how to use the inline assembly facility in an Ada program.
- Appendix F [Compatibility and Porting Guide], page 333, contains sections on compatibility of GNAT with other Ada development environments (including Ada 83 systems), to assist in porting code from those environments.
- Appendix G [Microsoft Windows Topics], page 343, presents information relevant to the Microsoft Windows platform.

What You Should Know before Reading This Guide

This guide assumes a basic familiarity with the Ada 95 language, as described in the International Standard ANSI/ISO/IEC-8652:1995, January 1995. It does not require knowledge of the new features introduced by Ada 2005, (officially known as ISO/IEC 8652:1995 with Technical Corrigendum 1 and Amendment 1). Both reference manuals are included in the GNAT documentation package.

Related Information

For further information about related tools, refer to the following documents:

- *GNAT Reference Manual*, which contains all reference material for the GNAT implementation of Ada.
- *Using the GNAT Programming Studio*, which describes the GPS Integrated Development Environment.
- *GNAT Programming Studio Tutorial*, which introduces the main GPS features through examples.
- *Ada 95 Reference Manual*, which contains reference material for the Ada 95 programming language.
- *Ada 2005 Reference Manual*, which contains reference material for the Ada 2005 programming language.
- *Debugging with GDB* contains all details on the use of the GNU source-level debugger.
- *GNU Emacs Manual* contains full information on the extensible editor and programming environment Emacs.

Conventions

Following are examples of the typographical and graphic conventions used in this guide:

- `Functions`, `utility program` names, `standard` names, and `classes`.
- 'Option flags'
- 'File Names', 'button names', and 'field names'.
- *Variables*.
- *Emphasis*.
- [optional information or parameters]
- Examples are described by text
        `and then shown this way.`

Commands that are entered by the user are preceded in this manual by the characters "$ " (dollar sign followed by space). If your system uses this sequence as a prompt, then the commands will appear exactly as you see them in the manual. If your system uses some other prompt, then the command will appear with the $ replaced by whatever prompt character you are using.

Full file names are shown with the "/" character as the directory separator; e.g., 'parent-dir/subdir/myfile.adb'. If you are using GNAT on a Windows platform, please note that the "\" character should be used instead.

1 Getting Started with GNAT

This chapter describes some simple ways of using GNAT to build executable Ada programs. Section 1.1 [Running GNAT], page 5, through Section 1.4 [Using the gnatmake Utility], page 8, show how to use the command line environment. Section 1.5 [Introduction to GPS], page 8, provides a brief introduction to the GNAT Programming Studio, a visually-oriented Integrated Development Environment for GNAT. GPS offers a graphical "look and feel", support for development in other programming languages, comprehensive browsing features, and many other capabilities. For information on GPS please refer to *Using the GNAT Programming Studio*.

1.1 Running GNAT

Three steps are needed to create an executable file from an Ada source file:

1. The source file(s) must be compiled.
2. The file(s) must be bound using the GNAT binder.
3. All appropriate object files must be linked to produce an executable.

All three steps are most commonly handled by using the `gnatmake` utility program that, given the name of the main program, automatically performs the necessary compilation, binding and linking steps.

1.2 Running a Simple Ada Program

Any text editor may be used to prepare an Ada program. (If `Emacs` is used, the optional Ada mode may be helpful in laying out the program.) The program text is a normal text file. We will assume in our initial example that you have used your editor to prepare the following standard format text file:

```
with Ada.Text_IO; use Ada.Text_IO;
procedure Hello is
begin
   Put_Line ("Hello WORLD!");
end Hello;
```

This file should be named 'hello.adb'. With the normal default file naming conventions, GNAT requires that each file contain a single compilation unit whose file name is the unit name, with periods replaced by hyphens; the extension is 'ads' for a spec and 'adb' for a body. You can override this default file naming convention by use of the special pragma `Source_File_Name` (see Section 2.4 [Using Other File Names], page 17). Alternatively, if you want to rename your files according to this default convention, which is probably more convenient if you will be using GNAT for all your compilations, then the `gnatchop` utility can be used to generate correctly-named source files (see Chapter 8 [Renaming Files Using gnatchop], page 115).

You can compile the program using the following command (`$` is used as the command prompt in the examples in this document):

```
$ gcc -c hello.adb
```

`gcc` is the command used to run the compiler. This compiler is capable of compiling programs in several languages, including Ada and C. It assumes that you have given it an Ada program if the file extension is either '`.ads`' or '`.adb`', and it will then call the GNAT compiler to compile the specified file.

The '`-c`' switch is required. It tells `gcc` to only do a compilation. (For C programs, `gcc` can also do linking, but this capability is not used directly for Ada programs, so the '`-c`' switch must always be present.)

This compile command generates a file '`hello.o`', which is the object file corresponding to your Ada program. It also generates an "Ada Library Information" file '`hello.ali`', which contains additional information used to check that an Ada program is consistent. To build an executable file, use `gnatbind` to bind the program and `gnatlink` to link it. The argument to both `gnatbind` and `gnatlink` is the name of the '`ALI`' file, but the default extension of '`.ali`' can be omitted. This means that in the most common case, the argument is simply the name of the main program:

```
$ gnatbind hello
$ gnatlink hello
```

A simpler method of carrying out these steps is to use `gnatmake`, a master program that invokes all the required compilation, binding and linking tools in the correct order. In particular, `gnatmake` automatically recompiles any sources that have been modified since they were last compiled, or sources that depend on such modified sources, so that "version skew" is avoided.

```
$ gnatmake hello.adb
```

The result is an executable program called '`hello`', which can be run by entering:

```
$ hello
```

assuming that the current directory is on the search path for executable programs.

and, if all has gone well, you will see

```
Hello WORLD!
```

appear in response to this command.

1.3 Running a Program with Multiple Units

Consider a slightly more complicated example that has three files: a main program, and the spec and body of a package:

```
package Greetings is
   procedure Hello;
   procedure Goodbye;
end Greetings;

with Ada.Text_IO; use Ada.Text_IO;
package body Greetings is
   procedure Hello is
   begin
      Put_Line ("Hello WORLD!");
   end Hello;

   procedure Goodbye is
   begin
      Put_Line ("Goodbye WORLD!");
   end Goodbye;
end Greetings;

with Greetings;
procedure Gmain is
begin
   Greetings.Hello;
   Greetings.Goodbye;
end Gmain;
```

Following the one-unit-per-file rule, place this program in the following three separate files:

'greetings.ads'
          spec of package Greetings

'greetings.adb'
          body of package Greetings

'gmain.adb'
          body of main program

To build an executable version of this program, we could use four separate steps to compile, bind, and link the program, as follows:

```
$ gcc -c gmain.adb
$ gcc -c greetings.adb
$ gnatbind gmain
$ gnatlink gmain
```

Note that there is no required order of compilation when using GNAT. In particular it is perfectly fine to compile the main program first. Also, it is not necessary to compile package specs in the case where there is an accompanying body; you only need to compile the body. If you want to submit these files to the compiler for semantic checking and not code generation, then use the '-gnatc' switch:

```
$ gcc -c greetings.ads -gnatc
```

Although the compilation can be done in separate steps as in the above example, in practice it is almost always more convenient to use the **gnatmake** tool. All you need to know in this case is the name of the main program's source file. The effect of the above four commands can be achieved with a single one:

```
$ gnatmake gmain.adb
```

In the next section we discuss the advantages of using **gnatmake** in more detail.

1.4 Using the gnatmake Utility

If you work on a program by compiling single components at a time using gcc, you typically keep track of the units you modify. In order to build a consistent system, you compile not only these units, but also any units that depend on the units you have modified. For example, in the preceding case, if you edit 'gmain.adb', you only need to recompile that file. But if you edit 'greetings.ads', you must recompile both 'greetings.adb' and 'gmain.adb', because both files contain units that depend on 'greetings.ads'.

gnatbind will warn you if you forget one of these compilation steps, so that it is impossible to generate an inconsistent program as a result of forgetting to do a compilation. Nevertheless it is tedious and error-prone to keep track of dependencies among units. One approach to handle the dependency-bookkeeping is to use a makefile. However, makefiles present maintenance problems of their own: if the dependencies change as you change the program, you must make sure that the makefile is kept up-to-date manually, which is also an error-prone process.

The gnatmake utility takes care of these details automatically. Invoke it using either one of the following forms:

```
$ gnatmake gmain.adb
$ gnatmake gmain
```

The argument is the name of the file containing the main program; you may omit the extension. gnatmake examines the environment, automatically recompiles any files that need recompiling, and binds and links the resulting set of object files, generating the executable file, 'gmain'. In a large program, it can be extremely helpful to use gnatmake, because working out by hand what needs to be recompiled can be difficult.

Note that gnatmake takes into account all the Ada rules that establish dependencies among units. These include dependencies that result from inlining subprogram bodies, and from generic instantiation. Unlike some other Ada make tools, gnatmake does not rely on the dependencies that were found by the compiler on a previous compilation, which may possibly be wrong when sources change. gnatmake determines the exact set of dependencies from scratch each time it is run.

1.5 Introduction to GPS

Although the command line interface (gnatmake, etc.) alone is sufficient, a graphical Interactive Development Environment can make it easier for you to compose, navigate, and debug programs. This section describes the main features of GPS ("GNAT Programming Studio"), the GNAT graphical IDE. You will see how to use GPS to build and debug an executable, and you will also learn some of the basics of the GNAT "project" facility.

GPS enables you to do much more than is presented here; e.g., you can produce a call graph, interface to a third-party Version Control System, and inspect the generated assembly language for a program. Indeed, GPS also supports languages other than Ada. Such additional information, and an explanation of all of the GPS menu items. may be found in the on-line help, which includes a user's guide and a tutorial (these are also accessible from the GNAT startup menu).

1.5.1 Building a New Program with GPS

GPS invokes the GNAT compilation tools using information contained in a *project* (also known as a *project file*): a collection of properties such as source directories, identities of main subprograms, tool switches, etc., and their associated values. See Chapter 11 [GNAT Project Manager], page 125 for details. In order to run GPS, you will need to either create a new project or else open an existing one.

This section will explain how you can use GPS to create a project, to associate Ada source files with a project, and to build and run programs.

1. *Creating a project*

   Invoke GPS, either from the command line or the platform's IDE. After it starts, GPS will display a "Welcome" screen with three radio buttons:

   - `Start with default project in directory`
   - `Create new project with wizard`
   - `Open existing project`

   Select `Create new project with wizard` and press OK. A new window will appear. In the text box labeled with `Enter the name of the project to create`, type 'sample' as the project name. In the next box, browse to choose the directory in which you would like to create the project file. After selecting an appropriate directory, press `Forward`.

   A window will appear with the title `Version Control System Configuration`. Simply press `Forward`.

   A window will appear with the title `Please select the source directories for this project`. The directory that you specified for the project file will be selected by default as the one to use for sources; simply press `Forward`.

   A window will appear with the title `Please select the build directory for this project`. The directory that you specified for the project file will be selected by default for object files and executables; simply press `Forward`.

   A window will appear with the title `Please select the main units for this project`. You will supply this information later, after creating the source file. Simply press `Forward` for now.

   A window will appear with the title `Please select the switches to build the project`. Press `Apply`. This will create a project file named 'sample.prj' in the directory that you had specified.

2. *Creating and saving the source file*

   After you create the new project, a GPS window will appear, which is partitioned into two main sections:

   - A *Workspace area*, initially greyed out, which you will use for creating and editing source files
   - Directly below, a *Messages area*, which initially displays a "Welcome" message. (If the Messages area is not visible, drag its border upward to expand it.)

   Select `File` on the menu bar, and then the `New` command. The Workspace area will become white, and you can now enter the source program explicitly. Type the following text

```
with Ada.Text_IO; use Ada.Text_IO;
procedure Hello is
begin
   Put_Line("Hello from GPS!");
end Hello;
```

Select `File`, then `Save As`, and enter the source file name 'hello.adb'. The file will be saved in the same directory you specified as the location of the default project file.

3. *Updating the project file*

   You need to add the new source file to the project. To do this, select the `Project` menu and then `Edit project properties`. Click the `Main files` tab on the left, and then the `Add` button. Choose 'hello.adb' from the list, and press `Open`. The project settings window will reflect this action. Click `OK`.

4. *Building and running the program*

   In the main GPS window, now choose the `Build` menu, then `Make`, and select 'hello.adb'. The Messages window will display the resulting invocations of `gcc`, `gnatbind`, and `gnatlink` (reflecting the default switch settings from the project file that you created) and then a "successful compilation/build" message.

   To run the program, choose the `Build` menu, then `Run`, and select `hello`. An *Arguments Selection* window will appear. There are no command line arguments, so just click `OK`.

   The Messages window will now display the program's output (the string `Hello from GPS`), and at the bottom of the GPS window a status update is displayed (`Run: hello`). Close the GPS window (or select `File`, then `Exit`) to terminate this GPS session.

1.5.2 Simple Debugging with GPS

This section illustrates basic debugging techniques (setting breakpoints, examining/modifying variables, single stepping).

1. *Opening a project*

   Start GPS and select `Open existing project`; browse to specify the project file 'sample.prj' that you had created in the earlier example.

2. *Creating a source file*

   Select `File`, then `New`, and type in the following program:

```
with Ada.Text_IO; use Ada.Text_IO;
procedure Example is
   Line : String (1..80);
   N    : Natural;
begin
   Put_Line("Type a line of text at each prompt; an empty line to exit");
   loop
      Put(": ");
      Get_Line (Line, N);
      Put_Line (Line (1..N) );
      exit when N=0;
   end loop;
end Example;
```

   Select `File`, then `Save as`, and enter the file name 'example.adb'.

3. *Updating the project file*

   Add `Example` as a new main unit for the project:

    a. Select `Project`, then `Edit Project Properties`.

    b. Select the `Main files` tab, click `Add`, then select the file 'example.adb' from the list, and click `Open`. You will see the file name appear in the list of main units

    c. Click `OK`

4. *Building/running the executable*

To build the executable select `Build`, then `Make`, and then choose 'example.adb'.

Run the program to see its effect (in the Messages area). Each line that you enter is displayed; an empty line will cause the loop to exit and the program to terminate.

5. *Debugging the program*

Note that the '-g' switches to `gcc` and `gnatlink`, which are required for debugging, are on by default when you create a new project. Thus unless you intentionally remove these settings, you will be able to debug any program that you develop using GPS.

    a. *Initializing*

Select `Debug`, then `Initialize`, then 'example'

    b. *Setting a breakpoint*

After performing the initialization step, you will observe a small icon to the right of each line number. This serves as a toggle for breakpoints; clicking the icon will set a breakpoint at the corresponding line (the icon will change to a red circle with an "x"), and clicking it again will remove the breakpoint / reset the icon.

For purposes of this example, set a breakpoint at line 10 (the statement `Put_Line (Line (1..N));`

    c. *Starting program execution*

Select `Debug`, then `Run`. When the `Program Arguments` window appears, click `OK`. A console window will appear; enter some line of text, e.g. `abcde`, at the prompt. The program will pause execution when it gets to the breakpoint, and the corresponding line is highlighted.

    d. *Examining a variable*

Move the mouse over one of the occurrences of the variable N. You will see the value (5) displayed, in "tool tip" fashion. Right click on N, select `Debug`, then select `Display N`. You will see information about N appear in the `Debugger Data` pane, showing the value as 5.

    e. *Assigning a new value to a variable*

Right click on the N in the `Debugger Data` pane, and select `Set value of N`. When the input window appears, enter the value 4 and click `OK`. This value does not automatically appear in the `Debugger Data` pane; to see it, right click again on the N in the `Debugger Data` pane and select `Update value`. The new value, 4, will appear in red.

    f. *Single stepping*

Select `Debug`, then `Next`. This will cause the next statement to be executed, in this case the call of `Put_Line` with the string slice. Notice in the console window that the displayed string is simply `abcd` and not `abcde` which you had entered. This is because the upper bound of the slice is now 4 rather than 5.

g. *Removing a breakpoint*

   Toggle the breakpoint icon at line 10.

h. *Resuming execution from a breakpoint*

   Select `Debug`, then `Continue`. The program will reach the next iteration of the loop, and wait for input after displaying the prompt. This time, just hit the `Enter` key. The value of `N` will be 0, and the program will terminate. The console window will disappear.

2 The GNAT Compilation Model

This chapter describes the compilation model used by GNAT. Although similar to that used by other languages, such as C and C++, this model is substantially different from the traditional Ada compilation models, which are based on a library. The model is initially described without reference to the library-based model. If you have not previously used an Ada compiler, you need only read the first part of this chapter. The last section describes and discusses the differences between the GNAT model and the traditional Ada compiler models. If you have used other Ada compilers, this section will help you to understand those differences, and the advantages of the GNAT model.

2.1 Source Representation

Ada source programs are represented in standard text files, using Latin-1 coding. Latin-1 is an 8-bit code that includes the familiar 7-bit ASCII set, plus additional characters used for representing foreign languages (see Section 2.2 [Foreign Language Representation], page 13 for support of non-USA character sets). The format effector characters are represented using their standard ASCII encodings, as follows:

VT   Vertical tab, `16#0B#`

HT   Horizontal tab, `16#09#`

CR   Carriage return, `16#0D#`

LF   Line feed, `16#0A#`

FF   Form feed, `16#0C#`

Source files are in standard text file format. In addition, GNAT will recognize a wide variety of stream formats, in which the end of physical lines is marked by any of the following sequences: `LF`, `CR`, `CR-LF`, or `LF-CR`. This is useful in accommodating files that are imported from other operating systems.

The end of a source file is normally represented by the physical end of file. However, the control character `16#1A#` (`SUB`) is also recognized as signalling the end of the source file. Again, this is provided for compatibility with other operating systems where this code is used to represent the end of file.

Each file contains a single Ada compilation unit, including any pragmas associated with the unit. For example, this means you must place a package declaration (a package *spec*) and the corresponding body in separate files. An Ada *compilation* (which is a sequence of compilation units) is represented using a sequence of files. Similarly, you will place each subunit or child unit in a separate file.

2.2 Foreign Language Representation

GNAT supports the standard character sets defined in Ada as well as several other non-standard character sets for use in localized versions of the compiler (see Section 3.2.10 [Character Set Control], page 67).

2.2.1 Latin-1

The basic character set is Latin-1. This character set is defined by ISO standard 8859, part 1. The lower half (character codes `16#00#` ... `16#7F#`) is identical to standard ASCII coding, but the upper half is used to represent additional characters. These include extended letters used by European languages, such as French accents, the vowels with umlauts used in German, and the extra letter A-ring used in Swedish.

For a complete list of Latin-1 codes and their encodings, see the source file of library unit `Ada.Characters.Latin_1` in file 'a-chlat1.ads'. You may use any of these extended characters freely in character or string literals. In addition, the extended characters that represent letters can be used in identifiers.

2.2.2 Other 8-Bit Codes

GNAT also supports several other 8-bit coding schemes:

ISO 8859-2 (Latin-2)
> Latin-2 letters allowed in identifiers, with uppercase and lowercase equivalence.

ISO 8859-3 (Latin-3)
> Latin-3 letters allowed in identifiers, with uppercase and lowercase equivalence.

ISO 8859-4 (Latin-4)
> Latin-4 letters allowed in identifiers, with uppercase and lowercase equivalence.

ISO 8859-5 (Cyrillic)
> ISO 8859-5 letters (Cyrillic) allowed in identifiers, with uppercase and lowercase equivalence.

ISO 8859-15 (Latin-9)
> ISO 8859-15 (Latin-9) letters allowed in identifiers, with uppercase and lowercase equivalence

IBM PC (code page 437)
> This code page is the normal default for PCs in the U.S. It corresponds to the original IBM PC character set. This set has some, but not all, of the extended Latin-1 letters, but these letters do not have the same encoding as Latin-1. In this mode, these letters are allowed in identifiers with uppercase and lowercase equivalence.

IBM PC (code page 850)
> This code page is a modification of 437 extended to include all the Latin-1 letters, but still not with the usual Latin-1 encoding. In this mode, all these letters are allowed in identifiers with uppercase and lowercase equivalence.

Full Upper 8-bit
> Any character in the range 80-FF allowed in identifiers, and all are considered distinct. In other words, there are no uppercase and lowercase equivalences in this range. This is useful in conjunction with certain encoding schemes used for some foreign character sets (e.g. the typical method of representing Chinese characters on the PC).

No Upper-Half

> No upper-half characters in the range 80-FF are allowed in identifiers. This gives Ada 83 compatibility for identifier names.

For precise data on the encodings permitted, and the uppercase and lowercase equivalences that are recognized, see the file 'csets.adb' in the GNAT compiler sources. You will need to obtain a full source release of GNAT to obtain this file.

2.2.3 Wide Character Encodings

GNAT allows wide character codes to appear in character and string literals, and also optionally in identifiers, by means of the following possible encoding schemes:

Hex Coding

> In this encoding, a wide character is represented by the following five character sequence:
>
> ```
> ESC a b c d
> ```
>
> Where a, b, c, d are the four hexadecimal characters (using uppercase letters) of the wide character code. For example, ESC A345 is used to represent the wide character with code 16#A345#. This scheme is compatible with use of the full Wide_Character set.

Upper-Half Coding

> The wide character with encoding 16#abcd# where the upper bit is on (in other words, "a" is in the range 8-F) is represented as two bytes, 16#ab# and 16#cd#. The second byte cannot be a format control character, but is not required to be in the upper half. This method can be also used for shift-JIS or EUC, where the internal coding matches the external coding.

Shift JIS Coding

> A wide character is represented by a two-character sequence, 16#ab# and 16#cd#, with the restrictions described for upper-half encoding as described above. The internal character code is the corresponding JIS character according to the standard algorithm for Shift-JIS conversion. Only characters defined in the JIS code set table can be used with this encoding method.

EUC Coding

> A wide character is represented by a two-character sequence 16#ab# and 16#cd#, with both characters being in the upper half. The internal character code is the corresponding JIS character according to the EUC encoding algorithm. Only characters defined in the JIS code set table can be used with this encoding method.

UTF-8 Coding

> A wide character is represented using UCS Transformation Format 8 (UTF-8) as defined in Annex R of ISO 10646-1/Am.2. Depending on the character value, the representation is a one, two, or three byte sequence:

```
16#0000#-16#007f#: 2#0xxxxxxx#
16#0080#-16#07ff#: 2#110xxxxx# 2#10xxxxxx#
16#0800#-16#ffff#: 2#1110xxxx# 2#10xxxxxx# 2#10xxxxxx#
```

where the xxx bits correspond to the left-padded bits of the 16-bit character value. Note that all lower half ASCII characters are represented as ASCII bytes and all upper half characters and other wide characters are represented as sequences of upper-half (The full UTF-8 scheme allows for encoding 31-bit characters as 6-byte sequences, but in this implementation, all UTF-8 sequences of four or more bytes length will be treated as illegal).

Brackets Coding

In this encoding, a wide character is represented by the following eight character sequence:

```
[ " a b c d " ]
```

Where a, b, c, d are the four hexadecimal characters (using uppercase letters) of the wide character code. For example, ["A345"] is used to represent the wide character with code 16#A345#. It is also possible (though not required) to use the Brackets coding for upper half characters. For example, the code 16#A3# can be represented as [''A3''].

This scheme is compatible with use of the full Wide_Character set, and is also the method used for wide character encoding in the standard ACVC (Ada Compiler Validation Capability) test suite distributions.

Note: Some of these coding schemes do not permit the full use of the Ada character set. For example, neither Shift JIS, nor EUC allow the use of the upper half of the Latin-1 set.

2.3 File Naming Rules

The default file name is determined by the name of the unit that the file contains. The name is formed by taking the full expanded name of the unit and replacing the separating dots with hyphens and using lowercase for all letters.

An exception arises if the file name generated by the above rules starts with one of the characters a,g,i, or s, and the second character is a minus. In this case, the character tilde is used in place of the minus. The reason for this special rule is to avoid clashes with the standard names for child units of the packages System, Ada, Interfaces, and GNAT, which use the prefixes s- a- i- and g- respectively.

The file extension is '.ads' for a spec and '.adb' for a body. The following list shows some examples of these rules.

'main.ads'

        Main (spec)

'main.adb'

        Main (body)

'arith_functions.ads'

        Arith_Functions (package spec)

'arith_functions.adb'

        Arith_Functions (package body)

'func-spec.ads'

        Func.Spec (child package spec)

'`func-spec.adb`'
> Func.Spec (child package body)

'`main-sub.adb`'
> Sub (subunit of Main)

'`a~bad.adb`'
> A.Bad (child package body)

Following these rules can result in excessively long file names if corresponding unit names are long (for example, if child units or subunits are heavily nested). An option is available to shorten such long file names (called file name "krunching"). This may be particularly useful when programs being developed with GNAT are to be used on operating systems with limited file name lengths. See Section 15.2 [Using gnatkr], page 195.

Of course, no file shortening algorithm can guarantee uniqueness over all possible unit names; if file name krunching is used, it is your responsibility to ensure no name clashes occur. Alternatively you can specify the exact file names that you want used, as described in the next section. Finally, if your Ada programs are migrating from a compiler with a different naming convention, you can use the gnatchop utility to produce source files that follow the GNAT naming conventions. (For details see Chapter 8 [Renaming Files Using gnatchop], page 115.)

Note: in the case of `Windows NT/XP` or `OpenVMS` operating systems, case is not significant. So for example on `Windows XP` if the canonical name is `main-sub.adb`, you can use the file name `Main-Sub.adb` instead. However, case is significant for other operating systems, so for example, if you want to use other than canonically cased file names on a Unix system, you need to follow the procedures described in the next section.

2.4 Using Other File Names

In the previous section, we have described the default rules used by GNAT to determine the file name in which a given unit resides. It is often convenient to follow these default rules, and if you follow them, the compiler knows without being explicitly told where to find all the files it needs.

However, in some cases, particularly when a program is imported from another Ada compiler environment, it may be more convenient for the programmer to specify which file names contain which units. GNAT allows arbitrary file names to be used by means of the Source_File_Name pragma. The form of this pragma is as shown in the following examples:

```
pragma Source_File_Name (My_Utilities.Stacks,
  Spec_File_Name => "myutilst_a.ada");
pragma Source_File_name (My_Utilities.Stacks,
  Body_File_Name => "myutilst.ada");
```

As shown in this example, the first argument for the pragma is the unit name (in this example a child unit). The second argument has the form of a named association. The identifier indicates whether the file name is for a spec or a body; the file name itself is given by a string literal.

The source file name pragma is a configuration pragma, which means that normally it will be placed in the 'gnat.adc' file used to hold configuration pragmas that apply to a complete compilation environment. For more details on how the 'gnat.adc' file is created and used see Section 9.1 [Handling of Configuration Pragmas], page 119.

GNAT allows completely arbitrary file names to be specified using the source file name pragma. However, if the file name specified has an extension other than '.ads' or '.adb' it is necessary to use a special syntax when compiling the file. The name in this case must be preceded by the special sequence -x followed by a space and the name of the language, here ada, as in:

```
$ gcc -c -x ada peculiar_file_name.sim
```

gnatmake handles non-standard file names in the usual manner (the non-standard file name for the main program is simply used as the argument to gnatmake). Note that if the extension is also non-standard, then it must be included in the gnatmake command, it may not be omitted.

2.5 Alternative File Naming Schemes

In the previous section, we described the use of the Source_File_Name pragma to allow arbitrary names to be assigned to individual source files. However, this approach requires one pragma for each file, and especially in large systems can result in very long 'gnat.adc' files, and also create a maintenance problem.

GNAT also provides a facility for specifying systematic file naming schemes other than the standard default naming scheme previously described. An alternative scheme for naming is specified by the use of Source_File_Name pragmas having the following format:

```
pragma Source_File_Name (
   Spec_File_Name  => FILE_NAME_PATTERN
[,Casing          => CASING_SPEC]
[,Dot_Replacement => STRING_LITERAL]);

pragma Source_File_Name (
   Body_File_Name  => FILE_NAME_PATTERN
[,Casing          => CASING_SPEC]
[,Dot_Replacement => STRING_LITERAL]);

pragma Source_File_Name (
   Subunit_File_Name  => FILE_NAME_PATTERN
[,Casing             => CASING_SPEC]
[,Dot_Replacement    => STRING_LITERAL]);

FILE_NAME_PATTERN ::= STRING_LITERAL
CASING_SPEC ::= Lowercase | Uppercase | Mixedcase
```

The FILE_NAME_PATTERN string shows how the file name is constructed. It contains a single asterisk character, and the unit name is substituted systematically for this asterisk. The optional parameter Casing indicates whether the unit name is to be all upper-case letters, all lower-case letters, or mixed-case. If no Casing parameter is used, then the default is all lower-case.

The optional Dot_Replacement string is used to replace any periods that occur in subunit or child unit names. If no Dot_Replacement argument is used then separating dots appear unchanged in the resulting file name. Although the above syntax indicates that the Casing argument must appear before the `Dot_Replacement` argument, but it is also permissible to write these arguments in the opposite order.

As indicated, it is possible to specify different naming schemes for bodies, specs, and subunits. Quite often the rule for subunits is the same as the rule for bodies, in which case, there is no need to give a separate `Subunit_File_Name` rule, and in this case the `Body_File_name` rule is used for subunits as well.

The separate rule for subunits can also be used to implement the rather unusual case of a compilation environment (e.g. a single directory) which contains a subunit and a child unit with the same unit name. Although both units cannot appear in the same partition, the Ada Reference Manual allows (but does not require) the possibility of the two units coexisting in the same environment.

The file name translation works in the following steps:

- If there is a specific `Source_File_Name` pragma for the given unit, then this is always used, and any general pattern rules are ignored.

- If there is a pattern type `Source_File_Name` pragma that applies to the unit, then the resulting file name will be used if the file exists. If more than one pattern matches, the latest one will be tried first, and the first attempt resulting in a reference to a file that exists will be used.

- If no pattern type `Source_File_Name` pragma that applies to the unit for which the corresponding file exists, then the standard GNAT default naming rules are used.

As an example of the use of this mechanism, consider a commonly used scheme in which file names are all lower case, with separating periods copied unchanged to the resulting file name, and specs end with '.1.ada', and bodies end with '.2.ada'. GNAT will follow this scheme if the following two pragmas appear:

```
pragma Source_File_Name
  (Spec_File_Name => "*.1.ada");
pragma Source_File_Name
  (Body_File_Name => "*.2.ada");
```

The default GNAT scheme is actually implemented by providing the following default pragmas internally:

```
pragma Source_File_Name
  (Spec_File_Name => "*.ads", Dot_Replacement => "-");
pragma Source_File_Name
  (Body_File_Name => "*.adb", Dot_Replacement => "-");
```

Our final example implements a scheme typically used with one of the Ada 83 compilers, where the separator character for subunits was "__" (two underscores), specs were identified by adding '_.ADA', bodies by adding '.ADA', and subunits by adding '.SEP'. All file names were upper case. Child units were not present of course since this was an Ada 83 compiler, but it seems reasonable to extend this scheme to use the same double underscore separator for child units.

```
pragma Source_File_Name
  (Spec_File_Name => "*_.ADA",
   Dot_Replacement => "__",
   Casing = Uppercase);
pragma Source_File_Name
  (Body_File_Name => "*.ADA",
   Dot_Replacement => "__",
```

```
    Casing = Uppercase);
pragma Source_File_Name
  (Subunit_File_Name => "*.SEP",
   Dot_Replacement => "__",
   Casing = Uppercase);
```

2.6 Generating Object Files

An Ada program consists of a set of source files, and the first step in compiling the program is to generate the corresponding object files. These are generated by compiling a subset of these source files. The files you need to compile are the following:

- If a package spec has no body, compile the package spec to produce the object file for the package.

- If a package has both a spec and a body, compile the body to produce the object file for the package. The source file for the package spec need not be compiled in this case because there is only one object file, which contains the code for both the spec and body of the package.

- For a subprogram, compile the subprogram body to produce the object file for the subprogram. The spec, if one is present, is as usual in a separate file, and need not be compiled.

- In the case of subunits, only compile the parent unit. A single object file is generated for the entire subunit tree, which includes all the subunits.

- Compile child units independently of their parent units (though, of course, the spec of all the ancestor unit must be present in order to compile a child unit).

- Compile generic units in the same manner as any other units. The object files in this case are small dummy files that contain at most the flag used for elaboration checking. This is because GNAT always handles generic instantiation by means of macro expansion. However, it is still necessary to compile generic units, for dependency checking and elaboration purposes.

The preceding rules describe the set of files that must be compiled to generate the object files for a program. Each object file has the same name as the corresponding source file, except that the extension is '.o' as usual.

You may wish to compile other files for the purpose of checking their syntactic and semantic correctness. For example, in the case where a package has a separate spec and body, you would not normally compile the spec. However, it is convenient in practice to compile the spec to make sure it is error-free before compiling clients of this spec, because such compilations will fail if there is an error in the spec.

GNAT provides an option for compiling such files purely for the purposes of checking correctness; such compilations are not required as part of the process of building a program. To compile a file in this checking mode, use the '-gnatc' switch.

2.7 Source Dependencies

A given object file clearly depends on the source file which is compiled to produce it. Here we are using *depends* in the sense of a typical make utility; in other words, an object file depends on a source file if changes to the source file require the object file to be recompiled.

In addition to this basic dependency, a given object may depend on additional source files as follows:

- If a file being compiled `with`'s a unit *X*, the object file depends on the file containing the spec of unit *X*. This includes files that are `with`'ed implicitly either because they are parents of `with`'ed child units or they are run-time units required by the language constructs used in a particular unit.

- If a file being compiled instantiates a library level generic unit, the object file depends on both the spec and body files for this generic unit.

- If a file being compiled instantiates a generic unit defined within a package, the object file depends on the body file for the package as well as the spec file.

- If a file being compiled contains a call to a subprogram for which pragma `Inline` applies and inlining is activated with the '`-gnatn`' switch, the object file depends on the file containing the body of this subprogram as well as on the file containing the spec. Note that for inlining to actually occur as a result of the use of this switch, it is necessary to compile in optimizing mode.

  The use of '`-gnatN`' activates a more extensive inlining optimization that is performed by the front end of the compiler. This inlining does not require that the code generation be optimized. Like '`-gnatn`', the use of this switch generates additional dependencies. Note that '`-gnatN`' automatically implies '`-gnatn`' so it is not necessary to specify both options.

- If an object file '`O`' depends on the proper body of a subunit through inlining or instantiation, it depends on the parent unit of the subunit. This means that any modification of the parent unit or one of its subunits affects the compilation of '`O`'.

- The object file for a parent unit depends on all its subunit body files.

- The previous two rules meant that for purposes of computing dependencies and recompilation, a body and all its subunits are treated as an indivisible whole.

  These rules are applied transitively: if unit `A` `with`'s unit B, whose elaboration calls an inlined procedure in package C, the object file for unit `A` will depend on the body of C, in file '`c.adb`'.

  The set of dependent files described by these rules includes all the files on which the unit is semantically dependent, as dictated by the Ada language standard. However, it is a superset of what the standard describes, because it includes generic, inline, and subunit dependencies.

  An object file must be recreated by recompiling the corresponding source file if any of the source files on which it depends are modified. For example, if the `make` utility is used to control compilation, the rule for an Ada object file must mention all the source files on which the object file depends, according to the above definition. The determination of the necessary recompilations is done automatically when one uses `gnatmake`.

2.8 The Ada Library Information Files

Each compilation actually generates two output files. The first of these is the normal object file that has a '`.o`' extension. The second is a text file containing full dependency information. It has the same name as the source file, but an '`.ali`' extension. This file is known as the Ada Library Information ('`ALI`') file. The following information is contained in the '`ALI`' file.

- Version information (indicates which version of GNAT was used to compile the unit(s) in question)
- Main program information (including priority and time slice settings, as well as the wide character encoding used during compilation).
- List of arguments used in the `gcc` command for the compilation
- Attributes of the unit, including configuration pragmas used, an indication of whether the compilation was successful, exception model used etc.
- A list of relevant restrictions applying to the unit (used for consistency) checking.
- Categorization information (e.g. use of pragma `Pure`).
- Information on all `with`'ed units, including presence of `Elaborate` or `Elaborate_All` pragmas.
- Information from any `Linker_Options` pragmas used in the unit
- Information on the use of `Body_Version` or `Version` attributes in the unit.
- Dependency information. This is a list of files, together with time stamp and checksum information. These are files on which the unit depends in the sense that recompilation is required if any of these units are modified.
- Cross-reference data. Contains information on all entities referenced in the unit. Used by tools like `gnatxref` and `gnatfind` to provide cross-reference information.

For a full detailed description of the format of the '`ALI`' file, see the source of the body of unit `Lib.Writ`, contained in file '`lib-writ.adb`' in the GNAT compiler sources.

2.9 Binding an Ada Program

When using languages such as C and C++, once the source files have been compiled the only remaining step in building an executable program is linking the object modules together. This means that it is possible to link an inconsistent version of a program, in which two units have included different versions of the same header.

The rules of Ada do not permit such an inconsistent program to be built. For example, if two clients have different versions of the same package, it is illegal to build a program containing these two clients. These rules are enforced by the GNAT binder, which also determines an elaboration order consistent with the Ada rules.

The GNAT binder is run after all the object files for a program have been created. It is given the name of the main program unit, and from this it determines the set of units required by the program, by reading the corresponding ALI files. It generates error messages if the program is inconsistent or if no valid order of elaboration exists.

If no errors are detected, the binder produces a main program, in Ada by default, that contains calls to the elaboration procedures of those compilation unit that require them, followed by a call to the main program. This Ada program is compiled to generate the object file for the main program. The name of the Ada file is '`b~xxx.adb`' (with the corresponding spec '`b~xxx.ads`') where *xxx* is the name of the main program unit.

Finally, the linker is used to build the resulting executable program, using the object from the main program from the bind step as well as the object files for the Ada units of the program.

2.10 Mixed Language Programming

This section describes how to develop a mixed-language program, specifically one that comprises units in both Ada and C.

2.10.1 Interfacing to C

Interfacing Ada with a foreign language such as C involves using compiler directives to import and/or export entity definitions in each language—using **extern** statements in C, for instance, and the **Import**, **Export**, and **Convention** pragmas in Ada. A full treatment of these topics is provided in Appendix B, section 1 of the Ada Reference Manual.

There are two ways to build a program using GNAT that contains some Ada sources and some foreign language sources, depending on whether or not the main subprogram is written in Ada. Here is a source example with the main subprogram in Ada:

```
/* file1.c */
#include <stdio.h>

void print_num (int num)
{
  printf ("num is %d.\n", num);
  return;
}

/* file2.c */

/* num_from_Ada is declared in my_main.adb */
extern int num_from_Ada;

int get_num (void)
{
  return num_from_Ada;
}
--  my_main.adb
procedure My_Main is

   --  Declare then export an Integer entity called num_from_Ada
   My_Num : Integer := 10;
   pragma Export (C, My_Num, "num_from_Ada");

   --  Declare an Ada function spec for Get_Num, then use
   --  C function get_num for the implementation.
   function Get_Num return Integer;
   pragma Import (C, Get_Num, "get_num");

   --  Declare an Ada procedure spec for Print_Num, then use
   --  C function print_num for the implementation.
   procedure Print_Num (Num : Integer);
   pragma Import (C, Print_Num, "print_num");

begin
   Print_Num (Get_Num);
end My_Main;
```

1. To build this example, first compile the foreign language files to generate object files:

```
gcc -c file1.c
gcc -c file2.c
```

2. Then, compile the Ada units to produce a set of object files and ALI files:

```
gnatmake -c my_main.adb
```

3. Run the Ada binder on the Ada main program:

```
gnatbind my_main.ali
```

4. Link the Ada main program, the Ada objects and the other language objects:

```
gnatlink my_main.ali file1.o file2.o
```

The last three steps can be grouped in a single command:

```
gnatmake my_main.adb -largs file1.o file2.o
```

If the main program is in a language other than Ada, then you may have more than one entry point into the Ada subsystem. You must use a special binder option to generate callable routines that initialize and finalize the Ada units (see Section 4.2.5 [Binding with Non-Ada Main Programs], page 86). Calls to the initialization and finalization routines must be inserted in the main program, or some other appropriate point in the code. The call to initialize the Ada units must occur before the first Ada subprogram is called, and the call to finalize the Ada units must occur after the last Ada subprogram returns. The binder will place the initialization and finalization subprograms into the 'b~xxx.adb' file where they can be accessed by your C sources. To illustrate, we have the following example:

```
/* main.c */
extern void adainit (void);
extern void adafinal (void);
extern int add (int, int);
extern int sub (int, int);

int main (int argc, char *argv[])
{
  int a = 21, b = 7;

  adainit();

  /* Should print "21 + 7 = 28" */
  printf ("%d + %d = %d\n", a, b, add (a, b));
  /* Should print "21 - 7 = 14" */
  printf ("%d - %d = %d\n", a, b, sub (a, b));

  adafinal();
}
--  unit1.ads
package Unit1 is
   function Add (A, B : Integer) return Integer;
   pragma Export (C, Add, "add");
end Unit1;

--  unit1.adb
package body Unit1 is
   function Add (A, B : Integer) return Integer is
   begin
      return A + B;
   end Add;
end Unit1;

--  unit2.ads
package Unit2 is
   function Sub (A, B : Integer) return Integer;
```

```
      pragma Export (C, Sub, "sub");
   end Unit2;

   --  unit2.adb
   package body Unit2 is
      function Sub (A, B : Integer) return Integer is
      begin
         return A - B;
      end Sub;
   end Unit2;
```

1. The build procedure for this application is similar to the last example's. First, compile the foreign language files to generate object files:

   ```
   gcc -c main.c
   ```

2. Next, compile the Ada units to produce a set of object files and ALI files:

   ```
   gnatmake -c unit1.adb
   gnatmake -c unit2.adb
   ```

3. Run the Ada binder on every generated ALI file. Make sure to use the '-n' option to specify a foreign main program:

   ```
   gnatbind -n unit1.ali unit2.ali
   ```

4. Link the Ada main program, the Ada objects and the foreign language objects. You need only list the last ALI file here:

   ```
   gnatlink unit2.ali main.o -o exec_file
   ```

   This procedure yields a binary executable called 'exec_file'.

Depending on the circumstances (for example when your non-Ada main object does not provide symbol main), you may also need to instruct the GNAT linker not to include the standard startup objects by passing the '-nostartfiles' switch to gnatlink.

2.10.2 Calling Conventions

GNAT follows standard calling sequence conventions and will thus interface to any other language that also follows these conventions. The following Convention identifiers are recognized by GNAT:

Ada   This indicates that the standard Ada calling sequence will be used and all Ada data items may be passed without any limitations in the case where GNAT is used to generate both the caller and callee. It is also possible to mix GNAT generated code and code generated by another Ada compiler. In this case, the data types should be restricted to simple cases, including primitive types. Whether complex data types can be passed depends on the situation. Probably it is safe to pass simple arrays, such as arrays of integers or floats. Records may or may not work, depending on whether both compilers lay them out identically. Complex structures involving variant records, access parameters, tasks, or protected types, are unlikely to be able to be passed.

Note that in the case of GNAT running on a platform that supports HP Ada 83, a higher degree of compatibility can be guaranteed, and in particular records are laid out in an identical manner in the two compilers. Note also that if output from two different compilers is mixed, the program is responsible for dealing with elaboration issues. Probably the safest approach is to write the main program in the version of Ada other than GNAT, so that it takes care of its own elaboration requirements, and then call the GNAT-generated adainit procedure to ensure elaboration of the GNAT components. Consult the documentation of the other Ada compiler for further details on elaboration.

However, it is not possible to mix the tasking run time of GNAT and HP Ada 83, All the tasking operations must either be entirely within GNAT compiled sections of the program, or entirely within HP Ada 83 compiled sections of the program.

Assembler

Specifies assembler as the convention. In practice this has the same effect as convention Ada (but is not equivalent in the sense of being considered the same convention).

Asm   Equivalent to Assembler.

COBOL   Data will be passed according to the conventions described in section B.4 of the Ada Reference Manual.

C   Data will be passed according to the conventions described in section B.3 of the Ada Reference Manual.

A note on interfacing to a C "varargs" function:

- In C, varargs allows a function to take a variable number of arguments. There is no direct equivalent in this to Ada. One approach that can be used is to create a C wrapper for each different profile and then interface to this C wrapper. For example, to print an int value using printf, create a C function printfi that takes two arguments, a pointer to a string and an int, and calls printf. Then in the Ada program, use pragma Import to interface to printfi.

- It may work on some platforms to directly interface to a varargs function by providing a specific Ada profile for a particular call. However, this does not work on all platforms, since there is no guarantee that the calling sequence for a two argument normal C function is the same as for calling a varargs C function with the same two arguments.

Default   Equivalent to C.

External   Equivalent to C.

C_Plus_Plus (or CPP)

This stands for C++. For most purposes this is identical to C. See the separate description of the specialized GNAT pragmas relating to C++ interfacing for further details.

Fortran   Data will be passed according to the conventions described in section B.5 of the Ada Reference Manual.

Intrinsic

This applies to an intrinsic operation, as defined in the Ada Reference Manual. If a pragma Import (Intrinsic) applies to a subprogram, this means that the body of the subprogram is provided by the compiler itself, usually by means of an efficient code sequence, and that the user does not supply an explicit body for it. In an application program, the pragma can only be applied to the following two sets of names, which the GNAT compiler recognizes.

- Rotate_Left, Rotate_Right, Shift_Left, Shift_Right, Shift_Right_Arithmetic. The corresponding subprogram declaration must have two formal parameters. The first one must be a signed integer type or a modular type with a binary modulus, and the second parameter must be of type Natural. The return type must be the same as the type of the first argument. The size of this type can only be 8, 16, 32, or 64.

- binary arithmetic operators: "+", "-", "*", "/" The corresponding operator declaration must have parameters and result type that have the same root numeric type (for example, all three are long_float types). This simplifies the definition of operations that use type checking to perform dimensional checks:

```
type Distance is new Long_Float;
type Time     is new Long_Float;
type Velocity is new Long_Float;
function "/" (D : Distance; T : Time)
  return Velocity;
pragma Import (Intrinsic, "/");
```

This common idiom is often programmed with a generic definition and an explicit body. The pragma makes it simpler to introduce such declarations. It incurs no overhead in compilation time or code size, because it is implemented as a single machine instruction.

Stdcall   This is relevant only to Windows XP/2000/NT implementations of GNAT, and specifies that the Stdcall calling sequence will be used, as defined by the NT API. Nevertheless, to ease building cross-platform bindings this convention will be handled as a C calling convention on non Windows platforms.

DLL   This is equivalent to Stdcall.

Win32   This is equivalent to Stdcall.

Stubbed   This is a special convention that indicates that the compiler should provide a stub body that raises Program_Error.

GNAT additionally provides a useful pragma Convention_Identifier that can be used to parametrize conventions and allow additional synonyms to be specified. For example if you have legacy code in which the convention identifier Fortran77 was used for Fortran, you can use the configuration pragma:

```
pragma Convention_Identifier (Fortran77, Fortran);
```

And from now on the identifier Fortran77 may be used as a convention identifier (for example in an Import pragma) with the same meaning as Fortran.

2.11 Building Mixed Ada and C++ Programs

A programmer inexperienced with mixed-language development may find that building an application containing both Ada and C++ code can be a challenge. This section gives a few hints that should make this task easier. The first section addresses the differences between interfacing with C and interfacing with C++. The second section looks into the delicate problem of linking the complete application from its Ada and C++ parts. The last section gives some hints on how the GNAT run-time library can be adapted in order to allow inter-language dispatching with a new C++ compiler.

2.11.1 Interfacing to C++

GNAT supports interfacing with the G++ compiler (or any C++ compiler generating code that is compatible with the G++ Application Binary Interface —see http://www.codesourcery.com/archives/cxx-abi).

Interfacing can be done at 3 levels: simple data, subprograms, and classes. In the first two cases, GNAT offers a specific *Convention C_Plus_Plus* (or *CPP*) that behaves exactly like *Convention C*. Usually, C++ mangles the names of subprograms, and currently, GNAT does not provide any help to solve the demangling problem. This problem can be addressed in two ways:

- by modifying the C++ code in order to force a C convention using the `extern "C"` syntax.

- by figuring out the mangled name and use it as the Link_Name argument of the pragma import.

Interfacing at the class level can be achieved by using the GNAT specific pragmas such as `CPP_Constructor`. See the GNAT Reference Manual for additional information.

2.11.2 Linking a Mixed C++ & Ada Program

Usually the linker of the C++ development system must be used to link mixed applications because most C++ systems will resolve elaboration issues (such as calling constructors on global class instances) transparently during the link phase. GNAT has been adapted to ease the use of a foreign linker for the last phase. Three cases can be considered:

1. Using GNAT and G++ (GNU C++ compiler) from the same GCC installation: The C++ linker can simply be called by using the C++ specific driver called `c++`. Note that this setup is not very common because it may involve recompiling the whole GCC tree from sources, which makes it harder to upgrade the compilation system for one language without destabilizing the other.

   ```
   $ c++ -c file1.C
   $ c++ -c file2.C
   $ gnatmake ada_unit -largs file1.o file2.o --LINK=c++
   ```

2. Using GNAT and G++ from two different GCC installations: If both compilers are on the PATH, the previous method may be used. It is important to note that environment variables such as C_INCLUDE_PATH, GCC_EXEC_PREFIX, BINUTILS_ROOT, and GCC_ROOT will affect both compilers at the same time and may make one of the two compilers operate improperly if set during invocation of the wrong compiler. It is also very important that the linker uses the proper 'libgcc.a' GCC library – that is, the one from the C++ compiler installation. The implicit link command as suggested in the gnatmake command from the former example can be replaced by an explicit link command with the full-verbosity option in order to verify which library is used:

   ```
   $ gnatbind ada_unit
   $ gnatlink -v -v ada_unit file1.o file2.o --LINK=c++
   ```

If there is a problem due to interfering environment variables, it can be worked around by using an intermediate script. The following example shows the proper script to use when GNAT has not been installed at its default location and g++ has been installed at its default location:

```
$ cat ./my_script
#!/bin/sh
unset BINUTILS_ROOT
unset GCC_ROOT
c++ $*
$ gnatlink -v -v ada_unit file1.o file2.o --LINK=./my_script
```

3. Using a non-GNU C++ compiler: The commands previously described can be used to insure that the C++ linker is used. Nonetheless, you need to add a few more parameters to the link command line, depending on the exception mechanism used.

   If the `setjmp/longjmp` exception mechanism is used, only the paths to the libgcc libraries are required:

```
$ cat ./my_script
#!/bin/sh
CC $* `gcc -print-file-name=libgcc.a` `gcc -print-file-name=libgcc_eh.a`
$ gnatlink ada_unit file1.o file2.o --LINK=./my_script
```

   Where CC is the name of the non-GNU C++ compiler.

   If the `zero cost` exception mechanism is used, and the platform supports automatic registration of exception tables (e.g. Solaris or IRIX), paths to more objects are required:

```
$ cat ./my_script
#!/bin/sh
CC `gcc -print-file-name=crtbegin.o` $* \
`gcc -print-file-name=libgcc.a` `gcc -print-file-name=libgcc_eh.a` \
`gcc -print-file-name=crtend.o`
$ gnatlink ada_unit file1.o file2.o --LINK=./my_script
```

   If the `zero cost` exception mechanism is used, and the platform doesn't support automatic registration of exception tables (e.g. HP-UX, Tru64 or AIX), the simple approach described above will not work and a pre-linking phase using GNAT will be necessary.

2.11.3 A Simple Example

The following example, provided as part of the GNAT examples, shows how to achieve procedural interfacing between Ada and C++ in both directions. The C++ class A has two methods. The first method is exported to Ada by the means of an extern C wrapper function. The second method calls an Ada subprogram. On the Ada side, The C++ calls are modelled by a limited record with a layout comparable to the C++ class. The Ada subprogram, in turn, calls the C++ method. So, starting from the C++ main program, the process passes back and forth between the two languages.

Here are the compilation commands:

```
$ gnatmake -c simple_cpp_interface
$ c++ -c cpp_main.C
$ c++ -c ex7.C
$ gnatbind -n simple_cpp_interface
$ gnatlink simple_cpp_interface -o cpp_main --LINK=$(CPLUSPLUS)
      -lstdc++ ex7.o cpp_main.o
```

Here are the corresponding sources:

```
//cpp_main.C

#include "ex7.h"

extern "C" {
  void adainit (void);
  void adafinal (void);
  void method1 (A *t);
}

void method1 (A *t)
{
  t->method1 ();
}

int main ()
{
  A obj;
  adainit ();
  obj.method2 (3030);
  adafinal ();
}

//ex7.h

class Origin {
 public:
  int o_value;
};
class A : public Origin {
 public:
  void method1 (void);
  void method2 (int v);
  A();
  int    a_value;
};

//ex7.C

#include "ex7.h"
#include <stdio.h>

extern "C" { void ada_method2 (A *t, int v);}

void A::method1 (void)
{
  a_value = 2020;
  printf ("in A::method1, a_value = %d \n",a_value);

}

void A::method2 (int v)
{
   ada_method2 (this, v);
   printf ("in A::method2, a_value = %d \n",a_value);

}
```

```
A::A(void)
{
   a_value = 1010;
  printf ("in A::A, a_value = %d \n",a_value);
}
-- Ada sources
package body Simple_Cpp_Interface is

   procedure Ada_Method2 (This : in out A; V : Integer) is
   begin
      Method1 (This);
      This.A_Value := V;
   end Ada_Method2;

end Simple_Cpp_Interface;

with System;
package Simple_Cpp_Interface is
   type A is limited
      record
         Vptr    : System.Address;
         O_Value : Integer;
         A_Value : Integer;
      end record;
   pragma Convention (C, A);

   procedure Method1 (This : in out A);
   pragma Import (C, Method1);

   procedure Ada_Method2 (This : in out A; V : Integer);
   pragma Export (C, Ada_Method2);

end Simple_Cpp_Interface;
```

2.11.4 Interfacing with C++ at the Class Level

In this section we demonstrate the GNAT features for interfacing with C++ by means of an example making use of Ada 2005 abstract interface types. This example consists of a classification of animals; classes have been used to model our main classification of animals, and interfaces provide support for the management of secondary classifications. We first demonstrate a case in which the types and constructors are defined on the C++ side and imported from the Ada side, and latter the reverse case.

The root of our derivation will be the Animal class, with a single private attribute (the Age of the animal) and two public primitives to set and get the value of this attribute.

```
class Animal {
 public:
    virtual void Set_Age (int New_Age);
    virtual int Age ();
 private:
    int Age_Count;
};
```

Abstract interface types are defined in C++ by means of classes with pure virtual functions and no data members. In our example we will use two interfaces that provide support for the common management of Carnivore and Domestic animals:

```
class Carnivore {
public:
    virtual int Number_Of_Teeth () = 0;
};

class Domestic {
public:
    virtual void Set_Owner (char* Name) = 0;
};
```

Using these declarations, we can now say that a `Dog` is an animal that is both Carnivore and Domestic, that is:

```
class Dog : Animal, Carnivore, Domestic {
 public:
   virtual int  Number_Of_Teeth ();
   virtual void Set_Owner (char* Name);

   Dog(); // Constructor
 private:
   int  Tooth_Count;
   char *Owner;
};
```

In the following examples we will assume that the previous declarations are located in a file named `animals.h`. The following package demonstrates how to import these C++ declarations from the Ada side:

```
with Interfaces.C.Strings; use Interfaces.C.Strings;
package Animals is
  type Carnivore is interface;
  pragma Convention (C_Plus_Plus, Carnivore);
  function Number_Of_Teeth (X : Carnivore)
     return Natural is abstract;

  type Domestic is interface;
  pragma Convention (C_Plus_Plus, Set_Owner);
  procedure Set_Owner
    (X      : in out Domestic;
     Name : Chars_Ptr) is abstract;

  type Animal is tagged record
    Age : Natural := 0;
  end record;
  pragma Import (C_Plus_Plus, Animal);

  procedure Set_Age (X : in out Animal; Age : Integer);
  pragma Import (C_Plus_Plus, Set_Age);

  function Age (X : Animal) return Integer;
  pragma Import (C_Plus_Plus, Age);

  type Dog is new Animal and Carnivore and Domestic with record
    Tooth_Count : Natural;
    Owner       : String (1 .. 30);
  end record;
  pragma Import (C_Plus_Plus, Dog);

  function Number_Of_Teeth (A : Dog) return Integer;
  pragma Import (C_Plus_Plus, Number_Of_Teeth);
```

```
   procedure Set_Owner (A : in out Dog; Name : Chars_Ptr);
   pragma Import (C_Plus_Plus, Set_Owner);

   function New_Dog return Dog'Class;
   pragma CPP_Constructor (New_Dog);
   pragma Import (CPP, New_Dog, "_ZN3DogC2Ev");
end Animals;
```

Thanks to the compatibility between GNAT run-time structures and the C++ ABI, interfacing with these C++ classes is easy. The only requirement is that all the primitives and components must be declared exactly in the same order in the two languages.

Regarding the abstract interfaces, we must indicate to the GNAT compiler by means of a **pragma Convention (C_Plus_Plus)**, the convention used to pass the arguments to the called primitives will be the same as for C++. For the imported classes we use **pragma Import** with convention **C_Plus_Plus** to indicate that they have been defined on the C++ side; this is required because the dispatch table associated with these tagged types will be built in the C++ side and therefore will not contain the predefined Ada primitives which Ada would otherwise expect.

As the reader can see there is no need to indicate the C++ mangled names associated with each subprogram because it is assumed that all the calls to these primitives will be dispatching calls. The only exception is the constructor, which must be registered with the compiler by means of **pragma CPP_Constructor** and needs to provide its associated C++ mangled name because the Ada compiler generates direct calls to it.

With the above packages we can now declare objects of type Dog on the Ada side and dispatch calls to the corresponding subprograms on the C++ side. We can also extend the tagged type Dog with further fields and primitives, and override some of its C++ primitives on the Ada side. For example, here we have a type derivation defined on the Ada side that inherits all the dispatching primitives of the ancestor from the C++ side.

```
with Animals; use Animals;
package Vaccinated_Animals is
  type Vaccinated_Dog is new Dog with null record;
  function Vaccination_Expired (A : Vaccinated_Dog) return Boolean;
end Vaccinated_Animals;
```

It is important to note that, because of the ABI compatibility, the programmer does not need to add any further information to indicate either the object layout or the dispatch table entry associated with each dispatching operation.

Now let us define all the types and constructors on the Ada side and export them to C++, using the same hierarchy of our previous example:

```
with Interfaces.C.Strings;
use Interfaces.C.Strings;
package Animals is
  type Carnivore is interface;
  pragma Convention (C_Plus_Plus, Carnivore);
  function Number_Of_Teeth (X : Carnivore)
    return Natural is abstract;

  type Domestic is interface;
  pragma Convention (C_Plus_Plus, Set_Owner);
  procedure Set_Owner
    (X     : in out Domestic;
```

```
    Name : Chars_Ptr) is abstract;

  type Animal is tagged record
    Age : Natural := 0;
  end record;
  pragma Convention (C_Plus_Plus, Animal);

  procedure Set_Age (X : in out Animal; Age : Integer);
  pragma Export (C_Plus_Plus, Set_Age);

  function Age (X : Animal) return Integer;
  pragma Export (C_Plus_Plus, Age);

  type Dog is new Animal and Carnivore and Domestic with record
    Tooth_Count : Natural;
    Owner       : String (1 .. 30);
  end record;
  pragma Convention (C_Plus_Plus, Dog);

  function Number_Of_Teeth (A : Dog) return Integer;
  pragma Export (C_Plus_Plus, Number_Of_Teeth);

  procedure Set_Owner (A : in out Dog; Name : Chars_Ptr);
  pragma Export (C_Plus_Plus, Set_Owner);

  function New_Dog return Dog'Class;
  pragma Export (C_Plus_Plus, New_Dog);
end Animals;
```

Compared with our previous example the only difference is the use of `pragma Export` to indicate to the GNAT compiler that the primitives will be available to C++. Thanks to the ABI compatibility, on the C++ side there is nothing else to be done; as explained above, the only requirement is that all the primitives and components are declared in exactly the same order.

For completeness, let us see a brief C++ main program that uses the declarations available in `animals.h` (presented in our first example) to import and use the declarations from the Ada side, properly initializing and finalizing the Ada run-time system along the way:

```
#include "animals.h"
#include <iostream>
using namespace std;

void Check_Carnivore (Carnivore *obj) { ... }
void Check_Domestic (Domestic *obj)  { ... }
void Check_Animal (Animal *obj)       { ... }
void Check_Dog (Dog *obj)             { ... }

extern "C" {
  void adainit (void);
  void adafinal (void);
  Dog* new_dog ();
}

void test ()
{
  Dog *obj = new_dog();  // Ada constructor
  Check_Carnivore (obj); // Check secondary DT
  Check_Domestic (obj);  // Check secondary DT
```

```
    Check_Animal (obj);    // Check primary DT
    Check_Dog (obj);       // Check primary DT
  }

  int main ()
  {
    adainit ();  test();  adafinal ();
    return 0;
  }
```

2.12 Comparison between GNAT and C/C++ Compilation Models

The GNAT model of compilation is close to the C and C++ models. You can think of Ada specs as corresponding to header files in C. As in C, you don't need to compile specs; they are compiled when they are used. The Ada `with` is similar in effect to the `#include` of a C header.

One notable difference is that, in Ada, you may compile specs separately to check them for semantic and syntactic accuracy. This is not always possible with C headers because they are fragments of programs that have less specific syntactic or semantic rules.

The other major difference is the requirement for running the binder, which performs two important functions. First, it checks for consistency. In C or C++, the only defense against assembling inconsistent programs lies outside the compiler, in a makefile, for example. The binder satisfies the Ada requirement that it be impossible to construct an inconsistent program when the compiler is used in normal mode.

The other important function of the binder is to deal with elaboration issues. There are also elaboration issues in C++ that are handled automatically. This automatic handling has the advantage of being simpler to use, but the C++ programmer has no control over elaboration. Where `gnatbind` might complain there was no valid order of elaboration, a C++ compiler would simply construct a program that malfunctioned at run time.

2.13 Comparison between GNAT and Conventional Ada Library Models

This section is intended for Ada programmers who have used an Ada compiler implementing the traditional Ada library model, as described in the Ada Reference Manual.

In GNAT, there is no "library" in the normal sense. Instead, the set of source files themselves acts as the library. Compiling Ada programs does not generate any centralized information, but rather an object file and a ALI file, which are of interest only to the binder and linker. In a traditional system, the compiler reads information not only from the source file being compiled, but also from the centralized library. This means that the effect of a compilation depends on what has been previously compiled. In particular:

- When a unit is `with`'ed, the unit seen by the compiler corresponds to the version of the unit most recently compiled into the library.

- Inlining is effective only if the necessary body has already been compiled into the library.

- Compiling a unit may obsolete other units in the library.

In GNAT, compiling one unit never affects the compilation of any other units because the compiler reads only source files. Only changes to source files can affect the results of a compilation. In particular:

- When a unit is `with`'ed, the unit seen by the compiler corresponds to the source version of the unit that is currently accessible to the compiler.

- Inlining requires the appropriate source files for the package or subprogram bodies to be available to the compiler. Inlining is always effective, independent of the order in which units are complied.

- Compiling a unit never affects any other compilations. The editing of sources may cause previous compilations to be out of date if they depended on the source file being modified.

The most important result of these differences is that order of compilation is never significant in GNAT. There is no situation in which one is required to do one compilation before another. What shows up as order of compilation requirements in the traditional Ada library becomes, in GNAT, simple source dependencies; in other words, there is only a set of rules saying what source files must be present when a file is compiled.

3 Compiling Using gcc

This chapter discusses how to compile Ada programs using the `gcc` command. It also describes the set of switches that can be used to control the behavior of the compiler.

3.1 Compiling Programs

The first step in creating an executable program is to compile the units of the program using the `gcc` command. You must compile the following files:

- the body file ('`.adb`') for a library level subprogram or generic subprogram
- the spec file ('`.ads`') for a library level package or generic package that has no body
- the body file ('`.adb`') for a library level package or generic package that has a body

You need *not* compile the following files

- the spec of a library unit which has a body
- subunits

because they are compiled as part of compiling related units. GNAT package specs when the corresponding body is compiled, and subunits when the parent is compiled.

If you attempt to compile any of these files, you will get one of the following error messages (where fff is the name of the file you compiled):

```
cannot generate code for file fff (package spec)
to check package spec, use -gnatc

cannot generate code for file fff (missing subunits)
to check parent unit, use -gnatc

cannot generate code for file fff (subprogram spec)
to check subprogram spec, use -gnatc

cannot generate code for file fff (subunit)
to check subunit, use -gnatc
```

As indicated by the above error messages, if you want to submit one of these files to the compiler to check for correct semantics without generating code, then use the '`-gnatc`' switch.

The basic command for compiling a file containing an Ada unit is

```
$ gcc -c [switches] 'file name'
```

where *file name* is the name of the Ada file (usually having an extension '`.ads`' for a spec or '`.adb`' for a body). You specify the '`-c`' switch to tell `gcc` to compile, but not link, the file. The result of a successful compilation is an object file, which has the same name as the source file but an extension of '`.o`' and an Ada Library Information (ALI) file, which also has the same name as the source file, but with '`.ali`' as the extension. GNAT creates these two output files in the current directory, but you may specify a source file in any directory using an absolute or relative path specification containing the directory information.

`gcc` is actually a driver program that looks at the extensions of the file arguments and loads the appropriate compiler. For example, the GNU C compiler is '`cc1`', and the Ada compiler is '`gnat1`'. These programs are in directories known to the driver program (in some configurations via environment variables you set), but need not be in your path. The gcc driver also calls the assembler and any other utilities needed to complete the generation of the required object files.

It is possible to supply several file names on the same gcc command. This causes gcc to call the appropriate compiler for each file. For example, the following command lists three separate files to be compiled:

```
$ gcc -c x.adb y.adb z.c
```

calls gnat1 (the Ada compiler) twice to compile 'x.adb' and 'y.adb', and cc1 (the C compiler) once to compile 'z.c'. The compiler generates three object files 'x.o', 'y.o' and 'z.o' and the two ALI files 'x.ali' and 'y.ali' from the Ada compilations. Any switches apply to all the files listed, except for '-gnatx' switches, which apply only to Ada compilations.

3.2 Switches for gcc

The gcc command accepts switches that control the compilation process. These switches are fully described in this section. First we briefly list all the switches, in alphabetical order, then we describe the switches in more detail in functionally grouped sections.

More switches exist for GCC than those documented here, especially for specific targets. However, their use is not recommended as they may change code generation in ways that are incompatible with the Ada run-time library, or can cause inconsistencies between compilation units.

'-b target'

    Compile your program to run on target, which is the name of a system configuration. You must have a GNAT cross-compiler built if target is not the same as your host system.

'-Bdir'

    Load compiler executables (for example, gnat1, the Ada compiler) from dir instead of the default location. Only use this switch when multiple versions of the GNAT compiler are available. See the gcc manual page for further details. You would normally use the '-b' or '-V' switch instead.

'-c'

    Compile. Always use this switch when compiling Ada programs.

    Note: for some other languages when using gcc, notably in the case of C and C++, it is possible to use use gcc without a '-c' switch to compile and link in one step. In the case of GNAT, you cannot use this approach, because the binder must be run and gcc cannot be used to run the GNAT binder.

'-fno-inline'

    Suppresses all back-end inlining, even if other optimization or inlining switches are set. This includes suppression of inlining that results from the use of the pragma Inline_Always. Any occurrences of pragma Inline or Inline_Always are ignored, and '-gnatn' and '-gnatN' have no effect if this switch is present.

'-fno-strict-aliasing'

    Causes the compiler to avoid assumptions regarding non-aliasing of objects of different types. See Section 7.1.7 [Optimization and Strict Aliasing], page 108 for details.

'-fstack-check'

> Activates stack checking. See Section 22.1 [Stack Overflow Checking], page 231 for details.

'-fstack-usage'

> Makes the compiler output stack usage information for the program, on a per-function basis. See Section 22.2 [Static Stack Usage Analysis], page 231 for details.

'-fcallgraph-info[=su]'

> Makes the compiler output callgraph information for the program, on a per-file basis. The information is generated in the VCG format. It can be decorated with stack-usage per-node information.

'-g'   Generate debugging information. This information is stored in the object file and copied from there to the final executable file by the linker, where it can be read by the debugger. You must use the '-g' switch if you plan on using the debugger.

'-gnat83' Enforce Ada 83 restrictions.

'-gnat95' Enforce Ada 95 restrictions.

'-gnat05' Allow full Ada 2005 features.

'-gnata'   Assertions enabled. Pragma Assert and pragma Debug to be activated. Note that these pragmas can also be controlled using the configuration pragmas Assertion_Policy and Debug_Policy.

'-gnatA'   Avoid processing 'gnat.adc'. If a gnat.adc file is present, it will be ignored.

'-gnatb'   Generate brief messages to 'stderr' even if verbose mode set.

'-gnatc'   Check syntax and semantics only (no code generation attempted).

'-gnatd'   Specify debug options for the compiler. The string of characters after the '-gnatd' specify the specific debug options. The possible characters are 0-9, a-z, A-Z, optionally preceded by a dot. See compiler source file 'debug.adb' for details of the implemented debug options. Certain debug options are relevant to applications programmers, and these are documented at appropriate points in this users guide.

'-gnatD'   Create expanded source files for source level debugging. This switch also suppress generation of cross-reference information (see '-gnatx').

'-gnatec=path'

> Specify a configuration pragma file (the equal sign is optional) (see Section 9.2 [The Configuration Pragmas Files], page 120).

'-gnateDsymbol[=value]'

> Defines a symbol, associated with value, for preprocessing. (see Section 3.2.17 [Integrated Preprocessing], page 74).

'-gnatef' Display full source path name in brief error messages.

'-gnatem=*path*'

  Specify a mapping file (the equal sign is optional) (see Section 3.2.16 [Units to Sources Mapping Files], page 73).

'-gnatep=*file*'

  Specify a preprocessing data file (the equal sign is optional) (see Section 3.2.17 [Integrated Preprocessing], page 74).

'-gnatE' Full dynamic elaboration checks.

'-gnatf' Full errors. Multiple errors per line, all undefined references, do not attempt to suppress cascaded errors.

'-gnatF' Externals names are folded to all uppercase.

'-gnatg' Internal GNAT implementation mode. This should not be used for applications programs, it is intended only for use by the compiler and its run-time library. For documentation, see the GNAT sources. Note that '-gnatg' implies '-gnatwae' and '-gnatyg' so that all standard warnings and all standard style options are turned on. All warnings and style error messages are treated as errors.

'-gnatG' List generated expanded code in source form.

'-gnath' Output usage information. The output is written to 'stdout'.

'-gnatic' Identifier character set (c=1/2/3/4/8/9/p/f/n/w). For details of the possible selections for c, see Section 3.2.10 [Character Set Control], page 67.

'-gnatI' Ignore representation clauses. When this switch is used, all representation clauses are treated as comments. This is useful when initially porting code where you want to ignore rep clause problems, and also for compiling foreign code (particularly for use with ASIS).

'-gnatj*nn*'

  Reformat error messages to fit on nn character lines

'-gnatk=*n*'

  Limit file names to n (1-999) characters (k = krunch).

'-gnatl' Output full source listing with embedded error messages.

'-gnatL' Used in conjunction with -gnatG or -gnatD to intersperse original source lines (as comment lines with line numbers) in the expanded source output.

'-gnatm=*n*'

  Limit number of detected error or warning messages to n where n is in the range 1..999_999. The default setting if no switch is given is 9999. Compilation is terminated if this limit is exceeded. The equal sign here is optional.

'-gnatn' Activate inlining for subprograms for which pragma inline is specified. This inlining is performed by the GCC back-end.

'-gnatN' Activate front end inlining for subprograms for which pragma Inline is specified. This inlining is performed by the front end and will be visible in the '-gnatG' output. In some cases, this has proved more effective than the back end inlining resulting from the use of '-gnatn'. Note that '-gnatN' automatically implies '-gnatn' so it is not necessary to specify both options. There are a few cases that the back-end inlining catches that cannot be dealt with in the front-end.

'-gnato'   Enable numeric overflow checking (which is not normally enabled by default). Not that division by zero is a separate check that is not controlled by this switch (division by zero checking is on by default).

'-gnatp'   Suppress all checks.

'-gnatP'   Enable polling. This is required on some systems (notably Windows NT) to obtain asynchronous abort and asynchronous transfer of control capability. See the description of pragma Polling in the GNAT Reference Manual for full details.

'-gnatq'   Don't quit; try semantics, even if parse errors.

'-gnatQ'   Don't quit; generate 'ALI' and tree files even if illegalities.

'-gnatR[0/1/2/3[s]]'
              Output representation information for declared types and objects.

'-gnats'   Syntax check only.

'-gnatS'   Print package Standard.

'-gnatt'   Generate tree output file.

'-gnatT*nnn*'
              All compiler tables start at *nnn* times usual starting size.

'-gnatu'   List units for this compilation.

'-gnatU'   Tag all error messages with the unique string "error:"

'-gnatv'   Verbose mode. Full error output with source lines to 'stdout'.

'-gnatV'   Control level of validity checking. See separate section describing this feature.

'-gnatw*xxx*'
              Warning mode where *xxx* is a string of option letters that denotes the exact warnings that are enabled or disabled (see Section 3.2.2 [Warning Message Control], page 46).

'-gnatWe'   Wide character encoding method (e=n/h/u/s/e/8).

'-gnatx'   Suppress generation of cross-reference information.

'-gnaty'   Enable built-in style checks (see Section 3.2.5 [Style Checking], page 58).

'-gnatz*m*'   Distribution stub generation and compilation (*m*=r/c for receiver/caller stubs).

'-I*dir*'   Direct GNAT to search the *dir* directory for source files needed by the current compilation (see Section 3.3 [Search Paths and the Run-Time Library (RTL)], page 76).

'-I-'   Except for the source file named in the command line, do not look for source files in the directory containing the source file named in the command line (see Section 3.3 [Search Paths and the Run-Time Library (RTL)], page 76).

'-mbig-switch'

This standard gcc switch causes the compiler to use larger offsets in its jump table representation for **case** statements. This may result in less efficient code, but is sometimes necessary (for example on HP-UX targets) in order to compile large and/or nested **case** statements.

'-o *file*'   This switch is used in gcc to redirect the generated object file and its associated ALI file. Beware of this switch with GNAT, because it may cause the object file and ALI file to have different names which in turn may confuse the binder and the linker.

'-nostdinc'

Inhibit the search of the default location for the GNAT Run Time Library (RTL) source files.

'-nostdlib'

Inhibit the search of the default location for the GNAT Run Time Library (RTL) ALI files.

'-O[*n*]'   *n* controls the optimization level.

    n = 0   No optimization, the default setting if no '-O' appears

    n = 1   Normal optimization, the default if you specify '-O' without an operand. A good compromise between code quality and compilation time.

    n = 2   Extensive optimization, may improve execution time, possibly at the cost of substantially increased compilation time.

    n = 3   Same as '-O2', and also includes inline expansion for small subprograms in the same unit.

    n = s   Optimize space usage

    See also Section 7.1.3 [Optimization Levels], page 104.

'-pass-exit-codes'

Catch exit codes from the compiler and use the most meaningful as exit status.

'--RTS=*rts-path*'

Specifies the default location of the runtime library. Same meaning as the equivalent **gnatmake** flag (see Section 6.2 [Switches for gnatmake], page 94).

'-S'   Used in place of '-c' to cause the assembler source file to be generated, using '.s' as the extension, instead of the object file. This may be useful if you need to examine the generated assembly code.

'-fverbose-asm'

Used in conjunction with '-S' to cause the generated assembly code file to be annotated with variable names, making it significantly easier to follow.

'-v'   Show commands generated by the gcc driver. Normally used only for debugging purposes or if you need to be sure what version of the compiler you are executing.

'-V *ver*' Execute *ver* version of the compiler. This is the gcc version, not the GNAT version.

'-w' Turn off warnings generated by the back end of the compiler. Use of this switch also causes the default for front end warnings to be set to suppress (as though '-gnatws' had appeared at the start of the options).

You may combine a sequence of GNAT switches into a single switch. For example, the combined switch

    -gnatofi3

is equivalent to specifying the following sequence of switches:

    -gnato -gnatf -gnati3

The following restrictions apply to the combination of switches in this manner:

- The switch '-gnatc' if combined with other switches must come first in the string.
- The switch '-gnats' if combined with other switches must come first in the string.
- The switches '-gnatz', '-gnatzc', and '-gnatzr' may not be combined with any other switches.
- Once a "y" appears in the string (that is a use of the '-gnaty' switch), then all further characters in the switch are interpreted as style modifiers (see description of '-gnaty').
- Once a "d" appears in the string (that is a use of the '-gnatd' switch), then all further characters in the switch are interpreted as debug flags (see description of '-gnatd').
- Once a "w" appears in the string (that is a use of the '-gnatw' switch), then all further characters in the switch are interpreted as warning mode modifiers (see description of '-gnatw').
- Once a "V" appears in the string (that is a use of the '-gnatV' switch), then all further characters in the switch are interpreted as validity checking options (see description of '-gnatV').

3.2.1 Output and Error Message Control

The standard default format for error messages is called "brief format". Brief format messages are written to 'stderr' (the standard error file) and have the following form:

    e.adb:3:04: Incorrect spelling of keyword "function"
    e.adb:4:20: ";" should be "is"

The first integer after the file name is the line number in the file, and the second integer is the column number within the line. GPS can parse the error messages and point to the referenced character. The following switches provide control over the error message format:

'-gnatv' The v stands for verbose. The effect of this setting is to write long-format error messages to 'stdout' (the standard output file. The same program compiled with the '-gnatv' switch would generate:

```
3. funcion X (Q : Integer)
   |
>>> Incorrect spelling of keyword "function"
4. return Integer;
              |
>>> ";" should be "is"
```

The vertical bar indicates the location of the error, and the '>>>' prefix can be used to search for error messages. When this switch is used the only source lines output are those with errors.

'-gnatl'   The l stands for list. This switch causes a full listing of the file to be generated. In the case where a body is compiled, the corresponding spec is also listed, along with any subunits. Typical output from compiling a package body 'p.adb' might look like:

```
Compiling: p.adb

   1. package body p is
   2.    procedure a;
   3.    procedure a is separate;
   4. begin
   5.    null
            |
      >>> missing ";"

   6. end;

Compiling: p.ads

   1. package p is
   2.    pragma Elaborate_Body
                             |
      >>> missing ";"

   3. end p;

Compiling: p-a.adb

   1. separate p
                |
      >>> missing "("

   2. procedure a is
   3. begin
   4.    null
            |
      >>> missing ";"

   5. end;
```

When you specify the '-gnatv' or '-gnatl' switches and standard output is redirected, a brief summary is written to 'stderr' (standard error) giving the number of error messages and warning messages generated.

'-gnatl=file'
            This has the same effect as -gnatl except that the output is written to a file instead of to standard output. If the given name 'fname' does not start with a period, then it is the full name of the file to be written. If 'fname' is an extension, it is appended to the name of the file being compiled. For example, if file 'xyz.adb' is compiled with '-gnatl=.lst', then the output is written to file xyz.adb.lst.

'-gnatU'   This switch forces all error messages to be preceded by the unique string "error:". This means that error messages take a few more characters in space, but allows easy searching for and identification of error messages.

'-gnatb'   The b stands for brief. This switch causes GNAT to generate the brief format error messages to 'stderr' (the standard error file) as well as the verbose format message or full listing (which as usual is written to 'stdout' (the standard output file).

'-gnatm=n'

The m stands for maximum. n is a decimal integer in the range of 1 to 999 and limits the number of error messages to be generated. For example, using '-gnatm2' might yield

```
e.adb:3:04: Incorrect spelling of keyword "function"
e.adb:5:35: missing ".."
fatal error: maximum errors reached
compilation abandoned
```

Note that the equal sign is optional, so the switches '-gnatm2' and '-gnatm=2' are equivalent.

'-gnatf'   The f stands for full. Normally, the compiler suppresses error messages that are likely to be redundant. This switch causes all error messages to be generated. In particular, in the case of references to undefined variables. If a given variable is referenced several times, the normal format of messages is

```
e.adb:7:07: "V" is undefined (more references follow)
```

where the parenthetical comment warns that there are additional references to the variable V. Compiling the same program with the '-gnatf' switch yields

```
e.adb:7:07: "V" is undefined
e.adb:8:07: "V" is undefined
e.adb:8:12: "V" is undefined
e.adb:8:16: "V" is undefined
e.adb:9:07: "V" is undefined
e.adb:9:12: "V" is undefined
```

The '-gnatf' switch also generates additional information for some error messages. Some examples are:

- Full details on entities not available in high integrity mode
- Details on possibly non-portable unchecked conversion
- List possible interpretations for ambiguous calls
- Additional details on incorrect parameters

'-gnatjnn'

In normal operation mode (or if '-gnatj0' is used, then error messages with continuation lines are treated as though the continuation lines were separate messages (and so a warning with two continuation lines counts as three warnings, and is listed as three separate messages).

If the '-gnatjnn' switch is used with a positive value for nn, then messages are output in a different manner. A message and all its continuation lines are treated as a unit, and count as only one warning or message in the statistics totals. Furthermore, the message is reformatted so that no line is longer than nn characters.

'-gnatq'   The q stands for quit (really "don't quit"). In normal operation mode, the
            compiler first parses the program and determines if there are any syntax errors.
            If there are, appropriate error messages are generated and compilation is imme-
            diately terminated. This switch tells GNAT to continue with semantic analysis
            even if syntax errors have been found. This may enable the detection of more
            errors in a single run. On the other hand, the semantic analyzer is more likely
            to encounter some internal fatal error when given a syntactically invalid tree.

'-gnatQ'   In normal operation mode, the 'ALI' file is not generated if any illegalities are
            detected in the program. The use of '-gnatQ' forces generation of the 'ALI' file.
            This file is marked as being in error, so it cannot be used for binding purposes,
            but it does contain reasonably complete cross-reference information, and thus
            may be useful for use by tools (e.g. semantic browsing tools or integrated
            development environments) that are driven from the 'ALI' file. This switch
            implies '-gnatq', since the semantic phase must be run to get a meaningful
            ALI file.

            In addition, if '-gnatt' is also specified, then the tree file is generated even
            if there are illegalities. It may be useful in this case to also specify '-gnatq'
            to ensure that full semantic processing occurs. The resulting tree file can be
            processed by ASIS, for the purpose of providing partial information about illegal
            units, but if the error causes the tree to be badly malformed, then ASIS may
            crash during the analysis.

            When '-gnatQ' is used and the generated 'ALI' file is marked as being in error,
            gnatmake will attempt to recompile the source when it finds such an 'ALI' file,
            including with switch '-gnatc'.

            Note that '-gnatQ' has no effect if '-gnats' is specified, since ALI files are never
            generated if '-gnats' is set.

3.2.2 Warning Message Control

In addition to error messages, which correspond to illegalities as defined in the Ada Reference Manual, the compiler detects two kinds of warning situations.

First, the compiler considers some constructs suspicious and generates a warning message
to alert you to a possible error. Second, if the compiler detects a situation that is sure to
raise an exception at run time, it generates a warning message. The following shows an
example of warning messages:

```
e.adb:4:24: warning: creation of object may raise Storage_Error
e.adb:10:17: warning: static value out of range
e.adb:10:17: warning: "Constraint_Error" will be raised at run time
```

GNAT considers a large number of situations as appropriate for the generation of warning
messages. As always, warnings are not definite indications of errors. For example, if you
do an out-of-range assignment with the deliberate intention of raising a Constraint_Error
exception, then the warning that may be issued does not indicate an error. Some of the
situations for which GNAT issues warnings (at least some of the time) are given in the
following list. This list is not complete, and new warnings are often added to subsequent
versions of GNAT. The list is intended to give a general idea of the kinds of warnings that
are generated.

- Possible infinitely recursive calls
- Out-of-range values being assigned
- Possible order of elaboration problems
- Assertions (pragma Assert) that are sure to fail
- Unreachable code
- Address clauses with possibly unaligned values, or where an attempt is made to overlay a smaller variable with a larger one.
- Fixed-point type declarations with a null range
- Direct_IO or Sequential_IO instantiated with a type that has access values
- Variables that are never assigned a value
- Variables that are referenced before being initialized
- Task entries with no corresponding `accept` statement
- Duplicate accepts for the same task entry in a `select`
- Objects that take too much storage
- Unchecked conversion between types of differing sizes
- Missing `return` statement along some execution path in a function
- Incorrect (unrecognized) pragmas
- Incorrect external names
- Allocation from empty storage pool
- Potentially blocking operation in protected type
- Suspicious parenthesization of expressions
- Mismatching bounds in an aggregate
- Attempt to return local value by reference
- Premature instantiation of a generic body
- Attempt to pack aliased components
- Out of bounds array subscripts
- Wrong length on string assignment
- Violations of style rules if style checking is enabled
- Unused `with` clauses
- `Bit_Order` usage that does not have any effect
- `Standard.Duration` used to resolve universal fixed expression
- Dereference of possibly null value
- Declaration that is likely to cause storage error
- Internal GNAT unit `with`'ed by application unit
- Values known to be out of range at compile time
- Unreferenced labels and variables
- Address overlays that could clobber memory
- Unexpected initialization when address clause present
- Bad alignment for address clause

- Useless type conversions
- Redundant assignment statements and other redundant constructs
- Useless exception handlers
- Accidental hiding of name by child unit
- Access before elaboration detected at compile time
- A range in a `for` loop that is known to be null or might be null

The following section lists compiler switches that are available to control the handling of warning messages. It is also possible to exercise much finer control over what warnings are issued and suppressed using the GNAT pragma Warnings, which is documented in the GNAT Reference manual.

'-gnatwa'   *Activate all optional errors.* This switch activates most optional warning messages, see remaining list in this section for details on optional warning messages that can be individually controlled. The warnings that are not turned on by this switch are '-gnatwd' (implicit dereferencing), '-gnatwh' (hiding), '-gnatwl' (elaboration warnings), '-gnatw.o' (warn on values set by out parameters ignored) and '-gnatwt' (tracking of deleted conditional code). All other optional warnings are turned on.

'-gnatwA'   *Suppress all optional errors.* This switch suppresses all optional warning messages, see remaining list in this section for details on optional warning messages that can be individually controlled.

'-gnatw.a'

    Activate warnings on failing assertions. This switch activates warnings for assertions where the compiler can tell at compile time that the assertion will fail. Note that this warning is given even if assertions are disabled. The default is that such warnings are generated.

'-gnatw.A'

    Suppress warnings on failing assertions. This switch suppresses warnings for assertions where the compiler can tell at compile time that the assertion will fail.

'-gnatwb'   *Activate warnings on bad fixed values.* This switch activates warnings for static fixed-point expressions whose value is not an exact multiple of Small. Such values are implementation dependent, since an implementation is free to choose either of the multiples that surround the value. GNAT always chooses the closer one, but this is not required behavior, and it is better to specify a value that is an exact multiple, ensuring predictable execution. The default is that such warnings are not generated.

'-gnatwB'   *Suppress warnings on bad fixed values.* This switch suppresses warnings for static fixed-point expressions whose value is not an exact multiple of Small.

'-gnatwc'   *Activate warnings on conditionals.* This switch activates warnings for conditional expressions used in tests that are known to be True or False at compile time. The default is that such warnings are not generated. Note that this warning does not get issued for the use of boolean variables or constants whose values are known at compile time, since this is a standard technique for conditional compilation in Ada, and this would generate too many false positive warnings.

This warning option also activates a special test for comparisons using the operators ">=" and " <=". If the compiler can tell that only the equality condition is possible, then it will warn that the ">" or "<" part of the test is useless and that the operator could be replaced by "=". An example would be comparing a `Natural` variable <= 0.

This warning option also generates warnings if one or both tests is optimized away in a membership test for integer values if the result can be determined at compile time. Range tests on enumeration types are not included, since it is common for such tests to include an end point.

This warning can also be turned on using '`-gnatwa`'.

'`-gnatwC`' *Suppress warnings on conditionals.* This switch suppresses warnings for conditional expressions used in tests that are known to be True or False at compile time.

'`-gnatw.c`'

    Activate warnings on missing component clauses. This switch activates warnings for record components where a record representation clause is present and has component clauses for the majority, but not all, of the components. A warning is given for each component for which no component clause is present.

    This warning can also be turned on using '`-gnatwa`'.

'`-gnatw.C`'

    Suppress warnings on missing component clauses. This switch suppresses warnings for record components that are missing a component clause in the situation described above.

'`-gnatwd`' *Activate warnings on implicit dereferencing.* If this switch is set, then the use of a prefix of an access type in an indexed component, slice, or selected component without an explicit `.all` will generate a warning. With this warning enabled, access checks occur only at points where an explicit `.all` appears in the source code (assuming no warnings are generated as a result of this switch). The default is that such warnings are not generated. Note that '`-gnatwa`' does not affect the setting of this warning option.

'`-gnatwD`' *Suppress warnings on implicit dereferencing.* This switch suppresses warnings for implicit dereferences in indexed components, slices, and selected components.

'`-gnatwe`' *Treat warnings as errors.* This switch causes warning messages to be treated as errors. The warning string still appears, but the warning messages are counted as errors, and prevent the generation of an object file.

'`-gnatwf`' *Activate warnings on unreferenced formals.* This switch causes a warning to be generated if a formal parameter is not referenced in the body of the subprogram. This warning can also be turned on using '`-gnatwa`' or '`-gnatwu`'. The default is that these warnings are not generated.

'-gnatwF'   *Suppress warnings on unreferenced formals.* This switch suppresses warnings for unreferenced formal parameters. Note that the combination '-gnatwu' followed by '-gnatwF' has the effect of warning on unreferenced entities other than subprogram formals.

'-gnatwg'   *Activate warnings on unrecognized pragmas.* This switch causes a warning to be generated if an unrecognized pragma is encountered. Apart from issuing this warning, the pragma is ignored and has no effect. This warning can also be turned on using '-gnatwa'. The default is that such warnings are issued (satisfying the Ada Reference Manual requirement that such warnings appear).

'-gnatwG'   *Suppress warnings on unrecognized pragmas.* This switch suppresses warnings for unrecognized pragmas.

'-gnatwh'   *Activate warnings on hiding.* This switch activates warnings on hiding declarations. A declaration is considered hiding if it is for a non-overloadable entity, and it declares an entity with the same name as some other entity that is directly or use-visible. The default is that such warnings are not generated. Note that '-gnatwa' does not affect the setting of this warning option.

'-gnatwH'   *Suppress warnings on hiding.* This switch suppresses warnings on hiding declarations.

'-gnatwi'   *Activate warnings on implementation units.* This switch activates warnings for a `with` of an internal GNAT implementation unit, defined as any unit from the `Ada`, `Interfaces`, `GNAT`, or `System` hierarchies that is not documented in either the Ada Reference Manual or the GNAT Programmer's Reference Manual. Such units are intended only for internal implementation purposes and should not be `with`'ed by user programs. The default is that such warnings are generated This warning can also be turned on using '-gnatwa'.

'-gnatwI'   *Disable warnings on implementation units.* This switch disables warnings for a `with` of an internal GNAT implementation unit.

'-gnatwj'   *Activate warnings on obsolescent features (Annex J).* If this warning option is activated, then warnings are generated for calls to subprograms marked with `pragma Obsolescent` and for use of features in Annex J of the Ada Reference Manual. In the case of Annex J, not all features are flagged. In particular use of the renamed packages (like `Text_IO`) and use of package `ASCII` are not flagged, since these are very common and would generate many annoying positive warnings. The default is that such warnings are not generated. This warning is also turned on by the use of '-gnatwa'.

             In addition to the above cases, warnings are also generated for GNAT features that have been provided in past versions but which have been superseded (typically by features in the new Ada standard). For example, `pragma Ravenscar` will be flagged since its function is replaced by `pragma Profile(Ravenscar)`.

             Note that this warning option functions differently from the restriction `No_Obsolescent_Features` in two respects. First, the restriction applies only to annex J features. Second, the restriction does flag uses of package `ASCII`.

'-gnatwJ'   *Suppress warnings on obsolescent features (Annex J).* This switch disables warnings on use of obsolescent features.

'-gnatwk'   *Activate warnings on variables that could be constants.* This switch activates warnings for variables that are initialized but never modified, and then could be declared constants. The default is that such warnings are not given. This warning can also be turned on using '-gnatwa'.

'-gnatwK'   *Suppress warnings on variables that could be constants.* This switch disables warnings on variables that could be declared constants.

'-gnatwl'   *Activate warnings for missing elaboration pragmas.* This switch activates warnings on missing `Elaborate_All` and `Elaborate` pragmas. See the section in this guide on elaboration checking for details on when such pragmas should be used. Warnings are also generated if you are using the static mode of elaboration, and a `pragma Elaborate` is encountered. The default is that such warnings are not generated. This warning is not automatically turned on by the use of '-gnatwa'.

'-gnatwL'   *Suppress warnings for missing elaboration pragmas.* This switch suppresses warnings on missing Elaborate and Elaborate_All pragmas. See the section in this guide on elaboration checking for details on when such pragmas should be used.

'-gnatwm'   *Activate warnings on modified but unreferenced variables.* This switch activates warnings for variables that are assigned (using an initialization value or with one or more assignment statements) but whose value is never read. The warning is suppressed for volatile variables and also for variables that are renamings of other variables or for which an address clause is given. This warning can also be turned on using '-gnatwa'. The default is that these warnings are not given.

'-gnatwM'   *Disable warnings on modified but unreferenced variables.* This switch disables warnings for variables that are assigned or initialized, but never read.

'-gnatwn'   *Set normal warnings mode.* This switch sets normal warning mode, in which enabled warnings are issued and treated as warnings rather than errors. This is the default mode. the switch '-gnatwn' can be used to cancel the effect of an explicit '-gnatws' or '-gnatwe'. It also cancels the effect of the implicit '-gnatwe' that is activated by the use of '-gnatg'.

'-gnatwo'   *Activate warnings on address clause overlays.* This switch activates warnings for possibly unintended initialization effects of defining address clauses that cause one variable to overlap another. The default is that such warnings are generated. This warning can also be turned on using '-gnatwa'.

'-gnatwO'   *Suppress warnings on address clause overlays.* This switch suppresses warnings on possibly unintended initialization effects of defining address clauses that cause one variable to overlap another.

'-gnatw.o'

    Activate warnings on modified but unreferenced out parameters. This switch activates warnings for variables that are modified by using them as actuals for a call to a procedure with an out mode formal, where the resulting assigned value is never read. It is applicable in the case where there is more than one out mode formal. If there is only one out mode formal, the warning is issued by default (controlled by -gnatwu). The warning is suppressed for volatile variables and also for variables that are renamings of other variables or for which an address clause is given. The default is that these warnings are not given. Note that this warning is not included in -gnatwa, it must be activated explicitly.

'-gnatw.O'

> *Disable warnings on modified but unreferenced out parameters.* This switch suppresses warnings for variables that are modified by using them as actuals for a call to a procedure with an out mode formal, where the resulting assigned value is never read.

'-gnatwp'

> *Activate warnings on ineffective pragma Inlines.* This switch activates warnings for failure of front end inlining (activated by '-gnatN') to inline a particular call. There are many reasons for not being able to inline a call, including most commonly that the call is too complex to inline. The default is that such warnings are not given. This warning can also be turned on using '-gnatwa'. Warnings on ineffective inlining by the gcc back-end can be activated separately, using the gcc switch -Winline.

'-gnatwP'

> *Suppress warnings on ineffective pragma Inlines.* This switch suppresses warnings on ineffective pragma Inlines. If the inlining mechanism cannot inline a call, it will simply ignore the request silently.

'-gnatwq'

> *Activate warnings on questionable missing parentheses.* This switch activates warnings for cases where parentheses are not used and the result is potential ambiguity from a readers point of view. For example (not a > b) when a and b are modular means ((not a) > b) and very likely the programmer intended (not (a > b)). Similarly (-x mod 5) means (-(x mod 5)) and quite likely ((-x) mod 5) was intended. In such situations it seems best to follow the rule of always parenthesizing to make the association clear, and this warning switch warns if such parentheses are not present. The default is that these warnings are given. This warning can also be turned on using '-gnatwa'.

'-gnatwQ'

> *Suppress warnings on questionable missing parentheses.* This switch suppresses warnings for cases where the association is not clear and the use of parentheses is preferred.

'-gnatwr'

> *Activate warnings on redundant constructs.* This switch activates warnings for redundant constructs. The following is the current list of constructs regarded as redundant:
>
> * Assignment of an item to itself.
> * Type conversion that converts an expression to its own type.
> * Use of the attribute Base where typ'Base is the same as typ.
> * Use of pragma Pack when all components are placed by a record representation clause.
> * Exception handler containing only a reraise statement (raise with no operand) which has no effect.
> * Use of the operator abs on an operand that is known at compile time to be non-negative
> * Comparison of boolean expressions to an explicit True value.

This warning can also be turned on using '`-gnatwa`'. The default is that warnings for redundant constructs are not given.

'`-gnatwR`' *Suppress warnings on redundant constructs.* This switch suppresses warnings for redundant constructs.

'`-gnatws`' *Suppress all warnings.* This switch completely suppresses the output of all warning messages from the GNAT front end. Note that it does not suppress warnings from the `gcc` back end. To suppress these back end warnings as well, use the switch '`-w`' in addition to '`-gnatws`'.

'`-gnatwt`' *Activate warnings for tracking of deleted conditional code.* This switch activates warnings for tracking of code in conditionals (IF and CASE statements) that is detected to be dead code which cannot be executed, and which is removed by the front end. This warning is off by default, and is not turned on by '`-gnatwa`', it has to be turned on explicitly. This may be useful for detecting deactivated code in certified applications.

'`-gnatwT`' *Suppress warnings for tracking of deleted conditional code.* This switch suppresses warnings for tracking of deleted conditional code.

'`-gnatwu`' *Activate warnings on unused entities.* This switch activates warnings to be generated for entities that are declared but not referenced, and for units that are `with`'ed and not referenced. In the case of packages, a warning is also generated if no entities in the package are referenced. This means that if the package is referenced but the only references are in `use` clauses or `renames` declarations, a warning is still generated. A warning is also generated for a generic package that is `with`'ed but never instantiated. In the case where a package or subprogram body is compiled, and there is a `with` on the corresponding spec that is only referenced in the body, a warning is also generated, noting that the `with` can be moved to the body. The default is that such warnings are not generated. This switch also activates warnings on unreferenced formals (it includes the effect of '`-gnatwf`'). This warning can also be turned on using '`-gnatwa`'.

'`-gnatwU`' *Suppress warnings on unused entities.* This switch suppresses warnings for unused entities and packages. It also turns off warnings on unreferenced formals (and thus includes the effect of '`-gnatwF`').

'`-gnatwv`' *Activate warnings on unassigned variables.* This switch activates warnings for access to variables which may not be properly initialized. The default is that such warnings are generated. This warning can also be turned on using '`-gnatwa`'.

'`-gnatwV`' *Suppress warnings on unassigned variables.* This switch suppresses warnings for access to variables which may not be properly initialized. For variables of a composite type, the warning can also be suppressed in Ada 2005 by using a default initialization with a box. For example, if Table is an array of records whose components are only partially uninitialized, then the following code:

```
Tab : Table := (others => <>);
```

will suppress warnings on subsequent statements that access components of variable Tab.

'-gnatww'   *Activate warnings on wrong low bound assumption.* This switch activates warnings for indexing an unconstrained string parameter with a literal or S'Length.
This is a case where the code is assuming that the low bound is one, which is in
general not true (for example when a slice is passed). The default is that such
warnings are generated. This warning can also be turned on using '-gnatwa'.

'-gnatwW'   *Suppress warnings on wrong low bound assumption.* This switch activates warnings for indexing an unconstrained string parameter with a literal or S'Length.
This warning can also be suppressed by providing an Assert pragma that checks
the low bound, for example:

```
procedure K (S : String) is
   pragma Assert (S'First = 1);
   ...
```

'-gnatwx'   *Activate warnings on Export/Import pragmas.* This switch activates warnings
on Export/Import pragmas when the compiler detects a possible conflict between the Ada and foreign language calling sequences. For example, the use
of default parameters in a convention C procedure is dubious because the C
compiler cannot supply the proper default, so a warning is issued. The default
is that such warnings are generated. This warning can also be turned on using
'-gnatwa'.

'-gnatwX'   *Suppress warnings on Export/Import pragmas.* This switch suppresses warnings
on Export/Import pragmas. The sense of this is that you are telling the compiler that you know what you are doing in writing the pragma, and it should
not complain at you.

'-gnatw.x'
             Activate warnings for No_Exception_Propagation mode. This switch
activates warnings for exception usage when pragma Restrictions
(No_Exception_Propagation) is in effect. Warnings are given for implicit or
explicit exception raises which are not covered by a local handler, and for
exception handlers which do not cover a local raise. The default is that these
warnings are not given.

'-gnatw.X'
             Disable warnings for No_Exception_Propagation mode. This switch
disables warnings for exception usage when pragma Restrictions
(No_Exception_Propagation) is in effect.

'-gnatwy'   *Activate warnings for Ada 2005 compatibility issues.* For the most part Ada
2005 is upwards compatible with Ada 95, but there are some exceptions (for
example the fact that interface is now a reserved word in Ada 2005). This
switch activates several warnings to help in identifying and correcting such
incompatibilities. The default is that these warnings are generated. Note that
at one point Ada 2005 was called Ada 0Y, hence the choice of character. This
warning can also be turned on using '-gnatwa'.

'-gnatwY'   *Disable warnings for Ada 2005 compatibility issues.* This switch suppresses
several warnings intended to help in identifying incompatibilities between Ada
95 and Ada 2005.

'`-gnatwz`'   *Activate warnings on unchecked conversions.* This switch activates warnings
                for unchecked conversions where the types are known at compile time to have
                different sizes. The default is that such warnings are generated. This warning
                can also be turned on using '`-gnatwa`'.

'`-gnatwZ`'   *Suppress warnings on unchecked conversions.* This switch suppresses warnings
                for unchecked conversions where the types are known at compile time to have
                different sizes.

'`-Wuninitialized`'

                The warnings controlled by the '`-gnatw`' switch are generated by the front end of
                the compiler. In some cases, the '`gcc`' back end can provide additional warnings.
                One such useful warning is provided by '`-Wuninitialized`'. This must be
                used in conjunction with turning on optimization mode. This causes the flow
                analysis circuits of the back end optimizer to output additional warnings about
                uninitialized variables.

'`-w`'   This switch suppresses warnings from the '`gcc`' back end. The code generator
                detects a number of warning situations that are missed by the '`GNAT`' front end,
                and this switch can be used to suppress them. The use of this switch also sets
                the default front end warning mode to '`-gnatws`', that is, front end warnings
                suppressed as well.

A string of warning parameters can be used in the same parameter. For example:

    -gnatwaLe

will turn on all optional warnings except for elaboration pragma warnings, and also specify that warnings should be treated as errors. When no switch '`-gnatw`' is used, this is equivalent to:

'`-gnatwC`'

'`-gnatwD`'

'`-gnatwF`'

'`-gnatwg`'

'`-gnatwH`'

'`-gnatwi`'

'`-gnatwJ`'

'`-gnatwK`'

'`-gnatwL`'

'`-gnatwM`'

'`-gnatwn`'

'`-gnatwo`'

'`-gnatwP`'

'`-gnatwR`'

'-gnatwU'

'-gnatwv'

'-gnatwz'

'-gnatwx'

3.2.3 Debugging and Assertion Control

'-gnata'

> The pragmas `Assert` and `Debug` normally have no effect and are ignored. This switch, where 'a' stands for assert, causes `Assert` and `Debug` pragmas to be activated.

> The pragmas have the form:

```
pragma Assert (Boolean-expression [,
                        static-string-expression])
pragma Debug (procedure call)
```

> The `Assert` pragma causes *Boolean-expression* to be tested. If the result is `True`, the pragma has no effect (other than possible side effects from evaluating the expression). If the result is `False`, the exception `Assert_Failure` declared in the package `System.Assertions` is raised (passing *static-string-expression*, if present, as the message associated with the exception). If no string expression is given the default is a string giving the file name and line number of the pragma.

> The `Debug` pragma causes *procedure* to be called. Note that `pragma Debug` may appear within a declaration sequence, allowing debugging procedures to be called between declarations.

3.2.4 Validity Checking

The Ada Reference Manual has specific requirements for checking for invalid values. In particular, RM 13.9.1 requires that the evaluation of invalid values (for example from unchecked conversions), not result in erroneous execution. In GNAT, the result of such an evaluation in normal default mode is to either use the value unmodified, or to raise Constraint_Error in those cases where use of the unmodified value would cause erroneous execution. The cases where unmodified values might lead to erroneous execution are case statements (where a wild jump might result from an invalid value), and subscripts on the left hand side (where memory corruption could occur as a result of an invalid value).

The '-gnatVx' switch allows more control over the validity checking mode. The x argument is a string of letters that indicate validity checks that are performed or not performed in addition to the default checks described above.

'-gnatVa'   *All validity checks.* All validity checks are turned on. That is, '-gnatVa' is equivalent to 'gnatVcdfimorst'.

'-gnatVc'   *Validity checks for copies.* The right hand side of assignments, and the initializing values of object declarations are validity checked.

'-gnatVd'   *Default (RM) validity checks.* Some validity checks are done by default fol-
             lowing normal Ada semantics (RM 13.9.1 (9-11)). A check is done in case
             statements that the expression is within the range of the subtype. If it is not,
             Constraint_Error is raised. For assignments to array components, a check is
             done that the expression used as index is within the range. If it is not, Con-
             straint_Error is raised. Both these validity checks may be turned off using
             switch '-gnatVD'. They are turned on by default. If '-gnatVD' is specified, a
             subsequent switch '-gnatVd' will leave the checks turned on. Switch '-gnatVD'
             should be used only if you are sure that all such expressions have valid val-
             ues. If you use this switch and invalid values are present, then the program is
             erroneous, and wild jumps or memory overwriting may occur.

'-gnatVe'   *Validity checks for elementary components.* In the absence of this switch, assign-
             ments to record or array components are not validity checked, even if validity
             checks for assignments generally ('-gnatVc') are turned on. In Ada, assignment
             of composite values do not require valid data, but assignment of individual com-
             ponents does. So for example, there is a difference between copying the elements
             of an array with a slice assignment, compared to assigning element by element
             in a loop. This switch allows you to turn off validity checking for components,
             even when they are assigned component by component.

'-gnatVf'   *Validity checks for floating-point values.* In the absence of this switch, validity
             checking occurs only for discrete values. If '-gnatVf' is specified, then validity
             checking also applies for floating-point values, and NaNs and infinities are con-
             sidered invalid, as well as out of range values for constrained types. Note that
             this means that standard IEEE infinity mode is not allowed. The exact con-
             texts in which floating-point values are checked depends on the setting of other
             options. For example, '-gnatVif' or '-gnatVfi' (the order does not matter)
             specifies that floating-point parameters of mode in should be validity checked.

'-gnatVi'   *Validity checks for* in *mode parameters* Arguments for parameters of mode in
             are validity checked in function and procedure calls at the point of call.

'-gnatVm'   *Validity checks for* in out *mode parameters.* Arguments for parameters of mode
             in out are validity checked in procedure calls at the point of call. The 'm' here
             stands for modify, since this concerns parameters that can be modified by the
             call. Note that there is no specific option to test out parameters, but any
             reference within the subprogram will be tested in the usual manner, and if
             an invalid value is copied back, any reference to it will be subject to validity
             checking.

'-gnatVn'   *No validity checks.* This switch turns off all validity checking, including the
             default checking for case statements and left hand side subscripts. Note that
             the use of the switch '-gnatp' suppresses all run-time checks, including validity
             checks, and thus implies '-gnatVn'. When this switch is used, it cancels any
             other '-gnatV' previously issued.

'-gnatVo'   *Validity checks for operator and attribute operands.* Arguments for prede-
             fined operators and attributes are validity checked. This includes all opera-
             tors in package Standard, the shift operators defined as intrinsic in package

Interfaces and operands for attributes such as Pos. Checks are also made on individual component values for composite comparisons, and on the expressions in type conversions and qualified expressions. Checks are also made on explicit ranges using .. (e.g. slices, loops etc).

'-gnatVp' *Validity checks for parameters.* This controls the treatment of parameters within a subprogram (as opposed to '-gnatVi' and '-gnatVm' which control validity testing of parameters on a call. If either of these call options is used, then normally an assumption is made within a subprogram that the input arguments have been validity checking at the point of call, and do not need checking again within a subprogram). If '-gnatVp' is set, then this assumption is not made, and parameters are not assumed to be valid, so their validity will be checked (or rechecked) within the subprogram.

'-gnatVr' *Validity checks for function returns.* The expression in return statements in functions is validity checked.

'-gnatVs' *Validity checks for subscripts.* All subscripts expressions are checked for validity, whether they appear on the right side or left side (in default mode only left side subscripts are validity checked).

'-gnatVt' *Validity checks for tests.* Expressions used as conditions in if, while or exit statements are checked, as well as guard expressions in entry calls.

The '-gnatV' switch may be followed by a string of letters to turn on a series of validity checking options. For example, '-gnatVcr' specifies that in addition to the default validity checking, copies and function return expressions are to be validity checked. In order to make it easier to specify the desired combination of effects, the upper case letters CDFIMORST may be used to turn off the corresponding lower case option. Thus '-gnatVaM' turns on all validity checking options except for checking of **in out** procedure arguments.

The specification of additional validity checking generates extra code (and in the case of '-gnatVa' the code expansion can be substantial. However, these additional checks can be very useful in detecting uninitialized variables, incorrect use of unchecked conversion, and other errors leading to invalid values. The use of pragma Initialize_Scalars is useful in conjunction with the extra validity checking, since this ensures that wherever possible uninitialized variables have invalid values.

See also the pragma Validity_Checks which allows modification of the validity checking mode at the program source level, and also allows for temporary disabling of validity checks.

3.2.5 Style Checking

The '-gnatyx' switch causes the compiler to enforce specified style rules. A limited set of style rules has been used in writing the GNAT sources themselves. This switch allows user programs to activate all or some of these checks. If the source program fails a specified style check, an appropriate warning message is given, preceded by the character sequence "(style)". The string x is a sequence of letters or digits indicating the particular style checks to be performed. The following checks are defined:

'1-9' *Specify indentation level.* If a digit from 1-9 appears in the string after '-gnaty' then proper indentation is checked, with the digit indicating the indentation level required. The general style of required indentation is as specified by the examples in the Ada Reference Manual. Full line comments must be aligned with the -- starting on a column that is a multiple of the alignment level, or they may be aligned the same way as the following non-blank line (this is useful when full line comments appear in the middle of a statement.

'a'   *Check attribute casing.* If the letter a appears in the string after '-gnaty' then attribute names, including the case of keywords such as digits used as attributes names, must be written in mixed case, that is, the initial letter and any letter following an underscore must be uppercase. All other letters must be lowercase.

'A'   *Use of array index numbers in array attributes.* If the letter A appears in the string after '-gnaty' then when using the array attributes First, Last, Range, or Length, the index number must be omitted for one-dimensional arrays and is required for multi-dimensional arrays.

'b'   *Blanks not allowed at statement end.* If the letter b appears in the string after '-gnaty' then trailing blanks are not allowed at the end of statements. The purpose of this rule, together with h (no horizontal tabs), is to enforce a canonical format for the use of blanks to separate source tokens.

'c'   *Check comments.* If the letter c appears in the string after '-gnaty' then comments must meet the following set of rules:

- The "--" that starts the column must either start in column one, or else at least one blank must precede this sequence.

- Comments that follow other tokens on a line must have at least one blank following the "--" at the start of the comment.

- Full line comments must have two blanks following the "--" that starts the comment, with the following exceptions.

- A line consisting only of the "--" characters, possibly preceded by blanks is permitted.

- A comment starting with "--x" where x is a special character is permitted. This allows proper processing of the output generated by specialized tools including gnatprep (where "--!" is used) and the SPARK annotation language (where "--#" is used). For the purposes of this rule, a special character is defined as being in one of the ASCII ranges 16#21#..16#2F# or 16#3A#..16#3F#. Note that this usage is not permitted in GNAT implementation units (i.e. when '-gnatg' is used).

- A line consisting entirely of minus signs, possibly preceded by blanks, is permitted. This allows the construction of box comments where lines of minus signs are used to form the top and bottom of the box.

- A comment that starts and ends with "--" is permitted as long as at least one blank follows the initial "--". Together with the preceding rule, this allows the construction of box comments, as shown in the following example:

```
--------------------------
-- This is a box comment --
-- with two text lines.  --
--------------------------
```

'd'   *Check no DOS line terminators present.* If the letter d appears in the string
         after '-gnaty' then all lines must be terminated by a single ASCII.LF character
         (in particular the DOS line terminator sequence CR/LF is not allowed).

'e'   *Check end/exit labels.* If the letter e appears in the string after '-gnaty' then
         optional labels on **end** statements ending subprograms and on **exit** statements
         exiting named loops, are required to be present.

'f'   *No form feeds or vertical tabs.* If the letter f appears in the string after '-gnaty'
         then neither form feeds nor vertical tab characters are permitted in the source
         text.

'g'   *GNAT style mode* If the letter g appears in the string after '-gnaty' then the
         set of style check switches is set to match that used by the GNAT sources.
         This may be useful when developing code that is eventually intended to be
         incorporated into GNAT. For further details, see GNAT sources.

'h'   *No horizontal tabs.* If the letter h appears in the string after '-gnaty' then
         horizontal tab characters are not permitted in the source text. Together with
         the b (no blanks at end of line) check, this enforces a canonical form for the
         use of blanks to separate source tokens.

'i'   *Check if-then layout.* If the letter i appears in the string after '-gnaty', then
         the keyword **then** must appear either on the same line as corresponding **if**, or
         on a line on its own, lined up under the **if** with at least one non-blank line in
         between containing all or part of the condition to be tested.

'I'   *check mode IN keywords* If the letter I (upper case) appears in the string after
         '-gnaty' then mode **in** (the default mode) is not allowed to be given explicitly.
         in out is fine, but not **in** on its own.

'k'   *Check keyword casing.* If the letter k appears in the string after '-gnaty' then
         all keywords must be in lower case (with the exception of keywords such as
         digits used as attribute names to which this check does not apply).

'l'   *Check layout.* If the letter l appears in the string after '-gnaty' then layout
         of statement and declaration constructs must follow the recommendations in
         the Ada Reference Manual, as indicated by the form of the syntax rules. For
         example an **else** keyword must be lined up with the corresponding **if** keyword.

         There are two respects in which the style rule enforced by this check option
         are more liberal than those in the Ada Reference Manual. First in the case of
         record declarations, it is permissible to put the **record** keyword on the same
         line as the **type** keyword, and then the **end** in **end record** must line up under
         type. This is also permitted when the type declaration is split on two lines.
         For example, any of the following three layouts is acceptable:

```
type q is record
   a : integer;
   b : integer;
end record;

type q is
   record
      a : integer;
      b : integer;
   end record;

type q is
   record
      a : integer;
      b : integer;
end record;
```

Second, in the case of a block statement, a permitted alternative is to put the block label on the same line as the `declare` or `begin` keyword, and then line the `end` keyword up under the block label. For example both the following are permitted:

```
Block : declare
   A : Integer := 3;
begin
   Proc (A, A);
end Block;

Block :
   declare
      A : Integer := 3;
   begin
      Proc (A, A);
   end Block;
```

The same alternative format is allowed for loops. For example, both of the following are permitted:

```
Clear : while J < 10 loop
   A (J) := 0;
end loop Clear;

Clear :
   while J < 10 loop
      A (J) := 0;
   end loop Clear;
```

'Lnnn'   *Set maximum nesting level* If the sequence Lnnn, where nnn is a decimal number in the range 0-999, appears in the string after '`-gnaty`' then the maximum level of nesting of constructs (including subprograms, loops, blocks, packages, and conditionals) may not exceed the given value. A value of zero disconnects this style check.

'm'   *Check maximum line length.* If the letter m appears in the string after '-gnaty'
then the length of source lines must not exceed 79 characters, including any
trailing blanks. The value of 79 allows convenient display on an 80 character
wide device or window, allowing for possible special treatment of 80 character
lines. Note that this count is of characters in the source text. This means
that a tab character counts as one character in this count but a wide character
sequence counts as a single character (however many bytes are needed in the
encoding).

'Mnnn'   *Set maximum line length.* If the sequence Mnnn, where nnn is a decimal number, appears in the string after '-gnaty' then the length of lines must not exceed
the given value. The maximum value that can be specified is 32767.

'n'   *Check casing of entities in Standard.* If the letter n appears in the string after
'-gnaty' then any identifier from Standard must be cased to match the presentation in the Ada Reference Manual (for example, Integer and ASCII.NUL).

'o'   *Check order of subprogram bodies.* If the letter o appears in the string after
'-gnaty' then all subprogram bodies in a given scope (e.g. a package body)
must be in alphabetical order. The ordering rule uses normal Ada rules for
comparing strings, ignoring casing of letters, except that if there is a trailing
numeric suffix, then the value of this suffix is used in the ordering (e.g. Junk2
comes before Junk10).

'p'   *Check pragma casing.* If the letter p appears in the string after '-gnaty' then
pragma names must be written in mixed case, that is, the initial letter and any
letter following an underscore must be uppercase. All other letters must be
lowercase.

'r'   *Check references.* If the letter r appears in the string after '-gnaty' then all
identifier references must be cased in the same way as the corresponding declaration. No specific casing style is imposed on identifiers. The only requirement
is for consistency of references with declarations.

'S'   *Check no statements after THEN/ELSE.* If the letter S appears in the string
after '-gnaty' then it is not permitted to write any statements on the same
line as a THEN OR ELSE keyword following the keyword in an IF statement.
OR ELSE and AND THEN are not affected, and a special exception allows a
pragma to appear after ELSE.

's'   *Check separate specs.* If the letter s appears in the string after '-gnaty' then
separate declarations ("specs") are required for subprograms (a body is not allowed to serve as its own declaration). The only exception is that parameterless
library level procedures are not required to have a separate declaration. This
exception covers the most frequent form of main program procedures.

't'   *Check token spacing.* If the letter t appears in the string after '-gnaty' then
the following token spacing rules are enforced:

- The keywords **abs** and **not** must be followed by a space.
- The token => must be surrounded by spaces.
- The token <> must be preceded by a space or a left parenthesis.

- Binary operators other than ** must be surrounded by spaces. There is no restriction on the layout of the ** binary operator.

- Colon must be surrounded by spaces.

- Colon-equal (assignment, initialization) must be surrounded by spaces.

- Comma must be the first non-blank character on the line, or be immediately preceded by a non-blank character, and must be followed by a space.

- If the token preceding a left parenthesis ends with a letter or digit, then a space must separate the two tokens.

- A right parenthesis must either be the first non-blank character on a line, or it must be preceded by a non-blank character.

- A semicolon must not be preceded by a space, and must not be followed by a non-blank character.

- A unary plus or minus may not be followed by a space.

- A vertical bar must be surrounded by spaces.

'u'   *Check unnecessary blank lines.* Check for unnecessary blank lines. A blank line is considered unnecessary if it appears at the end of the file, or if more than one blank line occurs in sequence.

'x'   *Check extra parentheses.* Check for the use of an unnecessary extra level of parentheses (C-style) around conditions in `if` statements, `while` statements and `exit` statements.

In the above rules, appearing in column one is always permitted, that is, counts as meeting either a requirement for a required preceding space, or as meeting a requirement for no preceding space.

Appearing at the end of a line is also always permitted, that is, counts as meeting either a requirement for a following space, or as meeting a requirement for no following space.

If any of these style rules is violated, a message is generated giving details on the violation. The initial characters of such messages are always "`(style)`". Note that these messages are treated as warning messages, so they normally do not prevent the generation of an object file. The '`-gnatwe`' switch can be used to treat warning messages, including style messages, as fatal errors.

The switch '`-gnaty`' on its own (that is not followed by any letters or digits), is equivalent to `gnaty3aAbcefhiklmnprst`, that is all checking options enabled with the exception of '`-gnatyo`', '`-gnatyd`', '`-gnatyu`', and '`-gnatyx`'. an indentation level of 3 is set. This is similar to the standard checking option that is used for the GNAT sources.

The switch '`-gnatyN`' clears any previously set style checks.

3.2.6 Run-Time Checks

If you compile with the default options, GNAT will insert many run-time checks into the compiled code, including code that performs range checking against constraints, but not arithmetic overflow checking for integer operations (including division by zero), checks for access before elaboration on subprogram calls, or stack overflow checking. All other run-time checks, as required by the Ada Reference Manual, are generated by default. The following `gcc` switches refine this default behavior:

'-gnatp'   Suppress all run-time checks as though `pragma Suppress (all_checks)` had been present in the source. Validity checks are also suppressed (in other words '-gnatp' also implies '-gnatVn'. Use this switch to improve the performance of the code at the expense of safety in the presence of invalid data or program bugs.

'-gnato'   Enables overflow checking for integer operations. This causes GNAT to generate slower and larger executable programs by adding code to check for overflow (resulting in raising `Constraint_Error` as required by standard Ada semantics). These overflow checks correspond to situations in which the true value of the result of an operation may be outside the base range of the result type. The following example shows the distinction:

```
X1 : Integer := Integer'Last;
X2 : Integer range 1 .. 5 := 5;
X3 : Integer := Integer'Last;
X4 : Integer range 1 .. 5 := 5;
F  : Float := 2.0E+20;
...
X1 := X1 + 1;
X2 := X2 + 1;
X3 := Integer (F);
X4 := Integer (F);
```

Here the first addition results in a value that is outside the base range of Integer, and hence requires an overflow check for detection of the constraint error. Thus the first assignment to `X1` raises a `Constraint_Error` exception only if '-gnato' is set.

The second increment operation results in a violation of the explicit range constraint, and such range checks are always performed (unless specifically suppressed with a pragma `suppress` or the use of '-gnatp').

The two conversions of `F` both result in values that are outside the base range of type `Integer` and thus will raise `Constraint_Error` exceptions only if '-gnato' is used. The fact that the result of the second conversion is assigned to variable `X4` with a restricted range is irrelevant, since the problem is in the conversion, not the assignment.

Basically the rule is that in the default mode ('-gnato' not used), the generated code assures that all integer variables stay within their declared ranges, or within the base range if there is no declared range. This prevents any serious problems like indexes out of range for array operations.

What is not checked in default mode is an overflow that results in an in-range, but incorrect value. In the above example, the assignments to `X1`, `X2`, `X3` all give results that are within the range of the target variable, but the result is wrong in the sense that it is too large to be represented correctly. Typically the assignment to `X1` will result in wrap around to the largest negative number. The conversions of `F` will result in some `Integer` value and if that integer value is out of the `X4` range then the subsequent assignment would generate an exception.

Note that the '-gnato' switch does not affect the code generated for any floating-point operations; it applies only to integer semantics). For floating-point, GNAT has the `Machine_Overflows` attribute set to `False` and the normal mode of operation is to generate IEEE NaN and infinite values on overflow or invalid operations (such as dividing 0.0 by 0.0).

The reason that we distinguish overflow checking from other kinds of range constraint checking is that a failure of an overflow check can generate an incorrect value, but cannot cause erroneous behavior. This is unlike the situation with a constraint check on an array subscript, where failure to perform the check can result in random memory description, or the range check on a case statement, where failure to perform the check can cause a wild jump.

Note again that '`-gnato`' is off by default, so overflow checking is not performed in default mode. This means that out of the box, with the default settings, GNAT does not do all the checks expected from the language description in the Ada Reference Manual. If you want all constraint checks to be performed, as described in this Manual, then you must explicitly use the -gnato switch either on the `gnatmake` or `gcc` command.

'`-gnatE`'   Enables dynamic checks for access-before-elaboration on subprogram calls and generic instantiations. For full details of the effect and use of this switch, See Chapter 3 [Compiling Using gcc], page 37.

'`-fstack-check`'
            Activates stack overflow checking. For full details of the effect and use of this switch see Section 22.1 [Stack Overflow Checking], page 231.

The setting of these switches only controls the default setting of the checks. You may modify them using either **Suppress** (to remove checks) or **Unsuppress** (to add back suppressed checks) pragmas in the program source.

3.2.7 Using `gcc` for Syntax Checking

'`-gnats`'
            The **s** stands for "syntax".

            Run GNAT in syntax checking only mode. For example, the command

                $ gcc -c -gnats x.adb

            compiles file '`x.adb`' in syntax-check-only mode. You can check a series of files in a single command , and can use wild cards to specify such a group of files. Note that you must specify the '`-c`' (compile only) flag in addition to the '`-gnats`' flag. . You may use other switches in conjunction with '`-gnats`'. In particular, '`-gnatl`' and '`-gnatv`' are useful to control the format of any generated error messages.

            When the source file is empty or contains only empty lines and/or comments, the output is a warning:

                $ gcc -c -gnats -x ada toto.txt
                toto.txt:1:01: warning: empty file, contains no compilation units
                $

            Otherwise, the output is simply the error messages, if any. No object file or ALI file is generated by a syntax-only compilation. Also, no units other than the one specified are accessed. For example, if a unit X with's a unit Y, compiling unit X in syntax check only mode does not access the source file containing unit Y.

Normally, GNAT allows only a single unit in a source file. However, this restriction does not apply in syntax-check-only mode, and it is possible to check a file containing multiple compilation units concatenated together. This is primarily used by the gnatchop utility (see Chapter 8 [Renaming Files Using gnatchop], page 115).

3.2.8 Using gcc for Semantic Checking

'-gnatc'

The c stands for "check". Causes the compiler to operate in semantic check mode, with full checking for all illegalities specified in the Ada Reference Manual, but without generation of any object code (no object file is generated).

Because dependent files must be accessed, you must follow the GNAT semantic restrictions on file structuring to operate in this mode:

- The needed source files must be accessible (see Section 3.3 [Search Paths and the Run-Time Library (RTL)], page 76).
- Each file must contain only one compilation unit.
- The file name and unit name must match (see Section 2.3 [File Naming Rules], page 16).

The output consists of error messages as appropriate. No object file is generated. An 'ALI' file is generated for use in the context of cross-reference tools, but this file is marked as not being suitable for binding (since no object file is generated). The checking corresponds exactly to the notion of legality in the Ada Reference Manual.

Any unit can be compiled in semantics-checking-only mode, including units that would not normally be compiled (subunits, and specifications where a separate body is present).

3.2.9 Compiling Different Versions of Ada

The switches described in this section allow you to explicitly specify the version of the Ada language that your programs are written in. By default GNAT assumes Ada 2005, but you can also specify Ada 95 or indicate Ada 83 compatibility mode.

'-gnat83 (Ada 83 Compatibility Mode)'

Although GNAT is primarily an Ada 95 / Ada 2005 compiler, this switch specifies that the program is to be compiled in Ada 83 mode. With '-gnat83', GNAT rejects most post-Ada 83 extensions and applies Ada 83 semantics where this can be done easily. It is not possible to guarantee this switch does a perfect job; some subtle tests, such as are found in earlier ACVC tests (and that have been removed from the ACATS suite for Ada 95), might not compile correctly. Nevertheless, this switch may be useful in some circumstances, for example where, due to contractual reasons, existing code needs to be maintained using only Ada 83 features.

With few exceptions (most notably the need to use <> on unconstrained generic formal parameters, the use of the new Ada 95 / Ada 2005 reserved words, and the use of packages with optional bodies), it is not necessary to specify the '`-gnat83`' switch when compiling Ada 83 programs, because, with rare exceptions, Ada 95 and Ada 2005 are upwardly compatible with Ada 83. Thus a correct Ada 83 program is usually also a correct program in these later versions of the language standard. For further information, please refer to Appendix F [Compatibility and Porting Guide], page 333.

'`-gnat95 (Ada 95 mode)`'

This switch directs the compiler to implement the Ada 95 version of the language. Since Ada 95 is almost completely upwards compatible with Ada 83, Ada 83 programs may generally be compiled using this switch (see the description of the '`-gnat83`' switch for further information about Ada 83 mode). If an Ada 2005 program is compiled in Ada 95 mode, uses of the new Ada 2005 features will cause error messages or warnings.

This switch also can be used to cancel the effect of a previous '`-gnat83`' or '`-gnat05`' switch earlier in the command line.

'`-gnat05 (Ada 2005 mode)`'

This switch directs the compiler to implement the Ada 2005 version of the language. Since Ada 2005 is almost completely upwards compatible with Ada 95 (and thus also with Ada 83), Ada 83 and Ada 95 programs may generally be compiled using this switch (see the description of the '`-gnat83`' and '`-gnat95`' switches for further information).

For information about the approved "Ada Issues" that have been incorporated into Ada 2005, see `http://www.ada-auth.org/cgi-bin/cvsweb.cgi/AIs`. Included with GNAT releases is a file '`features-ada0y`' that describes the set of implemented Ada 2005 features.

3.2.10 Character Set Control

'`-gnatic`'

Normally GNAT recognizes the Latin-1 character set in source program identifiers, as described in the Ada Reference Manual. This switch causes GNAT to recognize alternate character sets in identifiers. c is a single character indicating the character set, as follows:

1	ISO 8859-1 (Latin-1) identifiers
2	ISO 8859-2 (Latin-2) letters allowed in identifiers
3	ISO 8859-3 (Latin-3) letters allowed in identifiers
4	ISO 8859-4 (Latin-4) letters allowed in identifiers
5	ISO 8859-5 (Cyrillic) letters allowed in identifiers
9	ISO 8859-15 (Latin-9) letters allowed in identifiers
p	IBM PC letters (code page 437) allowed in identifiers
8	IBM PC letters (code page 850) allowed in identifiers
f	Full upper-half codes allowed in identifiers
n	No upper-half codes allowed in identifiers

w   Wide-character codes (that is, codes greater than 255) allowed in identifiers

See Section 2.2 [Foreign Language Representation], page 13, for full details on the implementation of these character sets.

'-gnatW*e*'   Specify the method of encoding for wide characters. *e* is one of the following:

h   Hex encoding (brackets coding also recognized)

u   Upper half encoding (brackets encoding also recognized)

s   Shift/JIS encoding (brackets encoding also recognized)

e   EUC encoding (brackets encoding also recognized)

8   UTF-8 encoding (brackets encoding also recognized)

b   Brackets encoding only (default value)

For full details on these encoding methods see Section 2.2.3 [Wide Character Encodings], page 15. Note that brackets coding is always accepted, even if one of the other options is specified, so for example '-gnatW8' specifies that both brackets and UTF-8 encodings will be recognized. The units that are with'ed directly or indirectly will be scanned using the specified representation scheme, and so if one of the non-brackets scheme is used, it must be used consistently throughout the program. However, since brackets encoding is always recognized, it may be conveniently used in standard libraries, allowing these libraries to be used with any of the available coding schemes. scheme.

If no '-gnatW?' parameter is present, then the default representation is normally Brackets encoding only. However, if the first three characters of the file are 16#EF# 16#BB# 16#BF# (the standard byte order mark or BOM for UTF-8), then these three characters are skipped and the default representation for the file is set to UTF-8.

Note that the wide character representation that is specified (explicitly or by default) for the main program also acts as the default encoding used for Wide_Text_IO files if not specifically overridden by a WCEM form parameter.

3.2.11 File Naming Control

'-gnatk*n*'   Activates file name "krunching". *n*, a decimal integer in the range 1-999, indicates the maximum allowable length of a file name (not including the '.ads' or '.adb' extension). The default is not to enable file name krunching.

For the source file naming rules, See Section 2.3 [File Naming Rules], page 16.

3.2.12 Subprogram Inlining Control

'-gnatn'   The n here is intended to suggest the first syllable of the word "inline". GNAT recognizes and processes Inline pragmas. However, for the inlining to actually occur, optimization must be enabled. To enable inlining of subprograms specified by pragma Inline, you must also specify this switch. In the absence of this switch, GNAT does not attempt inlining and does not need to access the bodies of subprograms for which pragma Inline is specified if they are not in the current unit.

If you specify this switch the compiler will access these bodies, creating an extra source dependency for the resulting object file, and where possible, the call will be inlined. For further details on when inlining is possible see Section 7.1.5 [Inlining of Subprograms], page 106.

'-gnatN'   The front end inlining activated by this switch is generally more extensive, and quite often more effective than the standard '-gnatn' inlining mode. It will also generate additional dependencies. Note that '-gnatN' automatically implies '-gnatn' so it is not necessary to specify both options.

3.2.13 Auxiliary Output Control

'-gnatt'   Causes GNAT to write the internal tree for a unit to a file (with the extension '.adt'. This not normally required, but is used by separate analysis tools. Typically these tools do the necessary compilations automatically, so you should not have to specify this switch in normal operation.

'-gnatu'   Print a list of units required by this compilation on 'stdout'. The listing includes all units on which the unit being compiled depends either directly or indirectly.

'-pass-exit-codes'

If this switch is not used, the exit code returned by gcc when compiling multiple files indicates whether all source files have been successfully used to generate object files or not.

When '-pass-exit-codes' is used, gcc exits with an extended exit status and allows an integrated development environment to better react to a compilation failure. Those exit status are:

5   There was an error in at least one source file.

3   At least one source file did not generate an object file.

2   The compiler died unexpectedly (internal error for example).

0   An object file has been generated for every source file.

3.2.14 Debugging Control

'-gnatdx'   Activate internal debugging switches. x is a letter or digit, or string of letters or digits, which specifies the type of debugging outputs desired. Normally these are used only for internal development or system debugging purposes. You can find full documentation for these switches in the body of the Debug unit in the compiler source file 'debug.adb'.

'-gnatG'   This switch causes the compiler to generate auxiliary output containing a pseudo-source listing of the generated expanded code. Like most Ada compilers, GNAT works by first transforming the high level Ada code into lower level constructs. For example, tasking operations are transformed into calls to the tasking run-time routines. A unique capability of GNAT is to list this expanded code in a form very close to normal Ada source. This is very useful in understanding the implications of various Ada usage on the efficiency of the generated code. There are many cases in Ada (e.g. the use of controlled types), where simple Ada statements can generate a lot of run-time code. By using '-gnatG' you can identify these cases, and consider whether it may be desirable to modify the coding approach to improve efficiency.

The format of the output is very similar to standard Ada source, and is easily understood by an Ada programmer. The following special syntactic additions correspond to low level features used in the generated code that do not have any exact analogies in pure Ada source form. The following is a partial list of these special constructions. See the specification of package Sprint in file 'sprint.ads' for a full list.

If the switch '-gnatL' is used in conjunction with '-gnatG', then the original source lines are interspersed in the expanded source (as comment lines with the original line number).

new *xxx* [storage_pool = *yyy*]
> Shows the storage pool being used for an allocator.

at end *procedure-name*;
> Shows the finalization (cleanup) procedure for a scope.

(if *expr* then *expr* else *expr*)
> Conditional expression equivalent to the x?y:z construction in C.

target^(*source*)
> A conversion with floating-point truncation instead of rounding.

target?(*source*)
> A conversion that bypasses normal Ada semantic checking. In particular enumeration types and fixed-point types are treated simply as integers.

target?^(*source*)
> Combines the above two cases.

x #/ *y*
x #mod *y*
x #* *y*
x #rem *y*   A division or multiplication of fixed-point values which are treated as integers without any kind of scaling.

free *expr* [storage_pool = *xxx*]
> Shows the storage pool associated with a free statement.

[subtype or type declaration]
> Used to list an equivalent declaration for an internally generated type that is referenced elsewhere in the listing.

freeze *type-name* [*actions*]
> Shows the point at which *type-name* is frozen, with possible associated actions to be performed at the freeze point.

reference *itype*
> Reference (and hence definition) to internal type *itype*.

function-name! (arg, arg, arg)
> Intrinsic function call.

label-name : label
> Declaration of label *labelname*.

#$ *subprogram-name*
> An implicit call to a run-time support routine (to meet the requirement of H.3.1(9) in a convenient manner).

expr && *expr* && *expr* ... && *expr*
> A multiple concatenation (same effect as *expr* & *expr* & *expr*, but handled more efficiently).

[constraint_error]
> Raise the Constraint_Error exception.

expression'reference
> A pointer to the result of evaluating *expression*.

target-type!(*source-expression*)
> An unchecked conversion of *source-expression* to *target-type*.

[*numerator/denominator*]
> Used to represent internal real literals (that) have no exact representation in base 2-16 (for example, the result of compile time evaluation of the expression 1.0/27.0).

'-gnatD'
> When used in conjunction with '-gnatG', this switch causes the expanded source, as described above for '-gnatG' to be written to files with names 'xxx.dg', where 'xxx' is the normal file name, instead of to the standard output file. For example, if the source file name is 'hello.adb', then a file 'hello.adb.dg' will be written. The debugging information generated by the gcc '-g' switch will refer to the generated 'xxx.dg' file. This allows you to do source level debugging using the generated code which is sometimes useful for complex code, for example to find out exactly which part of a complex construction raised an exception. This switch also suppress generation of cross-reference information (see '-gnatx') since otherwise the cross-reference information would refer to the '.dg' file, which would cause confusion since this is not the original source file.
>
> Note that '-gnatD' actually implies '-gnatG' automatically, so it is not necessary to give both options. In other words '-gnatD' is equivalent to '-gnatDG').
>
> If the switch '-gnatL' is used in conjunction with '-gnatDG', then the original source lines are interspersed in the expanded source (as comment lines with the original line number).

'-gnatR[0|1|2|3[s]]'
> This switch controls output from the compiler of a listing showing representation information for declared types and objects. For '-gnatR0', no information

is output (equivalent to omitting the '-gnatR' switch). For '-gnatR1' (which is the default, so '-gnatR' with no parameter has the same effect), size and alignment information is listed for declared array and record types. For '-gnatR2', size and alignment information is listed for all declared types and objects. Finally -gnatR3 includes symbolic expressions for values that are computed at run time for variant records. These symbolic expressions have a mostly obvious format with #n being used to represent the value of the n'th discriminant. See source files 'repinfo.ads/adb' in the GNAT sources for full details on the format of '-gnatR3' output. If the switch is followed by an s (e.g. '-gnatR2s'), then the output is to a file with the name 'file.rep' where file is the name of the corresponding source file. Note that it is possible for record components to have zero size. In this case, the component clause uses an obvious extension of permitted Ada syntax, for example at 0 range 0 .. -1.

Representation information requires that code be generated (since it is the code generator that lays out complex data structures). If an attempt is made to output representation information when no code is generated, for example when a subunit is compiled on its own, then no information can be generated and the compiler outputs a message to this effect.

'-gnatS'   The use of the switch '-gnatS' for an Ada compilation will cause the compiler to output a representation of package Standard in a form very close to standard Ada. It is not quite possible to do this entirely in standard Ada (since new numeric base types cannot be created in standard Ada), but the output is easily readable to any Ada programmer, and is useful to determine the characteristics of target dependent types in package Standard.

'-gnatx'   Normally the compiler generates full cross-referencing information in the 'ALI' file. This information is used by a number of tools, including gnatfind and gnatxref. The '-gnatx' switch suppresses this information. This saves some space and may slightly speed up compilation, but means that these tools cannot be used.

3.2.15 Exception Handling Control

GNAT uses two methods for handling exceptions at run-time. The setjmp/longjmp method saves the context when entering a frame with an exception handler. Then when an exception is raised, the context can be restored immediately, without the need for tracing stack frames. This method provides very fast exception propagation, but introduces significant overhead for the use of exception handlers, even if no exception is raised.

The other approach is called "zero cost" exception handling. With this method, the compiler builds static tables to describe the exception ranges. No dynamic code is required when entering a frame containing an exception handler. When an exception is raised, the tables are used to control a back trace of the subprogram invocation stack to locate the required exception handler. This method has considerably poorer performance for the propagation of exceptions, but there is no overhead for exception handlers if no exception is raised. Note that in this mode and in the context of mixed Ada and C/C++ programming, to propagate an exception through a C/C++ code, the C/C++ code must be compiled with the '-funwind-tables' GCC's option.

The following switches may be used to control which of the two exception handling methods is used.

'`--RTS=sjlj`'

This switch causes the setjmp/longjmp run-time (when available) to be used for exception handling. If the default mechanism for the target is zero cost exceptions, then this switch can be used to modify this default, and must be used for all units in the partition. This option is rarely used. One case in which it may be advantageous is if you have an application where exception raising is common and the overall performance of the application is improved by favoring exception propagation.

'`--RTS=zcx`'

This switch causes the zero cost approach to be used for exception handling. If this is the default mechanism for the target (see below), then this switch is unneeded. If the default mechanism for the target is setjmp/longjmp exceptions, then this switch can be used to modify this default, and must be used for all units in the partition. This option can only be used if the zero cost approach is available for the target in use, otherwise it will generate an error.

The same option '`--RTS`' must be used both for `gcc` and `gnatbind`. Passing this option to `gnatmake` (see Section 6.2 [Switches for gnatmake], page 94) will ensure the required consistency through the compilation and binding steps.

3.2.16 Units to Sources Mapping Files

'`-gnatem`*path*'

A mapping file is a way to communicate to the compiler two mappings: from unit names to file names (without any directory information) and from file names to path names (with full directory information). These mappings are used by the compiler to short-circuit the path search.

The use of mapping files is not required for correct operation of the compiler, but mapping files can improve efficiency, particularly when sources are read over a slow network connection. In normal operation, you need not be concerned with the format or use of mapping files, and the '`-gnatem`' switch is not a switch that you would use explicitly. it is intended only for use by automatic tools such as `gnatmake` running under the project file facility. The description here of the format of mapping files is provided for completeness and for possible use by other tools.

A mapping file is a sequence of sets of three lines. In each set, the first line is the unit name, in lower case, with "%s" appended for specifications and "%b" appended for bodies; the second line is the file name; and the third line is the path name.

Example:

```
main%b
main.2.ada
/gnat/project1/sources/main.2.ada
```

When the switch '-gnatem' is specified, the compiler will create in memory the two mappings from the specified file. If there is any problem (non existent file, truncated file or duplicate entries), no mapping will be created.

Several '-gnatem' switches may be specified; however, only the last one on the command line will be taken into account.

When using a project file, gnatmake create a temporary mapping file and communicates it to the compiler using this switch.

3.2.17 Integrated Preprocessing

GNAT sources may be preprocessed immediately before compilation. In this case, the actual text of the source is not the text of the source file, but is derived from it through a process called preprocessing. Integrated preprocessing is specified through switches '-gnatep' and/or '-gnateD'. '-gnatep' indicates, through a text file, the preprocessing data to be used. '-gnateD' specifies or modifies the values of preprocessing symbol.

Note that when integrated preprocessing is used, the output from the preprocessor is not written to any external file. Instead it is passed internally to the compiler. If you need to preserve the result of preprocessing in a file, then you should use gnatprep to perform the desired preprocessing in stand-alone mode.

It is recommended that gnatmake switch -s should be used when Integrated Preprocessing is used. The reason is that preprocessing with another Preprocessing Data file without changing the sources will not trigger recompilation without this switch.

Note that gnatmake switch -m will almost always trigger recompilation for sources that are preprocessed, because gnatmake cannot compute the checksum of the source after preprocessing.

The actual preprocessing function is described in details in section Chapter 16 [Preprocessing Using gnatprep], page 199. This section only describes how integrated preprocessing is triggered and parameterized.

-gnatep=*file*

This switch indicates to the compiler the file name (without directory information) of the preprocessor data file to use. The preprocessor data file should be found in the source directories.

A preprocessing data file is a text file with significant lines indicating how should be preprocessed either a specific source or all sources not mentioned in other lines. A significant line is a non empty, non comment line. Comments are similar to Ada comments.

Each significant line starts with either a literal string or the character '*'. A literal string is the file name (without directory information) of the source to preprocess. A character '*' indicates the preprocessing for all the sources that are not specified explicitly on other lines (order of the lines is not significant). It is an error to have two lines with the same file name or two lines starting with the character '*'.

After the file name or the character '*', another optional literal string indicating the file name of the definition file to be used for preprocessing (see Section 16.3 [Form of Definitions File], page 200). The definition files are found by the compiler in one of the source directories. In some cases, when compiling a source in a directory other than the current directory, if the definition file is in the current directory, it may be necessary to add the current directory as a source directory through switch -I., otherwise the compiler would not find the definition file.

Then, optionally, switches similar to those of `gnatprep` may be found. Those switches are:

-b
: Causes both preprocessor lines and the lines deleted by preprocessing to be replaced by blank lines, preserving the line number. This switch is always implied; however, if specified after '-c' it cancels the effect of '-c'.

-c
: Causes both preprocessor lines and the lines deleted by preprocessing to be retained as comments marked with the special string "--! ".

-Dsymbol=value
: Define or redefine a symbol, associated with value. A symbol is an Ada identifier, or an Ada reserved word, with the exception of `if`, `else`, `elsif`, `end`, `and`, `or` and `then`. value is either a literal string, an Ada identifier or any Ada reserved word. A symbol declared with this switch replaces a symbol with the same name defined in a definition file.

-s
: Causes a sorted list of symbol names and values to be listed on the standard output file.

-u
: Causes undefined symbols to be treated as having the value `FALSE` in the context of a preprocessor test. In the absence of this option, an undefined symbol in a `#if` or `#elsif` test will be treated as an error.

Examples of valid lines in a preprocessor data file:

```
"toto.adb"  "prep.def" -u
--  preprocess "toto.adb", using definition file "prep.def",
--  undefined symbol are False.

*  -c -DVERSION=V101
--  preprocess all other sources without a definition file;
--  suppressed lined are commented; symbol VERSION has the value V101.

"titi.adb" "prep2.def" -s
--  preprocess "titi.adb", using definition file "prep2.def";
--  list all symbols with their values.
```

-gnateDsymbol[=value]
: Define or redefine a preprocessing symbol, associated with value. If no value is given on the command line, then the value of the symbol is `True`. A symbol is an identifier, following normal Ada (case-insensitive) rules for its syntax, and value is any sequence (including an empty sequence) of characters from the set (letters, digits, period, underline). Ada reserved words may be used as symbols, with the exceptions of `if`, `else`, `elsif`, `end`, `and`, `or` and `then`.

A symbol declared with this switch on the command line replaces a symbol with the same name either in a definition file or specified with a switch -D in the preprocessor data file.

This switch is similar to switch '-D' of `gnatprep`.

3.2.18 Code Generation Control

The GCC technology provides a wide range of target dependent '-m' switches for controlling details of code generation with respect to different versions of architectures. This includes variations in instruction sets (e.g. different members of the power pc family), and different requirements for optimal arrangement of instructions (e.g. different members of the x86 family). The list of available '-m' switches may be found in the GCC documentation.

Use of these '-m' switches may in some cases result in improved code performance.

The GNAT Pro technology is tested and qualified without any '-m' switches, so generally the most reliable approach is to avoid the use of these switches. However, we generally expect most of these switches to work successfully with GNAT Pro, and many customers have reported successful use of these options.

Our general advice is to avoid the use of '-m' switches unless special needs lead to requirements in this area. In particular, there is no point in using '-m' switches to improve performance unless you actually see a performance improvement.

3.3 Search Paths and the Run-Time Library (RTL)

With the GNAT source-based library system, the compiler must be able to find source files for units that are needed by the unit being compiled. Search paths are used to guide this process.

The compiler compiles one source file whose name must be given explicitly on the command line. In other words, no searching is done for this file. To find all other source files that are needed (the most common being the specs of units), the compiler examines the following directories, in the following order:

1. The directory containing the source file of the main unit being compiled (the file name on the command line).

2. Each directory named by an '-I' switch given on the `gcc` command line, in the order given.

3. Each of the directories listed in the text file whose name is given by the `ADA_PRJ_INCLUDE_FILE` environment variable.

   `ADA_PRJ_INCLUDE_FILE` is normally set by gnatmake or by the gnat driver when project files are used. It should not normally be set by other means.

4. Each of the directories listed in the value of the `ADA_INCLUDE_PATH` environment variable. Construct this value exactly as the `PATH` environment variable: a list of directory names separated by colons (semicolons when working with the NT version).

5. The content of the 'ada_source_path' file which is part of the GNAT installation tree and is used to store standard libraries such as the GNAT Run Time Library (RTL) source files. Section 19.2.2 [Installing a library], page 211

Specifying the switch '-I-' inhibits the use of the directory containing the source file named in the command line. You can still have this directory on your search path, but in this case it must be explicitly requested with a '-I' switch.

Specifying the switch '-nostdinc' inhibits the search of the default location for the GNAT Run Time Library (RTL) source files.

The compiler outputs its object files and ALI files in the current working directory. Caution: The object file can be redirected with the '-o' switch; however, `gcc` and `gnat1` have not been coordinated on this so the 'ALI' file will not go to the right place. Therefore, you should avoid using the '-o' switch.

The packages `Ada`, `System`, and `Interfaces` and their children make up the GNAT RTL, together with the simple `System.IO` package used in the "Hello World" example. The sources for these units are needed by the compiler and are kept together in one directory. Not all of the bodies are needed, but all of the sources are kept together anyway. In a normal installation, you need not specify these directory names when compiling or binding. Either the environment variables or the built-in defaults cause these files to be found.

In addition to the language-defined hierarchies (`System`, `Ada` and `Interfaces`), the GNAT distribution provides a fourth hierarchy, consisting of child units of `GNAT`. This is a collection of generally useful types, subprograms, etc. See the *GNAT Reference Manual* for further details.

Besides simplifying access to the RTL, a major use of search paths is in compiling sources from multiple directories. This can make development environments much more flexible.

3.4 Order of Compilation Issues

If, in our earlier example, there was a spec for the `hello` procedure, it would be contained in the file 'hello.ads'; yet this file would not have to be explicitly compiled. This is the result of the model we chose to implement library management. Some of the consequences of this model are as follows:

- There is no point in compiling specs (except for package specs with no bodies) because these are compiled as needed by clients. If you attempt a useless compilation, you will receive an error message. It is also useless to compile subunits because they are compiled as needed by the parent.

- There are no order of compilation requirements: performing a compilation never obsoletes anything. The only way you can obsolete something and require recompilations is to modify one of the source files on which it depends.

- There is no library as such, apart from the ALI files (see Section 2.8 [The Ada Library Information Files], page 21, for information on the format of these files). For now we find it convenient to create separate ALI files, but eventually the information therein may be incorporated into the object file directly.

- When you compile a unit, the source files for the specs of all units that it `with`'s, all its subunits, and the bodies of any generics it instantiates must be available (reachable by the search-paths mechanism described above), or you will receive a fatal error message.

3.5 Examples

The following are some typical Ada compilation command line examples:

`$ gcc -c xyz.adb`
> Compile body in file 'xyz.adb' with all default options.

`$ gcc -c -O2 -gnata xyz-def.adb`
> Compile the child unit package in file 'xyz-def.adb' with extensive optimizations, and pragma `Assert`/`Debug` statements enabled.

`$ gcc -c -gnatc abc-def.adb`
> Compile the subunit in file 'abc-def.adb' in semantic-checking-only mode.

4 Binding Using gnatbind

This chapter describes the GNAT binder, gnatbind, which is used to bind compiled GNAT objects.

Note: to invoke gnatbind with a project file, use the gnat driver (see Section 11.15.2 [The GNAT Driver and Project Files], page 157).

The gnatbind program performs four separate functions:

1. Checks that a program is consistent, in accordance with the rules in Chapter 10 of the Ada Reference Manual. In particular, error messages are generated if a program uses inconsistent versions of a given unit.

2. Checks that an acceptable order of elaboration exists for the program and issues an error message if it cannot find an order of elaboration that satisfies the rules in Chapter 10 of the Ada Language Manual.

3. Generates a main program incorporating the given elaboration order. This program is a small Ada package (body and spec) that must be subsequently compiled using the GNAT compiler. The necessary compilation step is usually performed automatically by gnatlink. The two most important functions of this program are to call the elaboration routines of units in an appropriate order and to call the main program.

4. Determines the set of object files required by the given main program. This information is output in the forms of comments in the generated program, to be read by the gnatlink utility used to link the Ada application.

4.1 Running gnatbind

The form of the gnatbind command is

```
$ gnatbind [switches] mainprog[.ali] [switches]
```

where 'mainprog.adb' is the Ada file containing the main program unit body. If no switches are specified, gnatbind constructs an Ada package in two files whose names are 'b~mainprog.ads', and 'b~mainprog.adb'. For example, if given the parameter 'hello.ali', for a main program contained in file 'hello.adb', the binder output files would be 'b~hello.ads' and 'b~hello.adb'.

When doing consistency checking, the binder takes into consideration any source files it can locate. For example, if the binder determines that the given main program requires the package Pack, whose '.ALI' file is 'pack.ali' and whose corresponding source spec file is 'pack.ads', it attempts to locate the source file 'pack.ads' (using the same search path conventions as previously described for the gcc command). If it can locate this source file, it checks that the time stamps or source checksums of the source and its references to in 'ALI' files match. In other words, any 'ALI' files that mentions this spec must have resulted from compiling this version of the source file (or in the case where the source checksums match, a version close enough that the difference does not matter).

The effect of this consistency checking, which includes source files, is that the binder ensures that the program is consistent with the latest version of the source files that can be located at bind time. Editing a source file without compiling files that depend on the source file cause error messages to be generated by the binder.

For example, suppose you have a main program 'hello.adb' and a package P, from file 'p.ads' and you perform the following steps:

1. Enter gcc -c hello.adb to compile the main program.
2. Enter gcc -c p.ads to compile package P.
3. Edit file 'p.ads'.
4. Enter gnatbind hello.

At this point, the file 'p.ali' contains an out-of-date time stamp because the file 'p.ads' has been edited. The attempt at binding fails, and the binder generates the following error messages:

```
error: "hello.adb" must be recompiled ("p.ads" has been modified)
error: "p.ads" has been modified and must be recompiled
```

Now both files must be recompiled as indicated, and then the bind can succeed, generating a main program. You need not normally be concerned with the contents of this file, but for reference purposes a sample binder output file is given in Appendix B [Example of Binder Output File], page 277.

In most normal usage, the default mode of gnatbind which is to generate the main package in Ada, as described in the previous section. In particular, this means that any Ada programmer can read and understand the generated main program. It can also be debugged just like any other Ada code provided the '-g' switch is used for gnatbind and gnatlink.

However for some purposes it may be convenient to generate the main program in C rather than Ada. This may for example be helpful when you are generating a mixed language program with the main program in C. The GNAT compiler itself is an example. The use of the '-C' switch for both gnatbind and gnatlink will cause the program to be generated in C (and compiled using the gnu C compiler).

4.2 Switches for gnatbind

The following switches are available with gnatbind; details will be presented in subsequent sections.

'--version'
    Display Copyright and version, then exit disregarding all other options.

'--help'   If '--version' was not used, display usage, then exit disregarding all other options.

'-a'   Indicates that, if supported by the platform, the adainit procedure should be treated as an initialisation routine by the linker (a constructor). This is intended to be used by the Project Manager to automatically initialize shared Stand-Alone Libraries.

'-aO'   Specify directory to be searched for ALI files.

'-aI'   Specify directory to be searched for source file.

'-A'   Generate binder program in Ada (default)

'-b'   Generate brief messages to 'stderr' even if verbose mode set.

'-c'   Check only, no generation of binder output file.

'-C'   Generate binder program in C

'`-dnn[k|m]`'
:   This switch can be used to change the default task stack size value to a specified size *nn*, which is expressed in bytes by default, or in kilobytes when suffixed with *k* or in megabytes when suffixed with *m*. In the absence of a [k|m] suffix, this switch is equivalent, in effect, to completing all task specs with

    ```
    pragma Storage_Size (nn);
    ```

    When they do not already have such a pragma.

'`-Dnn[k|m]`'
:   This switch can be used to change the default secondary stack size value to a specified size *nn*, which is expressed in bytes by default, or in kilobytes when suffixed with *k* or in megabytes when suffixed with *m*.

    The secondary stack is used to deal with functions that return a variable sized result, for example a function returning an unconstrained String. There are two ways in which this secondary stack is allocated.

    For most targets, the secondary stack is growing on demand and is allocated as a chain of blocks in the heap. The -D option is not very relevant. It only give some control over the size of the allocated blocks (whose size is the minimum of the default secondary stack size value, and the actual size needed for the current allocation request).

    For certain targets, notably VxWorks 653, the secondary stack is allocated by carving off a fixed ratio chunk of the primary task stack. The -D option is used to define the size of the environment task's secondary stack.

'`-e`'
:   Output complete list of elaboration-order dependencies.

'`-E`'
:   Store tracebacks in exception occurrences when the target supports it. This is the default with the zero cost exception mechanism. See also the packages `GNAT.Traceback` and `GNAT.Traceback.Symbolic` for more information. Note that on x86 ports, you must not use '`-fomit-frame-pointer`' gcc option.

'`-F`'
:   Force the checks of elaboration flags. `gnatbind` does not normally generate checks of elaboration flags for the main executable, except when a Stand-Alone Library is used. However, there are cases when this cannot be detected by gnatbind. An example is importing an interface of a Stand-Alone Library through a pragma Import and only specifying through a linker switch this Stand-Alone Library. This switch is used to guarantee that elaboration flag checks are generated.

'`-h`'
:   Output usage (help) information

'`-I`'
:   Specify directory to be searched for source and ALI files.

'`-I-`'
:   Do not look for sources in the current directory where `gnatbind` was invoked, and do not look for ALI files in the directory containing the ALI file named in the `gnatbind` command line.

'`-l`'
:   Output chosen elaboration order.

'`-Lxxx`'
:   Bind the units for library building. In this case the adainit and adafinal procedures (see Section 4.2.5 [Binding with Non-Ada Main Programs], page 86)

are renamed to xxxinit and xxxfinal. Implies -n. (See Chapter 19 [GNAT and Libraries], page 209, for more details.)

'-Mxyz'   Rename generated main program from main to xyz. This option is supported on cross environments only.

'-mn'   Limit number of detected errors to *n*, where *n* is in the range 1..999_999. The default value if no switch is given is 9999. Binding is terminated if the limit is exceeded. Furthermore, under Windows, the sources pointed to by the libraries path set in the registry are not searched for.

'-n'   No main program.

'-nostdinc'
             Do not look for sources in the system default directory.

'-nostdlib'
             Do not look for library files in the system default directory.

'--RTS=rts-path'
             Specifies the default location of the runtime library. Same meaning as the equivalent **gnatmake** flag (see Section 6.2 [Switches for gnatmake], page 94).

'-o file'   Name the output file *file* (default is 'b~xxx.adb'). Note that if this option is used, then linking must be done manually, gnatlink cannot be used.

'-O'   Output object list.

'-p'   Pessimistic (worst-case) elaboration order

'-R'   Output closure source list.

'-s'   Require all source files to be present.

'-Sxxx'   Specifies the value to be used when detecting uninitialized scalar objects with pragma Initialize_Scalars. The *xxx* string specified with the switch may be either

             • "'in'" requesting an invalid value where possible
             • "'lo'" for the lowest possible value
             • "'hi'" for the highest possible value
             • "'xx'" for a value consisting of repeated bytes with the value 16#xx# (i.e. xx is a string of two hexadecimal digits).

             In addition, you can specify '-Sev' to indicate that the value is to be set at run time. In this case, the program will look for an environment variable of the form GNAT_INIT_SCALARS=xx, where xx is one of 'in/lo/hi/xx' with the same meanings as above. If no environment variable is found, or if it does not have a valid value, then the default is 'in' (invalid values).

'-static'   Link against a static GNAT run time.

'-shared'   Link against a shared GNAT run time when available.

'-t'   Tolerate time stamp and other consistency errors

'-T*n*'   Set the time slice value to *n* milliseconds. If the system supports the specification of a specific time slice value, then the indicated value is used. If the system does not support specific time slice values, but does support some general notion of round-robin scheduling, then any nonzero value will activate round-robin scheduling.

A value of zero is treated specially. It turns off time slicing, and in addition, indicates to the tasking run time that the semantics should match as closely as possible the Annex D requirements of the Ada RM, and in particular sets the default scheduling policy to `FIFO_Within_Priorities`.

'-u*n*'   Enable dynamic stack usage, with *n* results stored and displayed at program termination. A result is generated when a task terminates. Results that can't be stored are displayed on the fly, at task termination. This option is currently not supported on Itanium platforms. (See Section 22.3 [Dynamic Stack Usage Analysis], page 232 for details.)

'-v'   Verbose mode. Write error messages, header, summary output to 'stdout'.

'-w*x*'   Warning mode (*x*=s/e for suppress/treat as error)

'-W*xe*'   Override default wide character encoding for standard Text_IO files.

'-x'   Exclude source files (check object consistency only).

'-y'   Enable leap seconds support in `Ada.Calendar` and its children.

'-z'   No main subprogram.

You may obtain this listing of switches by running `gnatbind` with no arguments.

4.2.1 Consistency-Checking Modes

As described earlier, by default `gnatbind` checks that object files are consistent with one another and are consistent with any source files it can locate. The following switches control binder access to sources.

'-s'   Require source files to be present. In this mode, the binder must be able to locate all source files that are referenced, in order to check their consistency. In normal mode, if a source file cannot be located it is simply ignored. If you specify this switch, a missing source file is an error.

'-W*xe*'   Override default wide character encoding for standard Text_IO files. Normally the default wide character encoding method used for standard [Wide_[Wide_]]Text_IO files is taken from the encoding specified for the main source input (see description of switch '-gnatW*x*' for the compiler). The use of this switch for the binder (which has the same set of possible arguments) overrides this default as specified.

'-x'   Exclude source files. In this mode, the binder only checks that ALI files are consistent with one another. Source files are not accessed. The binder runs faster in this mode, and there is still a guarantee that the resulting program is self-consistent. If a source file has been edited since it was last compiled, and you specify this switch, the binder will not detect that the object file is out of date with respect to the source file. Note that this is the mode that is automatically used by `gnatmake` because in this case the checking against sources has already been performed by `gnatmake` in the course of compilation (i.e. before binding).

4.2.2 Binder Error Message Control

The following switches provide control over the generation of error messages from the binder:

'`-v`'   Verbose mode. In the normal mode, brief error messages are generated to '`stderr`'. If this switch is present, a header is written to '`stdout`' and any error messages are directed to '`stdout`'. All that is written to '`stderr`' is a brief summary message.

'`-b`'   Generate brief error messages to '`stderr`' even if verbose mode is specified. This is relevant only when used with the '`-v`' switch.

'`-mn`'   Limits the number of error messages to *n*, a decimal integer in the range 1-999. The binder terminates immediately if this limit is reached.

'`-Mxxx`'   Renames the generated main program from `main` to `xxx`. This is useful in the case of some cross-building environments, where the actual main program is separate from the one generated by `gnatbind`.

'`-ws`'   Suppress all warning messages.

'`-we`'   Treat any warning messages as fatal errors.

'`-t`'   The binder performs a number of consistency checks including:
             - Check that time stamps of a given source unit are consistent
             - Check that checksums of a given source unit are consistent
             - Check that consistent versions of GNAT were used for compilation
             - Check consistency of configuration pragmas as required

             Normally failure of such checks, in accordance with the consistency requirements of the Ada Reference Manual, causes error messages to be generated which abort the binder and prevent the output of a binder file and subsequent link to obtain an executable.

             The '`-t`' switch converts these error messages into warnings, so that binding and linking can continue to completion even in the presence of such errors. The result may be a failed link (due to missing symbols), or a non-functional executable which has undefined semantics. *This means that '-t' should be used only in unusual situations, with extreme care.*

4.2.3 Elaboration Control

The following switches provide additional control over the elaboration order. For full details see Appendix C [Elaboration Order Handling in GNAT], page 291.

'`-p`'   Normally the binder attempts to choose an elaboration order that is likely to minimize the likelihood of an elaboration order error resulting in raising a `Program_Error` exception. This switch reverses the action of the binder, and requests that it deliberately choose an order that is likely to maximize the likelihood of an elaboration error. This is useful in ensuring portability and avoiding dependence on accidental fortuitous elaboration ordering.

Normally it only makes sense to use the '-p' switch if dynamic elaboration checking is used ('-gnatE' switch used for compilation). This is because in the default static elaboration mode, all necessary Elaborate and Elaborate_All pragmas are implicitly inserted. These implicit pragmas are still respected by the binder in '-p' mode, so a safe elaboration order is assured.

4.2.4 Output Control

The following switches allow additional control over the output generated by the binder.

'-A'   Generate binder program in Ada (default). The binder program is named 'b~mainprog.adb' by default. This can be changed with '-o' gnatbind option.

'-c'   Check only. Do not generate the binder output file. In this mode the binder performs all error checks but does not generate an output file.

'-C'   Generate binder program in C. The binder program is named 'b_mainprog.c'. This can be changed with '-o' gnatbind option.

'-e'   Output complete list of elaboration-order dependencies, showing the reason for each dependency. This output can be rather extensive but may be useful in diagnosing problems with elaboration order. The output is written to 'stdout'.

'-h'   Output usage information. The output is written to 'stdout'.

'-K'   Output linker options to 'stdout'. Includes library search paths, contents of pragmas Ident and Linker_Options, and libraries added by gnatbind.

'-l'   Output chosen elaboration order. The output is written to 'stdout'.

'-O'   Output full names of all the object files that must be linked to provide the Ada component of the program. The output is written to 'stdout'. This list includes the files explicitly supplied and referenced by the user as well as implicitly referenced run-time unit files. The latter are omitted if the corresponding units reside in shared libraries. The directory names for the run-time units depend on the system configuration.

'-o file'   Set name of output file to file instead of the normal 'b~mainprog.adb' default. Note that file denote the Ada binder generated body filename. In C mode you would normally give file an extension of '.c' because it will be a C source program. Note that if this option is used, then linking must be done manually. It is not possible to use gnatlink in this case, since it cannot locate the binder file.

'-r'   Generate list of pragma Restrictions that could be applied to the current unit. This is useful for code audit purposes, and also may be used to improve code generation in some cases.

4.2.5 Binding with Non-Ada Main Programs

In our description so far we have assumed that the main program is in Ada, and that the task of the binder is to generate a corresponding function `main` that invokes this Ada main program. GNAT also supports the building of executable programs where the main program is not in Ada, but some of the called routines are written in Ada and compiled using GNAT (see Section 2.10 [Mixed Language Programming], page 23). The following switch is used in this situation:

'-n'   No main program. The main program is not in Ada.

In this case, most of the functions of the binder are still required, but instead of generating a main program, the binder generates a file containing the following callable routines:

adainit   You must call this routine to initialize the Ada part of the program by calling the necessary elaboration routines. A call to `adainit` is required before the first call to an Ada subprogram.

              Note that it is assumed that the basic execution environment must be setup to be appropriate for Ada execution at the point where the first Ada subprogram is called. In particular, if the Ada code will do any floating-point operations, then the FPU must be setup in an appropriate manner. For the case of the x86, for example, full precision mode is required. The procedure GNAT.Float_Control.Reset may be used to ensure that the FPU is in the right state.

adafinal   You must call this routine to perform any library-level finalization required by the Ada subprograms. A call to `adafinal` is required after the last call to an Ada subprogram, and before the program terminates.

If the '-n' switch is given, more than one ALI file may appear on the command line for **gnatbind**. The normal *closure* calculation is performed for each of the specified units. Calculating the closure means finding out the set of units involved by tracing `with` references. The reason it is necessary to be able to specify more than one ALI file is that a given program may invoke two or more quite separate groups of Ada units.

The binder takes the name of its output file from the last specified ALI file, unless overridden by the use of the '-o file'. The output is an Ada unit in source form that can be compiled with GNAT unless the -C switch is used in which case the output is a C source file, which must be compiled using the C compiler. This compilation occurs automatically as part of the **gnatlink** processing.

Currently the GNAT run time requires a FPU using 80 bits mode precision. Under targets where this is not the default it is required to call GNAT.Float_Control.Reset before using floating point numbers (this include float computation, float input and output) in the Ada code. A side effect is that this could be the wrong mode for the foreign code where floating point computation could be broken after this call.

4.2.6 Binding Programs with No Main Subprogram

It is possible to have an Ada program which does not have a main subprogram. This program will call the elaboration routines of all the packages, then the finalization routines.

The following switch is used to bind programs organized in this manner:

'-z'   Normally the binder checks that the unit name given on the command line
            corresponds to a suitable main subprogram. When this switch is used, a list of
            ALI files can be given, and the execution of the program consists of elaboration
            of these units in an appropriate order. Note that the default wide character
            encoding method for standard Text_IO files is always set to Brackets if this
            switch is set (you can use the binder switch '-Wx' to override this default).

4.3 Command-Line Access

The package `Ada.Command_Line` provides access to the command-line arguments and program name. In order for this interface to operate correctly, the two variables

```
int gnat_argc;
char **gnat_argv;
```

are declared in one of the GNAT library routines. These variables must be set from the actual `argc` and `argv` values passed to the main program. With no 'n' present, `gnatbind` generates the C main program to automatically set these variables. If the 'n' switch is used, there is no automatic way to set these variables. If they are not set, the procedures in `Ada.Command_Line` will not be available, and any attempt to use them will raise `Constraint_Error`. If command line access is required, your main program must set `gnat_argc` and `gnat_argv` from the `argc` and `argv` values passed to it.

4.4 Search Paths for `gnatbind`

The binder takes the name of an ALI file as its argument and needs to locate source files as well as other ALI files to verify object consistency.

For source files, it follows exactly the same search rules as `gcc` (see Section 3.3 [Search Paths and the Run-Time Library (RTL)], page 76). For ALI files the directories searched are:

1. The directory containing the ALI file named in the command line, unless the switch '-I-' is specified.

2. All directories specified by '-I' switches on the `gnatbind` command line, in the order given.

3. Each of the directories listed in the text file whose name is given by the `ADA_PRJ_OBJECTS_FILE` environment variable.

   `ADA_PRJ_OBJECTS_FILE` is normally set by gnatmake or by the gnat driver when project files are used. It should not normally be set by other means.

4. Each of the directories listed in the value of the `ADA_OBJECTS_PATH` environment variable. Construct this value exactly as the `PATH` environment variable: a list of directory names separated by colons (semicolons when working with the NT version of GNAT).

5. The content of the 'ada_object_path' file which is part of the GNAT installation tree and is used to store standard libraries such as the GNAT Run Time Library (RTL) unless the switch '-nostdlib' is specified. Section 19.2.2 [Installing a library], page 211

In the binder the switch '-I' is used to specify both source and library file paths. Use '-aI' instead if you want to specify source paths only, and '-aO' if you want to specify library paths only. This means that for the binder '-I'*dir* is equivalent to '-aI'*dir* '-aO'*dir*. The binder generates the bind file (a C language source file) in the current working directory.

The packages `Ada`, `System`, and `Interfaces` and their children make up the GNAT Run-Time Library, together with the package GNAT and its children, which contain a set of useful additional library functions provided by GNAT. The sources for these units are needed by the compiler and are kept together in one directory. The ALI files and object files generated by compiling the RTL are needed by the binder and the linker and are kept together in one directory, typically different from the directory containing the sources. In a normal installation, you need not specify these directory names when compiling or binding. Either the environment variables or the built-in defaults cause these files to be found.

Besides simplifying access to the RTL, a major use of search paths is in compiling sources from multiple directories. This can make development environments much more flexible.

4.5 Examples of `gnatbind` Usage

This section contains a number of examples of using the GNAT binding utility `gnatbind`.

`gnatbind hello`

> The main program `Hello` (source program in 'hello.adb') is bound using the standard switch settings. The generated main program is 'b~hello.adb'. This is the normal, default use of the binder.

`gnatbind hello -o mainprog.adb`

> The main program `Hello` (source program in 'hello.adb') is bound using the standard switch settings. The generated main program is 'mainprog.adb' with the associated spec in 'mainprog.ads'. Note that you must specify the body here not the spec, in the case where the output is in Ada. Note that if this option is used, then linking must be done manually, since gnatlink will not be able to find the generated file.

`gnatbind main -C -o mainprog.c -x`

> The main program `Main` (source program in 'main.adb') is bound, excluding source files from the consistency checking, generating the file 'mainprog.c'.

`gnatbind -x main_program -C -o mainprog.c`

> This command is exactly the same as the previous example. Switches may appear anywhere in the command line, and single letter switches may be combined into a single switch.

`gnatbind -n math dbase -C -o ada-control.c`

> The main program is in a language other than Ada, but calls to subprograms in packages `Math` and `Dbase` appear. This call to `gnatbind` generates the file 'ada-control.c' containing the adainit and adafinal routines to be called before and after accessing the Ada units.

5 Linking Using gnatlink

This chapter discusses **gnatlink**, a tool that links an Ada program and builds an executable file. This utility invokes the system linker (via the **gcc** command) with a correct list of object files and library references. **gnatlink** automatically determines the list of files and references for the Ada part of a program. It uses the binder file generated by the **gnatbind** to determine this list.

Note: to invoke **gnatlink** with a project file, use the **gnat** driver (see Section 11.15.2 [The GNAT Driver and Project Files], page 157).

5.1 Running gnatlink

The form of the **gnatlink** command is

```
$ gnatlink [switches] mainprog[.ali]
          [non-Ada objects] [linker options]
```

The arguments of **gnatlink** (switches, main 'ALI' file, non-Ada objects or linker options) may be in any order, provided that no non-Ada object may be mistaken for a main 'ALI' file. Any file name 'F' without the '.ali' extension will be taken as the main 'ALI' file if a file exists whose name is the concatenation of 'F' and '.ali'.

'*mainprog*.ali' references the ALI file of the main program. The '.ali' extension of this file can be omitted. From this reference, **gnatlink** locates the corresponding binder file 'b~*mainprog*.adb' and, using the information in this file along with the list of non-Ada objects and linker options, constructs a linker command file to create the executable.

The arguments other than the **gnatlink** switches and the main 'ALI' file are passed to the linker uninterpreted. They typically include the names of object files for units written in other languages than Ada and any library references required to resolve references in any of these foreign language units, or in **Import** pragmas in any Ada units.

linker options is an optional list of linker specific switches. The default linker called by gnatlink is *gcc* which in turn calls the appropriate system linker. Standard options for the linker such as '-lmy_lib' or '-Ldir' can be added as is. For options that are not recognized by *gcc* as linker options, use the *gcc* switches '-Xlinker' or '-Wl,'. Refer to the GCC documentation for details. Here is an example showing how to generate a linker map:

```
$ gnatlink my_prog -Wl,-Map,MAPFILE
```

Using *linker options* it is possible to set the program stack and heap size. See Section G.14 [Setting Stack Size from gnatlink], page 362 and Section G.15 [Setting Heap Size from gnatlink], page 362.

gnatlink determines the list of objects required by the Ada program and prepends them to the list of objects passed to the linker. **gnatlink** also gathers any arguments set by the use of **pragma Linker_Options** and adds them to the list of arguments presented to the linker.

5.2 Switches for gnatlink

The following switches are available with the **gnatlink** utility:

'--version'
          Display Copyright and version, then exit disregarding all other options.

'--help'   If '--version' was not used, display usage, then exit disregarding all other options.

'-A'   The binder has generated code in Ada. This is the default.

'-C'   If instead of generating a file in Ada, the binder has generated one in C, then the linker needs to know about it. Use this switch to signal to `gnatlink` that the binder has generated C code rather than Ada code.

'-f'   On some targets, the command line length is limited, and `gnatlink` will generate a separate file for the linker if the list of object files is too long. The '-f' switch forces this file to be generated even if the limit is not exceeded. This is useful in some cases to deal with special situations where the command line length is exceeded.

'-g'   The option to include debugging information causes the Ada bind file (in other words, 'b~*mainprog*.adb') to be compiled with '-g'. In addition, the binder does not delete the 'b~*mainprog*.adb', 'b~*mainprog*.o' and 'b~*mainprog*.ali' files. Without '-g', the binder removes these files by default. The same procedure apply if a C bind file was generated using '-C' gnatbind option, in this case the filenames are 'b_*mainprog*.c' and 'b_*mainprog*.o'.

'-n'   Do not compile the file generated by the binder. This may be used when a link is rerun with different options, but there is no need to recompile the binder file.

'-v'   Causes additional information to be output, including a full list of the included object files. This switch option is most useful when you want to see what set of object files are being used in the link step.

'-v -v'   Very verbose mode. Requests that the compiler operate in verbose mode when it compiles the binder file, and that the system linker run in verbose mode.

'-o *exec-name*'
              exec-name specifies an alternate name for the generated executable program. If this switch is omitted, the executable has the same name as the main unit. For example, `gnatlink try.ali` creates an executable called '`try`'.

'-b *target*'
              Compile your program to run on *target*, which is the name of a system configuration. You must have a GNAT cross-compiler built if *target* is not the same as your host system.

'-B*dir*'   Load compiler executables (for example, `gnat1`, the Ada compiler) from *dir* instead of the default location. Only use this switch when multiple versions of the GNAT compiler are available. See the `gcc` manual page for further details. You would normally use the '-b' or '-V' switch instead.

'--GCC=*compiler_name*'
              Program used for compiling the binder file. The default is `gcc`. You need to use quotes around *compiler_name* if `compiler_name` contains spaces or other separator characters. As an example '--GCC="foo -x -y"' will instruct `gnatlink` to use `foo -x -y` as your compiler. Note that switch '-c' is always inserted after your command name. Thus in the above example the compiler command

that will be used by `gnatlink` will be `foo -c -x -y`. A limitation of this syntax is that the name and path name of the executable itself must not include any embedded spaces. If several '`--GCC=compiler_name`' are used, only the last *compiler_name* is taken into account. However, all the additional switches are also taken into account. Thus, '`--GCC="foo -x -y" --GCC="bar -z -t"`' is equivalent to '`--GCC="bar -x -y -z -t"`'.

'`--LINK=name`'

name is the name of the linker to be invoked. This is especially useful in mixed language programs since languages such as C++ require their own linker to be used. When this switch is omitted, the default name for the linker is `gcc`. When this switch is used, the specified linker is called instead of `gcc` with exactly the same parameters that would have been passed to `gcc` so if the desired linker requires different parameters it is necessary to use a wrapper script that massages the parameters before invoking the real linker. It may be useful to control the exact invocation by using the verbose switch.

6 The GNAT Make Program gnatmake

A typical development cycle when working on an Ada program consists of the following steps:

1. Edit some sources to fix bugs.

2. Add enhancements.

3. Compile all sources affected.

4. Rebind and relink.

5. Test.

The third step can be tricky, because not only do the modified files have to be compiled, but any files depending on these files must also be recompiled. The dependency rules in Ada can be quite complex, especially in the presence of overloading, use clauses, generics and inlined subprograms.

gnatmake automatically takes care of the third and fourth steps of this process. It determines which sources need to be compiled, compiles them, and binds and links the resulting object files.

Unlike some other Ada make programs, the dependencies are always accurately recomputed from the new sources. The source based approach of the GNAT compilation model makes this possible. This means that if changes to the source program cause corresponding changes in dependencies, they will always be tracked exactly correctly by gnatmake.

6.1 Running gnatmake

The usual form of the gnatmake command is

```
$ gnatmake [switches] file_name
      [file_names] [mode_switches]
```

The only required argument is one *file_name*, which specifies a compilation unit that is a main program. Several *file_names* can be specified: this will result in several executables being built. If switches are present, they can be placed before the first *file_name*, between *file_names* or after the last *file_name*. If *mode_switches* are present, they must always be placed after the last *file_name* and all switches.

If you are using standard file extensions (.adb and .ads), then the extension may be omitted from the *file_name* arguments. However, if you are using non-standard extensions, then it is required that the extension be given. A relative or absolute directory path can be specified in a *file_name*, in which case, the input source file will be searched for in the specified directory only. Otherwise, the input source file will first be searched in the directory where gnatmake was invoked and if it is not found, it will be search on the source path of the compiler as described in Section 3.3 [Search Paths and the Run-Time Library (RTL)], page 76.

All gnatmake output (except when you specify '-M') is to 'stderr'. The output produced by the '-M' switch is send to 'stdout'.

6.2 Switches for gnatmake

You may specify any of the following switches to gnatmake:

'--version'

> Display Copyright and version, then exit disregarding all other options.

'--help'   If '--version' was not used, display usage, then exit disregarding all other options.

'--GCC=*compiler_name*'

> Program used for compiling. The default is 'gcc'. You need to use quotes around *compiler_name* if compiler_name contains spaces or other separator characters. As an example '--GCC="foo -x -y"' will instruct gnatmake to use foo -x -y as your compiler. A limitation of this syntax is that the name and path name of the executable itself must not include any embedded spaces. Note that switch '-c' is always inserted after your command name. Thus in the above example the compiler command that will be used by gnatmake will be foo -c -x -y. If several '--GCC=compiler_name' are used, only the last *compiler_name* is taken into account. However, all the additional switches are also taken into account. Thus, '--GCC="foo -x -y" --GCC="bar -z -t"' is equivalent to '--GCC="bar -x -y -z -t"'.

'--GNATBIND=*binder_name*'

> Program used for binding. The default is 'gnatbind'. You need to use quotes around *binder_name* if *binder_name* contains spaces or other separator characters. As an example '--GNATBIND="bar -x -y"' will instruct gnatmake to use bar -x -y as your binder. Binder switches that are normally appended by gnatmake to 'gnatbind' are now appended to the end of bar -x -y. A limitation of this syntax is that the name and path name of the executable itself must not include any embedded spaces.

'--GNATLINK=*linker_name*'

> Program used for linking. The default is 'gnatlink'. You need to use quotes around *linker_name* if *linker_name* contains spaces or other separator characters. As an example '--GNATLINK="lan -x -y"' will instruct gnatmake to use lan -x -y as your linker. Linker switches that are normally appended by gnatmake to 'gnatlink' are now appended to the end of lan -x -y. A limitation of this syntax is that the name and path name of the executable itself must not include any embedded spaces.

'-a'   Consider all files in the make process, even the GNAT internal system files (for example, the predefined Ada library files), as well as any locked files. Locked files are files whose ALI file is write-protected. By default, gnatmake does not check these files, because the assumption is that the GNAT internal files are properly up to date, and also that any write protected ALI files have been properly installed. Note that if there is an installation problem, such that one of these files is not up to date, it will be properly caught by the binder. You may have to specify this switch if you are working on GNAT itself. The switch '-a' is also useful in conjunction with '-f' if you need to recompile an entire application, including run-time files, using special configuration pragmas, such as a `Normalize_Scalars` pragma.

By default `gnatmake -a` compiles all GNAT internal files with `gcc -c -gnatpg` rather than `gcc -c`.

'-b'   Bind only. Can be combined with '-c' to do compilation and binding, but no link. Can be combined with '-l' to do binding and linking. When not combined with '-c' all the units in the closure of the main program must have been previously compiled and must be up to date. The root unit specified by *file_name* may be given without extension, with the source extension or, if no GNAT Project File is specified, with the ALI file extension.

'-c'   Compile only. Do not perform binding, except when '-b' is also specified. Do not perform linking, except if both '-b' and '-l' are also specified. If the root unit specified by *file_name* is not a main unit, this is the default. Otherwise `gnatmake` will attempt binding and linking unless all objects are up to date and the executable is more recent than the objects.

'-C'   Use a temporary mapping file. A mapping file is a way to communicate to the compiler two mappings: from unit names to file names (without any directory information) and from file names to path names (with full directory information). These mappings are used by the compiler to short-circuit the path search. When `gnatmake` is invoked with this switch, it will create a temporary mapping file, initially populated by the project manager, if '-P' is used, otherwise initially empty. Each invocation of the compiler will add the newly accessed sources to the mapping file. This will improve the source search during the next invocation of the compiler.

'-C=*file*' Use a specific mapping file. The file, specified as a path name (absolute or relative) by this switch, should already exist, otherwise the switch is ineffective. The specified mapping file will be communicated to the compiler. This switch is not compatible with a project file (-P*file*) or with multiple compiling processes (-jnnn, when nnn is greater than 1).

'-D *dir*' Put all object files and ALI file in directory *dir*. If the '-D' switch is not used, all object files and ALI files go in the current working directory.

This switch cannot be used when using a project file.

'-eL'   Follow all symbolic links when processing project files.

'-eS'   Output the commands for the compiler, the binder and the linker on standard output, instead of standard error.

'-f'   Force recompilations. Recompile all sources, even though some object files may be up to date, but don't recompile predefined or GNAT internal files or locked files (files with a write-protected ALI file), unless the '-a' switch is also specified.

'-F'   When using project files, if some errors or warnings are detected during parsing and verbose mode is not in effect (no use of switch -v), then error lines start with the full path name of the project file, rather than its simple file name.

'-g'   Enable debugging. This switch is simply passed to the compiler and to the linker.

'-i'   In normal mode, gnatmake compiles all object files and ALI files into the current
                directory. If the '-i' switch is used, then instead object files and ALI files that
                already exist are overwritten in place. This means that once a large project is
                organized into separate directories in the desired manner, then gnatmake will
                automatically maintain and update this organization. If no ALI files are found
                on the Ada object path (Section 3.3 [Search Paths and the Run-Time Library
                (RTL)], page 76), the new object and ALI files are created in the directory
                containing the source being compiled. If another organization is desired, where
                objects and sources are kept in different directories, a useful technique is to
                create dummy ALI files in the desired directories. When detecting such a
                dummy file, gnatmake will be forced to recompile the corresponding source file,
                and it will be put the resulting object and ALI files in the directory where it
                found the dummy file.

'-jn'   Use n processes to carry out the (re)compilations. On a multiprocessor machine
                compilations will occur in parallel. In the event of compilation errors, messages
                from various compilations might get interspersed (but gnatmake will give you
                the full ordered list of failing compiles at the end). If this is problematic, rerun
                the make process with n set to 1 to get a clean list of messages.

'-k'   Keep going. Continue as much as possible after a compilation error. To ease
                the programmer's task in case of compilation errors, the list of sources for which
                the compile fails is given when gnatmake terminates.

                If gnatmake is invoked with several 'file_names' and with this switch, if there
                are compilation errors when building an executable, gnatmake will not attempt
                to build the following executables.

'-l'   Link only. Can be combined with '-b' to binding and linking. Linking will not
                be performed if combined with '-c' but not with '-b'. When not combined with
                '-b' all the units in the closure of the main program must have been previously
                compiled and must be up to date, and the main program needs to have been
                bound. The root unit specified by file_name may be given without extension,
                with the source extension or, if no GNAT Project File is specified, with the ALI
                file extension.

'-m'   Specify that the minimum necessary amount of recompilations be performed. In
                this mode gnatmake ignores time stamp differences when the only modifications
                to a source file consist in adding/removing comments, empty lines, spaces or
                tabs. This means that if you have changed the comments in a source file or
                have simply reformatted it, using this switch will tell gnatmake not to recompile
                files that depend on it (provided other sources on which these files depend have
                undergone no semantic modifications). Note that the debugging information
                may be out of date with respect to the sources if the '-m' switch causes a
                compilation to be switched, so the use of this switch represents a trade-off
                between compilation time and accurate debugging information.

'-M'   Check if all objects are up to date. If they are, output the object dependences
                to 'stdout' in a form that can be directly exploited in a 'Makefile'. By default,
                each source file is prefixed with its (relative or absolute) directory name. This
                name is whatever you specified in the various '-aI' and '-I' switches. If you

use `gnatmake -M` '`-q`' (see below), only the source file names, without relative paths, are output. If you just specify the '`-M`' switch, dependencies of the GNAT internal system files are omitted. This is typically what you want. If you also specify the '`-a`' switch, dependencies of the GNAT internal files are also listed. Note that dependencies of the objects in external Ada libraries (see switch '`-aL`'*dir* in the following list) are never reported.

'`-n`'
: Don't compile, bind, or link. Checks if all objects are up to date. If they are not, the full name of the first file that needs to be recompiled is printed. Repeated use of this option, followed by compiling the indicated source file, will eventually result in recompiling all required units.

'`-o exec_name`'
: Output executable name. The name of the final executable program will be *exec_name*. If the '`-o`' switch is omitted the default name for the executable will be the name of the input file in appropriate form for an executable file on the host system.

: This switch cannot be used when invoking **gnatmake** with several '`file_names`'.

'`-p or --create-missing-dirs`'
: When using project files (-P*project*), create automatically missing object directories, library directories and exec directories.

'`-Pproject`'
: Use project file *project*. Only one such switch can be used. See Section 11.15.1 [gnatmake and Project Files], page 153.

'`-q`'
: Quiet. When this flag is not set, the commands carried out by **gnatmake** are displayed.

'`-s`'
: Recompile if compiler switches have changed since last compilation. All compiler switches but -I and -o are taken into account in the following way: orders between different "first letter" switches are ignored, but orders between same switches are taken into account. For example, '`-O -O2`' is different than '`-O2 -O`', but '`-g -O`' is equivalent to '`-O -g`'.

: This switch is recommended when Integrated Preprocessing is used.

'`-u`'
: Unique. Recompile at most the main files. It implies -c. Combined with -f, it is equivalent to calling the compiler directly. Note that using -u with a project file and no main has a special meaning (see Section 11.15.1.3 [Project Files and Main Subprograms], page 156).

'`-U`'
: When used without a project file or with one or several mains on the command line, is equivalent to -u. When used with a project file and no main on the command line, all sources of all project files are checked and compiled if not up to date, and libraries are rebuilt, if necessary.

'`-v`'
: Verbose. Display the reason for all recompilations **gnatmake** decides are necessary, with the highest verbosity level.

'`-vl`'
: Verbosity level Low. Display fewer lines than in verbosity Medium.

'`-vm`'
: Verbosity level Medium. Potentially display fewer lines than in verbosity High.

'-vh'   Verbosity level High. Equivalent to -v.

'-vPx'   Indicate the verbosity of the parsing of GNAT project files. See Section 11.14
               [Switches Related to Project Files], page 152.

'-x'   Indicate that sources that are not part of any Project File may be compiled.
               Normally, when using Project Files, only sources that are part of a Project
               File may be compile. When this switch is used, a source outside of all Project
               Files may be compiled. The ALI file and the object file will be put in the object
               directory of the main Project. The compilation switches used will only be those
               specified on the command line.

'-Xname=value'
               Indicate that external variable *name* has the value *value*. The Project Manager
               will use this value for occurrences of external(name) when parsing the project
               file. See Section 11.14 [Switches Related to Project Files], page 152.

'-z'   No main subprogram. Bind and link the program even if the unit name given
               on the command line is a package name. The resulting executable will execute
               the elaboration routines of the package and its closure, then the finalization
               routines.

gcc switches
               Any uppercase or multi-character switch that is not a **gnatmake** switch is passed
               to gcc (e.g. '-O', '-gnato,' etc.)

Source and library search path switches:

'-aIdir'   When looking for source files also look in directory *dir*. The order in which
               source files search is undertaken is described in Section 3.3 [Search Paths and
               the Run-Time Library (RTL)], page 76.

'-aLdir'   Consider *dir* as being an externally provided Ada library. Instructs **gnatmake**
               to skip compilation units whose '.ALI' files have been located in directory *dir*.
               This allows you to have missing bodies for the units in *dir* and to ignore out
               of date bodies for the same units. You still need to specify the location of the
               specs for these units by using the switches '-aIdir' or '-Idir'. Note: this
               switch is provided for compatibility with previous versions of **gnatmake**. The
               easier method of causing standard libraries to be excluded from consideration
               is to write-protect the corresponding ALI files.

'-aOdir'   When searching for library and object files, look in directory *dir*. The order
               in which library files are searched is described in Section 4.4 [Search Paths for
               gnatbind], page 87.

'-Adir'   Equivalent to '-aLdir -aIdir'.

'-Idir'   Equivalent to '-aOdir -aIdir'.

'-I-'   Do not look for source files in the directory containing the source file named in
               the command line. Do not look for ALI or object files in the directory where
               gnatmake was invoked.

'-L*dir*'   Add directory *dir* to the list of directories in which the linker will search for
                 libraries. This is equivalent to '-largs -L'*dir*. Furthermore, under Windows,
                 the sources pointed to by the libraries path set in the registry are not searched
                 for.

'-nostdinc'
                 Do not look for source files in the system default directory.

'-nostdlib'
                 Do not look for library files in the system default directory.

'--RTS=*rts-path*'
                 Specifies the default location of the runtime library. GNAT looks for
                 the runtime in the following directories, and stops as soon as a valid
                 runtime is found ('adainclude' or 'ada_source_path', and 'adalib' or
                 'ada_object_path' present):

                 • <current directory>/$rts_path
                 • <default-search-dir>/$rts_path
                 • <default-search-dir>/rts-$rts_path

                 The selected path is handled like a normal RTS path.

6.3 Mode Switches for gnatmake

The mode switches (referred to as mode_switches) allow the inclusion of switches that are
to be passed to the compiler itself, the binder or the linker. The effect of a mode switch is
to cause all subsequent switches up to the end of the switch list, or up to the next mode
switch, to be interpreted as switches to be passed on to the designated component of GNAT.

'-cargs *switches*'
                 Compiler switches. Here *switches* is a list of switches that are valid switches
                 for gcc. They will be passed on to all compile steps performed by gnatmake.

'-bargs *switches*'
                 Binder switches. Here *switches* is a list of switches that are valid switches for
                 gnatbind. They will be passed on to all bind steps performed by gnatmake.

'-largs *switches*'
                 Linker switches. Here *switches* is a list of switches that are valid switches for
                 gnatlink. They will be passed on to all link steps performed by gnatmake.

'-margs *switches*'
                 Make switches. The switches are directly interpreted by gnatmake, regardless
                 of any previous occurrence of '-cargs', '-bargs' or '-largs'.

6.4 Notes on the Command Line

This section contains some additional useful notes on the operation of the gnatmake command.

 • If gnatmake finds no ALI files, it recompiles the main program and all other units
   required by the main program. This means that gnatmake can be used for the initial
   compile, as well as during subsequent steps of the development cycle.

- If you enter gnatmake `file.adb`, where '`file.adb`' is a subunit or body of a generic unit, gnatmake recompiles '`file.adb`' (because it finds no ALI) and stops, issuing a warning.

- In gnatmake the switch '`-I`' is used to specify both source and library file paths. Use '`-aI`' instead if you just want to specify source paths only and '`-aO`' if you want to specify library paths only.

- gnatmake will ignore any files whose ALI file is write-protected. This may conveniently be used to exclude standard libraries from consideration and in particular it means that the use of the '`-f`' switch will not recompile these files unless '`-a`' is also specified.

- gnatmake has been designed to make the use of Ada libraries particularly convenient. Assume you have an Ada library organized as follows: *obj-dir* contains the objects and ALI files for of your Ada compilation units, whereas *include-dir* contains the specs of these units, but no bodies. Then to compile a unit stored in `main.adb`, which uses this Ada library you would just type

  ```
  $ gnatmake -aIinclude-dir  -aLobj-dir  main
  ```

- Using gnatmake along with the '`-m (minimal recompilation)`' switch provides a mechanism for avoiding unnecessary recompilations. Using this switch, you can update the comments/format of your source files without having to recompile everything. Note, however, that adding or deleting lines in a source files may render its debugging info obsolete. If the file in question is a spec, the impact is rather limited, as that debugging info will only be useful during the elaboration phase of your program. For bodies the impact can be more significant. In all events, your debugger will warn you if a source file is more recent than the corresponding object, and alert you to the fact that the debugging information may be out of date.

6.5 How gnatmake Works

Generally gnatmake automatically performs all necessary recompilations and you don't need to worry about how it works. However, it may be useful to have some basic understanding of the gnatmake approach and in particular to understand how it uses the results of previous compilations without incorrectly depending on them.

First a definition: an object file is considered *up to date* if the corresponding ALI file exists and if all the source files listed in the dependency section of this ALI file have time stamps matching those in the ALI file. This means that neither the source file itself nor any files that it depends on have been modified, and hence there is no need to recompile this file.

gnatmake works by first checking if the specified main unit is up to date. If so, no compilations are required for the main unit. If not, gnatmake compiles the main program to build a new ALI file that reflects the latest sources. Then the ALI file of the main unit is examined to find all the source files on which the main program depends, and gnatmake recursively applies the above procedure on all these files.

This process ensures that gnatmake only trusts the dependencies in an existing ALI file if they are known to be correct. Otherwise it always recompiles to determine a new, guaranteed accurate set of dependencies. As a result the program is compiled "upside down" from what may be more familiar as the required order of compilation in some other Ada systems. In particular, clients are compiled before the units on which they depend. The ability of GNAT to compile in any order is critical in allowing an order of compilation to be chosen that guarantees that gnatmake will recompute a correct set of new dependencies if necessary.

When invoking gnatmake with several *file_names*, if a unit is imported by several of the executables, it will be recompiled at most once.

Note: when using non-standard naming conventions (see Section 2.4 [Using Other File Names], page 17), changing through a configuration pragmas file the version of a source and invoking gnatmake to recompile may have no effect, if the previous version of the source is still accessible by gnatmake. It may be necessary to use the switch -f.

6.6 Examples of gnatmake Usage

gnatmake hello.adb

> Compile all files necessary to bind and link the main program 'hello.adb' (containing unit Hello) and bind and link the resulting object files to generate an executable file 'hello'.

gnatmake main1 main2 main3

> Compile all files necessary to bind and link the main programs 'main1.adb' (containing unit Main1), 'main2.adb' (containing unit Main2) and 'main3.adb' (containing unit Main3) and bind and link the resulting object files to generate three executable files 'main1', 'main2' and 'main3'.

gnatmake -q Main_Unit -cargs -O2 -bargs -l

> Compile all files necessary to bind and link the main program unit Main_Unit (from file 'main_unit.adb'). All compilations will be done with optimization level 2 and the order of elaboration will be listed by the binder. gnatmake will operate in quiet mode, not displaying commands it is executing.

7 Improving Performance

This chapter presents several topics related to program performance. It first describes some of the tradeoffs that need to be considered and some of the techniques for making your program run faster. It then documents the `gnatelim` tool and unused subprogram/data elimination feature, which can reduce the size of program executables.

Note: to invoke `gnatelim` with a project file, use the `gnat` driver (see Section 11.15.2 [The GNAT Driver and Project Files], page 157).

7.1 Performance Considerations

The GNAT system provides a number of options that allow a trade-off between

- performance of the generated code
- speed of compilation
- minimization of dependences and recompilation
- the degree of run-time checking.

The defaults (if no options are selected) aim at improving the speed of compilation and minimizing dependences, at the expense of performance of the generated code:

- no optimization
- no inlining of subprogram calls
- all run-time checks enabled except overflow and elaboration checks

These options are suitable for most program development purposes. This chapter describes how you can modify these choices, and also provides some guidelines on debugging optimized code.

7.1.1 Controlling Run-Time Checks

By default, GNAT generates all run-time checks, except arithmetic overflow checking for integer operations and checks for access before elaboration on subprogram calls. The latter are not required in default mode, because all necessary checking is done at compile time. Two gnat switches, '`-gnatp`' and '`-gnato`' allow this default to be modified. See Section 3.2.6 [Run-Time Checks], page 63.

Our experience is that the default is suitable for most development purposes.

We treat integer overflow specially because these are quite expensive and in our experience are not as important as other run-time checks in the development process. Note that division by zero is not considered an overflow check, and divide by zero checks are generated where required by default.

Elaboration checks are off by default, and also not needed by default, since GNAT uses a static elaboration analysis approach that avoids the need for run-time checking. This manual contains a full chapter discussing the issue of elaboration checks, and if the default is not satisfactory for your use, you should read this chapter.

For validity checks, the minimal checks required by the Ada Reference Manual (for case statements and assignments to array elements) are on by default. These can be suppressed by use of the '`-gnatVn`' switch. Note that in Ada 83, there were no validity checks, so if the Ada 83 mode is acceptable (or when comparing GNAT performance with an Ada 83 compiler), it may be reasonable to routinely use '-gnatVn'. Validity checks are also suppressed entirely if '-gnatp' is used.

Note that the setting of the switches controls the default setting of the checks. They may be modified using either pragma Suppress (to remove checks) or pragma Unsuppress (to add back suppressed checks) in the program source.

7.1.2 Use of Restrictions

The use of pragma Restrictions allows you to control which features are permitted in your program. Apart from the obvious point that if you avoid relatively expensive features like finalization (enforceable by the use of pragma Restrictions (No_Finalization), the use of this pragma does not affect the generated code in most cases.

One notable exception to this rule is that the possibility of task abort results in some distributed overhead, particularly if finalization or exception handlers are used. The reason is that certain sections of code have to be marked as non-abortable.

If you use neither the abort statement, nor asynchronous transfer of control (select .. then abort), then this distributed overhead is removed, which may have a general positive effect in improving overall performance. Especially code involving frequent use of tasking constructs and controlled types will show much improved performance. The relevant restrictions pragmas are

```
pragma Restrictions (No_Abort_Statements);
pragma Restrictions (Max_Asynchronous_Select_Nesting => 0);
```

It is recommended that these restriction pragmas be used if possible. Note that this also means that you can write code without worrying about the possibility of an immediate abort at any point.

7.1.3 Optimization Levels

The default is optimization off. This results in the fastest compile times, but GNAT makes absolutely no attempt to optimize, and the generated programs are considerably larger and slower than when optimization is enabled. You can use the '-O' switch (the permitted forms are '-O0', '-O1' '-O2', '-O3', and '-Os') to gcc to control the optimization level:

'-O0'   No optimization (the default); generates unoptimized code but has the fastest compilation time.

            Note that many other compilers do fairly extensive optimization even if "no optimization" is specified. When using gcc, it is very unusual to use -O0 for production if execution time is of any concern, since -O0 really does mean no optimization at all. This difference between gcc and other compilers should be kept in mind when doing performance comparisons.

'-O1'   Moderate optimization; optimizes reasonably well but does not degrade compilation time significantly.

'-O2'   Full optimization; generates highly optimized code and has the slowest compilation time.

'-O3'   Full optimization as in '-O2', and also attempts automatic inlining of small subprograms within a unit (see Section 7.1.5 [Inlining of Subprograms], page 106).

'-Os'   Optimize space usage of resulting program.

Higher optimization levels perform more global transformations on the program and apply more expensive analysis algorithms in order to generate faster and more compact code. The price in compilation time, and the resulting improvement in execution time, both depend on the particular application and the hardware environment. You should experiment to find the best level for your application.

The '-Os' switch is independent of the time optimizations, so you can specify both '-Os' and a time optimization on the same compile command.

Since the precise set of optimizations done at each level will vary from release to release (and sometime from target to target), it is best to think of the optimization settings in general terms. The *Using GNU GCC* manual contains details about the '-O' settings and a number of '-f' options that individually enable or disable specific optimizations.

Unlike some other compilation systems, `gcc` has been tested extensively at all optimization levels. There are some bugs which appear only with optimization turned on, but there have also been bugs which show up only in *unoptimized* code. Selecting a lower level of optimization does not improve the reliability of the code generator, which in practice is highly reliable at all optimization levels.

Note regarding the use of '-O3': The use of this optimization level is generally discouraged with GNAT, since it often results in larger executables which run more slowly. See further discussion of this point in Section 7.1.5 [Inlining of Subprograms], page 106.

7.1.4 Debugging Optimized Code

Although it is possible to do a reasonable amount of debugging at nonzero optimization levels, the higher the level the more likely that source-level constructs will have been eliminated by optimization. For example, if a loop is strength-reduced, the loop control variable may be completely eliminated and thus cannot be displayed in the debugger. This can only happen at '-O2' or '-O3'. Explicit temporary variables that you code might be eliminated at level '-O1' or higher.

The use of the '-g' switch, which is needed for source-level debugging, affects the size of the program executable on disk, and indeed the debugging information can be quite large. However, it has no effect on the generated code (and thus does not degrade performance)

Since the compiler generates debugging tables for a compilation unit before it performs optimizations, the optimizing transformations may invalidate some of the debugging data. You therefore need to anticipate certain anomalous situations that may arise while debugging optimized code. These are the most common cases:

1. *The "hopping Program Counter"*: Repeated `step` or `next` commands show the PC bouncing back and forth in the code. This may result from any of the following optimizations:

   - *Common subexpression elimination:* using a single instance of code for a quantity that the source computes several times. As a result you may not be able to stop on what looks like a statement.

   - *Invariant code motion:* moving an expression that does not change within a loop, to the beginning of the loop.

- *Instruction scheduling:* moving instructions so as to overlap loads and stores (typically) with other code, or in general to move computations of values closer to their uses. Often this causes you to pass an assignment statement without the assignment happening and then later bounce back to the statement when the value is actually needed. Placing a breakpoint on a line of code and then stepping over it may, therefore, not always cause all the expected side-effects.

2. *The "big leap":* More commonly known as *cross-jumping*, in which two identical pieces of code are merged and the program counter suddenly jumps to a statement that is not supposed to be executed, simply because it (and the code following) translates to the same thing as the code that *was* supposed to be executed. This effect is typically seen in sequences that end in a jump, such as a `goto`, a `return`, or a `break` in a C `switch` statement.

3. *The "roving variable":* The symptom is an unexpected value in a variable. There are various reasons for this effect:

   - In a subprogram prologue, a parameter may not yet have been moved to its "home".
   - A variable may be dead, and its register re-used. This is probably the most common cause.
   - As mentioned above, the assignment of a value to a variable may have been moved.
   - A variable may be eliminated entirely by value propagation or other means. In this case, GCC may incorrectly generate debugging information for the variable

In general, when an unexpected value appears for a local variable or parameter you should first ascertain if that value was actually computed by your program, as opposed to being incorrectly reported by the debugger. Record fields or array elements in an object designated by an access value are generally less of a problem, once you have ascertained that the access value is sensible. Typically, this means checking variables in the preceding code and in the calling subprogram to verify that the value observed is explainable from other values (one must apply the procedure recursively to those other values); or re-running the code and stopping a little earlier (perhaps before the call) and stepping to better see how the variable obtained the value in question; or continuing to step *from* the point of the strange value to see if code motion had simply moved the variable's assignments later.

In light of such anomalies, a recommended technique is to use '-O0' early in the software development cycle, when extensive debugging capabilities are most needed, and then move to '-O1' and later '-O2' as the debugger becomes less critical. Whether to use the '-g' switch in the release version is a release management issue. Note that if you use '-g' you can then use the `strip` program on the resulting executable, which removes both debugging information and global symbols.

7.1.5 Inlining of Subprograms

A call to a subprogram in the current unit is inlined if all the following conditions are met:

- The optimization level is at least '-O1'.
- The called subprogram is suitable for inlining: It must be small enough and not contain nested subprograms or anything else that `gcc` cannot support in inlined subprograms.

- The call occurs after the definition of the body of the subprogram.
- Either `pragma Inline` applies to the subprogram or it is small and automatic inlining (optimization level '-O3') is specified.

Calls to subprograms in `with`'ed units are normally not inlined. To achieve actual inlining (that is, replacement of the call by the code in the body of the subprogram), the following conditions must all be true.

- The optimization level is at least '-O1'.
- The called subprogram is suitable for inlining: It must be small enough and not contain nested subprograms or anything else `gcc` cannot support in inlined subprograms.
- The call appears in a body (not in a package spec).
- There is a `pragma Inline` for the subprogram.
- The '-gnatn' switch is used in the `gcc` command line

Even if all these conditions are met, it may not be possible for the compiler to inline the call, due to the length of the body, or features in the body that make it impossible for the compiler to do the inlining.

Note that specifying the '-gnatn' switch causes additional compilation dependencies. Consider the following:

```
package R is
   procedure Q;
   pragma Inline (Q);
end R;
package body R is
   ...
end R;

with R;
procedure Main is
begin
   ...
   R.Q;
end Main;
```

With the default behavior (no '-gnatn' switch specified), the compilation of the `Main` procedure depends only on its own source, 'main.adb', and the spec of the package in file 'r.ads'. This means that editing the body of R does not require recompiling `Main`.

On the other hand, the call `R.Q` is not inlined under these circumstances. If the '-gnatn' switch is present when `Main` is compiled, the call will be inlined if the body of Q is small enough, but now `Main` depends on the body of R in 'r.adb' as well as on the spec. This means that if this body is edited, the main program must be recompiled. Note that this extra dependency occurs whether or not the call is in fact inlined by `gcc`.

The use of front end inlining with '-gnatN' generates similar additional dependencies.

Note: The '-fno-inline' switch can be used to prevent all inlining. This switch overrides all other conditions and ensures that no inlining occurs. The extra dependences resulting from '-gnatn' will still be active, even if this switch is used to suppress the resulting inlining actions.

Note regarding the use of '-O3': There is no difference in inlining behavior between '-O2' and '-O3' for subprograms with an explicit pragma `Inline` assuming the use of '-gnatn' or '-gnatN' (the switches that activate inlining). If you have used pragma `Inline` in appropriate cases, then it is usually much better to use '-O2' and '-gnatn' and avoid the use of '-O3' which in this case only has the effect of inlining subprograms you did not think should be inlined. We often find that the use of '-O3' slows down code by performing excessive inlining, leading to increased instruction cache pressure from the increased code size. So the bottom line here is that you should not automatically assume that '-O3' is better than '-O2', and indeed you should use '-O3' only if tests show that it actually improves performance.

7.1.6 Other Optimization Switches

Since `GNAT` uses the `gcc` back end, all the specialized `gcc` optimization switches are potentially usable. These switches have not been extensively tested with GNAT but can generally be expected to work. Examples of switches in this category are '-funroll-loops' and the various target-specific '-m' options (in particular, it has been observed that '-march=pentium4' can significantly improve performance on appropriate machines). For full details of these switches, see the `gcc` manual.

7.1.7 Optimization and Strict Aliasing

The strong typing capabilities of Ada allow an optimizer to generate efficient code in situations where other languages would be forced to make worst case assumptions preventing such optimizations. Consider the following example:

```
procedure R is
   type Int1 is new Integer;
   type Int2 is new Integer;
   type Int1A is access Int1;
   type Int2A is access Int2;
   Int1V : Int1A;
   Int2V : Int2A;
   ...

begin
   ...
   for J in Data'Range loop
      if Data (J) = Int1V.all then
         Int2V.all := Int2V.all + 1;
      end if;
   end loop;
   ...
end R;
```

In this example, since the variable `Int1V` can only access objects of type `Int1`, and `Int2V` can only access objects of type `Int2`, there is no possibility that the assignment to `Int2V.all` affects the value of `Int1V.all`. This means that the compiler optimizer can "know" that the value `Int1V.all` is constant for all iterations of the loop and avoid the extra memory reference required to dereference it each time through the loop.

This kind of optimization, called strict aliasing analysis, is triggered by specifying an optimization level of '-O2' or higher and allows `GNAT` to generate more efficient code when access values are involved.

However, although this optimization is always correct in terms of the formal semantics of the Ada Reference Manual, difficulties can arise if features like `Unchecked_Conversion` are used to break the typing system. Consider the following complete program example:

```
package p1 is
   type int1 is new integer;
   type int2 is new integer;
   type a1 is access int1;
   type a2 is access int2;
end p1;

with p1; use p1;
package p2 is
   function to_a2 (Input : a1) return a2;
end p2;

with Unchecked_Conversion;
package body p2 is
   function to_a2 (Input : a1) return a2 is
      function to_a2u is
         new Unchecked_Conversion (a1, a2);
   begin
      return to_a2u (Input);
   end to_a2;
end p2;

with p2; use p2;
with p1; use p1;
with Text_IO; use Text_IO;
procedure m is
   v1 : a1 := new int1;
   v2 : a2 := to_a2 (v1);
begin
   v1.all := 1;
   v2.all := 0;
   put_line (int1'image (v1.all));
end;
```

This program prints out 0 in -O0 or -O1 mode, but it prints out 1 in -O2 mode. That's because in strict aliasing mode, the compiler can and does assume that the assignment to `v2.all` could not affect the value of `v1.all`, since different types are involved.

This behavior is not a case of non-conformance with the standard, since the Ada RM specifies that an unchecked conversion where the resulting bit pattern is not a correct value of the target type can result in an abnormal value and attempting to reference an abnormal value makes the execution of a program erroneous. That's the case here since the result does not point to an object of type `int2`. This means that the effect is entirely unpredictable.

However, although that explanation may satisfy a language lawyer, in practice an applications programmer expects an unchecked conversion involving pointers to create true aliases and the behavior of printing 1 seems plain wrong. In this case, the strict aliasing optimization is unwelcome.

Indeed the compiler recognizes this possibility, and the unchecked conversion generates a warning:

```
p2.adb:5:07: warning: possible aliasing problem with type "a2"
```

```
p2.adb:5:07: warning: use -fno-strict-aliasing switch for references
p2.adb:5:07: warning:  or use "pragma No_Strict_Aliasing (a2);"
```

Unfortunately the problem is recognized when compiling the body of package p2, but the actual "bad" code is generated while compiling the body of m and this latter compilation does not see the suspicious Unchecked_Conversion.

As implied by the warning message, there are approaches you can use to avoid the unwanted strict aliasing optimization in a case like this.

One possibility is to simply avoid the use of -O2, but that is a bit drastic, since it throws away a number of useful optimizations that do not involve strict aliasing assumptions.

A less drastic approach is to compile the program using the option -fno-strict-aliasing. Actually it is only the unit containing the dereferencing of the suspicious pointer that needs to be compiled. So in this case, if we compile unit m with this switch, then we get the expected value of zero printed. Analyzing which units might need the switch can be painful, so a more reasonable approach is to compile the entire program with options -O2 and -fno-strict-aliasing. If the performance is satisfactory with this combination of options, then the advantage is that the entire issue of possible "wrong" optimization due to strict aliasing is avoided.

To avoid the use of compiler switches, the configuration pragma No_Strict_Aliasing with no parameters may be used to specify that for all access types, the strict aliasing optimization should be suppressed.

However, these approaches are still overkill, in that they causes all manipulations of all access values to be deoptimized. A more refined approach is to concentrate attention on the specific access type identified as problematic.

First, if a careful analysis of uses of the pointer shows that there are no possible problematic references, then the warning can be suppressed by bracketing the instantiation of Unchecked_Conversion to turn the warning off:

```
pragma Warnings (Off);
function to_a2u is
  new Unchecked_Conversion (a1, a2);
pragma Warnings (On);
```

Of course that approach is not appropriate for this particular example, since indeed there is a problematic reference. In this case we can take one of two other approaches.

The first possibility is to move the instantiation of unchecked conversion to the unit in which the type is declared. In this example, we would move the instantiation of Unchecked_Conversion from the body of package p2 to the spec of package p1. Now the warning disappears. That's because any use of the access type knows there is a suspicious unchecked conversion, and the strict aliasing optimization is automatically suppressed for the type.

If it is not practical to move the unchecked conversion to the same unit in which the destination access type is declared (perhaps because the source type is not visible in that unit), you may use pragma No_Strict_Aliasing for the type. This pragma must occur in the same declarative sequence as the declaration of the access type:

```
type a2 is access int2;
pragma No_Strict_Aliasing (a2);
```

Here again, the compiler now knows that the strict aliasing optimization should be suppressed for any reference to type a2 and the expected behavior is obtained.

Finally, note that although the compiler can generate warnings for simple cases of unchecked conversions, there are tricker and more indirect ways of creating type incorrect aliases which the compiler cannot detect. Examples are the use of address overlays and unchecked conversions involving composite types containing access types as components. In such cases, no warnings are generated, but there can still be aliasing problems. One safe coding practice is to forbid the use of address clauses for type overlaying, and to allow unchecked conversion only for primitive types. This is not really a significant restriction since any possible desired effect can be achieved by unchecked conversion of access values.

7.2 Reducing Size of Ada Executables with `gnatelim`

This section describes `gnatelim`, a tool which detects unused subprograms and helps the compiler to create a smaller executable for your program.

7.2.1 About `gnatelim`

When a program shares a set of Ada packages with other programs, it may happen that this program uses only a fraction of the subprograms defined in these packages. The code created for these unused subprograms increases the size of the executable.

`gnatelim` tracks unused subprograms in an Ada program and outputs a list of GNAT-specific pragmas `Eliminate` marking all the subprograms that are declared but never called. By placing the list of `Eliminate` pragmas in the GNAT configuration file 'gnat.adc' and recompiling your program, you may decrease the size of its executable, because the compiler will not generate the code for 'eliminated' subprograms. See GNAT Reference Manual for more information about this pragma.

`gnatelim` needs as its input data the name of the main subprogram and a bind file for a main subprogram.

To create a bind file for `gnatelim`, run gnatbind for the main subprogram. `gnatelim` can work with both Ada and C bind files; when both are present, it uses the Ada bind file. The following commands will build the program and create the bind file:

```
$ gnatmake -c Main_Prog
$ gnatbind main_prog
```

Note that `gnatelim` needs neither object nor ALI files.

7.2.2 Running `gnatelim`

gnatelim has the following command-line interface:

```
$ gnatelim [options] name
```

name should be a name of a source file that contains the main subprogram of a program (partition).

gnatelim has the following switches:

'-q'   Quiet mode: by default `gnatelim` outputs to the standard error stream the number of program units left to be processed. This option turns this trace off.

'-v'   Verbose mode: `gnatelim` version information is printed as Ada comments to the standard output stream. Also, in addition to the number of program units left `gnatelim` will output the name of the current unit being processed.

'-a'   Also look for subprograms from the GNAT run time that can be eliminated.
              Note that when 'gnat.adc' is produced using this switch, the entire program
              must be recompiled with switch '-a' to gnatmake.

'-Idir'   When looking for source files also look in directory *dir*. Specifying '-I-' in-
              structs gnatelim not to look for sources in the current directory.

'-bbind_file'
              Specifies *bind_file* as the bind file to process. If not set, the name of the bind
              file is computed from the full expanded Ada name of a main subprogram.

'-Cconfig_file'
              Specifies a file *config_file* that contains configuration pragmas. The file must
              be specified with full path.

'--GCC=compiler_name'
              Instructs gnatelim to use specific gcc compiler instead of one available on the
              path.

'--GNATMAKE=gnatmake_name'
              Instructs gnatelim to use specific gnatmake instead of one available on the
              path.

gnatelim sends its output to the standard output stream, and all the tracing and debug
information is sent to the standard error stream. In order to produce a proper GNAT
configuration file 'gnat.adc', redirection must be used:

```
$ gnatelim main_prog.adb > gnat.adc
```

or

```
$ gnatelim main_prog.adb >> gnat.adc
```

in order to append the gnatelim output to the existing contents of 'gnat.adc'.

7.2.3 Correcting the List of Eliminate Pragmas

In some rare cases gnatelim may try to eliminate subprograms that are actually called in
the program. In this case, the compiler will generate an error message of the form:

```
file.adb:106:07: cannot call eliminated subprogram "My_Prog"
```

You will need to manually remove the wrong Eliminate pragmas from the 'gnat.adc' file.
You should recompile your program from scratch after that, because you need a consistent
'gnat.adc' file during the entire compilation.

7.2.4 Making Your Executables Smaller

In order to get a smaller executable for your program you now have to recompile the program
completely with the new 'gnat.adc' file created by gnatelim in your current directory:

```
$ gnatmake -f main_prog
```

(Use the '-f' option for gnatmake to recompile everything with the set of pragmas
Eliminate that you have obtained with gnatelim).

Be aware that the set of Eliminate pragmas is specific to each program. It is not
recommended to merge sets of Eliminate pragmas created for different programs in one
'gnat.adc' file.

7.2.5 Summary of the gnatelim Usage Cycle

Here is a quick summary of the steps to be taken in order to reduce the size of your executables with gnatelim. You may use other GNAT options to control the optimization level, to produce the debugging information, to set search path, etc.

1. Produce a bind file

   ```
   $ gnatmake -c main_prog
   $ gnatbind main_prog
   ```

2. Generate a list of Eliminate pragmas

   ```
   $ gnatelim main_prog >[>] gnat.adc
   ```

3. Recompile the application

   ```
   $ gnatmake -f main_prog
   ```

7.3 Reducing Size of Executables with Unused Subprogram/Data Elimination

This section describes how you can eliminate unused subprograms and data from your executable just by setting options at compilation time.

7.3.1 About unused subprogram/data elimination

By default, an executable contains all code and data of its composing objects (directly linked or coming from statically linked libraries), even data or code never used by this executable.

This feature will allow you to eliminate such unused code from your executable, making it smaller (in disk and in memory).

This functionality is available on all Linux platforms except for the IA-64 architecture and on all cross platforms using the ELF binary file format. In both cases GNU binutils version 2.16 or later are required to enable it.

7.3.2 Compilation options

The operation of eliminating the unused code and data from the final executable is directly performed by the linker.

In order to do this, it has to work with objects compiled with the following options: '-ffunction-sections' '-fdata-sections'. These options are usable with C and Ada files. They will place respectively each function or data in a separate section in the resulting object file.

Once the objects and static libraries are created with these options, the linker can perform the dead code elimination. You can do this by setting the '-Wl,--gc-sections' option to gcc command or in the '-largs' section of gnatmake. This will perform a garbage collection of code and data never referenced.

If the linker performs a partial link ('-r' ld linker option), then you will need to provide one or several entry point using the '-e' / '--entry' ld option.

Note that objects compiled without the '-ffunction-sections' and '-fdata-sections' options can still be linked with the executable. However, no dead code elimination will be performed on those objects (they will be linked as is).

The GNAT static library is now compiled with -ffunction-sections and -fdata-sections on some platforms. This allows you to eliminate the unused code and data of the GNAT library from your executable.

7.3.3 Example of unused subprogram/data elimination

Here is a simple example:

```
with Aux;

procedure Test is
begin
   Aux.Used (10);
end Test;

package Aux is
   Used_Data   : Integer;
   Unused_Data : Integer;

   procedure Used   (Data : Integer);
   procedure Unused (Data : Integer);
end Aux;

package body Aux is
   procedure Used (Data : Integer) is
   begin
      Used_Data := Data;
   end Used;

   procedure Unused (Data : Integer) is
   begin
      Unused_Data := Data;
   end Unused;
end Aux;
```

Unused and Unused_Data are never referenced in this code excerpt, and hence they may be safely removed from the final executable.

```
$ gnatmake test

$ nm test | grep used
020015f0 T aux__unused
02005d88 B aux__unused_data
020015cc T aux__used
02005d84 B aux__used_data

$ gnatmake test -cargs -fdata-sections -ffunction-sections \
     -largs -Wl,--gc-sections

$ nm test | grep used
02005350 T aux__used
0201ffe0 B aux__used_data
```

It can be observed that the procedure Unused and the object Unused_Data are removed by the linker when using the appropriate options.

8 Renaming Files Using `gnatchop`

This chapter discusses how to handle files with multiple units by using the `gnatchop` utility. This utility is also useful in renaming files to meet the standard GNAT default file naming conventions.

8.1 Handling Files with Multiple Units

The basic compilation model of GNAT requires that a file submitted to the compiler have only one unit and there be a strict correspondence between the file name and the unit name.

The `gnatchop` utility allows both of these rules to be relaxed, allowing GNAT to process files which contain multiple compilation units and files with arbitrary file names. `gnatchop` reads the specified file and generates one or more output files, containing one unit per file. The unit and the file name correspond, as required by GNAT.

If you want to permanently restructure a set of "foreign" files so that they match the GNAT rules, and do the remaining development using the GNAT structure, you can simply use `gnatchop` once, generate the new set of files and work with them from that point on.

Alternatively, if you want to keep your files in the "foreign" format, perhaps to maintain compatibility with some other Ada compilation system, you can set up a procedure where you use `gnatchop` each time you compile, regarding the source files that it writes as temporary files that you throw away.

8.2 Operating gnatchop in Compilation Mode

The basic function of `gnatchop` is to take a file with multiple units and split it into separate files. The boundary between files is reasonably clear, except for the issue of comments and pragmas. In default mode, the rule is that any pragmas between units belong to the previous unit, except that configuration pragmas always belong to the following unit. Any comments belong to the following unit. These rules almost always result in the right choice of the split point without needing to mark it explicitly and most users will find this default to be what they want. In this default mode it is incorrect to submit a file containing only configuration pragmas, or one that ends in configuration pragmas, to `gnatchop`.

However, using a special option to activate "compilation mode", `gnatchop` can perform another function, which is to provide exactly the semantics required by the RM for handling of configuration pragmas in a compilation. In the absence of configuration pragmas (at the main file level), this option has no effect, but it causes such configuration pragmas to be handled in a quite different manner.

First, in compilation mode, if `gnatchop` is given a file that consists of only configuration pragmas, then this file is appended to the 'gnat.adc' file in the current directory. This behavior provides the required behavior described in the RM for the actions to be taken on submitting such a file to the compiler, namely that these pragmas should apply to all subsequent compilations in the same compilation environment. Using GNAT, the current directory, possibly containing a 'gnat.adc' file is the representation of a compilation environment. For more information on the 'gnat.adc' file, see Section 9.1 [Handling of Configuration Pragmas], page 119.

Second, in compilation mode, if `gnatchop` is given a file that starts with configuration pragmas, and contains one or more units, then these configuration pragmas are prepended to each of the chopped files. This behavior provides the required behavior described in the RM for the actions to be taken on compiling such a file, namely that the pragmas apply to all units in the compilation, but not to subsequently compiled units.

Finally, if configuration pragmas appear between units, they are appended to the previous unit. This results in the previous unit being illegal, since the compiler does not accept configuration pragmas that follow a unit. This provides the required RM behavior that forbids configuration pragmas other than those preceding the first compilation unit of a compilation.

For most purposes, `gnatchop` will be used in default mode. The compilation mode described above is used only if you need exactly accurate behavior with respect to compilations, and you have files that contain multiple units and configuration pragmas. In this circumstance the use of `gnatchop` with the compilation mode switch provides the required behavior, and is for example the mode in which GNAT processes the ACVC tests.

8.3 Command Line for `gnatchop`

The `gnatchop` command has the form:

```
$ gnatchop switches file name [file name file name ...]
      [directory]
```

The only required argument is the file name of the file to be chopped. There are no restrictions on the form of this file name. The file itself contains one or more Ada units, in normal GNAT format, concatenated together. As shown, more than one file may be presented to be chopped.

When run in default mode, `gnatchop` generates one output file in the current directory for each unit in each of the files.

directory, if specified, gives the name of the directory to which the output files will be written. If it is not specified, all files are written to the current directory.

For example, given a file called '`hellofiles`' containing

```
procedure hello;

with Text_IO; use Text_IO;
procedure hello is
begin
   Put_Line ("Hello");
end hello;
```

the command

```
$ gnatchop hellofiles
```

generates two files in the current directory, one called '`hello.ads`' containing the single line that is the procedure spec, and the other called '`hello.adb`' containing the remaining text. The original file is not affected. The generated files can be compiled in the normal manner.

When gnatchop is invoked on a file that is empty or that contains only empty lines and/or comments, gnatchop will not fail, but will not produce any new sources.

For example, given a file called '`toto.txt`' containing

```
--   Just a comment
```

the command

    $ gnatchop toto.txt

will not produce any new file and will result in the following warnings:

    toto.txt:1:01: warning: empty file, contains no compilation units
    no compilation units found
    no source files written

8.4 Switches for `gnatchop`

`gnatchop` recognizes the following switches:

'`--version`'
Display Copyright and version, then exit disregarding all other options.

'`--help`'
If '`--version`' was not used, display usage, then exit disregarding all other options.

'`-c`'
Causes `gnatchop` to operate in compilation mode, in which configuration pragmas are handled according to strict RM rules. See previous section for a full description of this mode.

'`-gnatxxx`'
This passes the given '`-gnatxxx`' switch to `gnat` which is used to parse the given file. Not all xxx options make sense, but for example, the use of '`-gnati2`' allows `gnatchop` to process a source file that uses Latin-2 coding for identifiers.

'`-h`'
Causes `gnatchop` to generate a brief help summary to the standard output file showing usage information.

'`-kmm`'
Limit generated file names to the specified number mm of characters. This is useful if the resulting set of files is required to be interoperable with systems which limit the length of file names. No space is allowed between the '`-k`' and the numeric value. The numeric value may be omitted in which case a default of '`-k8`', suitable for use with DOS-like file systems, is used. If no '`-k`' switch is present then there is no limit on the length of file names.

'`-p`'
Causes the file modification time stamp of the input file to be preserved and used for the time stamp of the output file(s). This may be useful for preserving coherency of time stamps in an environment where `gnatchop` is used as part of a standard build process.

'`-q`'
Causes output of informational messages indicating the set of generated files to be suppressed. Warnings and error messages are unaffected.

'`-r`'
Generate `Source_Reference` pragmas. Use this switch if the output files are regarded as temporary and development is to be done in terms of the original unchopped file. This switch causes `Source_Reference` pragmas to be inserted into each of the generated files to refers back to the original file name and line number. The result is that all error messages refer back to the original unchopped file. In addition, the debugging information placed into the object file (when the '`-g`' switch of `gcc` or `gnatmake` is specified) also refers back to

this original file so that tools like profilers and debuggers will give information in terms of the original unchopped file.

If the original file to be chopped itself contains a `Source_Reference` pragma referencing a third file, then gnatchop respects this pragma, and the generated `Source_Reference` pragmas in the chopped file refer to the original file, with appropriate line numbers. This is particularly useful when `gnatchop` is used in conjunction with `gnatprep` to compile files that contain preprocessing statements and multiple units.

'-v'   Causes `gnatchop` to operate in verbose mode. The version number and copyright notice are output, as well as exact copies of the gnat1 commands spawned to obtain the chop control information.

'-w'   Overwrite existing file names. Normally `gnatchop` regards it as a fatal error if there is already a file with the same name as a file it would otherwise output, in other words if the files to be chopped contain duplicated units. This switch bypasses this check, and causes all but the last instance of such duplicated units to be skipped.

'--GCC=xxxx'
                 Specify the path of the GNAT parser to be used. When this switch is used, no attempt is made to add the prefix to the GNAT parser executable.

8.5 Examples of gnatchop Usage

gnatchop -w hello_s.ada prerelease/files
                 Chops the source file 'hello_s.ada'. The output files will be placed in the directory 'prerelease/files', overwriting any files with matching names in that directory (no files in the current directory are modified).

gnatchop archive
                 Chops the source file 'archive' into the current directory. One useful application of `gnatchop` is in sending sets of sources around, for example in email messages. The required sources are simply concatenated (for example, using a Unix `cat` command), and then `gnatchop` is used at the other end to reconstitute the original file names.

gnatchop file1 file2 file3 direc
                 Chops all units in files 'file1', 'file2', 'file3', placing the resulting files in the directory 'direc'. Note that if any units occur more than once anywhere within this set of files, an error message is generated, and no files are written. To override this check, use the '-w' switch, in which case the last occurrence in the last file will be the one that is output, and earlier duplicate occurrences for a given unit will be skipped.

9 Configuration Pragmas

Configuration pragmas include those pragmas described as such in the Ada Reference Manual, as well as implementation-dependent pragmas that are configuration pragmas. See the individual descriptions of pragmas in the *GNAT Reference Manual* for details on these additional GNAT-specific configuration pragmas. Most notably, the pragma `Source_File_Name`, which allows specifying non-default names for source files, is a configuration pragma. The following is a complete list of configuration pragmas recognized by GNAT:

```
Ada_83
Ada_95
Ada_05
C_Pass_By_Copy
Component_Alignment
Detect_Blocking
Discard_Names
Elaboration_Checks
Eliminate
Extend_System
External_Name_Casing
Float_Representation
Initialize_Scalars
Interrupt_State
License
Locking_Policy
Long_Float
Normalize_Scalars
Persistent_BSS
Polling
Profile
Profile_Warnings
Propagate_Exceptions
Queuing_Policy
Ravenscar
Restricted_Run_Time
Restrictions
Restrictions_Warnings
Reviewable
Source_File_Name
Style_Checks
Suppress
Task_Dispatching_Policy
Universal_Data
Unsuppress
Use_VADS_Size
Warnings
Validity_Checks
```

9.1 Handling of Configuration Pragmas

Configuration pragmas may either appear at the start of a compilation unit, in which case they apply only to that unit, or they may apply to all compilations performed in a given compilation environment.

GNAT also provides the `gnatchop` utility to provide an automatic way to handle configuration pragmas following the semantics for compilations (that is, files with multiple units), described in the RM. See Section 8.2 [Operating gnatchop in Compilation Mode], page 115 for details. However, for most purposes, it will be more convenient to edit the 'gnat.adc' file that contains configuration pragmas directly, as described in the following section.

9.2 The Configuration Pragmas Files

In GNAT a compilation environment is defined by the current directory at the time that a compile command is given. This current directory is searched for a file whose name is 'gnat.adc'. If this file is present, it is expected to contain one or more configuration pragmas that will be applied to the current compilation. However, if the switch '-gnatA' is used, 'gnat.adc' is not considered.

Configuration pragmas may be entered into the 'gnat.adc' file either by running gnatchop on a source file that consists only of configuration pragmas, or more conveniently by direct editing of the 'gnat.adc' file, which is a standard format source file.

In addition to 'gnat.adc', additional files containing configuration pragmas may be applied to the current compilation using the switch '-gnatec'*path*. *path* must designate an existing file that contains only configuration pragmas. These configuration pragmas are in addition to those found in 'gnat.adc' (provided 'gnat.adc' is present and switch '-gnatA' is not used).

It is allowed to specify several switches '-gnatec', all of which will be taken into account.

If you are using project file, a separate mechanism is provided using project attributes, see Section 11.15.1.2 [Specifying Configuration Pragmas], page 155 for more details.

10 Handling Arbitrary File Naming Conventions Using gnatname

10.1 Arbitrary File Naming Conventions

The GNAT compiler must be able to know the source file name of a compilation unit. When using the standard GNAT default file naming conventions (.ads for specs, .adb for bodies), the GNAT compiler does not need additional information.

When the source file names do not follow the standard GNAT default file naming conventions, the GNAT compiler must be given additional information through a configuration pragmas file (see Chapter 9 [Configuration Pragmas], page 119) or a project file. When the non standard file naming conventions are well-defined, a small number of pragmas Source_File_Name specifying a naming pattern (see Section 2.5 [Alternative File Naming Schemes], page 18) may be sufficient. However, if the file naming conventions are irregular or arbitrary, a number of pragma Source_File_Name for individual compilation units must be defined. To help maintain the correspondence between compilation unit names and source file names within the compiler, GNAT provides a tool **gnatname** to generate the required pragmas for a set of files.

10.2 Running gnatname

The usual form of the **gnatname** command is

```
$ gnatname [switches] naming_pattern [naming_patterns]
```

All of the arguments are optional. If invoked without any argument, **gnatname** will display its usage.

When used with at least one naming pattern, **gnatname** will attempt to find all the compilation units in files that follow at least one of the naming patterns. To find these compilation units, **gnatname** will use the GNAT compiler in syntax-check-only mode on all regular files.

One or several Naming Patterns may be given as arguments to **gnatname**. Each Naming Pattern is enclosed between double quotes. A Naming Pattern is a regular expression similar to the wildcard patterns used in file names by the Unix shells or the DOS prompt.

Examples of Naming Patterns are

```
"*.[12].ada"
"*.ad[sb]*"
"body_*"    "spec_*"
```

For a more complete description of the syntax of Naming Patterns, see the second kind of regular expressions described in 'g-regexp.ads' (the "Glob" regular expressions).

When invoked with no switches, **gnatname** will create a configuration pragmas file 'gnat.adc' in the current working directory, with pragmas Source_File_Name for each file that contains a valid Ada unit.

10.3 Switches for gnatname

Switches for **gnatname** must precede any specified Naming Pattern.

You may specify any of the following switches to **gnatname**:

'--version'

        Display Copyright and version, then exit disregarding all other options.

'--help'   If '--version' was not used, display usage, then exit disregarding all other
               options.

'-c'file''
               Create a configuration pragmas file 'file' (instead of the default 'gnat.adc').
               There may be zero, one or more space between '-c' and 'file'. 'file' may
               include directory information. 'file' must be writable. There may be only one
               switch '-c'. When a switch '-c' is specified, no switch '-P' may be specified
               (see below).

'-d'dir''   Look for source files in directory 'dir'. There may be zero, one or more spaces
               between '-d' and 'dir'. When a switch '-d' is specified, the current working
               directory will not be searched for source files, unless it is explicitly specified
               with a '-d' or '-D' switch. Several switches '-d' may be specified. If 'dir' is
               a relative path, it is relative to the directory of the configuration pragmas file
               specified with switch '-c', or to the directory of the project file specified with
               switch '-P' or, if neither switch '-c' nor switch '-P' are specified, it is relative
               to the current working directory. The directory specified with switch '-d' must
               exist and be readable.

'-D'file''
               Look for source files in all directories listed in text file 'file'. There may be
               zero, one or more spaces between '-D' and 'file'. 'file' must be an existing,
               readable text file. Each non empty line in 'file' must be a directory. Specifying
               switch '-D' is equivalent to specifying as many switches '-d' as there are non
               empty lines in 'file'.

'-f'pattern''
               Foreign patterns. Using this switch, it is possible to add sources of languages
               other than Ada to the list of sources of a project file. It is only useful if a -P
               switch is used. For example,

                   gnatname -Pprj -f"*.c" "*.ada"

               will look for Ada units in all files with the '.ada' extension, and will add to the
               list of file for project 'prj.gpr' the C files with extension ".c".

'-h'   Output usage (help) information. The output is written to 'stdout'.

'-P'proj''
               Create or update project file 'proj'. There may be zero, one or more space
               between '-P' and 'proj'. 'proj' may include directory information. 'proj'
               must be writable. There may be only one switch '-P'. When a switch '-P' is
               specified, no switch '-c' may be specified.

'-v'   Verbose mode. Output detailed explanation of behavior to 'stdout'. This
               includes name of the file written, the name of the directories to search and, for
               each file in those directories whose name matches at least one of the Naming
               Patterns, an indication of whether the file contains a unit, and if so the name
               of the unit.

'-v -v'   Very Verbose mode. In addition to the output produced in verbose mode, for
               each file in the searched directories whose name matches none of the Naming
               Patterns, an indication is given that there is no match.

'-x'pattern''

Excluded patterns. Using this switch, it is possible to exclude some files that would match the name patterns. For example,

```
gnatname -x "*_nt.ada" "*.ada"
```

will look for Ada units in all files with the '.ada' extension, except those whose names end with '_nt.ada'.

10.4 Examples of gnatname Usage

```
$ gnatname -c /home/me/names.adc -d sources "[a-z]*.ada*"
```

In this example, the directory '/home/me' must already exist and be writable. In addition, the directory '/home/me/sources' (specified by '-d sources') must exist and be readable.

Note the optional spaces after '-c' and '-d'.

```
$ gnatname -P/home/me/proj -x "*_nt_body.ada"
  -dsources -dsources/plus -Dcommon_dirs.txt "body_*" "spec_*"
```

Note that several switches '-d' may be used, even in conjunction with one or several switches '-D'. Several Naming Patterns and one excluded pattern are used in this example.

11 GNAT Project Manager

11.1 Introduction

This chapter describes GNAT's *Project Manager*, a facility that allows you to manage complex builds involving a number of source files, directories, and compilation options for different system configurations. In particular, project files allow you to specify:

- The directory or set of directories containing the source files, and/or the names of the specific source files themselves

- The directory in which the compiler's output ('`ALI`' files, object files, tree files) is to be placed

- The directory in which the executable programs is to be placed

- Switch settings for any of the project-enabled tools (`gnatmake`, compiler, binder, linker, `gnatls`, `gnatxref`, `gnatfind`); you can apply these settings either globally or to individual compilation units.

- The source files containing the main subprogram(s) to be built

- The source programming language(s) (currently Ada and/or C)

- Source file naming conventions; you can specify these either globally or for individual compilation units

11.1.1 Project Files

Project files are written in a syntax close to that of Ada, using familiar notions such as packages, context clauses, declarations, default values, assignments, and inheritance. Finally, project files can be built hierarchically from other project files, simplifying complex system integration and project reuse.

A *project* is a specific set of values for various compilation properties. The settings for a given project are described by means of a *project file*, which is a text file written in an Ada-like syntax. Property values in project files are either strings or lists of strings. Properties that are not explicitly set receive default values. A project file may interrogate the values of *external variables* (user-defined command-line switches or environment variables), and it may specify property settings conditionally, based on the value of such variables.

In simple cases, a project's source files depend only on other source files in the same project, or on the predefined libraries. (*Dependence* is used in the Ada technical sense; as in one Ada unit `withing` another.) However, the Project Manager also allows more sophisticated arrangements, where the source files in one project depend on source files in other projects:

- One project can *import* other projects containing needed source files.

- You can organize GNAT projects in a hierarchy: a *child* project can extend a *parent* project, inheriting the parent's source files and optionally overriding any of them with alternative versions

More generally, the Project Manager lets you structure large development efforts into hierarchical subsystems, where build decisions are delegated to the subsystem level, and thus different compilation environments (switch settings) used for different subsystems.

The Project Manager is invoked through the '-P*projectfile*' switch to gnatmake or to the gnat front driver. There may be zero, one or more spaces between '-P' and '*project-file*'. If you want to define (on the command line) an external variable that is queried by the project file, you must use the '-X*vbl*=*value*' switch. The Project Manager parses and interprets the project file, and drives the invoked tool based on the project settings.

The Project Manager supports a wide range of development strategies, for systems of all sizes. Here are some typical practices that are easily handled:

- Using a common set of source files, but generating object files in different directories via different switch settings

- Using a mostly-shared set of source files, but with different versions of some unit or units

The destination of an executable can be controlled inside a project file using the '-o' switch. In the absence of such a switch either inside the project file or on the command line, any executable files generated by gnatmake are placed in the directory Exec_Dir specified in the project file. If no Exec_Dir is specified, they will be placed in the object directory of the project.

You can use project files to achieve some of the effects of a source versioning system (for example, defining separate projects for the different sets of sources that comprise different releases) but the Project Manager is independent of any source configuration management tools that might be used by the developers.

The next section introduces the main features of GNAT's project facility through a sequence of examples; subsequent sections will present the syntax and semantics in more detail. A more formal description of the project facility appears in the GNAT Reference Manual.

11.2 Examples of Project Files

This section illustrates some of the typical uses of project files and explains their basic structure and behavior.

11.2.1 Common Sources with Different Switches and Directories

Suppose that the Ada source files 'pack.ads', 'pack.adb', and 'proc.adb' are in the '/common' directory. The file 'proc.adb' contains an Ada main subprogram Proc that withs package Pack. We want to compile these source files under two sets of switches:

- When debugging, we want to pass the '-g' switch to gnatmake, and the '-gnata', '-gnato', and '-gnatE' switches to the compiler; the compiler's output is to appear in '/common/debug'

- When preparing a release version, we want to pass the '-O2' switch to the compiler; the compiler's output is to appear in '/common/release'

The GNAT project files shown below, respectively 'debug.gpr' and 'release.gpr' in the '/common' directory, achieve these effects.

Schematically:

```
/common
  debug.gpr
  release.gpr
  pack.ads
  pack.adb
  proc.adb
/common/debug
  proc.ali, proc.o
  pack.ali, pack.o
/common/release
  proc.ali, proc.o
  pack.ali, pack.o
```

Here are the corresponding project files:

```
project Debug is
  for Object_Dir use "debug";
  for Main use ("proc");

  package Builder is
    for Default_Switches ("Ada")
        use ("-g");
    for Executable ("proc.adb") use "proc1";
  end Builder;

  package Compiler is
    for Default_Switches ("Ada")
      use ("-fstack-check",
           "-gnata",
           "-gnato",
           "-gnatE");
  end Compiler;
end Debug;

project Release is
  for Object_Dir use "release";
  for Exec_Dir use ".";
  for Main use ("proc");

  package Compiler is
    for Default_Switches ("Ada")
        use ("-O2");
  end Compiler;
end Release;
```

The name of the project defined by 'debug.gpr' is "Debug" (case insensitive), and analogously the project defined by 'release.gpr' is "Release". For consistency the file should have the same name as the project, and the project file's extension should be "gpr". These conventions are not required, but a warning is issued if they are not followed.

If the current directory is '/temp', then the command

```
gnatmake -P/common/debug.gpr
```

generates object and ALI files in '/common/debug', as well as the proc1 executable, using the switch settings defined in the project file.

Likewise, the command

```
gnatmake -P/common/release.gpr
```

generates object and ALI files in '/common/release', and the proc executable in '/common', using the switch settings from the project file.

Source Files

If a project file does not explicitly specify a set of source directories or a set of source files, then by default the project's source files are the Ada source files in the project file directory. Thus 'pack.ads', 'pack.adb', and 'proc.adb' are the source files for both projects.

Specifying the Object Directory

Several project properties are modeled by Ada-style *attributes*; a property is defined by supplying the equivalent of an Ada attribute definition clause in the project file. A project's object directory is another such a property; the corresponding attribute is Object_Dir, and its value is also a string expression, specified either as absolute or relative. In the later case, it is relative to the project file directory. Thus the compiler's output is directed to '/common/debug' (for the Debug project) and to '/common/release' (for the Release project). If Object_Dir is not specified, then the default is the project file directory itself.

Specifying the Exec Directory

A project's exec directory is another property; the corresponding attribute is Exec_Dir, and its value is also a string expression, either specified as relative or absolute. If Exec_Dir is not specified, then the default is the object directory (which may also be the project file directory if attribute Object_Dir is not specified). Thus the executable is placed in '/common/debug' for the Debug project (attribute Exec_Dir not specified) and in '/common' for the Release project.

Project File Packages

A GNAT tool that is integrated with the Project Manager is modeled by a corresponding package in the project file. In the example above, The Debug project defines the packages Builder (for gnatmake) and Compiler; the Release project defines only the Compiler package.

The Ada-like package syntax is not to be taken literally. Although packages in project files bear a surface resemblance to packages in Ada source code, the notation is simply a way to convey a grouping of properties for a named entity. Indeed, the package names permitted in project files are restricted to a predefined set, corresponding to the project-aware tools, and the contents of packages are limited to a small set of constructs. The packages in the example above contain attribute definitions.

Specifying Switch Settings

Switch settings for a project-aware tool can be specified through attributes in the package that corresponds to the tool. The example above illustrates one of the relevant attributes, Default_Switches, which is defined in packages in both project files. Unlike simple attributes like Source_Dirs, Default_Switches is known as an *associative array*. When you define this attribute, you must supply an "index" (a literal string), and the effect of the attribute definition is to set the value of the array at the specified index. For the Default_Switches attribute, the index is a programming language (in our case, Ada), and the value specified (after use) must be a list of string expressions.

The attributes permitted in project files are restricted to a predefined set. Some may appear at project level, others in packages. For any attribute that is an associative array, the index must always be a literal string, but the restrictions on this string (e.g., a file name or a language name) depend on the individual attribute. Also depending on the attribute, its specified value will need to be either a string or a string list.

In the `Debug` project, we set the switches for two tools, `gnatmake` and the compiler, and thus we include the two corresponding packages; each package defines the `Default_Switches` attribute with index `"Ada"`. Note that the package corresponding to `gnatmake` is named `Builder`. The `Release` project is similar, but only includes the `Compiler` package.

In project `Debug` above, the switches starting with '`-gnat`' that are specified in package `Compiler` could have been placed in package `Builder`, since `gnatmake` transmits all such switches to the compiler.

Main Subprograms

One of the specifiable properties of a project is a list of files that contain main subprograms. This property is captured in the `Main` attribute, whose value is a list of strings. If a project defines the `Main` attribute, it is not necessary to identify the main subprogram(s) when invoking `gnatmake` (see Section 11.15.1 [gnatmake and Project Files], page 153).

Executable File Names

By default, the executable file name corresponding to a main source is deduced from the main source file name. Through the attributes `Executable` and `Executable_Suffix` of package `Builder`, it is possible to change this default. In project `Debug` above, the executable file name for main source '`proc.adb`' is '`proc1`'. Attribute `Executable_Suffix`, when specified, may change the suffix of the executable files, when no attribute `Executable` applies: its value replace the platform-specific executable suffix. Attributes `Executable` and `Executable_Suffix` are the only ways to specify a non default executable file name when several mains are built at once in a single `gnatmake` command.

Source File Naming Conventions

Since the project files above do not specify any source file naming conventions, the GNAT defaults are used. The mechanism for defining source file naming conventions – a package named `Naming` – is described below (see Section 11.11 [Naming Schemes], page 147).

Source Language(s)

Since the project files do not specify a `Languages` attribute, by default the GNAT tools assume that the language of the project file is Ada. More generally, a project can comprise source files in Ada, C, and/or other languages.

11.2.2 Using External Variables

Instead of supplying different project files for debug and release, we can define a single project file that queries an external variable (set either on the command line or via an environment variable) in order to conditionally define the appropriate settings. Again, assume that the source files '`pack.ads`', '`pack.adb`', and '`proc.adb`' are located in directory '`/common`'. The following project file, '`build.gpr`', queries the external variable named `STYLE` and defines an object directory and switch settings based on whether the value is `"deb"` (debug) or `"rel"` (release), and where the default is `"deb"`.

```
project Build is
  for Main use ("proc");

  type Style_Type is ("deb", "rel");
  Style : Style_Type := external ("STYLE", "deb");

  case Style is
    when "deb" =>
      for Object_Dir use "debug";

    when "rel" =>
      for Object_Dir use "release";
      for Exec_Dir use ".";
  end case;

  package Builder is

    case Style is
      when "deb" =>
        for Default_Switches ("Ada")
            use ("-g");
        for Executable ("proc") use "proc1";
      when others =>
        null;
    end case;

  end Builder;

  package Compiler is

    case Style is
      when "deb" =>
        for Default_Switches ("Ada")
            use ("-gnata",
                 "-gnato",
                 "-gnatE");

      when "rel" =>
        for Default_Switches ("Ada")
            use ("-O2");
    end case;

  end Compiler;

end Build;
```

Style_Type is an example of a *string type*, which is the project file analog of an Ada enumeration type but whose components are string literals rather than identifiers. Style is declared as a variable of this type.

The form external("STYLE", "deb") is known as an *external reference*; its first argument is the name of an *external variable*, and the second argument is a default value to be used if the external variable doesn't exist. You can define an external variable on the command line via the '-X' switch, or you can use an environment variable as an external variable.

Each case construct is expanded by the Project Manager based on the value of Style. Thus the command

```
gnatmake -P/common/build.gpr -XSTYLE=deb
```

is equivalent to the `gnatmake` invocation using the project file 'debug.gpr' in the earlier example. So is the command

```
gnatmake -P/common/build.gpr
```

since "deb" is the default for STYLE.

Analogously,

```
gnatmake -P/common/build.gpr -XSTYLE=rel
```

is equivalent to the `gnatmake` invocation using the project file 'release.gpr' in the earlier example.

11.2.3 Importing Other Projects

A compilation unit in a source file in one project may depend on compilation units in source files in other projects. To compile this unit under control of a project file, the dependent project must *import* the projects containing the needed source files. This effect is obtained using syntax similar to an Ada `with` clause, but where `with`ed entities are strings that denote project files.

As an example, suppose that the two projects GUI_Proj and Comm_Proj are defined in the project files 'gui_proj.gpr' and 'comm_proj.gpr' in directories '/gui' and '/comm', respectively. Suppose that the source files for GUI_Proj are 'gui.ads' and 'gui.adb', and that the source files for Comm_Proj are 'comm.ads' and 'comm.adb', where each set of files is located in its respective project file directory. Schematically:

```
/gui
  gui_proj.gpr
  gui.ads
  gui.adb

/comm
  comm_proj.gpr
  comm.ads
  comm.adb
```

We want to develop an application in directory '/app' that `with` the packages GUI and Comm, using the properties of the corresponding project files (e.g. the switch settings and object directory). Skeletal code for a main procedure might be something like the following:

```
with GUI, Comm;
procedure App_Main is
   ...
begin
   ...
end App_Main;
```

Here is a project file, 'app_proj.gpr', that achieves the desired effect:

```
with "/gui/gui_proj", "/comm/comm_proj";
project App_Proj is
   for Main use ("app_main");
end App_Proj;
```

Building an executable is achieved through the command:

```
gnatmake -P/app/app_proj
```

which will generate the `app_main` executable in the directory where 'app_proj.gpr' resides.

If an imported project file uses the standard extension (`gpr`) then (as illustrated above) the `with` clause can omit the extension.

Our example specified an absolute path for each imported project file. Alternatively, the directory name of an imported object can be omitted if either

- The imported project file is in the same directory as the importing project file, or
- You have defined an environment variable that includes the directory containing the needed project file. The syntax of `ADA_PROJECT_PATH` is the same as the syntax of `ADA_INCLUDE_PATH` and `ADA_OBJECTS_PATH`: a list of directory names separated by colons (semicolons on Windows).

Thus, if we define `ADA_PROJECT_PATH` to include '`/gui`' and '`/comm`', then our project file '`app_proj.gpr`' can be written as follows:

```
with "gui_proj", "comm_proj";
project App_Proj is
   for Main use ("app_main");
end App_Proj;
```

Importing other projects can create ambiguities. For example, the same unit might be present in different imported projects, or it might be present in both the importing project and in an imported project. Both of these conditions are errors. Note that in the current version of the Project Manager, it is illegal to have an ambiguous unit even if the unit is never referenced by the importing project. This restriction may be relaxed in a future release.

11.2.4 Extending a Project

In large software systems it is common to have multiple implementations of a common interface; in Ada terms, multiple versions of a package body for the same specification. For example, one implementation might be safe for use in tasking programs, while another might only be used in sequential applications. This can be modeled in GNAT using the concept of *project extension*. If one project (the "child") *extends* another project (the "parent") then by default all source files of the parent project are inherited by the child, but the child project can override any of the parent's source files with new versions, and can also add new files. This facility is the project analog of a type extension in Object-Oriented Programming. Project hierarchies are permitted (a child project may be the parent of yet another project), and a project that inherits one project can also import other projects.

As an example, suppose that directory '`/seq`' contains the project file '`seq_proj.gpr`' as well as the source files '`pack.ads`', '`pack.adb`', and '`proc.adb`':

```
/seq
  pack.ads
  pack.adb
  proc.adb
  seq_proj.gpr
```

Note that the project file can simply be empty (that is, no attribute or package is defined):

```
project Seq_Proj is
end Seq_Proj;
```

implying that its source files are all the Ada source files in the project directory.

Suppose we want to supply an alternate version of '`pack.adb`', in directory '`/tasking`', but use the existing versions of '`pack.ads`' and '`proc.adb`'. We can define a project `Tasking_Proj` that inherits `Seq_Proj`:

```
/tasking
  pack.adb
  tasking_proj.gpr

project Tasking_Proj extends "/seq/seq_proj" is
end Tasking_Proj;
```

The version of 'pack.adb' used in a build depends on which project file is specified.

Note that we could have obtained the desired behavior using project import rather than project inheritance; a base project would contain the sources for 'pack.ads' and 'proc.adb', a sequential project would import base and add 'pack.adb', and likewise a tasking project would import base and add a different version of 'pack.adb'. The choice depends on whether other sources in the original project need to be overridden. If they do, then project extension is necessary, otherwise, importing is sufficient.

In a project file that extends another project file, it is possible to indicate that an inherited source is not part of the sources of the extending project. This is necessary sometimes when a package spec has been overloaded and no longer requires a body: in this case, it is necessary to indicate that the inherited body is not part of the sources of the project, otherwise there will be a compilation error when compiling the spec.

For that purpose, the attribute `Excluded_Source_Files` is used. Its value is a string list: a list of file names.

```
project B extends "a" is
   for Source_Files use ("pkg.ads");
   -- New spec of Pkg does not need a completion
   for Excluded_Source_Files use ("pkg.adb");
end B;
```

Attribute `Excluded_Source_Files` may also be used to check if a source is still needed: if it is possible to build using `gnatmake` when such a source is put in attribute `Excluded_Source_Files` of a project P, then it is possible to remove the source completely from a system that includes project P.

11.3 Project File Syntax

This section describes the structure of project files.

A project may be an *independent project*, entirely defined by a single project file. Any Ada source file in an independent project depends only on the predefined library and other Ada source files in the same project.

A project may also *depend on* other projects, in either or both of the following ways:

- It may import any number of projects
- It may extend at most one other project

The dependence relation is a directed acyclic graph (the subgraph reflecting the "extends" relation is a tree).

A project's *immediate sources* are the source files directly defined by that project, either implicitly by residing in the project file's directory, or explicitly through any of the source-related attributes described below. More generally, a project *proj*'s *sources* are the immediate sources of *proj* together with the immediate sources (unless overridden) of any project on which *proj* depends (either directly or indirectly).

11.3.1 Basic Syntax

As seen in the earlier examples, project files have an Ada-like syntax. The minimal project file is:

```
project Empty is

end Empty;
```

The identifier `Empty` is the name of the project. This project name must be present after the reserved word `end` at the end of the project file, followed by a semi-colon.

Any name in a project file, such as the project name or a variable name, has the same syntax as an Ada identifier.

The reserved words of project files are the Ada reserved words plus `extends`, `external`, and `project`. Note that the only Ada reserved words currently used in project file syntax are:

- `case`
- `end`
- `for`
- `is`
- `others`
- `package`
- `renames`
- `type`
- `use`
- `when`
- `with`

Comments in project files have the same syntax as in Ada, two consecutive hyphens through the end of the line.

11.3.2 Packages

A project file may contain *packages*. The name of a package must be one of the identifiers from the following list. A package with a given name may only appear once in a project file. Package names are case insensitive. The following package names are legal:

- `Naming`
- `Builder`
- `Compiler`
- `Binder`
- `Linker`
- `Finder`
- `Cross_Reference`
- `Eliminate`
- `Pretty_Printer`
- `Metrics`

- gnatls

- gnatstub

- IDE

- Language_Processing

In its simplest form, a package may be empty:

```
project Simple is
  package Builder is
  end Builder;
end Simple;
```

A package may contain *attribute declarations*, *variable declarations* and *case constructions*, as will be described below.

When there is ambiguity between a project name and a package name, the name always designates the project. To avoid possible confusion, it is always a good idea to avoid naming a project with one of the names allowed for packages or any name that starts with gnat.

11.3.3 Expressions

An *expression* is either a *string expression* or a *string list expression*.

A *string expression* is either a *simple string expression* or a *compound string expression*.

A *simple string expression* is one of the following:

- A literal string; e.g."comm/my_proj.gpr"

- A string-valued variable reference (see Section 11.3.5 [Variables], page 136)

- A string-valued attribute reference (see Section 11.3.6 [Attributes], page 137)

- An external reference (see Section 11.8 [External References in Project Files], page 145)

A *compound string expression* is a concatenation of string expressions, using the operator "&"

```
            Path & "/" & File_Name & ".ads"
```

A *string list expression* is either a *simple string list expression* or a *compound string list expression*.

A *simple string list expression* is one of the following:

- A parenthesized list of zero or more string expressions, separated by commas

```
            File_Names := (File_Name, "gnat.adc", File_Name & ".orig");
            Empty_List := ();
```

- A string list-valued variable reference

- A string list-valued attribute reference

A *compound string list expression* is the concatenation (using "&") of a simple string list expression and an expression. Note that each term in a compound string list expression, except the first, may be either a string expression or a string list expression.

```
            File_Name_List := () & File_Name; --  One string in this list
            Extended_File_Name_List := File_Name_List & (File_Name & ".orig");
            --  Two strings
            Big_List := File_Name_List & Extended_File_Name_List;
            --  Concatenation of two string lists: three strings
            Illegal_List := "gnat.adc" & Extended_File_Name_List;
            --  Illegal: must start with a string list
```

11.3.4 String Types

A *string type declaration* introduces a discrete set of string literals. If a string variable is declared to have this type, its value is restricted to the given set of literals.

Here is an example of a string type declaration:

```
type OS is ("NT", "nt", "Unix", "GNU/Linux", "other OS");
```

Variables of a string type are called *typed variables*; all other variables are called *untyped variables*. Typed variables are particularly useful in `case` constructions, to support conditional attribute declarations. (see Section 11.3.8 [case Constructions], page 140).

The string literals in the list are case sensitive and must all be different. They may include any graphic characters allowed in Ada, including spaces.

A string type may only be declared at the project level, not inside a package.

A string type may be referenced by its name if it has been declared in the same project file, or by an expanded name whose prefix is the name of the project in which it is declared.

11.3.5 Variables

A variable may be declared at the project file level, or within a package. Here are some examples of variable declarations:

```
This_OS : OS := external ("OS"); --  a typed variable declaration
That_OS := "GNU/Linux";          --  an untyped variable declaration
```

The syntax of a *typed variable declaration* is identical to the Ada syntax for an object declaration. By contrast, the syntax of an untyped variable declaration is identical to an Ada assignment statement. In fact, variable declarations in project files have some of the characteristics of an assignment, in that successive declarations for the same variable are allowed. Untyped variable declarations do establish the expected kind of the variable (string or string list), and successive declarations for it must respect the initial kind.

A string variable declaration (typed or untyped) declares a variable whose value is a string. This variable may be used as a string expression.

```
File_Name       := "readme.txt";
Saved_File_Name := File_Name & ".saved";
```

A string list variable declaration declares a variable whose value is a list of strings. The list may contain any number (zero or more) of strings.

```
Empty_List := ();
List_With_One_Element := ("-gnaty");
List_With_Two_Elements := List_With_One_Element & "-gnatg";
Long_List := ("main.ada", "pack1_.ada", "pack1.ada", "pack2_.ada"
              "pack2.ada", "util_.ada", "util.ada");
```

The same typed variable may not be declared more than once at project level, and it may not be declared more than once in any package; it is in effect a constant.

The same untyped variable may be declared several times. Declarations are elaborated in the order in which they appear, so the new value replaces the old one, and any subsequent reference to the variable uses the new value. However, as noted above, if a variable has been declared as a string, all subsequent declarations must give it a string value. Similarly, if a variable has been declared as a string list, all subsequent declarations must give it a string list value.

A *variable reference* may take several forms:

- The simple variable name, for a variable in the current package (if any) or in the current project
- An expanded name, whose prefix is a context name.

A *context* may be one of the following:

- The name of an existing package in the current project
- The name of an imported project of the current project
- The name of an ancestor project (i.e., a project extended by the current project, either directly or indirectly)
- An expanded name whose prefix is an imported/parent project name, and whose selector is a package name in that project.

A variable reference may be used in an expression.

11.3.6 Attributes

A project (and its packages) may have *attributes* that define the project's properties. Some attributes have values that are strings; others have values that are string lists.

There are two categories of attributes: *simple attributes* and *associative arrays* (see Section 11.3.7 [Associative Array Attributes], page 139).

Legal project attribute names, and attribute names for each legal package are listed below. Attributes names are case-insensitive.

The following attributes are defined on projects (all are simple attributes):

Attribute Name	Value
Source_Files	string list
Source_Dirs	string list
Source_List_File	string
Object_Dir	string
Exec_Dir	string
Excluded_Source_Dirs	string list
Excluded_Source_Files	string list
Languages	string list
Main	string list
Library_Dir	string
Library_Name	string
Library_Kind	string
Library_Version	string
Library_Interface	string
Library_Auto_Init	string
Library_Options	string list
Library_Src_Dir	string
Library_ALI_Dir	string
Library_GCC	string
Library_Symbol_File	string
Library_Symbol_Policy	string
Library_Reference_Symbol_File	string
Externally_Built	string

The following attributes are defined for package `Naming` (see Section 11.11 [Naming Schemes], page 147):

Attribute Name	Category	Index	Value
Spec_Suffix	associative array	language name	string
Body_Suffix	associative array	language name	string
Separate_Suffix	simple attribute	n/a	string
Casing	simple attribute	n/a	string
Dot_Replacement	simple attribute	n/a	string
Spec	associative array	Ada unit name	string
Body	associative array	Ada unit name	string
Specification_Exceptions	associative array	language name	string list
Implementation_Exceptions	associative array	language name	string list

The following attributes are defined for packages `Builder`, `Compiler`, `Binder`, `Linker`, `Cross_Reference`, and `Finder` (see Section 11.15.1.1 [Switches and Project Files], page 153).

Attribute Name	Category	Index	Value
Default_Switches	associative array	language name	string list
Switches	associative array	file name	string list

In addition, package `Compiler` has a single string attribute `Local_Configuration_Pragmas` and package `Builder` has a single string attribute `Global_Configuration_Pragmas`.

Each simple attribute has a default value: the empty string (for string-valued attributes) and the empty list (for string list-valued attributes).

An attribute declaration defines a new value for an attribute.

Examples of simple attribute declarations:

```
for Object_Dir use "objects";
for Source_Dirs use ("units", "test/drivers");
```

The syntax of a *simple attribute declaration* is similar to that of an attribute definition clause in Ada.

Attributes references may be appear in expressions. The general form for such a reference is `<entity>'<attribute>`: Associative array attributes are functions. Associative array attribute references must have an argument that is a string literal.

Examples are:

```
project'Object_Dir
Naming'Dot_Replacement
Imported_Project'Source_Dirs
Imported_Project.Naming'Casing
Builder'Default_Switches("Ada")
```

The prefix of an attribute may be:

- `project` for an attribute of the current project
- The name of an existing package of the current project
- The name of an imported project
- The name of a parent project that is extended by the current project
- An expanded name whose prefix is imported/parent project name, and whose selector is a package name

Example:

```
project Prj is
  for Source_Dirs use project'Source_Dirs & "units";
  for Source_Dirs use project'Source_Dirs & "test/drivers"
end Prj;
```

In the first attribute declaration, initially the attribute `Source_Dirs` has the default value: an empty string list. After this declaration, `Source_Dirs` is a string list of one element: `"units"`. After the second attribute declaration `Source_Dirs` is a string list of two elements: `"units"` and `"test/drivers"`.

Note: this example is for illustration only. In practice, the project file would contain only one attribute declaration:

```
for Source_Dirs use ("units", "test/drivers");
```

11.3.7 Associative Array Attributes

Some attributes are defined as *associative arrays*. An associative array may be regarded as a function that takes a string as a parameter and delivers a string or string list value as its result.

Here are some examples of single associative array attribute associations:

```
for Body ("main") use "Main.ada";
for Switches ("main.ada")
    use ("-v",
         "-gnatv");
for Switches ("main.ada")
        use Builder'Switches ("main.ada")
          & "-g";
```

Like untyped variables and simple attributes, associative array attributes may be declared several times. Each declaration supplies a new value for the attribute, and replaces the previous setting.

An associative array attribute may be declared as a full associative array declaration, with the value of the same attribute in an imported or extended project.

```
package Builder is
    for Default_Switches use Default.Builder'Default_Switches;
end Builder;
```

In this example, `Default` must be either a project imported by the current project, or the project that the current project extends. If the attribute is in a package (in this case, in package `Builder`), the same package needs to be specified.

A full associative array declaration replaces any other declaration for the attribute, including other full associative array declaration. Single associative array associations may be declare after a full associative declaration, modifying the value for a single association of the attribute.

11.3.8 `case` Constructions

A `case` construction is used in a project file to effect conditional behavior. Here is a typical example:

```
project MyProj is
   type OS_Type is ("GNU/Linux", "Unix", "NT", "VMS");

   OS : OS_Type := external ("OS", "GNU/Linux");

   package Compiler is
     case OS is
       when "GNU/Linux" | "Unix" =>
         for Default_Switches ("Ada")
             use ("-gnath");
       when "NT" =>
         for Default_Switches ("Ada")
             use ("-gnatP");
       when others =>
     end case;
   end Compiler;
end MyProj;
```

The syntax of a `case` construction is based on the Ada case statement (although there is no `null` construction for empty alternatives).

The case expression must be a typed string variable. Each alternative comprises the reserved word `when`, either a list of literal strings separated by the `"|"` character or the reserved word `others`, and the `"=>"` token. Each literal string must belong to the string type that is the type of the case variable. An `others` alternative, if present, must occur last.

After each `=>`, there are zero or more constructions. The only constructions allowed in a case construction are other case constructions, attribute declarations and variable declarations. String type declarations and package declarations are not allowed. Variable declarations are restricted to variables that have already been declared before the case construction.

The value of the case variable is often given by an external reference (see Section 11.8 [External References in Project Files], page 145).

11.4 Objects and Sources in Project Files

Each project has exactly one object directory and one or more source directories. The source directories must contain at least one source file, unless the project file explicitly specifies that no source files are present (see Section 11.4.4 [Source File Names], page 142).

11.4.1 Object Directory

The object directory for a project is the directory containing the compiler's output (such as 'ALI' files and object files) for the project's immediate sources.

The object directory is given by the value of the attribute `Object_Dir` in the project file.

```
for Object_Dir use "objects";
```

The attribute *Object_Dir* has a string value, the path name of the object directory. The path name may be absolute or relative to the directory of the project file. This directory must already exist, and be readable and writable.

By default, when the attribute `Object_Dir` is not given an explicit value or when its value is the empty string, the object directory is the same as the directory containing the project file.

11.4.2 Exec Directory

The exec directory for a project is the directory containing the executables for the project's main subprograms.

The exec directory is given by the value of the attribute `Exec_Dir` in the project file.

```
for Exec_Dir use "executables";
```

The attribute *Exec_Dir* has a string value, the path name of the exec directory. The path name may be absolute or relative to the directory of the project file. This directory must already exist, and be writable.

By default, when the attribute `Exec_Dir` is not given an explicit value or when its value is the empty string, the exec directory is the same as the object directory of the project file.

11.4.3 Source Directories

The source directories of a project are specified by the project file attribute `Source_Dirs`.

This attribute's value is a string list. If the attribute is not given an explicit value, then there is only one source directory, the one where the project file resides.

A `Source_Dirs` attribute that is explicitly defined to be the empty list, as in

```
for Source_Dirs use ();
```

indicates that the project contains no source files.

Otherwise, each string in the string list designates one or more source directories.

```
for Source_Dirs use ("sources", "test/drivers");
```

If a string in the list ends with "/**", then the directory whose path name precedes the two asterisks, as well as all its subdirectories (recursively), are source directories.

```
for Source_Dirs use ("/system/sources/**");
```

Here the directory /system/sources and all of its subdirectories (recursively) are source directories.

To specify that the source directories are the directory of the project file and all of its subdirectories, you can declare `Source_Dirs` as follows:

```
for Source_Dirs use ("./**");
```

Each of the source directories must exist and be readable.

11.4.4 Source File Names

In a project that contains source files, their names may be specified by the attributes `Source_Files` (a string list) or `Source_List_File` (a string). Source file names never include any directory information.

If the attribute `Source_Files` is given an explicit value, then each element of the list is a source file name.

```
for Source_Files use ("main.adb");
for Source_Files use ("main.adb", "pack1.ads", "pack2.adb");
```

If the attribute `Source_Files` is not given an explicit value, but the attribute `Source_List_File` is given a string value, then the source file names are contained in the text file whose path name (absolute or relative to the directory of the project file) is the value of the attribute `Source_List_File`.

Each line in the file that is not empty or is not a comment contains a source file name.

```
for Source_List_File use "source_list.txt";
```

By default, if neither the attribute `Source_Files` nor the attribute `Source_List_File` is given an explicit value, then each file in the source directories that conforms to the project's naming scheme (see Section 11.11 [Naming Schemes], page 147) is an immediate source of the project.

A warning is issued if both attributes `Source_Files` and `Source_List_File` are given explicit values. In this case, the attribute `Source_Files` prevails.

Each source file name must be the name of one existing source file in one of the source directories.

A `Source_Files` attribute whose value is an empty list indicates that there are no source files in the project.

If the order of the source directories is known statically, that is if `"/**"` is not used in the string list `Source_Dirs`, then there may be several files with the same source file name. In this case, only the file in the first directory is considered as an immediate source of the project file. If the order of the source directories is not known statically, it is an error to have several files with the same source file name.

Projects can be specified to have no Ada source files: the value of (`Source_Dirs` or `Source_Files` may be an empty list, or the `"Ada"` may be absent from `Languages`:

```
for Source_Dirs use ();
for Source_Files use ();
for Languages use ("C", "C++");
```

Otherwise, a project must contain at least one immediate source.

Projects with no source files are useful as template packages (see Section 11.9 [Packages in Project Files], page 146) for other projects; in particular to define a package `Naming` (see Section 11.11 [Naming Schemes], page 147).

11.5 Importing Projects

An immediate source of a project P may depend on source files that are neither immediate sources of P nor in the predefined library. To get this effect, P must *import* the projects that contain the needed source files.

```
with "project1", "utilities.gpr";
with "/namings/apex.gpr";
project Main is
   ...
```

As can be seen in this example, the syntax for importing projects is similar to the syntax for importing compilation units in Ada. However, project files use literal strings instead of names, and the `with` clause identifies project files rather than packages.

Each literal string is the file name or path name (absolute or relative) of a project file. If a string corresponds to a file name, with no path or a relative path, then its location is determined by the *project path*. The latter can be queried using `gnatls -v`. It contains:

- In first position, the directory containing the current project file.

- In last position, the default project directory. This default project directory is part of the GNAT installation and is the standard place to install project files giving access to standard support libraries. Section 19.2.2 [Installing a library], page 211

- In between, all the directories referenced in the environment variable `ADA_PROJECT_PATH` if it exists.

If a relative pathname is used, as in

```
with "tests/proj";
```

then the full path for the project is constructed by concatenating this relative path to those in the project path, in order, until a matching file is found. Any symbolic link will be fully resolved in the directory of the importing project file before the imported project file is examined.

If the `with`'ed project file name does not have an extension, the default is '.gpr'. If a file with this extension is not found, then the file name as specified in the `with` clause (no extension) will be used. In the above example, if a file `project1.gpr` is found, then it will be used; otherwise, if a file `project1` exists then it will be used; if neither file exists, this is an error.

A warning is issued if the name of the project file does not match the name of the project; this check is case insensitive.

Any source file that is an immediate source of the imported project can be used by the immediate sources of the importing project, transitively. Thus if A imports B, and B imports C, the immediate sources of A may depend on the immediate sources of C, even if A does not import C explicitly. However, this is not recommended, because if and when B ceases to import C, some sources in A will no longer compile.

A side effect of this capability is that normally cyclic dependencies are not permitted: if A imports B (directly or indirectly) then B is not allowed to import A. However, there are cases when cyclic dependencies would be beneficial. For these cases, another form of import between projects exists, the `limited with`: a project A that imports a project B with a straight `with` may also be imported, directly or indirectly, by B on the condition that imports from B to A include at least one `limited with`.

```
with "../b/b.gpr";
with "../c/c.gpr";
project A is
end A;

limited with "../a/a.gpr";
```

```
project B is
end B;

with "../d/d.gpr";
project C is
end C;

limited with "../a/a.gpr";
project D is
end D;
```

In the above legal example, there are two project cycles:

- A-> B-> A
- A -> C -> D -> A

In each of these cycle there is one `limited with`: import of A from B and import of A from
D.

The difference between straight `with` and `limited with` is that the name of a project
imported with a `limited with` cannot be used in the project that imports it. In particular,
its packages cannot be renamed and its variables cannot be referred to.

An exception to the above rules for `limited with` is that for the main project specified
to `gnatmake` or to the `GNAT` driver a `limited with` is equivalent to a straight `with`. For
example, in the example above, projects B and D could not be main projects for `gnatmake`
or to the `GNAT` driver, because they each have a `limited with` that is the only one in a cycle
of importing projects.

11.6 Project Extension

During development of a large system, it is sometimes necessary to use modified versions
of some of the source files, without changing the original sources. This can be achieved
through the *project extension* facility.

```
project Modified_Utilities extends "/baseline/utilities.gpr" is ...
```

A project extension declaration introduces an extending project (the *child*) and a project
being extended (the *parent*).

By default, a child project inherits all the sources of its parent. However, inherited
sources can be overridden: a unit in a parent is hidden by a unit of the same name in the
child.

Inherited sources are considered to be sources (but not immediate sources) of the child
project; see Section 11.3 [Project File Syntax], page 133.

An inherited source file retains any switches specified in the parent project.

For example if the project `Utilities` contains the specification and the body of an
Ada package `Util_IO`, then the project `Modified_Utilities` can contain a new body for
package `Util_IO`. The original body of `Util_IO` will not be considered in program builds.
However, the package specification will still be found in the project `Utilities`.

A child project can have only one parent but it may import any number of other projects.

A project is not allowed to import directly or indirectly at the same time a child project
and any of its ancestors.

11.7 Project Hierarchy Extension

When extending a large system spanning multiple projects, it is often inconvenient to extend every project in the hierarchy that is impacted by a small change introduced. In such cases, it is possible to create a virtual extension of entire hierarchy using `extends all` relationship.

When the project is extended using `extends all` inheritance, all projects that are imported by it, both directly and indirectly, are considered virtually extended. That is, the Project Manager creates "virtual projects" that extend every project in the hierarchy; all these virtual projects have no sources of their own and have as object directory the object directory of the root of "extending all" project.

It is possible to explicitly extend one or more projects in the hierarchy in order to modify the sources. These extending projects must be imported by the "extending all" project, which will replace the corresponding virtual projects with the explicit ones.

When building such a project hierarchy extension, the Project Manager will ensure that both modified sources and sources in virtual extending projects that depend on them, are recompiled.

By means of example, consider the following hierarchy of projects.

1. project A, containing package P1
2. project B importing A and containing package P2 which depends on P1
3. project C importing B and containing package P3 which depends on P2

We want to modify packages P1 and P3.

This project hierarchy will need to be extended as follows:

1. Create project A1 that extends A, placing modified P1 there:
   ```
   project A1 extends "(...)/A" is
   end A1;
   ```
2. Create project C1 that "extends all" C and imports A1, placing modified P3 there:
   ```
   with "(...)/A1";
   project C1 extends all "(...)/C" is
   end C1;
   ```

When you build project C1, your entire modified project space will be recompiled, including the virtual project B1 that has been impacted by the "extending all" inheritance of project C.

Note that if a Library Project in the hierarchy is virtually extended, the virtual project that extends the Library Project is not a Library Project.

11.8 External References in Project Files

A project file may contain references to external variables; such references are called *external references*.

An external variable is either defined as part of the environment (an environment variable in Unix, for example) or else specified on the command line via the '`-Xvbl=value`' switch. If both, then the command line value is used.

The value of an external reference is obtained by means of the built-in function `external`, which returns a string value. This function has two forms:

- `external (external_variable_name)`
- `external (external_variable_name, default_value)`

Each parameter must be a string literal. For example:

```
external ("USER")
external ("OS", "GNU/Linux")
```

In the form with one parameter, the function returns the value of the external variable given as parameter. If this name is not present in the environment, the function returns an empty string.

In the form with two string parameters, the second argument is the value returned when the variable given as the first argument is not present in the environment. In the example above, if `"OS"` is not the name of an environment variable and is not passed on the command line, then the returned value is `"GNU/Linux"`.

An external reference may be part of a string expression or of a string list expression, and can therefore appear in a variable declaration or an attribute declaration.

```
type Mode_Type is ("Debug", "Release");
Mode : Mode_Type := external ("MODE");
case Mode is
  when "Debug" =>
     ...
```

11.9 Packages in Project Files

A *package* defines the settings for project-aware tools within a project. For each such tool one can declare a package; the names for these packages are preset (see Section 11.3.2 [Packages], page 134). A package may contain variable declarations, attribute declarations, and case constructions.

```
project Proj is
   package Builder is  -- used by gnatmake
      for Default_Switches ("Ada")
         use ("-v",
              "-g");
   end Builder;
end Proj;
```

The syntax of package declarations mimics that of package in Ada.

Most of the packages have an attribute `Default_Switches`. This attribute is an associative array, and its value is a string list. The index of the associative array is the name of a programming language (case insensitive). This attribute indicates the switch or switches to be used with the corresponding tool.

Some packages also have another attribute, `Switches`, an associative array whose value is a string list. The index is the name of a source file. This attribute indicates the switch or switches to be used by the corresponding tool when dealing with this specific file.

Further information on these switch-related attributes is found in Section 11.15.1.1 [Switches and Project Files], page 153.

A package may be declared as a *renaming* of another package; e.g., from the project file for an imported project.

```
with "/global/apex.gpr";
project Example is
  package Naming renames Apex.Naming;
  ...
end Example;
```

Packages that are renamed in other project files often come from project files that have no sources: they are just used as templates. Any modification in the template will be reflected automatically in all the project files that rename a package from the template.

In addition to the tool-oriented packages, you can also declare a package named `Naming` to establish specialized source file naming conventions (see Section 11.11 [Naming Schemes], page 147).

11.10 Variables from Imported Projects

An attribute or variable defined in an imported or parent project can be used in expressions in the importing / extending project. Such an attribute or variable is denoted by an expanded name whose prefix is either the name of the project or the expanded name of a package within a project.

```
with "imported";
project Main extends "base" is
   Var1 := Imported.Var;
   Var2 := Base.Var & ".new";

   package Builder is
      for Default_Switches ("Ada")
         use Imported.Builder'Ada_Switches &
            "-gnatg" &
            "-v";
   end Builder;

   package Compiler is
      for Default_Switches ("Ada")
         use Base.Compiler'Ada_Switches;
   end Compiler;
end Main;
```

In this example:

- The value of `Var1` is a copy of the variable `Var` defined in the project file '`"imported.gpr"`'
- the value of `Var2` is a copy of the value of variable `Var` defined in the project file 'base.gpr', concatenated with "`.new`"
- attribute `Default_Switches ("Ada")` in package `Builder` is a string list that includes in its value a copy of the value of `Ada_Switches` defined in the `Builder` package in project file 'imported.gpr' plus two new elements: '"`-gnatg`"' and '"`-v`"';
- attribute `Default_Switches ("Ada")` in package `Compiler` is a copy of the variable `Ada_Switches` defined in the `Compiler` package in project file 'base.gpr', the project being extended.

11.11 Naming Schemes

Sometimes an Ada software system is ported from a foreign compilation environment to GNAT, and the file names do not use the default GNAT conventions. Instead of changing all the file names (which for a variety of reasons might not be possible), you can define the relevant file naming scheme in the `Naming` package in your project file.

Note that the use of pragmas described in Section 2.5 [Alternative File Naming Schemes], page 18 by mean of a configuration pragmas file is not supported when using project files. You must use the features described in this paragraph. You can however use specify other configuration pragmas (see Section 11.15.1.2 [Specifying Configuration Pragmas], page 155).

For example, the following package models the Apex file naming rules:

```
package Naming is
   for Casing            use "lowercase";
   for Dot_Replacement   use ".";
   for Spec_Suffix ("Ada") use ".1.ada";
   for Body_Suffix ("Ada") use ".2.ada";
end Naming;
```

You can define the following attributes in package `Naming`:

Casing This must be a string with one of the three values `"lowercase"`, `"uppercase"` or `"mixedcase"`; these strings are case insensitive.

If *Casing* is not specified, then the default is `"lowercase"`.

Dot_Replacement

This must be a string whose value satisfies the following conditions:

- It must not be empty
- It cannot start or end with an alphanumeric character
- It cannot be a single underscore
- It cannot start with an underscore followed by an alphanumeric
- It cannot contain a dot '.' except if the entire string is "."

If `Dot_Replacement` is not specified, then the default is `"-"`.

Spec_Suffix

This is an associative array (indexed by the programming language name, case insensitive) whose value is a string that must satisfy the following conditions:

- It must not be empty
- It must include at least one dot

If `Spec_Suffix ("Ada")` is not specified, then the default is `".ads"`.

Body_Suffix

This is an associative array (indexed by the programming language name, case insensitive) whose value is a string that must satisfy the following conditions:

- It must not be empty
- It must include at least one dot
- It cannot be the same as `Spec_Suffix ("Ada")`

If `Body_Suffix ("Ada")` and `Spec_Suffix ("Ada")` end with the same string, then a file name that ends with the longest of these two suffixes will be a body if the longest suffix is `Body_Suffix ("Ada")` or a spec if the longest suffix is `Spec_Suffix ("Ada")`.

If `Body_Suffix ("Ada")` is not specified, then the default is `".adb"`.

Separate_Suffix

> This must be a string whose value satisfies the same conditions as `Body_Suffix`. The same "longest suffix" rules apply.
>
> If `Separate_Suffix ("Ada")` is not specified, then it defaults to same value as `Body_Suffix ("Ada")`.

Spec   You can use the associative array attribute `Spec` to define the source file name for an individual Ada compilation unit's spec. The array index must be a string literal that identifies the Ada unit (case insensitive). The value of this attribute must be a string that identifies the file that contains this unit's spec (case sensitive or insensitive depending on the operating system).

```
for Spec ("MyPack.MyChild") use "mypack.mychild.spec";
```

Body

> You can use the associative array attribute `Body` to define the source file name for an individual Ada compilation unit's body (possibly a subunit). The array index must be a string literal that identifies the Ada unit (case insensitive). The value of this attribute must be a string that identifies the file that contains this unit's body or subunit (case sensitive or insensitive depending on the operating system).

```
for Body ("MyPack.MyChild") use "mypack.mychild.body";
```

11.12 Library Projects

Library projects are projects whose object code is placed in a library. (Note that this facility is not yet supported on all platforms)

To create a library project, you need to define in its project file two project-level attributes: `Library_Name` and `Library_Dir`. Additionally, you may define other library-related attributes such as `Library_Kind`, `Library_Version`, `Library_Interface`, `Library_Auto_Init`, `Library_Options` and `Library_GCC`.

The `Library_Name` attribute has a string value. There is no restriction on the name of a library. It is the responsibility of the developer to choose a name that will be accepted by the platform. It is recommended to choose names that could be Ada identifiers; such names are almost guaranteed to be acceptable on all platforms.

The `Library_Dir` attribute has a string value that designates the path (absolute or relative) of the directory where the library will reside. It must designate an existing directory, and this directory must be writable, different from the project's object directory and from any source directory in the project tree.

If both `Library_Name` and `Library_Dir` are specified and are legal, then the project file defines a library project. The optional library-related attributes are checked only for such project files.

The `Library_Kind` attribute has a string value that must be one of the following (case insensitive): `"static"`, `"dynamic"` or `"relocatable"` (which is a synonym for `"dynamic"`). If this attribute is not specified, the library is a static library, that is an archive of object files that can be potentially linked into a static executable. Otherwise, the library may be dynamic or relocatable, that is a library that is loaded only at the start of execution.

If you need to build both a static and a dynamic library, you should use two different object directories, since in some cases some extra code needs to be generated for the latter. For such cases, it is recommended to either use two different project files, or a single one which uses external variables to indicate what kind of library should be build.

The `Library_ALI_Dir` attribute may be specified to indicate the directory where the ALI files of the library will be copied. When it is not specified, the ALI files are copied to the directory specified in attribute `Library_Dir`. The directory specified by `Library_ALI_Dir` must be writable and different from the project's object directory and from any source directory in the project tree.

The `Library_Version` attribute has a string value whose interpretation is platform dependent. It has no effect on VMS and Windows. On Unix, it is used only for dynamic/relocatable libraries as the internal name of the library (the `"soname"`). If the library file name (built from the `Library_Name`) is different from the `Library_Version`, then the library file will be a symbolic link to the actual file whose name will be `Library_Version`.

Example (on Unix):

```
project Plib is

   Version := "1";

   for Library_Dir use "lib_dir";
   for Library_Name use "dummy";
   for Library_Kind use "relocatable";
   for Library_Version use "libdummy.so." & Version;

end Plib;
```

Directory 'lib_dir' will contain the internal library file whose name will be 'libdummy.so.1', and 'libdummy.so' will be a symbolic link to 'libdummy.so.1'.

When **gnatmake** detects that a project file is a library project file, it will check all immediate sources of the project and rebuild the library if any of the sources have been recompiled.

Standard project files can import library project files. In such cases, the libraries will only be rebuilt if some of its sources are recompiled because they are in the closure of some other source in an importing project. Sources of the library project files that are not in such a closure will not be checked, unless the full library is checked, because one of its sources needs to be recompiled.

For instance, assume the project file **A** imports the library project file L. The immediate sources of A are 'a1.adb', 'a2.ads' and 'a2.adb'. The immediate sources of L are 'l1.ads', 'l1.adb', 'l2.ads', 'l2.adb'.

If 'l1.adb' has been modified, then the library associated with L will be rebuilt when compiling all the immediate sources of **A** only if 'a1.ads', 'a2.ads' or 'a2.adb' includes a statement `"with L1;"`.

To be sure that all the sources in the library associated with L are up to date, and that all the sources of project **A** are also up to date, the following two commands needs to be used:

```
gnatmake -Pl.gpr
gnatmake -Pa.gpr
```

When a library is built or rebuilt, an attempt is made first to delete all files in the library directory. All 'ALI' files will also be copied from the object directory to the library directory. To build executables, gnatmake will use the library rather than the individual object files.

It is also possible to create library project files for third-party libraries that are pre-compiled and cannot be compiled locally thanks to the externally_built attribute. (See Section 19.2.2 [Installing a library], page 211).

11.13 Stand-alone Library Projects

A Stand-alone Library is a library that contains the necessary code to elaborate the Ada units that are included in the library. A Stand-alone Library is suitable to be used in an executable when the main is not in Ada. However, Stand-alone Libraries may also be used with an Ada main subprogram.

A Stand-alone Library Project is a Library Project where the library is a Stand-alone Library.

To be a Stand-alone Library Project, in addition to the two attributes that make a project a Library Project (Library_Name and Library_Dir, see Section 11.12 [Library Projects], page 149), the attribute Library_Interface must be defined.

```
for Library_Dir use "lib_dir";
for Library_Name use "dummy";
for Library_Interface use ("int1", "int1.child");
```

Attribute Library_Interface has a non empty string list value, each string in the list designating a unit contained in an immediate source of the project file.

When a Stand-alone Library is built, first the binder is invoked to build a package whose name depends on the library name (b~dummy.ads/b in the example above). This binder-generated package includes initialization and finalization procedures whose names depend on the library name (dummyinit and dummyfinal in the example above). The object corresponding to this package is included in the library.

A dynamic or relocatable Stand-alone Library is automatically initialized if automatic initialization of Stand-alone Libraries is supported on the platform and if attribute Library_Auto_Init is not specified or is specified with the value "true". A static Stand-alone Library is never automatically initialized.

Single string attribute Library_Auto_Init may be specified with only two possible values: "false" or "true" (case-insensitive). Specifying "false" for attribute Library_Auto_Init will prevent automatic initialization of dynamic or relocatable libraries.

When a non automatically initialized Stand-alone Library is used in an executable, its initialization procedure must be called before any service of the library is used. When the main subprogram is in Ada, it may mean that the initialization procedure has to be called during elaboration of another package.

For a Stand-Alone Library, only the 'ALI' files of the Interface Units (those that are listed in attribute Library_Interface) are copied to the Library Directory. As a consequence, only the Interface Units may be imported from Ada units outside of the library. If other units are imported, the binding phase will fail.

When a Stand-Alone Library is bound, the switches that are specified in the attribute Default_Switches ("Ada") in package Binder are used in the call to gnatbind.

The string list attribute `Library_Options` may be used to specified additional switches to the call to `gcc` to link the library.

The attribute `Library_Src_Dir`, may be specified for a Stand-Alone Library. `Library_Src_Dir` is a simple attribute that has a single string value. Its value must be the path (absolute or relative to the project directory) of an existing directory. This directory cannot be the object directory or one of the source directories, but it can be the same as the library directory. The sources of the Interface Units of the library, necessary to an Ada client of the library, will be copied to the designated directory, called Interface Copy directory. These sources includes the specs of the Interface Units, but they may also include bodies and subunits, when pragmas `Inline` or `Inline_Always` are used, or when there is a generic units in the spec. Before the sources are copied to the Interface Copy directory, an attempt is made to delete all files in the Interface Copy directory.

11.14 Switches Related to Project Files

The following switches are used by GNAT tools that support project files:

'-P*project*'

> Indicates the name of a project file. This project file will be parsed with the verbosity indicated by '-vP*x*', if any, and using the external references indicated by '-X' switches, if any. There may zero, one or more spaces between '-P' and *project*.
>
> There must be only one '-P' switch on the command line.
>
> Since the Project Manager parses the project file only after all the switches on the command line are checked, the order of the switches '-P', '-vP*x*' or '-X' is not significant.

'-X*name=value*'

> Indicates that external variable *name* has the value *value*. The Project Manager will use this value for occurrences of `external(name)` when parsing the project file.
>
> If *name* or *value* includes a space, then *name=value* should be put between quotes.
>
> ```
> -XOS=NT
> -X"user=John Doe"
> ```
>
> Several '-X' switches can be used simultaneously. If several '-X' switches specify the same *name*, only the last one is used.
>
> An external variable specified with a '-X' switch takes precedence over the value of the same name in the environment.

'-vP*x*'   Indicates the verbosity of the parsing of GNAT project files.

> '-vP0' means Default; '-vP1' means Medium; '-vP2' means High.
>
> The default is Default: no output for syntactically correct project files. If several '-vP*x*' switches are present, only the last one is used.

11.15 Tools Supporting Project Files

11.15.1 gnatmake and Project Files

This section covers several topics related to **gnatmake** and project files: defining switches for **gnatmake** and for the tools that it invokes; specifying configuration pragmas; the use of the **Main** attribute; building and rebuilding library project files.

11.15.1.1 Switches and Project Files

For each of the packages **Builder**, **Compiler**, **Binder**, and **Linker**, you can specify a **Default_Switches** attribute, a **Switches** attribute, or both; as their names imply, these switch-related attributes affect the switches that are used for each of these GNAT components when **gnatmake** is invoked. As will be explained below, these component-specific switches precede the switches provided on the **gnatmake** command line.

The **Default_Switches** attribute is an associative array indexed by language name (case insensitive) whose value is a string list. For example:

```
package Compiler is
  for Default_Switches ("Ada")
      use ("-gnaty",
            "-v");
end Compiler;
```

The **Switches** attribute is also an associative array, indexed by a file name (which may or may not be case sensitive, depending on the operating system) whose value is a string list. For example:

```
package Builder is
    for Switches ("main1.adb")
        use ("-O2");
    for Switches ("main2.adb")
        use ("-g");
end Builder;
```

For the **Builder** package, the file names must designate source files for main subprograms. For the **Binder** and **Linker** packages, the file names must designate 'ALI' or source files for main subprograms. In each case just the file name without an explicit extension is acceptable.

For each tool used in a program build (**gnatmake**, the compiler, the binder, and the linker), the corresponding package *contributes* a set of switches for each file on which the tool is invoked, based on the switch-related attributes defined in the package. In particular, the switches that each of these packages contributes for a given file *f* comprise:

- the value of attribute **Switches (f)**, if it is specified in the package for the given file,

- otherwise, the value of **Default_Switches ("Ada")**, if it is specified in the package.

If neither of these attributes is defined in the package, then the package does not contribute any switches for the given file.

When **gnatmake** is invoked on a file, the switches comprise two sets, in the following order: those contributed for the file by the **Builder** package; and the switches passed on the command line.

When **gnatmake** invokes a tool (compiler, binder, linker) on a file, the switches passed to the tool comprise three sets, in the following order:

1. the applicable switches contributed for the file by the **Builder** package in the project file supplied on the command line;

2. those contributed for the file by the package (in the relevant project file – see below) corresponding to the tool; and

3. the applicable switches passed on the command line.

The term *applicable switches* reflects the fact that gnatmake switches may or may not be passed to individual tools, depending on the individual switch.

gnatmake may invoke the compiler on source files from different projects. The Project Manager will use the appropriate project file to determine the Compiler package for each source file being compiled. Likewise for the Binder and Linker packages.

As an example, consider the following package in a project file:

```
project Proj1 is
   package Compiler is
      for Default_Switches ("Ada")
         use ("-g");
      for Switches ("a.adb")
         use ("-O1");
      for Switches ("b.adb")
         use ("-O2",
              "-gnaty");
   end Compiler;
end Proj1;
```

If gnatmake is invoked with this project file, and it needs to compile, say, the files 'a.adb', 'b.adb', and 'c.adb', then 'a.adb' will be compiled with the switch '-O1', 'b.adb' with switches '-O2' and '-gnaty', and 'c.adb' with '-g'.

The following example illustrates the ordering of the switches contributed by different packages:

```
project Proj2 is
   package Builder is
      for Switches ("main.adb")
         use ("-g",
              "-O1",
              "-f");
   end Builder;

   package Compiler is
      for Switches ("main.adb")
         use ("-O2");
   end Compiler;
end Proj2;
```

If you issue the command:

```
gnatmake -Pproj2 -O0 main
```

then the compiler will be invoked on 'main.adb' with the following sequence of switches

```
-g -O1 -O2 -O0
```

with the last '-O' switch having precedence over the earlier ones; several other switches (such as '-c') are added implicitly.

The switches '-g' and '-O1' are contributed by package Builder, '-O2' is contributed by the package Compiler and '-O0' comes from the command line.

The '-g' switch will also be passed in the invocation of Gnatlink.

A final example illustrates switch contributions from packages in different project files:

```
project Proj3 is
   for Source_Files use ("pack.ads", "pack.adb");
   package Compiler is
      for Default_Switches ("Ada")
         use ("-gnata");
   end Compiler;
end Proj3;

with "Proj3";
project Proj4 is
   for Source_Files use ("foo_main.adb", "bar_main.adb");
   package Builder is
      for Switches ("foo_main.adb")
         use ("-s",
              "-g");
   end Builder;
end Proj4;

-- Ada source file:
with Pack;
procedure Foo_Main is
   ...
end Foo_Main;
```

If the command is

```
gnatmake -PProj4 foo_main.adb -cargs -gnato
```

then the switches passed to the compiler for 'foo_main.adb' are '-g' (contributed by the package Proj4.Builder) and '-gnato' (passed on the command line). When the imported package Pack is compiled, the switches used are '-g' from Proj4.Builder, '-gnata' (contributed from package Proj3.Compiler, and '-gnato' from the command line.

When using gnatmake with project files, some switches or arguments may be expressed as relative paths. As the working directory where compilation occurs may change, these relative paths are converted to absolute paths. For the switches found in a project file, the relative paths are relative to the project file directory, for the switches on the command line, they are relative to the directory where gnatmake is invoked. The switches for which this occurs are: -I, -A, -L, -aO, -aL, -aI, as well as all arguments that are not switches (arguments to switch -o, object files specified in package Linker or after -largs on the command line). The exception to this rule is the switch –RTS= for which a relative path argument is never converted.

11.15.1.2 Specifying Configuration Pragmas

When using gnatmake with project files, if there exists a file 'gnat.adc' that contains configuration pragmas, this file will be ignored.

Configuration pragmas can be defined by means of the following attributes in project files: Global_Configuration_Pragmas in package Builder and Local_Configuration_Pragmas in package Compiler.

Both these attributes are single string attributes. Their values is the path name of a file containing configuration pragmas. If a path name is relative, then it is relative to the project directory of the project file where the attribute is defined.

When compiling a source, the configuration pragmas used are, in order, those listed in the file designated by attribute Global_Configuration_Pragmas in package Builder of the main project file, if it is specified, and those listed in the file designated by attribute `Local_Configuration_Pragmas` in package `Compiler` of the project file of the source, if it exists.

11.15.1.3 Project Files and Main Subprograms

When using a project file, you can invoke **gnatmake** with one or several main subprograms, by specifying their source files on the command line.

```
gnatmake -Pprj main1 main2 main3
```

Each of these needs to be a source file of the same project, except when the switch -u is used.

When -u is not used, all the mains need to be sources of the same project, one of the project in the tree rooted at the project specified on the command line. The package `Builder` of this common project, the "main project" is the one that is considered by **gnatmake**.

When -u is used, the specified source files may be in projects imported directly or indirectly by the project specified on the command line. Note that if such a source file is not part of the project specified on the command line, the switches found in package `Builder` of the project specified on the command line, if any, that are transmitted to the compiler will still be used, not those found in the project file of the source file.

When using a project file, you can also invoke **gnatmake** without explicitly specifying any main, and the effect depends on whether you have defined the `Main` attribute. This attribute has a string list value, where each element in the list is the name of a source file (the file extension is optional) that contains a unit that can be a main subprogram.

If the `Main` attribute is defined in a project file as a non-empty string list and the switch '-u' is not used on the command line, then invoking **gnatmake** with this project file but without any main on the command line is equivalent to invoking **gnatmake** with all the file names in the `Main` attribute on the command line.

Example:

```
project Prj is
   for Main use ("main1", "main2", "main3");
end Prj;
```

With this project file, "**gnatmake -Pprj**" is equivalent to "**gnatmake -Pprj main1 main2 main3**".

When the project attribute `Main` is not specified, or is specified as an empty string list, or when the switch '-u' is used on the command line, then invoking **gnatmake** with no main on the command line will result in all immediate sources of the project file being checked, and potentially recompiled. Depending on the presence of the switch '-u', sources from other project files on which the immediate sources of the main project file depend are also checked and potentially recompiled. In other words, the '-u' switch is applied to all of the immediate sources of the main project file.

When no main is specified on the command line and attribute `Main` exists and includes several mains, or when several mains are specified on the command line, the default switches in package `Builder` will be used for all mains, even if there are specific switches specified for one or several mains.

But the switches from package `Binder` or `Linker` will be the specific switches for each main, if they are specified.

11.15.1.4 Library Project Files

When `gnatmake` is invoked with a main project file that is a library project file, it is not allowed to specify one or more mains on the command line.

When a library project file is specified, switches -b and -l have special meanings.

- -b is only allowed for stand-alone libraries. It indicates to `gnatmake` that `gnatbind` should be invoked for the library.

- -l may be used for all library projects. It indicates to `gnatmake` that the binder generated file should be compiled (in the case of a stand-alone library) and that the library should be built.

11.15.2 The GNAT Driver and Project Files

A number of GNAT tools, other than `gnatmake` can benefit from project files: `gnatbind`, `gnatcheck`), `gnatclean`), `gnatelim`, `gnatfind`, `gnatlink`, `gnatls`, `gnatmetric`, `gnatpp`, `gnatstub`, and `gnatxref`. However, none of these tools can be invoked directly with a project file switch ('-P'). They must be invoked through the `gnat` driver.

The **gnat** driver is a wrapper that accepts a number of commands and calls the corresponding tool. It was designed initially for VMS platforms (to convert VMS qualifiers to Unix-style switches), but it is now available on all GNAT platforms.

On non-VMS platforms, the **gnat** driver accepts the following commands (case insensitive):

- BIND to invoke `gnatbind`
- CHOP to invoke `gnatchop`
- CLEAN to invoke `gnatclean`
- COMP or COMPILE to invoke the compiler
- ELIM to invoke `gnatelim`
- FIND to invoke `gnatfind`
- KR or KRUNCH to invoke `gnatkr`
- LINK to invoke `gnatlink`
- LS or LIST to invoke `gnatls`
- MAKE to invoke `gnatmake`
- NAME to invoke `gnatname`
- PREP or PREPROCESS to invoke `gnatprep`
- PP or PRETTY to invoke `gnatpp`
- METRIC to invoke `gnatmetric`
- STUB to invoke `gnatstub`
- XREF to invoke `gnatxref`

(note that the compiler is invoked using the command `gnatmake -f -u -c`).

On non VMS platforms, between **gnat** and the command, two special switches may be used:

- `-v` to display the invocation of the tool.

- `-dn` to prevent the **gnat** driver from removing the temporary files it has created. These temporary files are configuration files and temporary file list files.

The command may be followed by switches and arguments for the invoked tool.

```
gnat bind -C main.ali
gnat ls -a main
gnat chop foo.txt
```

Switches may also be put in text files, one switch per line, and the text files may be specified with their path name preceded by '@'.

```
gnat bind @args.txt main.ali
```

In addition, for commands BIND, COMP or COMPILE, FIND, ELIM, LS or LIST, LINK, METRIC, PP or PRETTY, STUB and XREF, the project file related switches ('-P', '-X' and '-vPx') may be used in addition to the switches of the invoking tool.

When GNAT PP or GNAT PRETTY is used with a project file, but with no source specified on the command line, it invokes `gnatpp` with all the immediate sources of the specified project file.

When GNAT METRIC is used with a project file, but with no source specified on the command line, it invokes `gnatmetric` with all the immediate sources of the specified project file and with '-d' with the parameter pointing to the object directory of the project.

In addition, when GNAT PP, GNAT PRETTY or GNAT METRIC is used with a project file, no source is specified on the command line and switch -U is specified on the command line, then the underlying tool (gnatpp or gnatmetric) is invoked for all sources of all projects, not only for the immediate sources of the main project. (-U stands for Universal or Union of the project files of the project tree)

For each of the following commands, there is optionally a corresponding package in the main project.

- package `Binder` for command BIND (invoking `gnatbind`)
- package `Check` for command CHECK (invoking `gnatcheck`)
- package `Compiler` for command COMP or COMPILE (invoking the compiler)
- package `Cross_Reference` for command XREF (invoking `gnatxref`)
- package `Eliminate` for command ELIM (invoking `gnatelim`)
- package `Finder` for command FIND (invoking `gnatfind`)
- package `Gnatls` for command LS or LIST (invoking `gnatls`)
- package `Gnatstub` for command STUB (invoking `gnatstub`)
- package `Linker` for command LINK (invoking `gnatlink`)
- package `Metrics` for command METRIC (invoking `gnatmetric`)
- package `Pretty_Printer` for command PP or PRETTY (invoking `gnatpp`)

Package `Gnatls` has a unique attribute `Switches`, a simple variable with a string list value. It contains switches for the invocation of `gnatls`.

```
project Proj1 is
   package gnatls is
      for Switches
         use ("-a",
              "-v");
   end gnatls;
end Proj1;
```

All other packages have two attribute `Switches` and `Default_Switches`.

`Switches` is an associative array attribute, indexed by the source file name, that has a string list value: the switches to be used when the tool corresponding to the package is invoked for the specific source file.

`Default_Switches` is an associative array attribute, indexed by the programming language that has a string list value. `Default_Switches ("Ada")` contains the switches for the invocation of the tool corresponding to the package, except if a specific `Switches` attribute is specified for the source file.

```
project Proj is

   for Source_Dirs use ("./**");

   package gnatls is
      for Switches use
          ("-a",
           "-v");
   end gnatls;

   package Compiler is
      for Default_Switches ("Ada")
          use ("-gnatv",
               "-gnatwa");
   end Binder;

   package Binder is
      for Default_Switches ("Ada")
          use ("-C",
               "-e");
   end Binder;

   package Linker is
      for Default_Switches ("Ada")
          use ("-C");
      for Switches ("main.adb")
          use ("-C",
               "-v",
               "-v");
   end Linker;

   package Finder is
      for Default_Switches ("Ada")
          use ("-a",
               "-f");
   end Finder;

   package Cross_Reference is
      for Default_Switches ("Ada")
          use ("-a",
               "-f",
               "-d",
               "-u");
   end Cross_Reference;
end Proj;
```

With the above project file, commands such as

```
gnat comp -Pproj main
gnat ls -Pproj main
gnat xref -Pproj main
```

```
gnat bind -Pproj main.ali
gnat link -Pproj main.ali
```

will set up the environment properly and invoke the tool with the switches found in the package corresponding to the tool: `Default_Switches ("Ada")` for all tools, except `Switches ("main.adb")` for gnatlink. It is also possible to invoke some of the tools, gnatcheck), gnatmetric), and gnatpp) on a set of project units thanks to the combination of the switches -P, -U and possibly the main unit when one is interested in its closure. For instance,

```
gnat metric -Pproj
```

will compute the metrics for all the immediate units of project `proj`.

```
gnat metric -Pproj -U
```

will compute the metrics for all the units of the closure of projects rooted at `proj`.

```
gnat metric -Pproj -U main_unit
```

will compute the metrics for the closure of units rooted at `main_unit`. This last possibility relies implicitly on **gnatbind**'s option '-R'.

11.16 An Extended Example

Suppose that we have two programs, *prog1* and *prog2*, whose sources are in corresponding directories. We would like to build them with a single **gnatmake** command, and we want to place their object files into 'build' subdirectories of the source directories. Furthermore, we want to have to have two separate subdirectories in 'build' – 'release' and 'debug' – which will contain the object files compiled with different set of compilation flags.

In other words, we have the following structure:

```
main
 |- prog1
 |    |- build
 |          | debug
 |          | release
 |- prog2
      |- build
            | debug
            | release
```

Here are the project files that we must place in a directory 'main' to maintain this structure:

1. We create a `Common` project with a package `Compiler` that specifies the compilation switches:

```
File "common.gpr":
project Common is

    for Source_Dirs use (); -- No source files

    type Build_Type is ("release", "debug");
    Build : Build_Type := External ("BUILD", "debug");
```

```
package Compiler is
    case Build is
        when "release" =>
          for Default_Switches ("Ada")
                  use ("-O2");
        when "debug"   =>
          for Default_Switches ("Ada")
                    use ("-g");
    end case;
end Compiler;

end Common;
```

2. We create separate projects for the two programs:

```
File "prog1.gpr":

with "common";
project Prog1 is

    for Source_Dirs use ("prog1");
    for Object_Dir  use "prog1/build/" & Common.Build;

    package Compiler renames Common.Compiler;

end Prog1;
File "prog2.gpr":

with "common";
project Prog2 is

    for Source_Dirs use ("prog2");
    for Object_Dir  use "prog2/build/" & Common.Build;

    package Compiler renames Common.Compiler;

end Prog2;
```

3. We create a wrapping project Main:

```
File "main.gpr":

with "common";
with "prog1";
with "prog2";
project Main is

    package Compiler renames Common.Compiler;

end Main;
```

4. Finally we need to create a dummy procedure that **withs** (either explicitly or implicitly) all the sources of our two programs.

Now we can build the programs using the command

```
gnatmake -Pmain dummy
```

for the Debug mode, or

```
gnatmake -Pmain -XBUILD=release
```

for the Release mode.

11.17 Project File Complete Syntax

```
project ::=
  context_clause project_declaration

context_clause ::=
  {with_clause}

with_clause ::=
  with path_name { , path_name } ;

path_name ::=
   string_literal

project_declaration ::=
  simple_project_declaration | project_extension

simple_project_declaration ::=
  project <project_>simple_name is
    {declarative_item}
  end <project_>simple_name;

project_extension ::=
  project <project_>simple_name  extends path_name is
    {declarative_item}
  end <project_>simple_name;

declarative_item ::=
  package_declaration |
  typed_string_declaration |
  other_declarative_item

package_declaration ::=
  package_specification | package_renaming

package_specification ::=
  package package_identifier is
    {simple_declarative_item}
  end package_identifier ;

package_identifier ::=
  Naming | Builder | Compiler | Binder |
  Linker | Finder  | Cross_Reference |
  gnatls | IDE     | Pretty_Printer

package_renaming ::==
  package package_identifier renames
      <project_>simple_name.package_identifier ;

typed_string_declaration ::=
  type <typed_string_>_simple_name is
   ( string_literal {, string_literal} );

other_declarative_item ::=
  attribute_declaration |
  typed_variable_declaration |
  variable_declaration |
  case_construction
```

```
attribute_declaration ::=
  full_associative_array_declaration |
  for attribute_designator use expression ;

full_associative_array_declaration ::=
  for <associative_array_attribute_>simple_name use
  <project_>simple_name [ . <package_>simple_Name ] ' <attribute_>simple_name ;

attribute_designator ::=
  <simple_attribute_>simple_name |
  <associative_array_attribute_>simple_name ( string_literal )

typed_variable_declaration ::=
  <typed_variable_>simple_name : <typed_string_>name :=  string_expression ;

variable_declaration ::=
  <variable_>simple_name := expression;

expression ::=
  term {& term}

term ::=
  literal_string |
  string_list |
  <variable_>name |
  external_value |
  attribute_reference

string_literal ::=
  (same as Ada)

string_list ::=
  ( <string_>expression { , <string_>expression } )

external_value ::=
  external ( string_literal [, string_literal] )

attribute_reference ::=
  attribute_prefix ' <simple_attribute_>simple_name [ ( literal_string ) ]

attribute_prefix ::=
  project |
  <project_>simple_name | package_identifier |
  <project_>simple_name . package_identifier

case_construction ::=
  case <typed_variable_>name is
    {case_item}
  end case ;

case_item ::=
  when discrete_choice_list =>
      {case_construction | attribute_declaration}

discrete_choice_list ::=
  string_literal {| string_literal} |
  others
```

```
name ::=
  simple_name {. simple_name}

simple_name ::=
  identifier (same as Ada)
```

12 The Cross-Referencing Tools gnatxref and gnatfind

The compiler generates cross-referencing information (unless you set the '-gnatx' switch), which are saved in the '.ali' files. This information indicates where in the source each entity is declared and referenced. Note that entities in package Standard are not included, but entities in all other predefined units are included in the output.

Before using any of these two tools, you need to compile successfully your application, so that GNAT gets a chance to generate the cross-referencing information.

The two tools gnatxref and gnatfind take advantage of this information to provide the user with the capability to easily locate the declaration and references to an entity. These tools are quite similar, the difference being that gnatfind is intended for locating definitions and/or references to a specified entity or entities, whereas gnatxref is oriented to generating a full report of all cross-references.

To use these tools, you must not compile your application using the '-gnatx' switch on the gnatmake command line (see Chapter 6 [The GNAT Make Program gnatmake], page 93). Otherwise, cross-referencing information will not be generated.

Note: to invoke gnatxref or gnatfind with a project file, use the gnat driver (see Section 11.15.2 [The GNAT Driver and Project Files], page 157).

12.1 gnatxref Switches

The command invocation for gnatxref is:

    $ gnatxref [switches] sourcefile1 [sourcefile2 ...]

where

sourcefile1, sourcefile2

identifies the source files for which a report is to be generated. The "with"ed units will be processed too. You must provide at least one file.

These file names are considered to be regular expressions, so for instance specifying 'source*.adb' is the same as giving every file in the current directory whose name starts with 'source' and whose extension is 'adb'.

You shouldn't specify any directory name, just base names. gnatxref and gnatfind will be able to locate these files by themselves using the source path. If you specify directories, no result is produced.

The switches can be:

'--version'

Display Copyright and version, then exit disregarding all other options.

'--help'   If '--version' was not used, display usage, then exit disregarding all other options.

'-a'   If this switch is present, gnatfind and gnatxref will parse the read-only files found in the library search path. Otherwise, these files will be ignored. This option can be used to protect Gnat sources or your own libraries from being parsed, thus making gnatfind and gnatxref much faster, and their output much smaller. Read-only here refers to access or permissions status in the file system for the current user.

'-aIDIR'   When looking for source files also look in directory DIR. The order in which
                source file search is undertaken is the same as for **gnatmake**.

'-aODIR'   When searching for library and object files, look in directory DIR. The order
                in which library files are searched is the same as for **gnatmake**.

'-nostdinc'
                Do not look for sources in the system default directory.

'-nostdlib'
                Do not look for library files in the system default directory.

'--RTS=*rts-path*'
                Specifies the default location of the runtime library. Same meaning as the
                equivalent **gnatmake** flag (see Section 6.2 [Switches for gnatmake], page 94).

'-d'   If this switch is set **gnatxref** will output the parent type reference for each
                matching derived types.

'-f'   If this switch is set, the output file names will be preceded by their directory
                (if the file was found in the search path). If this switch is not set, the directory
                will not be printed.

'-g'   If this switch is set, information is output only for library-level entities, ignoring
                local entities. The use of this switch may accelerate **gnatfind** and **gnatxref**.

'-IDIR'   Equivalent to '-aODIR -aIDIR'.

'-pFILE'   Specify a project file to use See Section 11.1.1 [Project Files], page 125. If you
                need to use the '.gpr' project files, you should use gnatxref through the GNAT
                driver (gnat xref -Pproject).

                By default, **gnatxref** and **gnatfind** will try to locate a project file in the
                current directory.

                If a project file is either specified or found by the tools, then the content of
                the source directory and object directory lines are added as if they had been
                specified respectively by '-aI' and '-aO'.

'-u'   Output only unused symbols. This may be really useful if you give your main
                compilation unit on the command line, as **gnatxref** will then display every
                unused entity and 'with'ed package.

'-v'   Instead of producing the default output, **gnatxref** will generate a 'tags' file
                that can be used by vi. For examples how to use this feature, see Section 12.5
                [Examples of gnatxref Usage], page 171. The tags file is output to the standard
                output, thus you will have to redirect it to a file.

All these switches may be in any order on the command line, and may even appear after
the file names. They need not be separated by spaces, thus you can say 'gnatxref -ag'
instead of 'gnatxref -a -g'.

12.2 `gnatfind` Switches

The command line for `gnatfind` is:

```
$ gnatfind [switches] pattern[:sourcefile[:line[:column]]]
       [file1 file2 ...]
```

where

pattern   An entity will be output only if it matches the regular expression found in
          'pattern', see Section 12.4 [Regular Expressions in gnatfind and gnatxref],
          page 170.

          Omitting the pattern is equivalent to specifying '*', which will match any entity.
          Note that if you do not provide a pattern, you have to provide both a sourcefile
          and a line.

          Entity names are given in Latin-1, with uppercase/lowercase equivalence for
          matching purposes. At the current time there is no support for 8-bit codes
          other than Latin-1, or for wide characters in identifiers.

sourcefile
          `gnatfind` will look for references, bodies or declarations of symbols referenced in
          'sourcefile', at line 'line' and column 'column'. See Section 12.6 [Examples
          of gnatfind Usage], page 173 for syntax examples.

line   is a decimal integer identifying the line number containing the reference to the
          entity (or entities) to be located.

column   is a decimal integer identifying the exact location on the line of the first char-
          acter of the identifier for the entity reference. Columns are numbered from
          1.

file1 file2 ...
          The search will be restricted to these source files. If none are given, then the
          search will be done for every library file in the search path. These file must
          appear only after the pattern or sourcefile.

          These file names are considered to be regular expressions, so for instance speci-
          fying 'source*.adb' is the same as giving every file in the current directory whose
          name starts with 'source' and whose extension is 'adb'.

          The location of the spec of the entity will always be displayed, even if it isn't
          in one of file1, file2,... The occurrences of the entity in the separate units of the
          ones given on the command line will also be displayed.

          Note that if you specify at least one file in this part, `gnatfind` may sometimes
          not be able to find the body of the subprograms...

At least one of 'sourcefile' or 'pattern' has to be present on the command line.

The following switches are available:

          Display Copyright and version, then exit disregarding all other options.

'--help' If '--version' was not used, display usage, then exit disregarding all other
          options.

'-a'   If this switch is present, **gnatfind** and **gnatxref** will parse the read-only files found in the library search path. Otherwise, these files will be ignored. This option can be used to protect Gnat sources or your own libraries from being parsed, thus making **gnatfind** and **gnatxref** much faster, and their output much smaller. Read-only here refers to access or permission status in the file system for the current user.

'-aIDIR'   When looking for source files also look in directory DIR. The order in which source file search is undertaken is the same as for **gnatmake**.

'-aODIR'   When searching for library and object files, look in directory DIR. The order in which library files are searched is the same as for **gnatmake**.

'-nostdinc'
            Do not look for sources in the system default directory.

'-nostdlib'
            Do not look for library files in the system default directory.

'--RTS=*rts-path*'
            Specifies the default location of the runtime library. Same meaning as the equivalent **gnatmake** flag (see Section 6.2 [Switches for gnatmake], page 94).

'-d'   If this switch is set, then **gnatfind** will output the parent type reference for each matching derived types.

'-e'   By default, **gnatfind** accept the simple regular expression set for '**pattern**'. If this switch is set, then the pattern will be considered as full Unix-style regular expression.

'-f'   If this switch is set, the output file names will be preceded by their directory (if the file was found in the search path). If this switch is not set, the directory will not be printed.

'-g'   If this switch is set, information is output only for library-level entities, ignoring local entities. The use of this switch may accelerate **gnatfind** and **gnatxref**.

'-IDIR'   Equivalent to '-aODIR -aIDIR'.

'-pFILE'   Specify a project file (see Section 11.1.1 [Project Files], page 125) to use. By default, **gnatxref** and **gnatfind** will try to locate a project file in the current directory.

            If a project file is either specified or found by the tools, then the content of the source directory and object directory lines are added as if they had been specified respectively by '-aI' and '-aO'.

'-r'   By default, **gnatfind** will output only the information about the declaration, body or type completion of the entities. If this switch is set, the **gnatfind** will locate every reference to the entities in the files specified on the command line (or in every file in the search path if no file is given on the command line).

'-s'   If this switch is set, then **gnatfind** will output the content of the Ada source file lines were the entity was found.

'`-t`'   If this switch is set, then `gnatfind` will output the type hierarchy for the
             specified type. It act like -d option but recursively from parent type to parent
             type. When this switch is set it is not possible to specify more than one file.

All these switches may be in any order on the command line, and may even appear after
the file names. They need not be separated by spaces, thus you can say '`gnatxref -ag`'
instead of '`gnatxref -a -g`'.

As stated previously, gnatfind will search in every directory in the search path. You can
force it to look only in the current directory if you specify * at the end of the command
line.

12.3 Project Files for `gnatxref` and `gnatfind`

Project files allow a programmer to specify how to compile its application, where to find
sources, etc. These files are used primarily by GPS, but they can also be used by the two
tools `gnatxref` and `gnatfind`.

A project file name must end with '`.gpr`'. If a single one is present in the current
directory, then `gnatxref` and `gnatfind` will extract the information from it. If multiple
project files are found, none of them is read, and you have to use the '`-p`' switch to specify
the one you want to use.

The following lines can be included, even though most of them have default values which
can be used in most cases. The lines can be entered in any order in the file. Except for
'`src_dir`' and '`obj_dir`', you can only have one instance of each line. If you have multiple
instances, only the last one is taken into account.

`src_dir=DIR`
             [default: "`./`"] specifies a directory where to look for source files. Multiple
             `src_dir` lines can be specified and they will be searched in the order they are
             specified.

`obj_dir=DIR`
             [default: "`./`"] specifies a directory where to look for object and library files.
             Multiple `obj_dir` lines can be specified, and they will be searched in the order
             they are specified

`comp_opt=SWITCHES`
             [default: ""] creates a variable which can be referred to subsequently by using
             the `${comp_opt}` notation. This is intended to store the default switches given
             to `gnatmake` and `gcc`.

`bind_opt=SWITCHES`
             [default: ""] creates a variable which can be referred to subsequently by using
             the '`${bind_opt}`' notation. This is intended to store the default switches given
             to `gnatbind`.

`link_opt=SWITCHES`
             [default: ""] creates a variable which can be referred to subsequently by using
             the '`${link_opt}`' notation. This is intended to store the default switches given
             to `gnatlink`.

main=EXECUTABLE

> [default: ""] specifies the name of the executable for the application. This variable can be referred to in the following lines by using the '${main}' notation.

comp_cmd=COMMAND

> [default: "gcc -c -I${src_dir} -g -gnatq"] specifies the command used to compile a single file in the application.

make_cmd=COMMAND

> [default: "gnatmake ${main} -aI${src_dir} -aO${obj_dir} -g -gnatq -cargs ${comp_opt} -bargs ${bind_opt} -largs ${link_opt}"]   specifies the command used to recompile the whole application.

run_cmd=COMMAND

> [default: "${main}"] specifies the command used to run the application.

debug_cmd=COMMAND

> [default: "gdb ${main}"] specifies the command used to debug the application

gnatxref and gnatfind only take into account the src_dir and obj_dir lines, and ignore the others.

12.4 Regular Expressions in gnatfind and gnatxref

As specified in the section about gnatfind, the pattern can be a regular expression. Actually, there are to set of regular expressions which are recognized by the program:

globbing patterns

> These are the most usual regular expression. They are the same that you generally used in a Unix shell command line, or in a DOS session.
>
> Here is a more formal grammar:

```
regexp ::= term
term    ::= elmt            -- matches elmt
term    ::= elmt elmt       -- concatenation (elmt then elmt)
term    ::= *               -- any string of 0 or more characters
term    ::= ?               -- matches any character
term    ::= [char {char}]   -- matches any character listed
term    ::= [char - char]   -- matches any character in range
```

full regular expression

> The second set of regular expressions is much more powerful. This is the type of regular expressions recognized by utilities such a 'grep'.
>
> The following is the form of a regular expression, expressed in Ada reference manual style BNF is as follows

```
regexp ::= term {| term}    -- alternation (term or term ...)

term ::= item {item}        -- concatenation (item then item)

item ::= elmt               -- match elmt
item ::= elmt *             -- zero or more elmt's
item ::= elmt +             -- one or more elmt's
item ::= elmt ?             -- matches elmt or nothing
elmt ::= nschar             -- matches given character
elmt ::= [nschar {nschar}]    -- matches any character listed
elmt ::= [^ nschar {nschar}] -- matches any character not listed
elmt ::= [char - char]      -- matches chars in given range
elmt ::= \ char             -- matches given character
elmt ::= .                  -- matches any single character
elmt ::= ( regexp )         -- parens used for grouping

char ::= any character, including special characters
nschar ::= any character except ()[].*+?^
```

Following are a few examples:

'abcde|fghi'

> will match any of the two strings 'abcde' and 'fghi'.

'abc*d'   will match any string like 'abd', 'abcd', 'abccd', 'abcccd', and so on

'[a-z]+'   will match any string which has only lowercase characters in it (and at least one character.

12.5 Examples of gnatxref Usage

12.5.1 General Usage

For the following examples, we will consider the following units:

```
main.ads:
1: with Bar;
2: package Main is
3:     procedure Foo (B : in Integer);
4:     C : Integer;
5: private
6:     D : Integer;
7: end Main;

main.adb:
1: package body Main is
2:     procedure Foo (B : in Integer) is
3:     begin
4:         C := B;
5:         D := B;
6:         Bar.Print (B);
7:         Bar.Print (C);
8:     end Foo;
9: end Main;

bar.ads:
1: package Bar is
2:     procedure Print (B : Integer);
3: end bar;
```

The first thing to do is to recompile your application (for instance, in that case just by doing a 'gnatmake main', so that GNAT generates the cross-referencing information. You can then issue any of the following commands:

gnatxref main.adb

gnatxref generates cross-reference information for main.adb and every unit 'with'ed by main.adb.

The output would be:

```
B                                               Type: Integer
   Decl: bar.ads       2:22
B                                               Type: Integer
   Decl: main.ads      3:20
   Body: main.adb      2:20
   Ref:  main.adb      4:13    5:13    6:19
Bar                                             Type: Unit
   Decl: bar.ads       1:9
   Ref:  main.adb      6:8     7:8
         main.ads      1:6
C                                               Type: Integer
   Decl: main.ads      4:5
   Modi: main.adb      4:8
   Ref:  main.adb      7:19
D                                               Type: Integer
   Decl: main.ads      6:5
   Modi: main.adb      5:8
Foo                                             Type: Unit
   Decl: main.ads      3:15
   Body: main.adb      2:15
Main                                            Type: Unit
   Decl: main.ads      2:9
   Body: main.adb      1:14
```

```
Print                                              Type: Unit
  Decl: bar.ads          2:15
  Ref:  main.adb         6:12       7:12
```

that is the entity Main is declared in main.ads, line 2, column 9, its body is in main.adb, line 1, column 14 and is not referenced any where.

The entity Print is declared in bar.ads, line 2, column 15 and it it referenced in main.adb, line 6 column 12 and line 7 column 12.

`gnatxref package1.adb package2.ads`

gnatxref will generates cross-reference information for package1.adb, package2.ads and any other package 'with'ed by any of these.

12.5.2 Using gnatxref with vi

gnatxref can generate a tags file output, which can be used directly from vi. Note that the standard version of vi will not work properly with overloaded symbols. Consider using another free implementation of vi, such as vim.

```
$ gnatxref -v gnatfind.adb > tags
```

will generate the tags file for gnatfind itself (if the sources are in the search path!).

From vi, you can then use the command ':tag *entity*' (replacing *entity* by whatever you are looking for), and vi will display a new file with the corresponding declaration of entity.

12.6 Examples of gnatfind Usage

`gnatfind -f xyz:main.adb`

Find declarations for all entities xyz referenced at least once in main.adb. The references are search in every library file in the search path.

The directories will be printed as well (as the '-f' switch is set)

The output will look like:

```
directory/main.ads:106:14: xyz <= declaration
directory/main.adb:24:10: xyz <= body
directory/foo.ads:45:23: xyz <= declaration
```

that is to say, one of the entities xyz found in main.adb is declared at line 12 of main.ads (and its body is in main.adb), and another one is declared at line 45 of foo.ads

`gnatfind -fs xyz:main.adb`

This is the same command as the previous one, instead gnatfind will display the content of the Ada source file lines.

The output will look like:

```
directory/main.ads:106:14: xyz <= declaration
   procedure xyz;
directory/main.adb:24:10: xyz <= body
   procedure xyz is
directory/foo.ads:45:23: xyz <= declaration
   xyz : Integer;
```

This can make it easier to find exactly the location your are looking for.

`gnatfind -r "*x*":main.ads:123 foo.adb`

> Find references to all entities containing an x that are referenced on line 123 of main.ads. The references will be searched only in main.ads and foo.adb.

`gnatfind main.ads:123`

> Find declarations and bodies for all entities that are referenced on line 123 of main.ads.
>
> This is the same as `gnatfind "*":main.adb:123`.

`gnatfind mydir/main.adb:123:45`

> Find the declaration for the entity referenced at column 45 in line 123 of file main.adb in directory mydir. Note that it is usual to omit the identifier name when the column is given, since the column position identifies a unique reference.
>
> The column has to be the beginning of the identifier, and should not point to any character in the middle of the identifier.

13 The GNAT Pretty-Printer gnatpp

The gnatpp tool is an ASIS-based utility for source reformatting / pretty-printing. It takes an Ada source file as input and generates a reformatted version as output. You can specify various style directives via switches; e.g., identifier case conventions, rules of indentation, and comment layout.

To produce a reformatted file, gnatpp generates and uses the ASIS tree for the input source and thus requires the input to be syntactically and semantically legal. If this condition is not met, gnatpp will terminate with an error message; no output file will be generated.

If the source files presented to gnatpp contain preprocessing directives, then the output file will correspond to the generated source after all preprocessing is carried out. There is no way using gnatpp to obtain pretty printed files that include the preprocessing directives.

If the compilation unit contained in the input source depends semantically upon units located outside the current directory, you have to provide the source search path when invoking gnatpp, if these units are contained in files with names that do not follow the GNAT file naming rules, you have to provide the configuration file describing the corresponding naming scheme; see the description of the gnatpp switches below. Another possibility is to use a project file and to call gnatpp through the gnat driver

The gnatpp command has the form

```
$ gnatpp [switches] filename
```

where

- *switches* is an optional sequence of switches defining such properties as the formatting rules, the source search path, and the destination for the output source file

- *filename* is the name (including the extension) of the source file to reformat; "wildcards" or several file names on the same gnatpp command are allowed. The file name may contain path information; it does not have to follow the GNAT file naming rules

13.1 Switches for gnatpp

The following subsections describe the various switches accepted by gnatpp, organized by category.

You specify a switch by supplying a name and generally also a value. In many cases the values for a switch with a given name are incompatible with each other (for example the switch that controls the casing of a reserved word may have exactly one value: upper case, lower case, or mixed case) and thus exactly one such switch can be in effect for an invocation of gnatpp. If more than one is supplied, the last one is used. However, some values for the same switch are mutually compatible. You may supply several such switches to gnatpp, but then each must be specified in full, with both the name and the value. Abbreviated forms (the name appearing once, followed by each value) are not permitted. For example, to set the alignment of the assignment delimiter both in declarations and in assignment statements, you must write '-A2A3' (or '-A2 -A3'), but not '-A23'.

In most cases, it is obvious whether or not the values for a switch with a given name are compatible with each other. When the semantics might not be evident, the summaries below explicitly indicate the effect.

13.1.1 Alignment Control

Programs can be easier to read if certain constructs are vertically aligned. By default all alignments are set ON. Through the '-A0' switch you may reset the default to OFF, and then use one or more of the other '-An' switches to activate alignment for specific constructs.

'-A0'   Set all alignments to OFF

'-A1'   Align : in declarations

'-A2'   Align := in initializations in declarations

'-A3'   Align := in assignment statements

'-A4'   Align => in associations

'-A5'   Align at keywords in the component clauses in record representation clauses

The '-A' switches are mutually compatible; any combination is allowed.

13.1.2 Casing Control

gnatpp allows you to specify the casing for reserved words, pragma names, attribute designators and identifiers. For identifiers you may define a general rule for name casing but also override this rule via a set of dictionary files.

Three types of casing are supported: lower case, upper case, and mixed case. Lower and upper case are self-explanatory (but since some letters in Latin1 and other GNAT-supported character sets exist only in lower-case form, an upper case conversion will have no effect on them.) "Mixed case" means that the first letter, and also each letter immediately following an underscore, are converted to their uppercase forms; all the other letters are converted to their lowercase forms.

'-aL'   Attribute designators are lower case

'-aU'   Attribute designators are upper case

'-aM'   Attribute designators are mixed case (this is the default)

'-kL'   Keywords (technically, these are known in Ada as *reserved words*) are lower case (this is the default)

'-kU'   Keywords are upper case

'-nD'   Name casing for defining occurrences are as they appear in the source file (this is the default)

'-nU'   Names are in upper case

'-nL'   Names are in lower case

'-nM'   Names are in mixed case

'-pL'   Pragma names are lower case

'-pU'   Pragma names are upper case

'-pM'   Pragma names are mixed case (this is the default)

'`-Dfile`'   Use *file* as a *dictionary file* that defines the casing for a set of specified names, thereby overriding the effect on these names by any explicit or implicit -n switch. To supply more than one dictionary file, use several '`-D`' switches.

'`gnatpp`' implicitly uses a *default dictionary file* to define the casing for the Ada predefined names and the names declared in the GNAT libraries.

'`-D-`'   Do not use the default dictionary file; instead, use the casing defined by a '`-n`' switch and any explicit dictionary file(s)

The structure of a dictionary file, and details on the conventions used in the default dictionary file, are defined in Section 13.2.4 [Name Casing], page 183.

The '`-D-`' and '`-Dfile`' switches are mutually compatible.

13.1.3 Construct Layout Control

This group of `gnatpp` switches controls the layout of comments and complex syntactic constructs. See Section 13.2.2 [Formatting Comments], page 180 for details on their effect.

'`-c0`'   All the comments remain unchanged

'`-c1`'   GNAT-style comment line indentation (this is the default).

'`-c2`'   Reference-manual comment line indentation.

'`-c3`'   GNAT-style comment beginning

'`-c4`'   Reformat comment blocks

'`-c5`'   Keep unchanged special form comments
              Reformat comment blocks

'`-l1`'   GNAT-style layout (this is the default)

'`-l2`'   Compact layout

'`-l3`'   Uncompact layout

'`-N`'   All the VT characters are removed from the comment text. All the HT characters are expanded with the sequences of space characters to get to the next tab stops.

'`--no-separate-is`'
              Do not place the keyword `is` on a separate line in a subprogram body in case if the specification occupies more then one line.

'`--separate-loop-then`'
              Place the keyword `loop` in FOR and WHILE loop statements and the keyword `then` in IF statements on a separate line.

'`--no-separate-loop-then`'
              Do not place the keyword `loop` in FOR and WHILE loop statements and the keyword `then` in IF statements on a separate line. This option is incompatible with '`--separate-loop-then`' option.

'`--use-on-new-line`'
              Start each USE clause in a context clause from a separate line.

'`--separate-stmt-name`'
> Use a separate line for a loop or block statement name, but do not use an extra indentation level for the statement itself.

The '`-c1`' and '`-c2`' switches are incompatible. The '`-c3`' and '`-c4`' switches are compatible with each other and also with '`-c1`' and '`-c2`'. The '`-c0`' switch disables all the other comment formatting switches.

The '`-l1`', '`-l2`', and '`-l3`' switches are incompatible.

13.1.4 General Text Layout Control

These switches allow control over line length and indentation.

'`-Mnnn`'   Maximum line length, *nnn* from 32 ..256, the default value is 79

'`-innn`'   Indentation level, *nnn* from 1 .. 9, the default value is 3

'`-clnnn`'   Indentation level for continuation lines (relative to the line being continued), *nnn* from 1 .. 9. The default value is one less then the (normal) indentation level, unless the indentation is set to 1 (in which case the default value for continuation line indentation is also 1)

13.1.5 Other Formatting Options

These switches control the inclusion of missing end/exit labels, and the indentation level in **case** statements.

'`-e`'   Do not insert missing end/exit labels. An end label is the name of a construct that may optionally be repeated at the end of the construct's declaration; e.g., the names of packages, subprograms, and tasks. An exit label is the name of a loop that may appear as target of an exit statement within the loop. By default, **gnatpp** inserts these end/exit labels when they are absent from the original source. This option suppresses such insertion, so that the formatted source reflects the original.

'`-ff`'   Insert a Form Feed character after a pragma Page.

'`-Tnnn`'   Do not use an additional indentation level for **case** alternatives and variants if there are *nnn* or more (the default value is 10). If *nnn* is 0, an additional indentation level is used for **case** alternatives and variants regardless of their number.

13.1.6 Setting the Source Search Path

To define the search path for the input source file, **gnatpp** uses the same switches as the GNAT compiler, with the same effects.

'`-Idir`'   The same as the corresponding gcc switch

'`-I-`'   The same as the corresponding gcc switch

'`-gnatec=path`'
> The same as the corresponding gcc switch

'`--RTS=path`'
> The same as the corresponding gcc switch

13.1.7 Output File Control

By default the output is sent to the file whose name is obtained by appending the '.pp' suffix to the name of the input file (if the file with this name already exists, it is unconditionally overwritten). Thus if the input file is 'my_ada_proc.adb' then gnatpp will produce 'my_ada_proc.adb.pp' as output file. The output may be redirected by the following switches:

'-pipe' Send the output to Standard_Output

'-o output_file'

> Write the output into *output_file*. If *output_file* already exists, gnatpp terminates without reading or processing the input file.

'-of output_file'

> Write the output into *output_file*, overwriting the existing file (if one is present).

'-r'

> Replace the input source file with the reformatted output, and copy the original input source into the file whose name is obtained by appending the '.npp' suffix to the name of the input file. If a file with this name already exists, gnatpp terminates without reading or processing the input file.

'-rf'

> Like '-r' except that if the file with the specified name already exists, it is overwritten.

'-rnb'

> Replace the input source file with the reformatted output without creating any backup copy of the input source.

'--eol=xxx'

> Specifies the format of the reformatted output file. The xxx string specified with the switch may be either
>
> - "'dos'" MS DOS style, lines end with CR LF characters
> - "'crlf'" the same as 'crlf'
> - "'unix'" UNIX style, lines end with LF character
> - "'lf'" the same as 'unix'

'-We'

> Specify the wide character encoding method used to write the code in the result file *e* is one of the following:
>
> - h Hex encoding
> - u Upper half encoding
> - s Shift/JIS encoding
> - e EUC encoding
> - 8 UTF-8 encoding
> - b Brackets encoding (default value)

Options '-pipe', '-o' and '-of' are allowed only if the call to gnatpp contains only one file to reformat. Option '--eol' and '-W' cannot be used together with '-pipe' option.

13.1.8 Other gnatpp Switches

The additional **gnatpp** switches are defined in this subsection.

'-files *filename*'

Take the argument source files from the specified file. This file should be an ordinary textual file containing file names separated by spaces or line breaks. You can use this switch more then once in the same call to **gnatpp**. You also can combine this switch with explicit list of files.

'-v'   Verbose mode; **gnatpp** generates version information and then a trace of the actions it takes to produce or obtain the ASIS tree.

'-w'   Warning mode; **gnatpp** generates a warning whenever it cannot provide a required layout in the result source.

13.2 Formatting Rules

The following subsections show how **gnatpp** treats "white space", comments, program layout, and name casing. They provide the detailed descriptions of the switches shown above.

13.2.1 White Space and Empty Lines

gnatpp does not have an option to control space characters. It will add or remove spaces according to the style illustrated by the examples in the *Ada Reference Manual*.

The only format effectors (see *Ada Reference Manual*, paragraph 2.1(13)) that will appear in the output file are platform-specific line breaks, and also format effectors within (but not at the end of) comments. In particular, each horizontal tab character that is not inside a comment will be treated as a space and thus will appear in the output file as zero or more spaces depending on the reformatting of the line in which it appears. The only exception is a Form Feed character, which is inserted after a pragma **Page** when '-ff' is set.

The output file will contain no lines with trailing "white space" (spaces, format effectors).

Empty lines in the original source are preserved only if they separate declarations or statements. In such contexts, a sequence of two or more empty lines is replaced by exactly one empty line. Note that a blank line will be removed if it separates two "comment blocks" (a comment block is a sequence of whole-line comments). In order to preserve a visual separation between comment blocks, use an "empty comment" (a line comprising only hyphens) rather than an empty line. Likewise, if for some reason you wish to have a sequence of empty lines, use a sequence of empty comments instead.

13.2.2 Formatting Comments

Comments in Ada code are of two kinds:

- a *whole-line comment*, which appears by itself (possibly preceded by "white space") on a line
- an *end-of-line comment*, which follows some other Ada lexical element on the same line.

The indentation of a whole-line comment is that of either the preceding or following line in the formatted source, depending on switch settings as will be described below.

For an end-of-line comment, `gnatpp` leaves the same number of spaces between the end of the preceding Ada lexical element and the beginning of the comment as appear in the original source, unless either the comment has to be split to satisfy the line length limitation, or else the next line contains a whole line comment that is considered a continuation of this end-of-line comment (because it starts at the same position). In the latter two cases, the start of the end-of-line comment is moved right to the nearest multiple of the indentation level. This may result in a "line overflow" (the right-shifted comment extending beyond the maximum line length), in which case the comment is split as described below.

There is a difference between '`-c1`' (GNAT-style comment line indentation) and '`-c2`' (reference-manual comment line indentation). With reference-manual style, a whole-line comment is indented as if it were a declaration or statement at the same place (i.e., according to the indentation of the preceding line(s)). With GNAT style, a whole-line comment that is immediately followed by an **if** or **case** statement alternative, a record variant, or the reserved word **begin**, is indented based on the construct that follows it.

For example:

```
if A then
    null;
        -- some comment
else
    null;
end if;
```

Reference-manual indentation produces:

```
if A then
    null;
    --   some comment
else
    null;
end if;
```

while GNAT-style indentation produces:

```
if A then
    null;
--   some comment
else
    null;
end if;
```

The '`-c3`' switch (GNAT style comment beginning) has the following effect:

- For each whole-line comment that does not end with two hyphens, `gnatpp` inserts spaces if necessary after the starting two hyphens to ensure that there are at least two spaces between these hyphens and the first non-blank character of the comment.

For an end-of-line comment, if in the original source the next line is a whole-line comment that starts at the same position as the end-of-line comment, then the whole-line comment (and all whole-line comments that follow it and that start at the same position) will start at this position in the output file.

That is, if in the original source we have:

```
begin
A := B + C;                 --  B must be in the range Low1..High1
                            --  C must be in the range Low2..High2
              --B+C will be in the range Low1+Low2..High1+High2
X := X + 1;
```

Then in the formatted source we get:

```
begin
   A := B + C;              --  B must be in the range Low1..High1
                            --  C must be in the range Low2..High2
   --  B+C will be in the range Low1+Low2..High1+High2
   X := X + 1;
```

A comment that exceeds the line length limit will be split. Unless switch '-c4' (reformat comment blocks) is set and the line belongs to a reformattable block, splitting the line generates a gnatpp warning. The '-c4' switch specifies that whole-line comments may be reformatted in typical word processor style (that is, moving words between lines and putting as many words in a line as possible).

The '-c5' switch specifies, that comments that has a special format (that is, a character that is neither a letter nor digit not white space nor line break immediately following the leading -- of the comment) should be without any change moved from the argument source into reformatted source. This switch allows to preserve comments that are used as a special marks in the code (e.g. SPARK annotation).

13.2.3 Construct Layout

In several cases the suggested layout in the Ada Reference Manual includes an extra level of indentation that many programmers prefer to avoid. The affected cases include:

- Record type declaration (RM 3.8)
- Record representation clause (RM 13.5.1)
- Loop statement in case if a loop has a statement identifier (RM 5.6)
- Block statement in case if a block has a statement identifier (RM 5.6)

In compact mode (when GNAT style layout or compact layout is set), the pretty printer uses one level of indentation instead of two. This is achieved in the record definition and record representation clause cases by putting the record keyword on the same line as the start of the declaration or representation clause, and in the block and loop case by putting the block or loop header on the same line as the statement identifier.

The difference between GNAT style '-l1' and compact '-l2' layout on the one hand, and uncompact layout '-l3' on the other hand, can be illustrated by the following examples:

```
GNAT style, compact layout              Uncompact layout

type q is record                        type q is
   a : integer;                            record
   b : integer;                                  a : integer;
end record;                                      b : integer;
                                              end record;


for q use record                        for q use
   a at 0 range  0 .. 31;                  record
   b at 4 range  0 .. 31;                        a at 0 range  0 .. 31;
end record;                                      b at 4 range  0 .. 31;
                                              end record;


Block : declare                         Block :
   A : Integer := 3;                       declare
begin                                            A : Integer := 3;
   Proc (A, A);                          begin
end Block;                                       Proc (A, A);
                                              end Block;


Clear : for J in 1 .. 10 loop           Clear :
   A (J) := 0;                             for J in 1 .. 10 loop
end loop Clear;                                  A (J) := 0;
                                              end loop Clear;
```

A further difference between GNAT style layout and compact layout is that GNAT style layout inserts empty lines as separation for compound statements, return statements and bodies.

Note that the layout specified by '--separate-stmt-name' for named block and loop statements overrides the layout defined by these constructs by '-l1', '-l2' or '-l3' option.

13.2.4 Name Casing

`gnatpp` always converts the usage occurrence of a (simple) name to the same casing as the corresponding defining identifier.

You control the casing for defining occurrences via the '-n' switch. With '-nD' ("as declared", which is the default), defining occurrences appear exactly as in the source file where they are declared. The other values for this switch — '-nU', '-nL', '-nM' — result in upper, lower, or mixed case, respectively. If `gnatpp` changes the casing of a defining occurrence, it analogously changes the casing of all the usage occurrences of this name.

If the defining occurrence of a name is not in the source compilation unit currently being processed by `gnatpp`, the casing of each reference to this name is changed according to the value of the '-n' switch (subject to the dictionary file mechanism described below). Thus `gnatpp` acts as though the '-n' switch had affected the casing for the defining occurrence of the name.

Some names may need to be spelled with casing conventions that are not covered by the upper-, lower-, and mixed-case transformations. You can arrange correct casing by placing such names in a *dictionary file*, and then supplying a '-D' switch. The casing of names from dictionary files overrides any '-n' switch.

To handle the casing of Ada predefined names and the names from GNAT libraries, **gnatpp** assumes a default dictionary file. The name of each predefined entity is spelled with the same casing as is used for the entity in the *Ada Reference Manual*. The name of each entity in the GNAT libraries is spelled with the same casing as is used in the declaration of that entity.

The '**-D-**' switch suppresses the use of the default dictionary file. Instead, the casing for predefined and GNAT-defined names will be established by the '**-n**' switch or explicit dictionary files. For example, by default the names `Ada.Text_IO` and `GNAT.OS_Lib` will appear as just shown, even in the presence of a '**-nU**' switch. To ensure that even such names are rendered in uppercase, additionally supply the '**-D-**' switch (or else, less conveniently, place these names in upper case in a dictionary file).

A dictionary file is a plain text file; each line in this file can be either a blank line (containing only space characters and ASCII.HT characters), an Ada comment line, or the specification of exactly one *casing schema*.

A casing schema is a string that has the following syntax:

```
casing_schema ::= identifier | *simple_identifier*

simple_identifier ::= letter{letter_or_digit}
```

(See *Ada Reference Manual*, Section 2.3) for the definition of the *identifier* lexical element and the *letter_or_digit* category.)

The casing schema string can be followed by white space and/or an Ada-style comment; any amount of white space is allowed before the string.

If a dictionary file is passed as the value of a '**-D**file' switch then for every simple name and every identifier, **gnatpp** checks if the dictionary defines the casing for the name or for some of its parts (the term "subword" is used below to denote the part of a name which is delimited by "_" or by the beginning or end of the word and which does not contain any "_" inside):

- if the whole name is in the dictionary, **gnatpp** uses for this name the casing defined by the dictionary; no subwords are checked for this word

- for every subword **gnatpp** checks if the dictionary contains the corresponding string of the form `*simple_identifier*`, and if it does, the casing of this *simple_identifier* is used for this subword

- if the whole name does not contain any "_" inside, and if for this name the dictionary contains two entries - one of the form *identifier*, and another - of the form *simple_identifier*, then the first one is applied to define the casing of this name

- if more than one dictionary file is passed as **gnatpp** switches, each dictionary adds new casing exceptions and overrides all the existing casing exceptions set by the previous dictionaries

- when **gnatpp** checks if the word or subword is in the dictionary, this check is not case sensitive

For example, suppose we have the following source to reformat:

```
procedure test is
   name1 : integer := 1;
   name4_name3_name2 : integer := 2;
   name2_name3_name4 : Boolean;
   name1_var : Float;
begin
   name2_name3_name4 := name4_name3_name2 > name1;
end;
```

And suppose we have two dictionaries:

```
dict1:
   NAME1
   *NaMe3*
   *Name1*
```

```
dict2:
   *NAME3*
```

If gnatpp is called with the following switches:

```
gnatpp -nM -D dict1 -D dict2 test.adb
```

then we will get the following name casing in the gnatpp output:

```
procedure Test is
   NAME1             : Integer := 1;
   Name4_NAME3_Name2 : Integer := 2;
   Name2_NAME3_Name4 : Boolean;
   Name1_Var         : Float;
begin
   Name2_NAME3_Name4 := Name4_NAME3_Name2 > NAME1;
end Test;
```

14 The GNAT Metric Tool gnatmetric

The gnatmetric tool is an ASIS-based utility for computing various program metrics. It takes an Ada source file as input and generates a file containing the metrics data as output. Various switches control which metrics are computed and output.

gnatmetric generates and uses the ASIS tree for the input source and thus requires the input to be syntactically and semantically legal. If this condition is not met, gnatmetric will generate an error message; no metric information for this file will be computed and reported.

If the compilation unit contained in the input source depends semantically upon units in files located outside the current directory, you have to provide the source search path when invoking gnatmetric. If it depends semantically upon units that are contained in files with names that do not follow the GNAT file naming rules, you have to provide the configuration file describing the corresponding naming scheme (see the description of the gnatmetric switches below.) Alternatively, you may use a project file and invoke gnatmetric through the gnat driver.

The gnatmetric command has the form

```
$ gnatmetric [switches] {filename} [-cargs gcc_switches]
```

where

- *switches* specify the metrics to compute and define the destination for the output

- Each *filename* is the name (including the extension) of a source file to process. "Wild-cards" are allowed, and the file name may contain path information. If no *filename* is supplied, then the *switches* list must contain at least one '-files' switch (see Section 14.1.4 [Other gnatmetric Switches], page 193). Including both a '-files' switch and one or more *filename* arguments is permitted.

- *-cargs gcc_switches* is a list of switches for gcc. They will be passed on to all compiler invocations made by gnatmetric to generate the ASIS trees. Here you can provide '-I' switches to form the source search path, and use the '-gnatec' switch to set the configuration file.

14.1 Switches for gnatmetric

The following subsections describe the various switches accepted by gnatmetric, organized by category.

14.1.1 Output File Control

gnatmetric has two output formats. It can generate a textual (human-readable) form, and also XML. By default only textual output is generated.

When generating the output in textual form, gnatmetric creates for each Ada source file a corresponding text file containing the computed metrics, except for the case when the set of metrics specified by gnatmetric parameters consists only of metrics that are computed for the whole set of analyzed sources, but not for each Ada source. By default, this file is placed in the same directory as where the source file is located, and its name is obtained by appending the '.metrix' suffix to the name of the input file.

All the output information generated in XML format is placed in a single file. By default this file is placed in the current directory and has the name 'metrix.xml'.

Some of the computed metrics are summed over the units passed to gnatmetric; for example, the total number of lines of code. By default this information is sent to 'stdout', but a file can be specified with the '-og' switch.

The following switches control the gnatmetric output:

'-x'   Generate the XML output

'-nt'   Do not generate the output in text form (implies '-x')

'-d output_dir'
            Put textual files with detailed metrics into output_dir

'-o file_suffix'
            Use file_suffix, instead of '.metrix' in the name of the output file.

'-og file_name'
            Put global metrics into file_name

'-ox file_name'
            Put the XML output into file_name (also implies '-x')

'-sfn'   Use "short" source file names in the output. (The gnatmetric output includes the name(s) of the Ada source file(s) from which the metrics are computed. By default each name includes the absolute path. The '-sfn' switch causes gnatmetric to exclude all directory information from the file names that are output.)

14.1.2 Disable Metrics For Local Units

gnatmetric relies on the GNAT compilation model — one compilation unit per one source file. It computes line metrics for the whole source file, and it also computes syntax and complexity metrics for the file's outermost unit.

By default, gnatmetric will also compute all metrics for certain kinds of locally declared program units:

- subprogram (and generic subprogram) bodies;
- package (and generic package) specifications and bodies;
- task object and type specifications and bodies;
- protected object and type specifications and bodies.

These kinds of entities will be referred to as *eligible local program units*, or simply *eligible local units*, in the discussion below.

Note that a subprogram declaration, generic instantiation, or renaming declaration only receives metrics computation when it appear as the outermost entity in a source file.

Suppression of metrics computation for eligible local units can be obtained via the following switch:

'-nolocal'
            Do not compute detailed metrics for eligible local program units

14.1.3 Specifying a set of metrics to compute

By default all the metrics are computed and reported. The switches described in this subsection allow you to control, on an individual basis, whether metrics are computed and reported. If at least one positive metric switch is specified (that is, a switch that defines that a given metric or set of metrics is to be computed), then only explicitly specified metrics are reported.

14.1.3.1 Line Metrics Control

For any (legal) source file, and for each of its eligible local program units, `gnatmetric` computes the following metrics:

- the total number of lines;
- the total number of code lines (i.e., non-blank lines that are not comments)
- the number of comment lines
- the number of code lines containing end-of-line comments;
- the comment percentage: the ratio between the number of lines that contain comments and the number of all non-blank lines, expressed as a percentage;
- the number of empty lines and lines containing only space characters and/or format effectors (blank lines)
- the average number of code lines in subprogram bodies, task bodies, entry bodies and statement sequences in package bodies (this metric is only computed across the whole set of the analyzed units)

`gnatmetric` sums the values of the line metrics for all the files being processed and then generates the cumulative results. The tool also computes for all the files being processed the average number of code lines in bodies.

You can use the following switches to select the specific line metrics to be computed and reported.

'`--lines-all`'
> Report all the line metrics

'`--no-lines-all`'
> Do not report any of line metrics

'`--lines`'   Report the number of all lines

'`--no-lines`'
> Do not report the number of all lines

'`--lines-code`'
> Report the number of code lines

'`--no-lines-code`'
> Do not report the number of code lines

'`--lines-comment`'
> Report the number of comment lines

'`--no-lines-comment`'
> Do not report the number of comment lines

'--lines-eol-comment'
>   Report the number of code lines containing end-of-line comments

'--no-lines-eol-comment'
>   Do not report the number of code lines containing end-of-line comments

'--lines-ratio'
>   Report the comment percentage in the program text

'--no-lines-ratio'
>   Do not report the comment percentage in the program text

'--lines-blank'
>   Report the number of blank lines

'--no-lines-blank'
>   Do not report the number of blank lines

'--lines-average'
>   Report the average number of code lines in subprogram bodies, task bodies, entry bodies and statement sequences in package bodies. The metric is computed and reported for the whole set of processed Ada sources only.

'--no-lines-average'
>   Do not report the average number of code lines in subprogram bodies, task bodies, entry bodies and statement sequences in package bodies.

14.1.3.2 Syntax Metrics Control

gnatmetric computes various syntactic metrics for the outermost unit and for each eligible local unit:

LSLOC ("Logical Source Lines Of Code")
>   The total number of declarations and the total number of statements

Maximal static nesting level of inner program units
>   According to *Ada Reference Manual*, 10.1(1), "A program unit is either a package, a task unit, a protected unit, a protected entry, a generic unit, or an explicitly declared subprogram other than an enumeration literal."

Maximal nesting level of composite syntactic constructs
>   This corresponds to the notion of the maximum nesting level in the GNAT built-in style checks (see Section 3.2.5 [Style Checking], page 58)

For the outermost unit in the file, gnatmetric additionally computes the following metrics:

Public subprograms
>   This metric is computed for package specifications. It is the number of subprograms and generic subprograms declared in the visible part (including the visible part of nested packages, protected objects, and protected types).

All subprograms
>   This metric is computed for bodies and subunits. The metric is equal to a total number of subprogram bodies in the compilation unit. Neither generic instantiations nor renamings-as-a-body nor body stubs are counted. Any subprogram

body is counted, independently of its nesting level and enclosing constructs. Generic bodies and bodies of protected subprograms are counted in the same way as "usual" subprogram bodies.

Public types

This metric is computed for package specifications and generic package declarations. It is the total number of types that can be referenced from outside this compilation unit, plus the number of types from all the visible parts of all the visible generic packages. Generic formal types are not counted. Only types, not subtypes, are included.

Along with the total number of public types, the following types are counted and reported separately:

- Abstract types
- Root tagged types (abstract, non-abstract, private, non-private). Type extensions are *not* counted
- Private types (including private extensions)
- Task types
- Protected types

All types   This metric is computed for any compilation unit. It is equal to the total number of the declarations of different types given in the compilation unit. The private and the corresponding full type declaration are counted as one type declaration. Incomplete type declarations and generic formal types are not counted. No distinction is made among different kinds of types (abstract, private etc.); the total number of types is computed and reported.

By default, all the syntax metrics are computed and reported. You can use the following switches to select specific syntax metrics.

'--syntax-all'
        Report all the syntax metrics

'--no-syntax-all'
        Do not report any of syntax metrics

'--declarations'
        Report the total number of declarations

'--no-declarations'
        Do not report the total number of declarations

'--statements'
        Report the total number of statements

'--no-statements'
        Do not report the total number of statements

'--public-subprograms'
        Report the number of public subprograms in a compilation unit

'--no-public-subprograms'
        Do not report the number of public subprograms in a compilation unit

'`--all-subprograms`'
> Report the number of all the subprograms in a compilation unit

'`--no-all-subprograms`'
> Do not report the number of all the subprograms in a compilation unit

'`--public-types`'
> Report the number of public types in a compilation unit

'`--no-public-types`'
> Do not report the number of public types in a compilation unit

'`--all-types`'
> Report the number of all the types in a compilation unit

'`--no-all-types`'
> Do not report the number of all the types in a compilation unit

'`--unit-nesting`'
> Report the maximal program unit nesting level

'`--no-unit-nesting`'
> Do not report the maximal program unit nesting level

'`--construct-nesting`'
> Report the maximal construct nesting level

'`--no-construct-nesting`'
> Do not report the maximal construct nesting level

14.1.3.3 Complexity Metrics Control

For a program unit that is an executable body (a subprogram body (including generic bodies), task body, entry body or a package body containing its own statement sequence) `gnatmetric` computes the following complexity metrics:

- McCabe cyclomatic complexity;
- McCabe essential complexity;
- maximal loop nesting level

The McCabe complexity metrics are defined in `http://www.mccabe.com/pdf/nist235r.pdf`

According to McCabe, both control statements and short-circuit control forms should be taken into account when computing cyclomatic complexity. For each body, we compute three metric values:

- the complexity introduced by control statements only, without taking into account short-circuit forms,
- the complexity introduced by short-circuit control forms only, and
- the total cyclomatic complexity, which is the sum of these two values.

When computing cyclomatic and essential complexity, `gnatmetric` skips the code in the exception handlers and in all the nested program units.

By default, all the complexity metrics are computed and reported. For more fine-grained control you can use the following switches:

'--complexity-all'
> Report all the complexity metrics

'--no-complexity-all'
> Do not report any of complexity metrics

'--complexity-cyclomatic'
> Report the McCabe Cyclomatic Complexity

'--no-complexity-cyclomatic'
> Do not report the McCabe Cyclomatic Complexity

'--complexity-essential'
> Report the Essential Complexity

'--no-complexity-essential'
> Do not report the Essential Complexity

'--loop-nesting'
> Report maximal loop nesting level

'--no-loop-nesting'
> Do not report maximal loop nesting level

'--complexity-average'
> Report the average McCabe Cyclomatic Complexity for all the subprogram bodies, task bodies, entry bodies and statement sequences in package bodies. The metric is computed and reported for whole set of processed Ada sources only.

'--no-complexity-average'
> Do not report the average McCabe Cyclomatic Complexity for all the subprogram bodies, task bodies, entry bodies and statement sequences in package bodies

'-ne'
> Do not consider `exit` statements as `goto`s when computing Essential Complexity

14.1.4 Other gnatmetric Switches

Additional gnatmetric switches are as follows:

'-files *filename*'
> Take the argument source files from the specified file. This file should be an ordinary text file containing file names separated by spaces or line breaks. You can use this switch more then once in the same call to gnatmetric. You also can combine this switch with an explicit list of files.

'-v'
> Verbose mode; gnatmetric generates version information and then a trace of sources being processed.

'-dv'
> Debug mode; gnatmetric generates various messages useful to understand what happens during the metrics computation

'-q'
> Quiet mode.

14.1.5 Generate project-wide metrics

In order to compute metrics on all units of a given project, you can use the `gnat` driver along with the '`-P`' option:

```
gnat metric -Pproj
```

If the project `proj` depends upon other projects, you can compute the metrics on the project closure using the '`-U`' option:

```
gnat metric -Pproj -U
```

Finally, if not all the units are relevant to a particular main program in the project closure, you can generate metrics for the set of units needed to create a given main program (unit closure) using the '`-U`' option followed by the name of the main unit:

```
gnat metric -Pproj -U main
```

15 File Name Krunching Using gnatkr

This chapter discusses the method used by the compiler to shorten the default file names chosen for Ada units so that they do not exceed the maximum length permitted. It also describes the **gnatkr** utility that can be used to determine the result of applying this shortening.

15.1 About gnatkr

The default file naming rule in GNAT is that the file name must be derived from the unit name. The exact default rule is as follows:

- Take the unit name and replace all dots by hyphens.
- If such a replacement occurs in the second character position of a name, and the first character is a, g, s, or i then replace the dot by the character ~ (tilde) instead of a minus.

The reason for this exception is to avoid clashes with the standard names for children of System, Ada, Interfaces, and GNAT, which use the prefixes s- a- i- and g- respectively.

The '-gnatk*nn*' switch of the compiler activates a "krunching" circuit that limits file names to nn characters (where nn is a decimal integer). For example, using OpenVMS, where the maximum file name length is 39, the value of nn is usually set to 39, but if you want to generate a set of files that would be usable if ported to a system with some different maximum file length, then a different value can be specified. The default value of 39 for OpenVMS need not be specified.

The **gnatkr** utility can be used to determine the krunched name for a given file, when krunched to a specified maximum length.

15.2 Using gnatkr

The **gnatkr** command has the form

```
$ gnatkr name [length]
```

name is the uncrunched file name, derived from the name of the unit in the standard manner described in the previous section (i.e. in particular all dots are replaced by hyphens). The file name may or may not have an extension (defined as a suffix of the form period followed by arbitrary characters other than period). If an extension is present then it will be preserved in the output. For example, when krunching '`hellofile.ads`' to eight characters, the result will be hellofil.ads.

Note: for compatibility with previous versions of **gnatkr** dots may appear in the name instead of hyphens, but the last dot will always be taken as the start of an extension. So if **gnatkr** is given an argument such as '`Hello.World.adb`' it will be treated exactly as if the first period had been a hyphen, and for example krunching to eight characters gives the result '`hellworl.adb`'.

Note that the result is always all lower case (except on OpenVMS where it is all upper case). Characters of the other case are folded as required.

length represents the length of the krunched name. The default when no argument is given is 8 characters. A length of zero stands for unlimited, in other words do not chop except for system files where the implied crunching length is always eight characters.

The output is the krunched name. The output has an extension only if the original argument was a file name with an extension.

15.3 Krunching Method

The initial file name is determined by the name of the unit that the file contains. The name is formed by taking the full expanded name of the unit and replacing the separating dots with hyphens and using lowercase for all letters, except that a hyphen in the second character position is replaced by a tilde if the first character is a, i, g, or s. The extension is `.ads` for a specification and `.adb` for a body. Krunching does not affect the extension, but the file name is shortened to the specified length by following these rules:

- The name is divided into segments separated by hyphens, tildes or underscores and all hyphens, tildes, and underscores are eliminated. If this leaves the name short enough, we are done.

- If the name is too long, the longest segment is located (left-most if there are two of equal length), and shortened by dropping its last character. This is repeated until the name is short enough.

  As an example, consider the krunching of `our-strings-wide_fixed.adb` to fit the name into 8 characters as required by some operating systems.

```
      our-strings-wide_fixed 22
      our strings wide fixed 19
      our string  wide fixed 18
      our strin   wide fixed 17
      our stri    wide fixed 16
      our stri    wide fixe  15
      our str     wide fixe  14
      our str     wid  fixe  13
      our str     wid  fix   12
      ou  str     wid  fix   11
      ou  st      wid  fix   10
      ou  st      wi   fix   9
      ou  st      wi   fi    8
      Final file name: oustwifi.adb
```

- The file names for all predefined units are always krunched to eight characters. The krunching of these predefined units uses the following special prefix replacements:

  `ada-`   replaced by `a-`

  `gnat-`   replaced by `g-`

  `interfaces-`
                  replaced by `i-`

  `system-`   replaced by `s-`

  These system files have a hyphen in the second character position. That is why normal user files replace such a character with a tilde, to avoid confusion with system file names.

  As an example of this special rule, consider `ada-strings-wide_fixed.adb`, which gets krunched as follows:

```
      ada-strings-wide_fixed 22
      a-  strings wide fixed 18
      a-  string  wide fixed 17
      a-  strin   wide fixed 16
      a-  stri    wide fixed 15
      a-  stri    wide fixe  14
      a-  str     wide fixe  13
      a-  str     wid  fixe  12
      a-  str     wid  fix   11
      a-  st      wid  fix   10
      a-  st      wi   fix   9
      a-  st      wi   fi    8
      Final file name: a-stwifi.adb
```

Of course no file shortening algorithm can guarantee uniqueness over all possible unit names, and if file name krunching is used then it is your responsibility to ensure that no name clashes occur. The utility program **gnatkr** is supplied for conveniently determining the krunched name of a file.

15.4 Examples of gnatkr Usage

```
$ gnatkr very_long_unit_name.ads       --> velounna.ads
$ gnatkr grandparent-parent-child.ads --> grparchi.ads
$ gnatkr Grandparent.Parent.Child.ads --> grparchi.ads
$ gnatkr grandparent-parent-child     --> grparchi
$ gnatkr very_long_unit_name.ads/count=6 --> vlunna.ads
$ gnatkr very_long_unit_name.ads/count=0 --> very_long_unit_name.ads
```

16 Preprocessing Using gnatprep

This chapter discusses how to use GNAT's gnatprep utility for simple preprocessing. Although designed for use with GNAT, gnatprep does not depend on any special GNAT features. For further discussion of conditional compilation in general, see Appendix D [Conditional Compilation], page 317.

16.1 Using gnatprep

To call gnatprep use

```
$ gnatprep [switches] infile outfile [deffile]
```

where

switches   is an optional sequence of switches as described in the next section.

infile   is the full name of the input file, which is an Ada source file containing preprocessor directives.

outfile   is the full name of the output file, which is an Ada source in standard Ada form. When used with GNAT, this file name will normally have an ads or adb suffix.

deffile   is the full name of a text file containing definitions of symbols to be referenced by the preprocessor. This argument is optional, and can be replaced by the use of the '-D' switch.

16.2 Switches for gnatprep

'-b'   Causes both preprocessor lines and the lines deleted by preprocessing to be replaced by blank lines in the output source file, preserving line numbers in the output file.

'-c'   Causes both preprocessor lines and the lines deleted by preprocessing to be retained in the output source as comments marked with the special string "--! ". This option will result in line numbers being preserved in the output file.

'-C'   Causes comments to be scanned. Normally comments are ignored by gnatprep. If this option is specified, then comments are scanned and any $symbol substitutions performed as in program text. This is particularly useful when structured comments are used (e.g. when writing programs in the SPARK dialect of Ada). Note that this switch is not available when doing integrated preprocessing (it would be useless in this context since comments are ignored by the compiler in any case).

'-Dsymbol=value'
            Defines a new symbol, associated with value. If no value is given on the command line, then symbol is considered to be True. This switch can be used in place of a definition file.

'-r'   Causes a Source_Reference pragma to be generated that references the original input file, so that error messages will use the file name of this original file. The use of this switch implies that preprocessor lines are not to be removed from the file, so its use will force '-b' mode if '-c' has not been specified explicitly.

Note that if the file to be preprocessed contains multiple units, then it will be necessary to gnatchop the output file from gnatprep. If a Source_Reference pragma is present in the preprocessed file, it will be respected by gnatchop -r so that the final chopped files will correctly refer to the original input source file for gnatprep.

'-s'   Causes a sorted list of symbol names and values to be listed on the standard output file.

'-u'   Causes undefined symbols to be treated as having the value FALSE in the context of a preprocessor test. In the absence of this option, an undefined symbol in a #if or #elsif test will be treated as an error.

Note: if neither '-b' nor '-c' is present, then preprocessor lines and deleted lines are completely removed from the output, unless -r is specified, in which case -b is assumed.

16.3 Form of Definitions File

The definitions file contains lines of the form

```
symbol := value
```

where symbol is an identifier, following normal Ada (case-insensitive) rules for its syntax, and value is one of the following:

- Empty, corresponding to a null substitution
- A string literal using normal Ada syntax
- Any sequence of characters from the set (letters, digits, period, underline).

Comment lines may also appear in the definitions file, starting with the usual --, and comments may be added to the definitions lines.

16.4 Form of Input Text for gnatprep

The input text may contain preprocessor conditional inclusion lines, as well as general symbol substitution sequences.

The preprocessor conditional inclusion commands have the form

```
#if expression [then]
   lines
#elsif expression [then]
   lines
#elsif expression [then]
   lines
...
#else
   lines
#end if;
```

In this example, *expression* is defined by the following grammar:

```
expression ::=  <symbol>
expression ::=  <symbol> = "<value>"
expression ::=  <symbol> = <symbol>
expression ::=  <symbol> 'Defined
expression ::=  not expression
expression ::=  expression and expression
expression ::=  expression or expression
expression ::=  expression and then expression
expression ::=  expression or else expression
expression ::=  ( expression )
```

For the first test (*expression* ::= <symbol>) the symbol must have either the value true or false, that is to say the right-hand of the symbol definition must be one of the (case-insensitive) literals True or False. If the value is true, then the corresponding lines are included, and if the value is false, they are excluded.

The test (*expression* ::= <symbol> 'Defined) is true only if the symbol has been defined in the definition file or by a '-D' switch on the command line. Otherwise, the test is false.

The equality tests are case insensitive, as are all the preprocessor lines.

If the symbol referenced is not defined in the symbol definitions file, then the effect depends on whether or not switch '-u' is specified. If so, then the symbol is treated as if it had the value false and the test fails. If this switch is not specified, then it is an error to reference an undefined symbol. It is also an error to reference a symbol that is defined with a value other than True or False.

The use of the not operator inverts the sense of this logical test. The not operator cannot be combined with the or or and operators, without parentheses. For example, "if not X or Y then" is not allowed, but "if (not X) or Y then" and "if not (X or Y) then" are.

The then keyword is optional as shown

The # must be the first non-blank character on a line, but otherwise the format is free form. Spaces or tabs may appear between the # and the keyword. The keywords and the symbols are case insensitive as in normal Ada code. Comments may be used on a preprocessor line, but other than that, no other tokens may appear on a preprocessor line. Any number of elsif clauses can be present, including none at all. The else is optional, as in Ada.

The # marking the start of a preprocessor line must be the first non-blank character on the line, i.e. it must be preceded only by spaces or horizontal tabs.

Symbol substitution outside of preprocessor lines is obtained by using the sequence

```
$symbol
```

anywhere within a source line, except in a comment or within a string literal. The identifier following the $ must match one of the symbols defined in the symbol definition file, and the result is to substitute the value of the symbol in place of $symbol in the output file.

Note that although the substitution of strings within a string literal is not possible, it is possible to have a symbol whose defined value is a string literal. So instead of setting XYZ to hello and writing:

```
Header : String := "$XYZ";
```

you should set XYZ to "hello" and write:

```
Header : String := $XYZ;
```

and then the substitution will occur as desired.

17 The GNAT Library Browser gnatls

gnatls is a tool that outputs information about compiled units. It gives the relationship between objects, unit names and source files. It can also be used to check the source dependencies of a unit as well as various characteristics.

Note: to invoke gnatls with a project file, use the **gnat** driver (see Section 11.15.2 [The GNAT Driver and Project Files], page 157).

17.1 Running gnatls

The **gnatls** command has the form

```
$ gnatls switches object_or_ali_file
```

The main argument is the list of object or 'ali' files (see Section 2.8 [The Ada Library Information Files], page 21) for which information is requested.

In normal mode, without additional option, gnatls produces a four-column listing. Each line represents information for a specific object. The first column gives the full path of the object, the second column gives the name of the principal unit in this object, the third column gives the status of the source and the fourth column gives the full path of the source representing this unit. Here is a simple example of use:

```
$ gnatls *.o
./demo1.o            demo1            DIF demo1.adb
./demo2.o            demo2             OK demo2.adb
./hello.o            h1                OK hello.adb
./instr-child.o      instr.child      MOK instr-child.adb
./instr.o            instr             OK instr.adb
./tef.o              tef              DIF tef.adb
./text_io_example.o  text_io_example   OK text_io_example.adb
./tgef.o             tgef             DIF tgef.adb
```

The first line can be interpreted as follows: the main unit which is contained in object file 'demo1.o' is demo1, whose main source is in 'demo1.adb'. Furthermore, the version of the source used for the compilation of demo1 has been modified (DIF). Each source file has a status qualifier which can be:

OK (unchanged)

> The version of the source file used for the compilation of the specified unit corresponds exactly to the actual source file.

MOK (slightly modified)

> The version of the source file used for the compilation of the specified unit differs from the actual source file but not enough to require recompilation. If you use gnatmake with the qualifier '-m (minimal recompilation)', a file marked MOK will not be recompiled.

DIF (modified)

> No version of the source found on the path corresponds to the source used to build this object.

??? (file not found)

> No source file was found for this unit.

HID (hidden, unchanged version not first on PATH)
:   The version of the source that corresponds exactly to the source used for compilation has been found on the path but it is hidden by another version of the same source that has been modified.

17.2 Switches for `gnatls`

`gnatls` recognizes the following switches:

:   Display Copyright and version, then exit disregarding all other options.

'`--help`'
:   If '`--version`' was not used, display usage, then exit disregarding all other options.

'`-a`'
:   Consider all units, including those of the predefined Ada library. Especially useful with '`-d`'.

'`-d`'
:   List sources from which specified units depend on.

'`-h`'
:   Output the list of options.

'`-o`'
:   Only output information about object files.

'`-s`'
:   Only output information about source files.

'`-u`'
:   Only output information about compilation units.

'`-files=file`'
:   Take as arguments the files listed in text file *file*. Text file *file* may contain empty lines that are ignored. Each non empty line should contain the name of an existing file. Several such switches may be specified simultaneously.

'`-aOdir`'
'`-aIdir`'
'`-Idir`'
'`-I-`'
'`-nostdinc`'
:   Source path manipulation. Same meaning as the equivalent **gnatmake** flags (see Section 6.2 [Switches for gnatmake], page 94).

'`--RTS=rts-path`'
:   Specifies the default location of the runtime library. Same meaning as the equivalent **gnatmake** flag (see Section 6.2 [Switches for gnatmake], page 94).

'`-v`'
:   Verbose mode. Output the complete source, object and project paths. Do not use the default column layout but instead use long format giving as much as information possible on each requested units, including special characteristics such as:

Preelaborable
:   The unit is preelaborable in the Ada sense.

No_Elab_Code
:   No elaboration code has been produced by the compiler for this unit.

Pure   The unit is pure in the Ada sense.

Elaborate_Body
>The unit contains a pragma Elaborate_Body.

Remote_Types
>The unit contains a pragma Remote_Types.

Shared_Passive
>The unit contains a pragma Shared_Passive.

Predefined
>This unit is part of the predefined environment and cannot be modified by the user.

Remote_Call_Interface
>The unit contains a pragma Remote_Call_Interface.

17.3 Example of `gnatls` Usage

Example of using the verbose switch. Note how the source and object paths are affected by the -I switch.

```
$ gnatls -v -I.. demo1.o

GNATLS 5.03w (20041123-34)
Copyright 1997-2004 Free Software Foundation, Inc.

Source Search Path:
   <Current_Directory>
   ../
   /home/comar/local/adainclude/

Object Search Path:
   <Current_Directory>
   ../
   /home/comar/local/lib/gcc-lib/x86-linux/3.4.3/adalib/

Project Search Path:
   <Current_Directory>
   /home/comar/local/lib/gnat/

./demo1.o
   Unit =>
     Name   => demo1
     Kind   => subprogram body
     Flags  => No_Elab_Code
     Source => demo1.adb    modified
```

The following is an example of use of the dependency list. Note the use of the -s switch which gives a straight list of source files. This can be useful for building specialized scripts.

```
$ gnatls -d demo2.o
./demo2.o   demo2        OK demo2.adb
                         OK gen_list.ads
                         OK gen_list.adb
                         OK instr.ads
                         OK instr-child.ads
```

```
$ gnatls -d -s -a demo1.o
demo1.adb
/home/comar/local/adainclude/ada.ads
/home/comar/local/adainclude/a-finali.ads
/home/comar/local/adainclude/a-filico.ads
/home/comar/local/adainclude/a-stream.ads
/home/comar/local/adainclude/a-tags.ads
gen_list.ads
gen_list.adb
/home/comar/local/adainclude/gnat.ads
/home/comar/local/adainclude/g-io.ads
instr.ads
/home/comar/local/adainclude/system.ads
/home/comar/local/adainclude/s-exctab.ads
/home/comar/local/adainclude/s-finimp.ads
/home/comar/local/adainclude/s-finroo.ads
/home/comar/local/adainclude/s-secsta.ads
/home/comar/local/adainclude/s-stalib.ads
/home/comar/local/adainclude/s-stoele.ads
/home/comar/local/adainclude/s-stratt.ads
/home/comar/local/adainclude/s-tasoli.ads
/home/comar/local/adainclude/s-unstyp.ads
/home/comar/local/adainclude/unchconv.ads
```

18 Cleaning Up Using gnatclean

`gnatclean` is a tool that allows the deletion of files produced by the compiler, binder and linker, including ALI files, object files, tree files, expanded source files, library files, interface copy source files, binder generated files and executable files.

18.1 Running gnatclean

The `gnatclean` command has the form:

```
$ gnatclean switches names
```

names is a list of source file names. Suffixes `.ads` and `adb` may be omitted. If a project file is specified using switch -P, then *names* may be completely omitted.

In normal mode, `gnatclean` delete the files produced by the compiler and, if switch -c is not specified, by the binder and the linker. In informative-only mode, specified by switch -n, the list of files that would have been deleted in normal mode is listed, but no file is actually deleted.

18.2 Switches for gnatclean

`gnatclean` recognizes the following switches:

Display Copyright and version, then exit disregarding all other options.

'--help'   If '--version' was not used, display usage, then exit disregarding all other options.

'-c'   Only attempt to delete the files produced by the compiler, not those produced by the binder or the linker. The files that are not to be deleted are library files, interface copy files, binder generated files and executable files.

'-D dir'   Indicate that ALI and object files should normally be found in directory *dir*.

'-F'   When using project files, if some errors or warnings are detected during parsing and verbose mode is not in effect (no use of switch -v), then error lines start with the full path name of the project file, rather than its simple file name.

'-h'   Output a message explaining the usage of `gnatclean`.

'-n'   Informative-only mode. Do not delete any files. Output the list of the files that would have been deleted if this switch was not specified.

'-Pproject'
            Use project file *project*. Only one such switch can be used. When cleaning a project file, the files produced by the compilation of the immediate sources or inherited sources of the project files are to be deleted. This is not depending on the presence or not of executable names on the command line.

'-q'   Quiet output. If there are no errors, do not output anything, except in verbose mode (switch -v) or in informative-only mode (switch -n).

'-r'   When a project file is specified (using switch -P), clean all imported and extended project files, recursively. If this switch is not specified, only the files related to the main project file are to be deleted. This switch has no effect if no project file is specified.

'-v'   Verbose mode.

'-vP*x*'   Indicates the verbosity of the parsing of GNAT project files. See Section 11.14
                [Switches Related to Project Files], page 152.

'-X*name=value*'
                Indicates that external variable *name* has the value *value*. The Project Manager
                will use this value for occurrences of `external(name)` when parsing the project
                file. See Section 11.14 [Switches Related to Project Files], page 152.

'-aO*dir*'   When searching for ALI and object files, look in directory *dir*.

'-I*dir*'   Equivalent to '-aO*dir*'.

'-I-'   Do not look for ALI or object files in the directory where `gnatclean` was in-
                voked.

19 GNAT and Libraries

This chapter describes how to build and use libraries with GNAT, and also shows how to recompile the GNAT run-time library. You should be familiar with the Project Manager facility (see Chapter 11 [GNAT Project Manager], page 125) before reading this chapter.

19.1 Introduction to Libraries in GNAT

A library is, conceptually, a collection of objects which does not have its own main thread of execution, but rather provides certain services to the applications that use it. A library can be either statically linked with the application, in which case its code is directly included in the application, or, on platforms that support it, be dynamically linked, in which case its code is shared by all applications making use of this library.

GNAT supports both types of libraries. In the static case, the compiled code can be provided in different ways. The simplest approach is to provide directly the set of objects resulting from compilation of the library source files. Alternatively, you can group the objects into an archive using whatever commands are provided by the operating system. For the latter case, the objects are grouped into a shared library.

In the GNAT environment, a library has three types of components:

- Source files.
- 'ALI' files. See Section 2.8 [The Ada Library Information Files], page 21.
- Object files, an archive or a shared library.

A GNAT library may expose all its source files, which is useful for documentation purposes. Alternatively, it may expose only the units needed by an external user to make use of the library. That is to say, the specs reflecting the library services along with all the units needed to compile those specs, which can include generic bodies or any body implementing an inlined routine. In the case of *stand-alone libraries* those exposed units are called *interface units* (see Section 19.3 [Stand-alone Ada Libraries], page 213).

All compilation units comprising an application, including those in a library, need to be elaborated in an order partially defined by Ada's semantics. GNAT computes the elaboration order from the 'ALI' files and this is why they constitute a mandatory part of GNAT libraries. Except in the case of *stand-alone libraries*, where a specific library elaboration routine is produced independently of the application(s) using the library.

19.2 General Ada Libraries

19.2.1 Building a library

The easiest way to build a library is to use the Project Manager, which supports a special type of project called a *Library Project* (see Section 11.12 [Library Projects], page 149).

A project is considered a library project, when two project-level attributes are defined in it: `Library_Name` and `Library_Dir`. In order to control different aspects of library configuration, additional optional project-level attributes can be specified:

`Library_Kind`
        This attribute controls whether the library is to be static or dynamic

`Library_Version`

> This attribute specifies the library version; this value is used during dynamic linking of shared libraries to determine if the currently installed versions of the binaries are compatible.

`Library_Options`
`Library_GCC`

> These attributes specify additional low-level options to be used during library generation, and redefine the actual application used to generate library.

The GNAT Project Manager takes full care of the library maintenance task, including recompilation of the source files for which objects do not exist or are not up to date, assembly of the library archive, and installation of the library (i.e., copying associated source, object and 'ALI' files to the specified location).

Here is a simple library project file:

```
project My_Lib is
    for Source_Dirs use ("src1", "src2");
    for Object_Dir use "obj";
    for Library_Name use "mylib";
    for Library_Dir use "lib";
    for Library_Kind use "dynamic";
end My_lib;
```

and the compilation command to build and install the library:

```
$ gnatmake -Pmy_lib
```

It is not entirely trivial to perform manually all the steps required to produce a library. We recommend that you use the GNAT Project Manager for this task. In special cases where this is not desired, the necessary steps are discussed below.

There are various possibilities for compiling the units that make up the library: for example with a Makefile (see Chapter 20 [Using the GNU make Utility], page 217) or with a conventional script. For simple libraries, it is also possible to create a dummy main program which depends upon all the packages that comprise the interface of the library. This dummy main program can then be given to **gnatmake**, which will ensure that all necessary objects are built.

After this task is accomplished, you should follow the standard procedure of the underlying operating system to produce the static or shared library.

Here is an example of such a dummy program:

```
with My_Lib.Service1;
with My_Lib.Service2;
with My_Lib.Service3;
procedure My_Lib_Dummy is
begin
    null;
end;
```

Here are the generic commands that will build an archive or a shared library.

```
# compiling the library
$ gnatmake -c my_lib_dummy.adb

# we don't need the dummy object itself
$ rm my_lib_dummy.o my_lib_dummy.ali
```

```
# create an archive with the remaining objects
$ ar rc libmy_lib.a *.o
# some systems may require "ranlib" to be run as well

# or create a shared library
$ gcc -shared -o libmy_lib.so *.o
# some systems may require the code to have been compiled with -fPIC

# remove the object files that are now in the library
$ rm *.o

# Make the ALI files read-only so that gnatmake will not try to
# regenerate the objects that are in the library
$ chmod -w *.ali
```

Please note that the library must have a name of the form 'libxxx.a' or 'libxxx.so' (or 'libxxx.dll' on Windows) in order to be accessed by the directive '-lxxx' at link time.

19.2.2 Installing a library

If you use project files, library installation is part of the library build process. Thus no further action is needed in order to make use of the libraries that are built as part of the general application build. A usable version of the library is installed in the directory specified by the `Library_Dir` attribute of the library project file.

You may want to install a library in a context different from where the library is built. This situation arises with third party suppliers, who may want to distribute a library in binary form where the user is not expected to be able to recompile the library. The simplest option in this case is to provide a project file slightly different from the one used to build the library, by using the `externally_built` attribute. For instance, the project file used to build the library in the previous section can be changed into the following one when the library is installed:

```
project My_Lib is
    for Source_Dirs use ("src1", "src2");
    for Library_Name use "mylib";
    for Library_Dir use "lib";
    for Library_Kind use "dynamic";
    for Externally_Built use "true";
end My_lib;
```

This project file assumes that the directories 'src1', 'src2', and 'lib' exist in the directory containing the project file. The `externally_built` attribute makes it clear to the GNAT builder that it should not attempt to recompile any of the units from this library. It allows the library provider to restrict the source set to the minimum necessary for clients to make use of the library as described in the first section of this chapter. It is the responsibility of the library provider to install the necessary sources, ALI files and libraries in the directories mentioned in the project file. For convenience, the user's library project file should be installed in a location that will be searched automatically by the GNAT builder. These are the directories referenced in the `ADA_PROJECT_PATH` environment variable (see Section 11.5 [Importing Projects], page 142), and also the default GNAT library location that can be queried with `gnatls -v` and is usually of the form $gnat_install_root/lib/gnat.

When project files are not an option, it is also possible, but not recommended, to install the library so that the sources needed to use the library are on the Ada source path and the ALI files & libraries be on the Ada Object path (see Section 3.3 [Search Paths and the Run-Time Library (RTL)], page 76. Alternatively, the system administrator can place general-purpose libraries in the default compiler paths, by specifying the libraries' location in the configuration files 'ada_source_path' and 'ada_object_path'. These configuration files must be located in the GNAT installation tree at the same place as the gcc spec file. The location of the gcc spec file can be determined as follows:

```
$ gcc -v
```

The configuration files mentioned above have a simple format: each line must contain one unique directory name. Those names are added to the corresponding path in their order of appearance in the file. The names can be either absolute or relative; in the latter case, they are relative to where theses files are located.

The files 'ada_source_path' and 'ada_object_path' might not be present in a GNAT installation, in which case, GNAT will look for its run-time library in the directories 'adainclude' (for the sources) and 'adalib' (for the objects and 'ALI' files). When the files exist, the compiler does not look in 'adainclude' and 'adalib', and thus the 'ada_source_path' file must contain the location for the GNAT run-time sources (which can simply be 'adainclude'). In the same way, the 'ada_object_path' file must contain the location for the GNAT run-time objects (which can simply be 'adalib').

You can also specify a new default path to the run-time library at compilation time with the switch '--RTS=rts-path'. You can thus choose / change the run-time library you want your program to be compiled with. This switch is recognized by gcc, gnatmake, gnatbind, gnatls, gnatfind and gnatxref.

It is possible to install a library before or after the standard GNAT library, by reordering the lines in the configuration files. In general, a library must be installed before the GNAT library if it redefines any part of it.

19.2.3 Using a library

Once again, the project facility greatly simplifies the use of libraries. In this context, using a library is just a matter of adding a with clause in the user project. For instance, to make use of the library My_Lib shown in examples in earlier sections, you can write:

```
with "my_lib";
project My_Proj is
   ...
end My_Proj;
```

Even if you have a third-party, non-Ada library, you can still use GNAT's Project Manager facility to provide a wrapper for it. For example, the following project, when withed by your main project, will link with the third-party library 'liba.a':

```
project Liba is
   for Externally_Built use "true";
   for Source_Files use ();
   for Library_Dir use "lib";
   for Library_Name use "a";
   for Library_Kind use "static";
end Liba;
```

This is an alternative to the use of pragma Linker_Options. It is especially interesting in the context of systems with several interdependent static libraries where finding a proper linker order is not easy and best be left to the tools having visibility over project dependence information.

In order to use an Ada library manually, you need to make sure that this library is on both your source and object path (see Section 3.3 [Search Paths and the Run-Time Library (RTL)], page 76 and Section 4.4 [Search Paths for gnatbind], page 87). Furthermore, when the objects are grouped in an archive or a shared library, you need to specify the desired library at link time.

For example, you can use the library 'mylib' installed in '/dir/my_lib_src' and '/dir/my_lib_obj' with the following commands:

```
$ gnatmake -aI/dir/my_lib_src -aO/dir/my_lib_obj my_appl \
  -largs -lmy_lib
```

This can be expressed more simply:

```
$ gnatmake my_appl
```

when the following conditions are met:

- '/dir/my_lib_src' has been added by the user to the environment variable ADA_INCLUDE_PATH, or by the administrator to the file 'ada_source_path'

- '/dir/my_lib_obj' has been added by the user to the environment variable ADA_OBJECTS_PATH, or by the administrator to the file 'ada_object_path'

- a pragma Linker_Options has been added to one of the sources. For example:
  ```
  pragma Linker_Options ("-lmy_lib");
  ```

19.3 Stand-alone Ada Libraries

19.3.1 Introduction to Stand-alone Libraries

A Stand-alone Library (abbreviated "SAL") is a library that contains the necessary code to elaborate the Ada units that are included in the library. In contrast with an ordinary library, which consists of all sources, objects and 'ALI' files of the library, a SAL may specify a restricted subset of compilation units to serve as a library interface. In this case, the fully self-sufficient set of files will normally consist of an objects archive, the sources of interface units' specs, and the 'ALI' files of interface units. If an interface spec contains a generic unit or an inlined subprogram, the body's source must also be provided; if the units that must be provided in the source form depend on other units, the source and 'ALI' files of those must also be provided.

The main purpose of a SAL is to minimize the recompilation overhead of client applications when a new version of the library is installed. Specifically, if the interface sources have not changed, client applications do not need to be recompiled. If, furthermore, a SAL is provided in the shared form and its version, controlled by Library_Version attribute, is not changed, then the clients do not need to be relinked.

SALs also allow the library providers to minimize the amount of library source text exposed to the clients. Such "information hiding" might be useful or necessary for various reasons.

Stand-alone libraries are also well suited to be used in an executable whose main routine is not written in Ada.

19.3.2 Building a Stand-alone Library

GNAT's Project facility provides a simple way of building and installing stand-alone libraries; see Section 11.13 [Stand-alone Library Projects], page 151. To be a Stand-alone

Library Project, in addition to the two attributes that make a project a Library Project (`Library_Name` and `Library_Dir`; see Section 11.12 [Library Projects], page 149), the attribute `Library_Interface` must be defined. For example:

```
for Library_Dir use "lib_dir";
for Library_Name use "dummy";
for Library_Interface use ("int1", "int1.child");
```

Attribute `Library_Interface` has a non-empty string list value, each string in the list designating a unit contained in an immediate source of the project file.

When a Stand-alone Library is built, first the binder is invoked to build a package whose name depends on the library name ('`b~dummy.ads/b`' in the example above). This binder-generated package includes initialization and finalization procedures whose names depend on the library name (`dummyinit` and `dummyfinal` in the example above). The object corresponding to this package is included in the library.

You must ensure timely (e.g., prior to any use of interfaces in the SAL) calling of these procedures if a static SAL is built, or if a shared SAL is built with the project-level attribute `Library_Auto_Init` set to `"false"`.

For a Stand-Alone Library, only the 'ALI' files of the Interface Units (those that are listed in attribute `Library_Interface`) are copied to the Library Directory. As a consequence, only the Interface Units may be imported from Ada units outside of the library. If other units are imported, the binding phase will fail.

The attribute `Library_Src_Dir` may be specified for a Stand-Alone Library. `Library_Src_Dir` is a simple attribute that has a single string value. Its value must be the path (absolute or relative to the project directory) of an existing directory. This directory cannot be the object directory or one of the source directories, but it can be the same as the library directory. The sources of the Interface Units of the library that are needed by an Ada client of the library will be copied to the designated directory, called the Interface Copy directory. These sources include the specs of the Interface Units, but they may also include bodies and subunits, when pragmas `Inline` or `Inline_Always` are used, or when there is a generic unit in the spec. Before the sources are copied to the Interface Copy directory, an attempt is made to delete all files in the Interface Copy directory.

Building stand-alone libraries by hand is somewhat tedious, but for those occasions when it is necessary here are the steps that you need to perform:

- Compile all library sources.

- Invoke the binder with the switch '-n' (No Ada main program), with all the 'ALI' files of the interfaces, and with the switch '-L' to give specific names to the `init` and `final` procedures. For example:

  ```
  gnatbind -n int1.ali int2.ali -Lsal1
  ```

- Compile the binder generated file:

  ```
  gcc -c b~int2.adb
  ```

- Link the dynamic library with all the necessary object files, indicating to the linker the names of the `init` (and possibly `final`) procedures for automatic initialization (and finalization). The built library should be placed in a directory different from the object directory.

- Copy the `ALI` files of the interface to the library directory, add in this copy an indication that it is an interface to a SAL (i.e. add a word 'SL' on the line in the 'ALI' file that starts with letter "P") and make the modified copy of the 'ALI' file read-only.

Using SALs is not different from using other libraries (see Section 19.2.3 [Using a library], page 212).

19.3.3 Creating a Stand-alone Library to be used in a non-Ada context

It is easy to adapt the SAL build procedure discussed above for use of a SAL in a non-Ada context.

The only extra step required is to ensure that library interface subprograms are compatible with the main program, by means of `pragma Export` or `pragma Convention`.

Here is an example of simple library interface for use with C main program:

```
package Interface is

   procedure Do_Something;
   pragma Export (C, Do_Something, "do_something");

   procedure Do_Something_Else;
   pragma Export (C, Do_Something_Else, "do_something_else");

end Interface;
```

On the foreign language side, you must provide a "foreign" view of the library interface; remember that it should contain elaboration routines in addition to interface subprograms.

The example below shows the content of `mylib_interface.h` (note that there is no rule for the naming of this file, any name can be used)

```
/* the library elaboration procedure */
extern void mylibinit (void);

/* the library finalization procedure */
extern void mylibfinal (void);

/* the interface exported by the library */
extern void do_something (void);
extern void do_something_else (void);
```

Libraries built as explained above can be used from any program, provided that the elaboration procedures (named `mylibinit` in the previous example) are called before the library services are used. Any number of libraries can be used simultaneously, as long as the elaboration procedure of each library is called.

Below is an example of a C program that uses the `mylib` library.

```
#include "mylib_interface.h"

int
main (void)
{
   /* First, elaborate the library before using it */
   mylibinit ();

   /* Main program, using the library exported entities */
   do_something ();
```

```
      do_something_else ();

      /* Library finalization at the end of the program */
      mylibfinal ();
      return 0;
}
```

Note that invoking any library finalization procedure generated by `gnatbind` shuts down the Ada run-time environment. Consequently, the finalization of all Ada libraries must be performed at the end of the program. No call to these libraries or to the Ada run-time library should be made after the finalization phase.

19.3.4 Restrictions in Stand-alone Libraries

The pragmas listed below should be used with caution inside libraries, as they can create incompatibilities with other Ada libraries:

- pragma `Locking_Policy`
- pragma `Queuing_Policy`
- pragma `Task_Dispatching_Policy`
- pragma `Unreserve_All_Interrupts`

When using a library that contains such pragmas, the user must make sure that all libraries use the same pragmas with the same values. Otherwise, `Program_Error` will be raised during the elaboration of the conflicting libraries. The usage of these pragmas and its consequences for the user should therefore be well documented.

Similarly, the traceback in the exception occurrence mechanism should be enabled or disabled in a consistent manner across all libraries. Otherwise, Program_Error will be raised during the elaboration of the conflicting libraries.

If the `Version` or `Body_Version` attributes are used inside a library, then you need to perform a `gnatbind` step that specifies all 'ALI' files in all libraries, so that version identifiers can be properly computed. In practice these attributes are rarely used, so this is unlikely to be a consideration.

19.4 Rebuilding the GNAT Run-Time Library

It may be useful to recompile the GNAT library in various contexts, the most important one being the use of partition-wide configuration pragmas such as `Normalize_Scalars`. A special Makefile called `Makefile.adalib` is provided to that effect and can be found in the directory containing the GNAT library. The location of this directory depends on the way the GNAT environment has been installed and can be determined by means of the command:

```
$ gnatls -v
```

The last entry in the object search path usually contains the gnat library. This Makefile contains its own documentation and in particular the set of instructions needed to rebuild a new library and to use it.

20 Using the GNU make Utility

This chapter offers some examples of makefiles that solve specific problems. It does not explain how to write a makefile (see the GNU make documentation), nor does it try to replace the **gnatmake** utility (see Chapter 6 [The GNAT Make Program gnatmake], page 93).

All the examples in this section are specific to the GNU version of make. Although make is a standard utility, and the basic language is the same, these examples use some advanced features found only in GNU make.

20.1 Using gnatmake in a Makefile

Complex project organizations can be handled in a very powerful way by using GNU make combined with gnatmake. For instance, here is a Makefile which allows you to build each subsystem of a big project into a separate shared library. Such a makefile allows you to significantly reduce the link time of very big applications while maintaining full coherence at each step of the build process.

The list of dependencies are handled automatically by **gnatmake**. The Makefile is simply used to call gnatmake in each of the appropriate directories.

Note that you should also read the example on how to automatically create the list of directories (see Section 20.2 [Automatically Creating a List of Directories], page 218) which might help you in case your project has a lot of subdirectories.

```
## This Makefile is intended to be used with the following directory
## configuration:
##  - The sources are split into a series of csc (computer software components)
##    Each of these csc is put in its own directory.
##    Their name are referenced by the directory names.
##    They will be compiled into shared library (although this would also work
##    with static libraries
##  - The main program (and possibly other packages that do not belong to any
##    csc is put in the top level directory (where the Makefile is).
##       toplevel_dir __ first_csc  (sources) __ lib (will contain the library)
##                   \_ second_csc (sources) __ lib (will contain the library)
##                   \_ ...
## Although this Makefile is build for shared library, it is easy to modify
## to build partial link objects instead (modify the lines with -shared and
## gnatlink below)
##
## With this makefile, you can change any file in the system or add any new
## file, and everything will be recompiled correctly (only the relevant shared
## objects will be recompiled, and the main program will be re-linked).

# The list of computer software component for your project. This might be
# generated automatically.
CSC_LIST=aa bb cc

# Name of the main program (no extension)
MAIN=main

# If we need to build objects with -fPIC, uncomment the following line
```

```
#NEED_FPIC=-fPIC

# The following variable should give the directory containing libgnat.so
# You can get this directory through 'gnatls -v'. This is usually the last
# directory in the Object_Path.
GLIB=...

# The directories for the libraries
# (This macro expands the list of CSC to the list of shared libraries, you
# could simply use the expanded form:
# LIB_DIR=aa/lib/libaa.so bb/lib/libbb.so cc/lib/libcc.so
LIB_DIR=${foreach dir,${CSC_LIST},${dir}/lib/lib${dir}.so}

${MAIN}: objects ${LIB_DIR}
    gnatbind ${MAIN} ${CSC_LIST:%=-aO%/lib} -shared
    gnatlink ${MAIN} ${CSC_LIST:%=-l%}

objects::
    # recompile the sources
    gnatmake -c -i ${MAIN}.adb ${NEED_FPIC} ${CSC_LIST:%=-I%}

# Note: In a future version of GNAT, the following commands will be simplified
# by a new tool, gnatmlib:
${LIB_DIR}:
    mkdir -p ${dir $@ }
    cd ${dir $@ }; gcc -shared -o ${notdir $@ } ../*.o -L${GLIB} -lgnat
    cd ${dir $@ }; cp -f ../*.ali .

# The dependencies for the modules
# Note that we have to force the expansion of *.o, since in some cases
# make won't be able to do it itself.
aa/lib/libaa.so: ${wildcard aa/*.o}
bb/lib/libbb.so: ${wildcard bb/*.o}
cc/lib/libcc.so: ${wildcard cc/*.o}

# Make sure all of the shared libraries are in the path before starting the
# program
run::
    LD_LIBRARY_PATH=`pwd`/aa/lib:`pwd`/bb/lib:`pwd`/cc/lib ./${MAIN}

clean::
    ${RM} -rf ${CSC_LIST:%=%/lib}
    ${RM} ${CSC_LIST:%=%/*.ali}
    ${RM} ${CSC_LIST:%=%/*.o}
    ${RM} *.o *.ali ${MAIN}
```

20.2 Automatically Creating a List of Directories

In most makefiles, you will have to specify a list of directories, and store it in a variable. For small projects, it is often easier to specify each of them by hand, since you then have full control over what is the proper order for these directories, which ones should be included...

However, in larger projects, which might involve hundreds of subdirectories, it might be more convenient to generate this list automatically.

The example below presents two methods. The first one, although less general, gives you more control over the list. It involves wildcard characters, that are automatically expanded by make. Its shortcoming is that you need to explicitly specify some of the organization of your project, such as for instance the directory tree depth, whether some directories are found in a separate tree,...

The second method is the most general one. It requires an external program, called **find**, which is standard on all Unix systems. All the directories found under a given root directory will be added to the list.

```
# The examples below are based on the following directory hierarchy:
# All the directories can contain any number of files
# ROOT_DIRECTORY -> a -> aa -> aaa
#                     -> ab
#                     -> ac
#                -> b -> ba -> baa
#                     -> bb
#                     -> bc
# This Makefile creates a variable called DIRS, that can be reused any time
# you need this list (see the other examples in this section)

# The root of your project's directory hierarchy
ROOT_DIRECTORY=.

####
# First method: specify explicitly the list of directories
# This allows you to specify any subset of all the directories you need.
####

DIRS := a/aa/ a/ab/ b/ba/

####
# Second method: use wildcards
# Note that the argument(s) to wildcard below should end with a '/'.
# Since wildcards also return file names, we have to filter them out
# to avoid duplicate directory names.
# We thus use make's dir and sort functions.
# It sets DIRs to the following value (note that the directories aaa and baa
# are not given, unless you change the arguments to wildcard).
# DIRS= ./a/a/ ./b/ ./a/aa/ ./a/ab/ ./a/ac/ ./b/ba/ ./b/bb/ ./b/bc/
####

DIRS := ${sort ${dir ${wildcard ${ROOT_DIRECTORY}/*/
            ${ROOT_DIRECTORY}/*/*/}}}

####
# Third method: use an external program
# This command is much faster if run on local disks, avoiding NFS slowdowns.
# This is the most complete command: it sets DIRs to the following value:
# DIRS= ./a ./a/aa ./a/aa/aaa ./a/ab ./a/ac ./b ./b/ba ./b/ba/baa ./b/bb ./b/bc
####

DIRS := ${shell find ${ROOT_DIRECTORY} -type d -print}
```

20.3 Generating the Command Line Switches

Once you have created the list of directories as explained in the previous section (see
Section 20.2 [Automatically Creating a List of Directories], page 218), you can easily generate the command line arguments to pass to gnatmake.

For the sake of completeness, this example assumes that the source path is not the same
as the object path, and that you have two separate lists of directories.

```
# see "Automatically creating a list of directories" to create
# these variables
SOURCE_DIRS=
OBJECT_DIRS=

GNATMAKE_SWITCHES := ${patsubst %,-aI%,${SOURCE_DIRS}}
GNATMAKE_SWITCHES += ${patsubst %,-aO%,${OBJECT_DIRS}}

all:
        gnatmake ${GNATMAKE_SWITCHES} main_unit
```

20.4 Overcoming Command Line Length Limits

One problem that might be encountered on big projects is that many operating systems
limit the length of the command line. It is thus hard to give gnatmake the list of source
and object directories.

This example shows how you can set up environment variables, which will make gnatmake
behave exactly as if the directories had been specified on the command line, but have a much
higher length limit (or even none on most systems).

It assumes that you have created a list of directories in your Makefile, using one of the
methods presented in Section 20.2 [Automatically Creating a List of Directories], page 218.
For the sake of completeness, we assume that the object path (where the ALI files are found)
is different from the sources patch.

Note a small trick in the Makefile below: for efficiency reasons, we create two temporary
variables (SOURCE_LIST and OBJECT_LIST), that are expanded immediately by make.
This way we overcome the standard make behavior which is to expand the variables only
when they are actually used.

On Windows, if you are using the standard Windows command shell, you must replace
colons with semicolons in the assignments to these variables.

```
# In this example, we create both ADA_INCLUDE_PATH and ADA_OBJECT_PATH.
# This is the same thing as putting the -I arguments on the command line.
# (the equivalent of using -aI on the command line would be to define
#   only ADA_INCLUDE_PATH, the equivalent of -aO is ADA_OBJECT_PATH).
# You can of course have different values for these variables.
#
# Note also that we need to keep the previous values of these variables, since
# they might have been set before running 'make' to specify where the GNAT
# library is installed.

# see "Automatically creating a list of directories" to create these
```

```
# variables
SOURCE_DIRS=
OBJECT_DIRS=

empty:=
space:=${empty} ${empty}
SOURCE_LIST := ${subst ${space},:,${SOURCE_DIRS}}
OBJECT_LIST := ${subst ${space},:,${OBJECT_DIRS}}
ADA_INCLUDE_PATH += ${SOURCE_LIST}
ADA_OBJECT_PATH += ${OBJECT_LIST}
export ADA_INCLUDE_PATH
export ADA_OBJECT_PATH

all:
        gnatmake main_unit
```

21 Memory Management Issues

This chapter describes some useful memory pools provided in the GNAT library and in particular the GNAT Debug Pool facility, which can be used to detect incorrect uses of access values (including "dangling references"). It also describes the `gnatmem` tool, which can be used to track down "memory leaks".

21.1 Some Useful Memory Pools

The `System.Pool_Global` package offers the Unbounded_No_Reclaim_Pool storage pool. Allocations use the standard system call `malloc` while deallocations use the standard system call `free`. No reclamation is performed when the pool goes out of scope. For performance reasons, the standard default Ada allocators/deallocators do not use any explicit storage pools but if they did, they could use this storage pool without any change in behavior. That is why this storage pool is used when the user manages to make the default implicit allocator explicit as in this example:

```
type T1 is access Something;
 -- no Storage pool is defined for T2
type T2 is access Something_Else;
for T2'Storage_Pool use T1'Storage_Pool;
-- the above is equivalent to
for T2'Storage_Pool use System.Pool_Global.Global_Pool_Object;
```

The `System.Pool_Local` package offers the Unbounded_Reclaim_Pool storage pool. The allocation strategy is similar to `Pool_Local`'s except that the all storage allocated with this pool is reclaimed when the pool object goes out of scope. This pool provides a explicit mechanism similar to the implicit one provided by several Ada 83 compilers for allocations performed through a local access type and whose purpose was to reclaim memory when exiting the scope of a given local access. As an example, the following program does not leak memory even though it does not perform explicit deallocation:

```
with System.Pool_Local;
procedure Pooloc1 is
   procedure Internal is
      type A is access Integer;
      X : System.Pool_Local.Unbounded_Reclaim_Pool;
      for A'Storage_Pool use X;
      v : A;
   begin
      for I in  1 .. 50 loop
         v := new Integer;
      end loop;
   end Internal;
begin
   for I in  1 .. 100 loop
      Internal;
   end loop;
end Pooloc1;
```

The `System.Pool_Size` package implements the Stack_Bounded_Pool used when `Storage_Size` is specified for an access type. The whole storage for the pool is allocated at once, usually on the stack at the point where the access type is elaborated. It is automatically reclaimed when exiting the scope where the access type is defined. This package is not intended to be used directly by the user and it is implicitly used for each such declaration:

```
type T1 is access Something;
for T1'Storage_Size use 10_000;
```

21.2 The GNAT Debug Pool Facility

The use of unchecked deallocation and unchecked conversion can easily lead to incorrect memory references. The problems generated by such references are usually difficult to tackle because the symptoms can be very remote from the origin of the problem. In such cases, it is very helpful to detect the problem as early as possible. This is the purpose of the Storage Pool provided by `GNAT.Debug_Pools`.

In order to use the GNAT specific debugging pool, the user must associate a debug pool object with each of the access types that may be related to suspected memory problems. See Ada Reference Manual 13.11.

```
type Ptr is access Some_Type;
Pool : GNAT.Debug_Pools.Debug_Pool;
for Ptr'Storage_Pool use Pool;
```

`GNAT.Debug_Pools` is derived from a GNAT-specific kind of pool: the `Checked_Pool`. Such pools, like standard Ada storage pools, allow the user to redefine allocation and deallocation strategies. They also provide a checkpoint for each dereference, through the use of the primitive operation `Dereference` which is implicitly called at each dereference of an access value.

Once an access type has been associated with a debug pool, operations on values of the type may raise four distinct exceptions, which correspond to four potential kinds of memory corruption:

- `GNAT.Debug_Pools.Accessing_Not_Allocated_Storage`
- `GNAT.Debug_Pools.Accessing_Deallocated_Storage`
- `GNAT.Debug_Pools.Freeing_Not_Allocated_Storage`
- `GNAT.Debug_Pools.Freeing_Deallocated_Storage`

For types associated with a Debug_Pool, dynamic allocation is performed using the standard GNAT allocation routine. References to all allocated chunks of memory are kept in an internal dictionary. Several deallocation strategies are provided, whereupon the user can choose to release the memory to the system, keep it allocated for further invalid access checks, or fill it with an easily recognizable pattern for debug sessions. The memory pattern is the old IBM hexadecimal convention: `16#DEADBEEF#`.

See the documentation in the file g-debpoo.ads for more information on the various strategies.

Upon each dereference, a check is made that the access value denotes a properly allocated memory location. Here is a complete example of use of `Debug_Pools`, that includes typical instances of memory corruption:

```
with Gnat.Io; use Gnat.Io;
with Unchecked_Deallocation;
with Unchecked_Conversion;
with GNAT.Debug_Pools;
with System.Storage_Elements;
with Ada.Exceptions; use Ada.Exceptions;
```

```
procedure Debug_Pool_Test is

   type T is access Integer;
   type U is access all T;

   P : GNAT.Debug_Pools.Debug_Pool;
   for T'Storage_Pool use P;

   procedure Free is new Unchecked_Deallocation (Integer, T);
   function UC is new Unchecked_Conversion (U, T);
   A, B : aliased T;

   procedure Info is new GNAT.Debug_Pools.Print_Info(Put_Line);

begin
   Info (P);
   A := new Integer;
   B := new Integer;
   B := A;
   Info (P);
   Free (A);
   begin
      Put_Line (Integer'Image(B.all));
   exception
      when E : others => Put_Line ("raised: " & Exception_Name (E));
   end;
   begin
      Free (B);
   exception
      when E : others => Put_Line ("raised: " & Exception_Name (E));
   end;
   B := UC(A'Access);
   begin
      Put_Line (Integer'Image(B.all));
   exception
      when E : others => Put_Line ("raised: " & Exception_Name (E));
   end;
   begin
      Free (B);
   exception
      when E : others => Put_Line ("raised: " & Exception_Name (E));
   end;
   Info (P);
end Debug_Pool_Test;
```

The debug pool mechanism provides the following precise diagnostics on the execution of this erroneous program:

```
Debug Pool info:
  Total allocated bytes :  0
  Total deallocated bytes :  0
  Current Water Mark:  0
  High Water Mark:  0

Debug Pool info:
  Total allocated bytes :  8
  Total deallocated bytes :  0
  Current Water Mark:  8
  High Water Mark:  8
```

```
raised: GNAT.DEBUG_POOLS.ACCESSING_DEALLOCATED_STORAGE
raised: GNAT.DEBUG_POOLS.FREEING_DEALLOCATED_STORAGE
raised: GNAT.DEBUG_POOLS.ACCESSING_NOT_ALLOCATED_STORAGE
raised: GNAT.DEBUG_POOLS.FREEING_NOT_ALLOCATED_STORAGE
Debug Pool info:
  Total allocated bytes :  8
  Total deallocated bytes :  4
  Current Water Mark:  4
  High Water Mark:  8
```

21.3 The gnatmem Tool

The gnatmem utility monitors dynamic allocation and deallocation activity in a program, and displays information about incorrect deallocations and possible sources of memory leaks. It provides three type of information:

- General information concerning memory management, such as the total number of allocations and deallocations, the amount of allocated memory and the high water mark, i.e. the largest amount of allocated memory in the course of program execution.

- Backtraces for all incorrect deallocations, that is to say deallocations which do not correspond to a valid allocation.

- Information on each allocation that is potentially the origin of a memory leak.

21.3.1 Running gnatmem

gnatmem makes use of the output created by the special version of allocation and deallocation routines that record call information. This allows to obtain accurate dynamic memory usage history at a minimal cost to the execution speed. Note however, that gnatmem is not supported on all platforms (currently, it is supported on AIX, HP-UX, GNU/Linux, Solaris and Windows NT/2000/XP (x86).

The gnatmem command has the form

```
$ gnatmem [switches] user_program
```

The program must have been linked with the instrumented version of the allocation and deallocation routines. This is done by linking with the 'libgmem.a' library. For correct symbolic backtrace information, the user program should be compiled with debugging options (see Section 3.2 [Switches for gcc], page 38). For example to build 'my_program':

```
$ gnatmake -g my_program -largs -lgmem
```

As library 'libgmem.a' contains an alternate body for package System.Memory, 's-memory.adb' should not be compiled and linked when an executable is linked with library 'libgmem.a'. It is then not recommended to use gnatmake with switch '-a'.

When 'my_program' is executed, the file 'gmem.out' is produced. This file contains information about all allocations and deallocations performed by the program. It is produced by the instrumented allocations and deallocations routines and will be used by gnatmem.

In order to produce symbolic backtrace information for allocations and deallocations performed by the GNAT run-time library, you need to use a version of that library that has been compiled with the '-g' switch (see Section 19.4 [Rebuilding the GNAT Run-Time Library], page 216).

Gnatmem must be supplied with the 'gmem.out' file and the executable to examine. If the location of 'gmem.out' file was not explicitly supplied by -i switch, gnatmem will assume that this file can be found in the current directory. For example, after you have executed 'my_program', 'gmem.out' can be analyzed by gnatmem using the command:

```
$ gnatmem my_program
```

This will produce the output with the following format:

```
*************** debut cc

$ gnatmem my_program

Global information
------------------
   Total number of allocations        :  45
   Total number of deallocations      :   6
   Final Water Mark (non freed mem)   :  11.29 Kilobytes
   High Water Mark                    :  11.40 Kilobytes

   .
   .
   .

Allocation Root # 2
-------------------
 Number of non freed allocations    :  11
 Final Water Mark (non freed mem)   :  1.16 Kilobytes
 High Water Mark                    :  1.27 Kilobytes
 Backtrace                          :
   my_program.adb:23 my_program.alloc

   .
   .
   .
```

The first block of output gives general information. In this case, the Ada construct "**new**" was executed 45 times, and only 6 calls to an Unchecked_Deallocation routine occurred.

Subsequent paragraphs display information on all allocation roots. An allocation root is a specific point in the execution of the program that generates some dynamic allocation, such as a "**new**" construct. This root is represented by an execution backtrace (or subprogram call stack). By default the backtrace depth for allocations roots is 1, so that a root corresponds exactly to a source location. The backtrace can be made deeper, to make the root more specific.

21.3.2 Switches for gnatmem

gnatmem recognizes the following switches:

'-q'   Quiet. Gives the minimum output needed to identify the origin of the memory leaks. Omits statistical information.

'*N*'   N is an integer literal (usually between 1 and 10) which controls the depth of the backtraces defining allocation root. The default value for N is 1. The deeper the backtrace, the more precise the localization of the root. Note that the total number of roots can depend on this parameter. This parameter must be specified *before* the name of the executable to be analyzed, to avoid ambiguity.

'-b n'   This switch has the same effect as just depth parameter.

'-i *file*'   Do the gnatmem processing starting from 'file', rather than 'gmem.out' in the current directory.

'-m n'   This switch causes gnatmem to mask the allocation roots that have less than n leaks. The default value is 1. Specifying the value of 0 will allow to examine even the roots that didn't result in leaks.

'-s order' This switch causes gnatmem to sort the allocation roots according to the specified order of sort criteria, each identified by a single letter. The currently supported criteria are **n, h, w** standing respectively for number of unfreed allocations, high watermark, and final watermark corresponding to a specific root. The default order is **nwh**.

21.3.3 Example of gnatmem Usage

The following example shows the use of gnatmem on a simple memory-leaking program. Suppose that we have the following Ada program:

```
with Unchecked_Deallocation;
procedure Test_Gm is

   type T is array (1..1000) of Integer;
   type Ptr is access T;
   procedure Free is new Unchecked_Deallocation (T, Ptr);
   A : Ptr;

   procedure My_Alloc is
   begin
      A := new T;
   end My_Alloc;

   procedure My_DeAlloc is
      B : Ptr := A;
   begin
      Free (B);
   end My_DeAlloc;

begin
   My_Alloc;
   for I in 1 .. 5 loop
      for J in I .. 5 loop
         My_Alloc;
      end loop;
      My_Dealloc;
   end loop;
end;
```

The program needs to be compiled with debugging option and linked with **gmem** library:

```
$ gnatmake -g test_gm -largs -lgmem
```

Then we execute the program as usual:

```
$ test_gm
```

Then gnatmem is invoked simply with

```
$ gnatmem test_gm
```

which produces the following output (result may vary on different platforms):

```
      Global information
      ------------------
         Total number of allocations      :  18
         Total number of deallocations    :   5
         Final Water Mark (non freed mem) :  53.00 Kilobytes
         High Water Mark                  :  56.90 Kilobytes

      Allocation Root # 1
      -------------------
       Number of non freed allocations    :  11
       Final Water Mark (non freed mem)   :  42.97 Kilobytes
       High Water Mark                    :  46.88 Kilobytes
       Backtrace                          :
         test_gm.adb:11 test_gm.my_alloc

      Allocation Root # 2
      -------------------
       Number of non freed allocations    :   1
       Final Water Mark (non freed mem)   :  10.02 Kilobytes
       High Water Mark                    :  10.02 Kilobytes
       Backtrace                          :
         s-secsta.adb:81 system.secondary_stack.ss_init

      Allocation Root # 3
      -------------------
       Number of non freed allocations    :   1
       Final Water Mark (non freed mem)   :  12 Bytes
       High Water Mark                    :  12 Bytes
       Backtrace                          :
         s-secsta.adb:181 system.secondary_stack.ss_init
```

Note that the GNAT run time contains itself a certain number of allocations that have no corresponding deallocation, as shown here for root #2 and root #3. This is a normal behavior when the number of non freed allocations is one, it allocates dynamic data structures that the run time needs for the complete lifetime of the program. Note also that there is only one allocation root in the user program with a single line back trace: test_gm.adb:11 test_gm.my_alloc, whereas a careful analysis of the program shows that 'My_Alloc' is called at 2 different points in the source (line 21 and line 24). If those two allocation roots need to be distinguished, the backtrace depth parameter can be used:

```
      $ gnatmem 3 test_gm
```

which will give the following output:

```
      Global information
      ------------------
         Total number of allocations      :  18
         Total number of deallocations    :   5
         Final Water Mark (non freed mem) :  53.00 Kilobytes
         High Water Mark                  :  56.90 Kilobytes

      Allocation Root # 1
      -------------------
       Number of non freed allocations    :  10
       Final Water Mark (non freed mem)   :  39.06 Kilobytes
       High Water Mark                    :  42.97 Kilobytes
       Backtrace                          :
         test_gm.adb:11 test_gm.my_alloc
         test_gm.adb:24 test_gm
```

```
   b_test_gm.c:52 main

Allocation Root # 2
-------------------
 Number of non freed allocations     :    1
 Final Water Mark (non freed mem)    :   10.02 Kilobytes
 High Water Mark                     :   10.02 Kilobytes
 Backtrace                           :
   s-secsta.adb:81  system.secondary_stack.ss_init
   s-secsta.adb:283 <system__secondary_stack___elabb>
   b_test_gm.c:33   adainit

Allocation Root # 3
-------------------
 Number of non freed allocations     :    1
 Final Water Mark (non freed mem)    :    3.91 Kilobytes
 High Water Mark                     :    3.91 Kilobytes
 Backtrace                           :
   test_gm.adb:11 test_gm.my_alloc
   test_gm.adb:21 test_gm
   b_test_gm.c:52 main

Allocation Root # 4
-------------------
 Number of non freed allocations     :    1
 Final Water Mark (non freed mem)    :   12 Bytes
 High Water Mark                     :   12 Bytes
 Backtrace                           :
   s-secsta.adb:181 system.secondary_stack.ss_init
   s-secsta.adb:283 <system__secondary_stack___elabb>
   b_test_gm.c:33   adainit
```

The allocation root #1 of the first example has been split in 2 roots #1 and #3 thanks to the more precise associated backtrace.

22 Stack Related Facilities

This chapter describes some useful tools associated with stack checking and analysis. In particular, it deals with dynamic and static stack usage measurements.

22.1 Stack Overflow Checking

For most operating systems, `gcc` does not perform stack overflow checking by default. This means that if the main environment task or some other task exceeds the available stack space, then unpredictable behavior will occur. Most native systems offer some level of protection by adding a guard page at the end of each task stack. This mechanism is usually not enough for dealing properly with stack overflow situations because a large local variable could "jump" above the guard page. Furthermore, when the guard page is hit, there may not be any space left on the stack for executing the exception propagation code. Enabling stack checking avoids such situations.

To activate stack checking, compile all units with the gcc option '`-fstack-check`'. For example:

```
gcc -c -fstack-check package1.adb
```

Units compiled with this option will generate extra instructions to check that any use of the stack (for procedure calls or for declaring local variables in declare blocks) does not exceed the available stack space. If the space is exceeded, then a `Storage_Error` exception is raised.

For declared tasks, the stack size is controlled by the size given in an applicable `Storage_Size` pragma or by the value specified at bind time with '`-d`' (see Section 4.2 [Switches for gnatbind], page 80) or is set to the default size as defined in the GNAT runtime otherwise.

For the environment task, the stack size depends on system defaults and is unknown to the compiler. Stack checking may still work correctly if a fixed size stack is allocated, but this cannot be guaranteed. To ensure that a clean exception is signalled for stack overflow, set the environment variable `GNAT_STACK_LIMIT` to indicate the maximum stack area that can be used, as in:

```
SET GNAT_STACK_LIMIT 1600
```

The limit is given in kilobytes, so the above declaration would set the stack limit of the environment task to 1.6 megabytes. Note that the only purpose of this usage is to limit the amount of stack used by the environment task. If it is necessary to increase the amount of stack for the environment task, then this is an operating systems issue, and must be addressed with the appropriate operating systems commands.

22.2 Static Stack Usage Analysis

A unit compiled with '`-fstack-usage`' will generate an extra file that specifies the maximum amount of stack used, on a per-function basis. The file has the same basename as the target object file with a '`.su`' extension. Each line of this file is made up of three fields:

- The name of the function.
- A number of bytes.
- One or more qualifiers: `static`, `dynamic`, `bounded`.

The second field corresponds to the size of the known part of the function frame.

The qualifier `static` means that the function frame size is purely static. It usually means that all local variables have a static size. In this case, the second field is a reliable measure of the function stack utilization.

The qualifier `dynamic` means that the function frame size is not static. It happens mainly when some local variables have a dynamic size. When this qualifier appears alone, the second field is not a reliable measure of the function stack analysis. When it is qualified with `bounded`, it means that the second field is a reliable maximum of the function stack utilization.

22.3 Dynamic Stack Usage Analysis

It is possible to measure the maximum amount of stack used by a task, by adding a switch to gnatbind, as:

```
$ gnatbind -u0 file
```

With this option, at each task termination, its stack usage is output on 'stderr'. It is not always convenient to output the stack usage when the program is still running. Hence, it is possible to delay this output until program termination. for a given number of tasks specified as the argument of the -u option. For instance:

```
$ gnatbind -u100 file
```

will buffer the stack usage information of the first 100 tasks to terminate and output this info at program termination. Results are displayed in four columns:

Index | Task Name | Stack Size | Actual Use [min - max]

where:

Index   is a number associated with each task.

Task Name
              is the name of the task analyzed.

Stack Size is the maximum size for the stack.

Actual Use
              is the measure done by the stack analyzer. In order to prevent overflow, the stack is not entirely analyzed, and it's not possible to know exactly how much has actually been used. The real amount of stack used is between the min and max values.

The environment task stack, e.g. the stack that contains the main unit, is only processed when the environment variable GNAT_STACK_LIMIT is set.

23 Verifying Properties Using gnatcheck

The gnatcheck tool is an ASIS-based utility that checks properties of Ada source files according to a given set of semantic rules.

In order to check compliance with a given rule, gnatcheck has to semantically analyze the Ada sources. Therefore, checks can only be performed on legal Ada units. Moreover, when a unit depends semantically upon units located outside the current directory, the source search path has to be provided when calling gnatcheck, either through a specified project file or through gnatcheck switches as described below.

A number of rules are predefined in gnatcheck and are described later in this chapter. You can also add new rules, by modifying the gnatcheck code and rebuilding the tool. In order to add a simple rule making some local checks, a small amount of straightforward ASIS-based programming is usually needed.

Project support for gnatcheck is provided by the GNAT driver (see Section 11.15.2 [The GNAT Driver and Project Files], page 157).

Invoking gnatcheck on the command line has the form:

```
$ gnatcheck [switches]  {filename}
      [-files={arg_list_filename}]
      [-cargs gcc_switches] [-rules rule_options]
```

where

- *switches* specify the general tool options

- Each *filename* is the name (including the extension) of a source file to process. "Wild-cards" are allowed, and the file name may contain path information.

- Each *arg_list_filename* is the name (including the extension) of a text file containing the names of the source files to process, separated by spaces or line breaks.

- *gcc_switches* is a list of switches for gcc. They will be passed on to all compiler invocations made by gnatcheck to generate the ASIS trees. Here you can provide '-I' switches to form the source search path, and use the '-gnatec' switch to set the configuration file.

- *rule_options* is a list of options for controlling a set of rules to be checked by gnatcheck (see Section 23.3 [gnatcheck Rule Options], page 234).

Either a *filename* or an *arg_list_filename* must be supplied.

23.1 Format of the Report File

The gnatcheck tool outputs on 'stdout' all messages concerning rule violations. It also creates, in the current directory, a text file named 'gnatcheck.out' that contains the complete report of the last gnatcheck run. This report contains:

- a list of the Ada source files being checked,

- a list of enabled and disabled rules,

- a list of the diagnostic messages, ordered in three different ways and collected in three separate sections. Section 1 contains the raw list of diagnostic messages. It corresponds to the output going to 'stdout'. Section 2 contains messages ordered by rules. Section 3 contains messages ordered by source files.

23.2 General `gnatcheck` Switches

The following switches control the general **gnatcheck** behavior

'`-a`'   Process all units including those with read-only ALI files such as those from GNAT Run-Time library.

'`-dd`'   Progress indicator mode (for use in GPS)

'`-h`'   List the predefined and user-defined rules. For more details see Section 23.6 [Predefined Rules], page 236.

'`-l`'   Use full source locations references in the report file. For a construct from a generic instantiation a full source location is a chain from the location of this construct in the generic unit to the place where this unit is instantiated.

'`-q`'   Quiet mode. All the diagnoses about rule violations are placed in the **gnatcheck** report file only, without duplicating in '`stdout`'.

'`-s`'   Short format of the report file (no version information, no list of applied rules, no list of checked sources is included)

'`-s1`'   Include the compiler-style section in the report file

'`-s2`'   Include the section containing diagnoses ordered by rules in the report file

'`-s3`'   Include the section containing diagnoses ordered by files and then by rules in the report file

'`-v`'   Verbose mode; **gnatcheck** generates version information and then a trace of sources being processed.

Note that if any of the options '`-s1`', '`-s2`' or '`-s3`' is specified, then the **gnatcheck** report file will only contain sections explicitly denoted by these options.

23.3 `gnatcheck` Rule Options

The following options control the processing performed by **gnatcheck**.

'`+ALL`'   Turn all the rule checks ON.

'`-ALL`'   Turn all the rule checks OFF.

'`+Rrule_id[:param]`'
              Turn on the check for a specified rule with the specified parameter, if any. *rule_id* must be the identifier of one of the currently implemented rules (use '`-h`' for the list of implemented rules). Rule identifiers are not case-sensitive. The *param* item must be a string representing a valid parameter(s) for the specified rule. If it contains any space characters then this string must be enclosed in quotation marks.

'`-Rrule_id[:param]`'
              Turn off the check for a specified rule with the specified parameter, if any.

'`-from=rule_option_filename`'
              Read the rule options from the text file *rule_option_filename*, referred as "rule file" below.

The default behavior is that all the rule checks are enabled, except for the checks performed by the compiler.

A rule file is a text file containing a set of rule options. The file may contain empty lines and Ada-style comments (comment lines and end-of-line comments). The rule file has free format; that is, you do not have to start a new rule option on a new line.

A rule file may contain other '`-from=rule_option_filename`' options, each such option being replaced with the content of the corresponding rule file during the rule files processing. In case a cycle is detected (that is, *rule_file_1* reads rule options from *rule_file_2*, and *rule_file_2* reads (directly or indirectly) rule options from *rule_file_1*), the processing of rule files is interrupted and a part of their content is ignored.

23.4 Adding the Results of Compiler Checks to `gnatcheck` Output

The `gnatcheck` tool can include in the generated diagnostic messages and in the report file the results of the checks performed by the compiler. Though disabled by default, this effect may be obtained by using '`+R`' with the following rule identifiers and parameters:

'`Restrictions`'

>> To record restrictions violations (that are performed by the compiler if the pragma `Restrictions` or `Restriction_Warnings` are given), use the rule named `Restrictions` with the same parameters as pragma `Restrictions` or `Restriction_Warnings`.

'`Style_Checks`'

>> To record compiler style checks, use the rule named `Style_Checks`. A parameter of this rule can be either `All_Checks`, which enables all the style checks, or a string that has exactly the same structure and semantics as the `string_LITERAL` parameter of GNAT pragma `Style_Checks` (for further information about this pragma, please refer to the *GNAT Reference Manual*).

'`Warnings`'

>> To record compiler warnings (see Section 3.2.2 [Warning Message Control], page 46), use the rule named `Warnings` with a parameter that is a valid *static_string_expression* argument of GNAT pragma `Warnings` (for further information about this pragma, please refer to the *GNAT Reference Manual*).

23.5 Project-Wide Checks

In order to perform checks on all units of a given project, you can use the GNAT driver along with the '`-P`' option:

```
gnat check -Pproj -rules -from=my_rules
```

If the project `proj` depends upon other projects, you can perform checks on the project closure using the '`-U`' option:

```
gnat check -Pproj -U -rules -from=my_rules
```

Finally, if not all the units are relevant to a particular main program in the project closure, you can perform checks for the set of units needed to create a given main program (unit closure) using the '`-U`' option followed by the name of the main unit:

```
gnat check -Pproj -U main -rules -from=my_rules
```

23.6 Predefined Rules

The following subsections document the rules implemented in `gnatcheck`. The subsection title is the same as the rule identifier, which may be used as a parameter of the '+R' or '-R' options.

23.6.1 Abstract_Type_Declarations

Flag all declarations of abstract types. For an abstract private type, both the private and full type declarations are flagged.

This rule has no parameters.

23.6.2 Anonymous_Arrays

Flag all anonymous array type definitions (by Ada semantics these can only occur in object declarations).

This rule has no parameters.

23.6.3 Anonymous_Subtypes

Flag all uses of anonymous subtypes. A use of an anonymous subtype is any instance of a subtype indication with a constraint, other than one that occurs immediately within a subtype declaration. Any use of a range other than as a constraint used immediately within a subtype declaration is considered as an anonymous subtype.

An effect of this rule is that `for` loops such as the following are flagged (since `1..N` is formally a "range"):

```
for I in 1 .. N loop
   ...
end loop;
```

Declaring an explicit subtype solves the problem:

```
subtype S is Integer range 1..N;
...
for I in S loop
   ...
end loop;
```

This rule has no parameters.

23.6.4 Blocks

Flag each block statement.

This rule has no parameters.

23.6.5 Boolean_Relational_Operators

Flag each call to a predefined relational operator ("<", ">", "<=", ">=", "=" and "/=") for the predefined Boolean type. (This rule is useful in enforcing the SPARK language restrictions.)

Calls to predefined relational operators of any type derived from `Standard.Boolean` are not detected. Calls to user-defined functions with these designators, and uses of operators that are renamings of the predefined relational operators for `Standard.Boolean`, are likewise not detected.

This rule has no parameters.

23.6.6 Controlled_Type_Declarations

Flag all declarations of controlled types. A declaration of a private type is flagged if its full declaration declares a controlled type. A declaration of a derived type is flagged if its ancestor type is controlled. Subtype declarations are not checked. A declaration of a type that itself is not a descendant of a type declared in Ada.Finalization but has a controlled component is not checked.

This rule has no parameters.

23.6.7 Declarations_In_Blocks

Flag all block statements containing local declarations. A declare block with an empty *declarative_part* or with a *declarative part* containing only pragmas and/or use clauses is not flagged.

This rule has no parameters.

23.6.8 Default_Parameters

Flag all default expressions for subprogram parameters. Parameter declarations of formal and generic subprograms are also checked.

This rule has no parameters.

23.6.9 Discriminated_Records

Flag all declarations of record types with discriminants. Only the declarations of record and record extension types are checked. Incomplete, formal, private, derived and private extension type declarations are not checked. Task and protected type declarations also are not checked.

This rule has no parameters.

23.6.10 Enumeration_Ranges_In_CASE_Statements

Flag each use of a range of enumeration literals as a choice in a case statement. All forms for specifying a range (explicit ranges such as A .. B, subtype marks and 'Range attributes) are flagged. An enumeration range is flagged even if contains exactly one enumeration value or no values at all. A type derived from an enumeration type is considered as an enumeration type.

This rule helps prevent maintenance problems arising from adding an enumeration value to a type and having it implicitly handled by an existing case statement with an enumeration range that includes the new literal.

This rule has no parameters.

23.6.11 Exceptions_As_Control_Flow

Flag each place where an exception is explicitly raised and handled in the same subprogram body. A raise statement in an exception handler, package body, task body or entry body is not flagged.

The rule has no parameters.

23.6.12 EXIT_Statements_With_No_Loop_Name

Flag each `exit` statement that does not specify the name of the loop being exited.

The rule has no parameters.

23.6.13 Expanded_Loop_Exit_Names

Flag all expanded loop names in `exit` statements.

This rule has no parameters.

23.6.14 Explicit_Full_Discrete_Ranges

Flag each discrete range that has the form `A'First .. A'Last`.

This rule has no parameters.

23.6.15 Float_Equality_Checks

Flag all calls to the predefined equality operations for floating-point types. Both "=" and "/=" operations are checked. User-defined equality operations are not flagged, nor are "=" and "/=" operations for fixed-point types.

This rule has no parameters.

23.6.16 Forbidden_Pragmas

Flag each use of the specified pragmas. The pragmas to be detected are named in the rule's parameters.

This rule has the following parameters:

- For the '+R' option

Pragma_Name
    Adds the specified pragma to the set of pragmas to be checked and sets the checks for all the specified pragmas ON. *Pragma_Name* is treated as a name of a pragma. If it does not correspond to any pragma name defined in the Ada standard or to the name of a GNAT-specific pragma defined in the GNAT Reference Manual, it is treated as the name of unknown pragma.

GNAT
    All the GNAT-specific pragmas are detected; this sets the checks for all the specified pragmas ON.

ALL
    All pragmas are detected; this sets the rule ON.

- For the '-R' option

Pragma_Name
    Removes the specified pragma from the set of pragmas to be checked without affecting checks for other pragmas. *Pragma_Name* is treated as a name of a pragma. If it does not correspond to any pragma defined in the Ada standard or to any name defined in the GNAT Reference Manual, this option is treated as turning OFF detection of all unknown pragmas.

GNAT
    Turn OFF detection of all GNAT-specific pragmas

ALL
    Clear the list of the pragmas to be detected and turn the rule OFF.

Parameters are not case sensitive. If *Pragma_Name* does not have the syntax of an Ada identifier and therefore can not be considered as a pragma name, a diagnostic message is generated and the corresponding parameter is ignored.

When more then one parameter is given in the same rule option, the parameters must be separated by a comma.

If more then one option for this rule is specified for the `gnatcheck` call, a new option overrides the previous one(s).

The '+R' option with no parameters turns the rule ON with the set of pragmas to be detected defined by the previous rule options. (By default this set is empty, so if the only option specified for the rule is '+RForbidden_Pragmas' (with no parameter), then the rule is enabled, but it does not detect anything). The '-R' option with no parameter turns the rule OFF, but it does not affect the set of pragmas to be detected.

23.6.17 Function_Style_Procedures

Flag each procedure that can be rewritten as a function. A procedure can be converted into a function if it has exactly one parameter of mode `out` and no parameters of mode `in out`. Procedure declarations, formal procedure declarations, and generic procedure declarations are always checked. Procedure bodies and body stubs are flagged only if they do not have corresponding separate declarations. Procedure renamings and procedure instantiations are not flagged.

If a procedure can be rewritten as a function, but its `out` parameter is of a limited type, it is not flagged.

Protected procedures are not flagged. Null procedures also are not flagged.

This rule has no parameters.

23.6.18 Generics_In_Subprograms

Flag each declaration of a generic unit in a subprogram. Generic declarations in the bodies of generic subprograms are also flagged. A generic unit nested in another generic unit is not flagged. If a generic unit is declared in a local package that is declared in a subprogram body, the generic unit is flagged.

This rule has no parameters.

23.6.19 GOTO_Statements

Flag each occurrence of a `goto` statement.

This rule has no parameters.

23.6.20 Implicit_IN_Mode_Parameters

Flag each occurrence of a formal parameter with an implicit `in` mode. Note that `access` parameters, although they technically behave like `in` parameters, are not flagged.

This rule has no parameters.

23.6.21 Implicit_SMALL_For_Fixed_Point_Types

Flag each fixed point type declaration that lacks an explicit representation clause to define its `'Small` value. Since `'Small` can be defined only for ordinary fixed point types, decimal fixed point type declarations are not checked.

This rule has no parameters.

23.6.22 Improperly_Located_Instantiations

Flag all generic instantiations in library-level package specifications (including library generic packages) and in all subprogram bodies.

Instantiations in task and entry bodies are not flagged. Instantiations in the bodies of protected subprograms are flagged.

This rule has no parameters.

23.6.23 Improper_Returns

Flag each explicit **return** statement in procedures, and multiple **return** statements in functions. Diagnostic messages are generated for all **return** statements in a procedure (thus each procedure must be written so that it returns implicitly at the end of its statement part), and for all **return** statements in a function after the first one. This rule supports the stylistic convention that each subprogram should have no more than one point of normal return.

This rule has no parameters.

23.6.24 Library_Level_Subprograms

Flag all library-level subprograms (including generic subprogram instantiations).

This rule has no parameters.

23.6.25 Local_Packages

Flag all local packages declared in package and generic package specifications. Local packages in bodies are not flagged.

This rule has no parameters.

23.6.26 Misnamed_Identifiers

Flag the declaration of each identifier that does not have a suffix corresponding to the kind of entity being declared. The following declarations are checked:

- type declarations
- constant declarations (but not number declarations)
- package renaming declarations (but not generic package renaming declarations)

This rule may have parameters. When used without parameters, the rule enforces the following checks:

- type-defining names end with _T, unless the type is an access type, in which case the suffix must be _A
- constant names end with _C
- names defining package renamings end with _R

For a private or incomplete type declaration the following checks are made for the defining name suffix:

- For an incomplete type declaration: if the corresponding full type declaration is available, the defining identifier from the full type declaration is checked, but the defining identifier from the incomplete type declaration is not; otherwise the defining identifier from the incomplete type declaration is checked against the suffix specified for type declarations.

- For a private type declaration (including private extensions), the defining identifier from the private type declaration is checked against the type suffix (even if the corresponding full declaration is an access type declaration), and the defining identifier from the corresponding full type declaration is not checked.

For a deferred constant, the defining name in the corresponding full constant declaration is not checked.

Defining names of formal types are not checked.

The rule may have the following parameters:

- For the '+R' option:

  Default   Sets the default listed above for all the names to be checked.

  `Type_Suffix=string`
  Specifies the suffix for a type name.

  `Access_Suffix=string`
  Specifies the suffix for an access type name. If this parameter is set, it overrides for access types the suffix set by the `Type_Suffix` parameter.

  `Constant_Suffix=string`
  Specifies the suffix for a constant name.

  `Renaming_Suffix=string`
  Specifies the suffix for a package renaming name.

- For the '-R' option:

  `All_Suffixes`
  Remove all the suffixes specified for the identifier suffix checks, whether by default or as specified by other rule parameters. All the checks for this rule are disabled as a result.

  `Type_Suffix`
  Removes the suffix specified for types. This disables checks for types but does not disable any other checks for this rule (including the check for access type names if `Access_Suffix` is set).

  `Access_Suffix`
  Removes the suffix specified for access types. This disables checks for access type names but does not disable any other checks for this rule. If `Type_Suffix` is set, access type names are checked as ordinary type names.

  `Constant_Suffix`
  Removes the suffix specified for constants. This disables checks for constant names but does not disable any other checks for this rule.

`Renaming_Suffix`
> Removes the suffix specified for package renamings. This disables checks for package renamings but does not disable any other checks for this rule.

If more than one parameter is used, parameters must be separated by commas.

If more than one option is specified for the `gnatcheck` invocation, a new option overrides the previous one(s).

The '`+RMisnamed_Identifiers`' option (with no parameter) enables checks for all the name suffixes specified by previous options used for this rule.

The '`-RMisnamed_Identifiers`' option (with no parameter) disables all the checks but keeps all the suffixes specified by previous options used for this rule.

The *string* value must be a valid suffix for an Ada identifier (after trimming all the leading and trailing space characters, if any). Parameters are not case sensitive, except the *string* part.

If any error is detected in a rule parameter, the parameter is ignored. In such a case the options that are set for the rule are not specified.

23.6.27 `Multiple_Entries_In_Protected_Definitions`

Flag each protected definition (i.e., each protected object/type declaration) that defines more than one entry. Diagnostic messages are generated for all the entry declarations except the first one. An entry family is counted as one entry. Entries from the private part of the protected definition are also checked.

This rule has no parameters.

23.6.28 `Name_Clashes`

Check that certain names are not used as defining identifiers. To activate this rule, you need to supply a reference to the dictionary file(s) as a rule parameter(s) (more then one dictionary file can be specified). If no dictionary file is set, this rule will not cause anything to be flagged. Only defining occurrences, not references, are checked. The check is not case-sensitive.

This rule is enabled by default, but without setting any corresponding dictionary file(s); thus the default effect is to do no checks.

A dictionary file is a plain text file. The maximum line length for this file is 1024 characters. If the line is longer then this limit, extra characters are ignored.

Each line can be either an empty line, a comment line, or a line containing a list of identifiers separated by space or HT characters. A comment is an Ada-style comment (from `--` to end-of-line). Identifiers must follow the Ada syntax for identifiers. A line containing one or more identifiers may end with a comment.

23.6.29 `Non_Qualified_Aggregates`

Flag each non-qualified aggregate. A non-qualified aggregate is an aggregate that is not the expression of a qualified expression. A string literal is not considered an aggregate, but an array aggregate of a string type is considered as a normal aggregate. Aggregates of anonymous array types are not flagged.

This rule has no parameters.

23.6.30 Non_Short_Circuit_Operators

Flag all calls to predefined **and** and **or** operators for any boolean type. Calls to user-defined **and** and **or** and to operators defined by renaming declarations are not flagged. Calls to predefined **and** and **or** operators for modular types or boolean array types are not flagged.

This rule has no parameters.

23.6.31 Non_SPARK_Attributes

The SPARK language defines the following subset of Ada 95 attribute designators as those that can be used in SPARK programs. The use of any other attribute is flagged.

- 'Adjacent
- 'Aft
- 'Base
- 'Ceiling
- 'Component_Size
- 'Compose
- 'Copy_Sign
- 'Delta
- 'Denorm
- 'Digits
- 'Exponent
- 'First
- 'Floor
- 'Fore
- 'Fraction
- 'Last
- 'Leading_Part
- 'Length
- 'Machine
- 'Machine_Emax
- 'Machine_Emin
- 'Machine_Mantissa
- 'Machine_Overflows
- 'Machine_Radix
- 'Machine_Rounds
- 'Max
- 'Min
- 'Model
- 'Model_Emin
- 'Model_Epsilon

- 'Model_Mantissa
- 'Model_Small
- 'Modulus
- 'Pos
- 'Pred
- 'Range
- 'Remainder
- 'Rounding
- 'Safe_First
- 'Safe_Last
- 'Scaling
- 'Signed_Zeros
- 'Size
- 'Small
- 'Succ
- 'Truncation
- 'Unbiased_Rounding
- 'Val
- 'Valid

This rule has no parameters.

23.6.32 Non_Tagged_Derived_Types

Flag all derived type declarations that do not have a record extension part.

This rule has no parameters.

23.6.33 Non_Visible_Exceptions

Flag constructs leading to the possibility of propagating an exception out of the scope in which the exception is declared. Two cases are detected:

- An exception declaration in a subprogram body, task body or block statement is flagged if the body or statement does not contain a handler for that exception or a handler with an `others` choice.
- A `raise` statement in an exception handler of a subprogram body, task body or block statement is flagged if it (re)raises a locally declared exception. This may occur under the following circumstances:
    - it explicitly raises a locally declared exception, or
    - it does not specify an exception name (i.e., it is simply `raise;`) and the enclosing handler contains a locally declared exception in its exception choices.

Renamings of local exceptions are not flagged.

This rule has no parameters.

23.6.34 Numeric_Literals

Flag each use of a numeric literal in an index expression, and in any circumstance except for the following:

- a literal occurring in the initialization expression for a constant declaration or a named number declaration, or
- an integer literal that is less than or equal to a value specified by the 'N' rule parameter.

This rule may have the following parameters for the '+R' option:

N   *N* is an integer literal used as the maximal value that is not flagged (i.e., integer literals not exceeding this value are allowed)

ALL   All integer literals are flagged

If no parameters are set, the maximum unflagged value is 1.

The last specified check limit (or the fact that there is no limit at all) is used when multiple '+R' options appear.

The '-R' option for this rule has no parameters. It disables the rule but retains the last specified maximum unflagged value. If the '+R' option subsequently appears, this value is used as the threshold for the check.

23.6.35 OTHERS_In_Aggregates

Flag each use of an others choice in extension aggregates. In record and array aggregates, an others choice is flagged unless it is used to refer to all components, or to all but one component.

If, in case of a named array aggregate, there are two associations, one with an others choice and another with a discrete range, the others choice is flagged even if the discrete range specifies exactly one component; for example, (1..1 => 0, others => 1).

This rule has no parameters.

23.6.36 OTHERS_In_CASE_Statements

Flag any use of an others choice in a case statement.

This rule has no parameters.

23.6.37 OTHERS_In_Exception_Handlers

Flag any use of an others choice in an exception handler.

This rule has no parameters.

23.6.38 Outer_Loop_Exits

Flag each exit statement containing a loop name that is not the name of the immediately enclosing loop statement.

This rule has no parameters.

23.6.39 Overloaded_Operators

Flag each function declaration that overloads an operator symbol. A function body is checked only if the body does not have a separate spec. Formal functions are also checked. For a renaming declaration, only renaming-as-declaration is checked

This rule has no parameters.

23.6.40 Overly_Nested_Control_Structures

Flag each control structure whose nesting level exceeds the value provided in the rule parameter.

The control structures checked are the following:

- `if` statement
- `case` statement
- `loop` statement
- Selective accept statement
- Timed entry call statement
- Conditional entry call
- Asynchronous select statement

The rule may have the following parameter for the '+R' option:

N   Positive integer specifying the maximal control structure nesting level that is not flagged

If the parameter for the '+R' option is not a positive integer, the parameter is ignored and the rule is turned ON with the most recently specified maximal non-flagged nesting level.

If more then one option is specified for the gnatcheck call, the later option and new parameter override the previous one(s).

A '+R' option with no parameter turns the rule ON using the maximal non-flagged nesting level specified by the most recent '+R' option with a parameter, or the value 4 if there is no such previous '+R' option.

23.6.41 Parameters_Out_Of_Order

Flag each subprogram and entry declaration whose formal parameters are not ordered according to the following scheme:

- `in` and `access` parameters first, then `in out` parameters, and then `out` parameters;
- for `in` mode, parameters with default initialization expressions occur last

Only the first violation of the described order is flagged.

The following constructs are checked:

- subprogram declarations (including null procedures);
- generic subprogram declarations;
- formal subprogram declarations;
- entry declarations;
- subprogram bodies and subprogram body stubs that do not have separate specifications

Subprogram renamings are not checked.

This rule has no parameters.

23.6.42 Positional_Actuals_For_Defaulted_Generic_Parameters

Flag each generic actual parameter corresponding to a generic formal parameter with a default initialization, if positional notation is used.

This rule has no parameters.

23.6.43 Positional_Actuals_For_Defaulted_Parameters

Flag each actual parameter to a subprogram or entry call where the corresponding formal parameter has a default expression, if positional notation is used.

This rule has no parameters.

23.6.44 Positional_Components

Flag each array, record and extension aggregate that includes positional notation.

This rule has no parameters.

23.6.45 Positional_Generic_Parameters

Flag each instantiation using positional parameter notation.

This rule has no parameters.

23.6.46 Positional_Parameters

Flag each subprogram or entry call using positional parameter notation, except for the following:

- Invocations of prefix or infix operators are not flagged
- If the called subprogram or entry has only one formal parameter, the call is not flagged;
- If a subprogram call uses the *Object.Operation* notation, then
  - the first parameter (that is, *Object*) is not flagged;
  - if the called subprogram has only two parameters, the second parameter of the call is not flagged;

This rule has no parameters.

23.6.47 Predefined_Numeric_Types

Flag each explicit use of the name of any numeric type or subtype defined in package Standard.

The rationale for this rule is to detect when the program may depend on platform-specific characteristics of the implementation of the predefined numeric types. Note that this rule is over-pessimistic; for example, a program that uses String indexing likely needs a variable of type Integer. Another example is the flagging of predefined numeric types with explicit constraints:

```
subtype My_Integer is Integer range Left .. Right;
Vy_Var : My_Integer;
```

This rule detects only numeric types and subtypes defined in Standard. The use of numeric types and subtypes defined in other predefined packages (such as System.Any_Priority or Ada.Text_IO.Count) is not flagged

This rule has no parameters.

23.6.48 Raising_External_Exceptions

Flag any **raise** statement, in a program unit declared in a library package or in a generic library package, for an exception that is neither a predefined exception nor an exception that is also declared (or renamed) in the visible part of the package.

This rule has no parameters.

23.6.49 Raising_Predefined_Exceptions

Flag each **raise** statement that raises a predefined exception (i.e., one of the exceptions `Constraint_Error`, `Numeric_Error`, `Program_Error`, `Storage_Error`, or `Tasking_Error`).

This rule has no parameters.

23.6.50 Slices

Flag all uses of array slicing

This rule has no parameters.

23.6.51 Unassigned_OUT_Parameters

Flags procedures' **out** parameters that are not assigned, and identifies the contexts in which the assignments are missing.

An **out** parameter is flagged in the statements in the procedure body's handled sequence of statements (before the procedure body's **exception** part, if any) if this sequence of statements contains no assignments to the parameter.

An **out** parameter is flagged in an exception handler in the exception part of the procedure body's handled sequence of statements if the handler contains no assignment to the parameter.

Bodies of generic procedures are also considered.

The following are treated as assignments to an **out** parameter:

- an assignment statement, with the parameter or some component as the target;
- passing the parameter (or one of its components) as an **out** or **in out** parameter.

This rule does not have any parameters.

23.6.52 Uncommented_BEGIN_In_Package_Bodies

Flags each package body with declarations and a statement part that does not include a trailing comment on the line containing the **begin** keyword; this trailing comment needs to specify the package name and nothing else. The **begin** is not flagged if the package body does not contain any declarations.

If the **begin** keyword is placed on the same line as the last declaration or the first statement, it is flagged independently of whether the line contains a trailing comment. The diagnostic message is attached to the line containing the first statement.

This rule has no parameters.

23.6.53 Unconstrained_Array_Returns

Flag each function returning an unconstrained array. Function declarations, function bodies (and body stubs) having no separate specifications, and generic function instantiations are checked. Generic function declarations, function calls and function renamings are not checked.

This rule has no parameters.

23.6.54 Universal_Ranges

Flag discrete ranges that are a part of an index constraint, constrained array definition, or `for`-loop parameter specification, and whose bounds are both of type *universal_integer*. Ranges that have at least one bound of a specific type (such as 1 .. N, where N is a variable or an expression of non-universal type) are not flagged.

This rule has no parameters.

23.6.55 Unnamed_Blocks_And_Loops

Flag each unnamed block statement and loop statement.

The rule has no parameters.

23.6.56 USE_PACKAGE_Clauses

Flag all `use` clauses for packages; `use type` clauses are not flagged.

This rule has no parameters.

23.6.57 Volatile_Objects_Without_Address_Clauses

Flag each volatile object that does not have an address clause.

The following check is made: if the pragma `Volatile` is applied to a data object or to its type, then an address clause must be supplied for this object.

This rule does not check the components of data objects, array components that are volatile as a result of the pragma `Volatile_Components`, or objects that are volatile because they are atomic as a result of pragmas `Atomic` or `Atomic_Components`.

Only variable declarations, and not constant declarations, are checked.

This rule has no parameters.

24 Creating Sample Bodies Using gnatstub

gnatstub creates body stubs, that is, empty but compilable bodies for library unit declarations.

Note: to invoke gnatstub with a project file, use the gnat driver (see Section 11.15.2 [The GNAT Driver and Project Files], page 157).

To create a body stub, gnatstub has to compile the library unit declaration. Therefore, bodies can be created only for legal library units. Moreover, if a library unit depends semantically upon units located outside the current directory, you have to provide the source search path when calling gnatstub, see the description of gnatstub switches below.

24.1 Running gnatstub

gnatstub has the command-line interface of the form

```
$ gnatstub [switches] filename [directory]
```

where

filename   is the name of the source file that contains a library unit declaration for which a body must be created. The file name may contain the path information. The file name does not have to follow the GNAT file name conventions. If the name does not follow GNAT file naming conventions, the name of the body file must be provided explicitly as the value of the '-obody-name' option. If the file name follows the GNAT file naming conventions and the name of the body file is not provided, gnatstub creates the name of the body file from the argument file name by replacing the '.ads' suffix with the '.adb' suffix.

directory   indicates the directory in which the body stub is to be placed (the default is the current directory)

switches   is an optional sequence of switches as described in the next section

24.2 Switches for gnatstub

'-f'   If the destination directory already contains a file with the name of the body file for the argument spec file, replace it with the generated body stub.

'-hs'   Put the comment header (i.e., all the comments preceding the compilation unit) from the source of the library unit declaration into the body stub.

'-hg'   Put a sample comment header into the body stub.

'-IDIR'

'-I-'   These switches have the same meaning as in calls to gcc. They define the source search path in the call to gcc issued by gnatstub to compile an argument source file.

'-gnatecPATH'

     This switch has the same meaning as in calls to gcc. It defines the additional configuration file to be passed to the call to gcc issued by gnatstub to compile an argument source file.

'`-gnatyMn`'
> (*n* is a non-negative integer). Set the maximum line length in the body stub to *n*; the default is 79. The maximum value that can be specified is 32767. Note that in the special case of configuration pragma files, the maximum is always 32767 regardless of whether or not this switch appears.

'`-gnatyn`' (*n* is a non-negative integer from 1 to 9). Set the indentation level in the generated body sample to *n*. The default indentation is 3.

'`-gnatyo`' Order local bodies alphabetically. (By default local bodies are ordered in the same way as the corresponding local specs in the argument spec file.)

'`-in`' Same as '`-gnatyn`'

'`-k`' Do not remove the tree file (i.e., the snapshot of the compiler internal structures used by **gnatstub**) after creating the body stub.

'`-ln`' Same as '`-gnatyMn`'

'`-obody-name`'
> Body file name. This should be set if the argument file name does not follow the GNAT file naming conventions. If this switch is omitted the default name for the body will be obtained from the argument file name according to the GNAT file naming conventions.

'`-q`' Quiet mode: do not generate a confirmation when a body is successfully created, and do not generate a message when a body is not required for an argument unit.

'`-r`' Reuse the tree file (if it exists) instead of creating it. Instead of creating the tree file for the library unit declaration, **gnatstub** tries to find it in the current directory and use it for creating a body. If the tree file is not found, no body is created. This option also implies '`-k`', whether or not the latter is set explicitly.

'`-t`' Overwrite the existing tree file. If the current directory already contains the file which, according to the GNAT file naming rules should be considered as a tree file for the argument source file, **gnatstub** will refuse to create the tree file needed to create a sample body unless this option is set.

'`-v`' Verbose mode: generate version information.

25 Other Utility Programs

This chapter discusses some other utility programs available in the Ada environment.

25.1 Using Other Utility Programs with GNAT

The object files generated by GNAT are in standard system format and in particular the debugging information uses this format. This means programs generated by GNAT can be used with existing utilities that depend on these formats.

In general, any utility program that works with C will also often work with Ada programs generated by GNAT. This includes software utilities such as gprof (a profiling program), gdb (the FSF debugger), and utilities such as Purify.

25.2 The External Symbol Naming Scheme of GNAT

In order to interpret the output from GNAT, when using tools that are originally intended for use with other languages, it is useful to understand the conventions used to generate link names from the Ada entity names.

All link names are in all lowercase letters. With the exception of library procedure names, the mechanism used is simply to use the full expanded Ada name with dots replaced by double underscores. For example, suppose we have the following package spec:

```
package QRS is
   MN : Integer;
end QRS;
```

The variable MN has a full expanded Ada name of QRS.MN, so the corresponding link name is qrs__mn. Of course if a pragma Export is used this may be overridden:

```
package Exports is
   Var1 : Integer;
   pragma Export (Var1, C, External_Name => "var1_name");
   Var2 : Integer;
   pragma Export (Var2, C, Link_Name => "var2_link_name");
end Exports;
```

In this case, the link name for *Var1* is whatever link name the C compiler would assign for the C function *var1_name*. This typically would be either *var1_name* or *_var1_name*, depending on operating system conventions, but other possibilities exist. The link name for *Var2* is *var2_link_name*, and this is not operating system dependent.

One exception occurs for library level procedures. A potential ambiguity arises between the required name _main for the C main program, and the name we would otherwise assign to an Ada library level procedure called Main (which might well not be the main program).

To avoid this ambiguity, we attach the prefix _ada_ to such names. So if we have a library level procedure such as

```
procedure Hello (S : String);
```

the external name of this procedure will be *_ada_hello*.

25.3 Converting Ada Files to HTML with gnathtml

This **Perl** script allows Ada source files to be browsed using standard Web browsers. For installation procedure, see the section See Section 25.4 [Installing gnathtml], page 255.

Ada reserved keywords are highlighted in a bold font and Ada comments in a blue font. Unless your program was compiled with the gcc '**-gnatx**' switch to suppress the generation of cross-referencing information, user defined variables and types will appear in a different color; you will be able to click on any identifier and go to its declaration.

The command line is as follow:

```
$ perl gnathtml.pl [switches] ada-files
```

You can pass it as many Ada files as you want. **gnathtml** will generate an html file for every ada file, and a global file called '**index.htm**'. This file is an index of every identifier defined in the files.

The available switches are the following ones:

'-83'   Only the Ada 83 subset of keywords will be highlighted.

'-cc *color*'
                This option allows you to change the color used for comments. The default value is green. The color argument can be any name accepted by html.

'-d'   If the Ada files depend on some other files (for instance through **with** clauses, the latter files will also be converted to html. Only the files in the user project will be converted to html, not the files in the run-time library itself.

'-D'   This command is the same as '-d' above, but **gnathtml** will also look for files in the run-time library, and generate html files for them.

'-ext *extension*'
                This option allows you to change the extension of the generated HTML files. If you do not specify an extension, it will default to '**htm**'.

'-f'   By default, gnathtml will generate html links only for global entities ('with'ed units, global variables and types,...). If you specify '-f' on the command line, then links will be generated for local entities too.

'-l *number*'
                If this switch is provided and *number* is not 0, then **gnathtml** will number the html files every *number* line.

'-I *dir*'   Specify a directory to search for library files ('.**ALI**' files) and source files. You can provide several -I switches on the command line, and the directories will be parsed in the order of the command line.

'-o *dir*'   Specify the output directory for html files. By default, gnathtml will saved the generated html files in a subdirectory named '**html/**'.

'-p *file*'   If you are using Emacs and the most recent Emacs Ada mode, which provides a full Integrated Development Environment for compiling, checking, running and debugging applications, you may use '.**gpr**' files to give the directories where Emacs can find sources and object files.

Using this switch, you can tell gnathtml to use these files. This allows you to get an html version of your application, even if it is spread over multiple directories.

'-sc *color*'

This switch allows you to change the color used for symbol definitions. The default value is red. The color argument can be any name accepted by html.

'-t *file*'   This switch provides the name of a file. This file contains a list of file names to be converted, and the effect is exactly as though they had appeared explicitly on the command line. This is the recommended way to work around the command line length limit on some systems.

25.4 Installing gnathtml

`Perl` needs to be installed on your machine to run this script. `Perl` is freely available for almost every architecture and Operating System via the Internet.

On Unix systems, you may want to modify the first line of the script gnathtml, to explicitly tell the Operating system where Perl is. The syntax of this line is:

```
#!full_path_name_to_perl
```

Alternatively, you may run the script using the following command line:

```
$ perl gnathtml.pl [switches] files
```

26 Running and Debugging Ada Programs

This chapter discusses how to debug Ada programs.

An incorrect Ada program may be handled in three ways by the GNAT compiler:

1. The illegality may be a violation of the static semantics of Ada. In that case GNAT diagnoses the constructs in the program that are illegal. It is then a straightforward matter for the user to modify those parts of the program.

2. The illegality may be a violation of the dynamic semantics of Ada. In that case the program compiles and executes, but may generate incorrect results, or may terminate abnormally with some exception.

3. When presented with a program that contains convoluted errors, GNAT itself may terminate abnormally without providing full diagnostics on the incorrect user program.

26.1 The GNAT Debugger GDB

GDB is a general purpose, platform-independent debugger that can be used to debug mixed-language programs compiled with gcc, and in particular is capable of debugging Ada programs compiled with GNAT. The latest versions of GDB are Ada-aware and can handle complex Ada data structures.

The manual *Debugging with GDB* contains full details on the usage of GDB, including a section on its usage on programs. This manual should be consulted for full details. The section that follows is a brief introduction to the philosophy and use of GDB.

When GNAT programs are compiled, the compiler optionally writes debugging information into the generated object file, including information on line numbers, and on declared types and variables. This information is separate from the generated code. It makes the object files considerably larger, but it does not add to the size of the actual executable that will be loaded into memory, and has no impact on run-time performance. The generation of debug information is triggered by the use of the -g switch in the gcc or gnatmake command used to carry out the compilations. It is important to emphasize that the use of these options does not change the generated code.

The debugging information is written in standard system formats that are used by many tools, including debuggers and profilers. The format of the information is typically designed to describe C types and semantics, but GNAT implements a translation scheme which allows full details about Ada types and variables to be encoded into these standard C formats. Details of this encoding scheme may be found in the file exp_dbug.ads in the GNAT source distribution. However, the details of this encoding are, in general, of no interest to a user, since GDB automatically performs the necessary decoding.

When a program is bound and linked, the debugging information is collected from the object files, and stored in the executable image of the program. Again, this process significantly increases the size of the generated executable file, but it does not increase the size of the executable program itself. Furthermore, if this program is run in the normal manner, it runs exactly as if the debug information were not present, and takes no more actual memory.

However, if the program is run under control of GDB, the debugger is activated. The image of the program is loaded, at which point it is ready to run. If a run command is given, then the program will run exactly as it would have if GDB were not present. This is a crucial part of the GDB design philosophy. GDB is entirely non-intrusive until a breakpoint is encountered. If no breakpoint is ever hit, the program will run exactly as it would if no debugger were present. When a breakpoint is hit, GDB accesses the debugging information and can respond to user commands to inspect variables, and more generally to report on the state of execution.

26.2 Running GDB

This section describes how to initiate the debugger.

The debugger can be launched from a GPS menu or directly from the command line. The description below covers the latter use. All the commands shown can be used in the GPS debug console window, but there are usually more GUI-based ways to achieve the same effect.

The command to run GDB is

```
$ gdb program
```

where program is the name of the executable file. This activates the debugger and results in a prompt for debugger commands. The simplest command is simply run, which causes the program to run exactly as if the debugger were not present. The following section describes some of the additional commands that can be given to GDB.

26.3 Introduction to GDB Commands

GDB contains a large repertoire of commands. The manual *Debugging with GDB* includes extensive documentation on the use of these commands, together with examples of their use. Furthermore, the command *help* invoked from within GDB activates a simple help facility which summarizes the available commands and their options. In this section we summarize a few of the most commonly used commands to give an idea of what GDB is about. You should create a simple program with debugging information and experiment with the use of these GDB commands on the program as you read through the following section.

set args *arguments*

> The *arguments* list above is a list of arguments to be passed to the program on a subsequent run command, just as though the arguments had been entered on a normal invocation of the program. The set args command is not needed if the program does not require arguments.

run

> The run command causes execution of the program to start from the beginning. If the program is already running, that is to say if you are currently positioned at a breakpoint, then a prompt will ask for confirmation that you want to abandon the current execution and restart.

breakpoint *location*

> The breakpoint command sets a breakpoint, that is to say a point at which execution will halt and GDB will await further commands. *location* is either a line number within a file, given in the format file:linenumber, or it is the name of a subprogram. If you request that a breakpoint be set on a subprogram that is overloaded, a prompt will ask you to specify on which of those subprograms you want to breakpoint. You can also specify that all of them should be

breakpointed. If the program is run and execution encounters the breakpoint, then the program stops and GDB signals that the breakpoint was encountered by printing the line of code before which the program is halted.

breakpoint exception *name*

A special form of the breakpoint command which breakpoints whenever exception *name* is raised. If *name* is omitted, then a breakpoint will occur when any exception is raised.

print *expression*

This will print the value of the given expression. Most simple Ada expression formats are properly handled by GDB, so the expression can contain function calls, variables, operators, and attribute references.

continue   Continues execution following a breakpoint, until the next breakpoint or the termination of the program.

step   Executes a single line after a breakpoint. If the next statement is a subprogram call, execution continues into (the first statement of) the called subprogram.

next   Executes a single line. If this line is a subprogram call, executes and returns from the call.

list   Lists a few lines around the current source location. In practice, it is usually more convenient to have a separate edit window open with the relevant source file displayed. Successive applications of this command print subsequent lines. The command can be given an argument which is a line number, in which case it displays a few lines around the specified one.

backtrace

Displays a backtrace of the call chain. This command is typically used after a breakpoint has occurred, to examine the sequence of calls that leads to the current breakpoint. The display includes one line for each activation record (frame) corresponding to an active subprogram.

up   At a breakpoint, GDB can display the values of variables local to the current frame. The command up can be used to examine the contents of other active frames, by moving the focus up the stack, that is to say from callee to caller, one frame at a time.

down   Moves the focus of GDB down from the frame currently being examined to the frame of its callee (the reverse of the previous command),

frame *n*   Inspect the frame with the given number. The value 0 denotes the frame of the current breakpoint, that is to say the top of the call stack.

The above list is a very short introduction to the commands that GDB provides. Important additional capabilities, including conditional breakpoints, the ability to execute command sequences on a breakpoint, the ability to debug at the machine instruction level and many other features are described in detail in *Debugging with GDB*. Note that most commands can be abbreviated (for example, c for continue, bt for backtrace).

26.4 Using Ada Expressions

GDB supports a fairly large subset of Ada expression syntax, with some extensions. The
philosophy behind the design of this subset is

- That GDB should provide basic literals and access to operations for arithmetic, dereferencing, field selection, indexing, and subprogram calls, leaving more sophisticated
  computations to subprograms written into the program (which therefore may be called
  from GDB).

- That type safety and strict adherence to Ada language restrictions are not particularly
  important to the GDB user.

- That brevity is important to the GDB user.

Thus, for brevity, the debugger acts as if there were implicit **with** and **use** clauses in effect
for all user-written packages, thus making it unnecessary to fully qualify most names with
their packages, regardless of context. Where this causes ambiguity, GDB asks the user's
intent.

For details on the supported Ada syntax, see *Debugging with GDB*.

26.5 Calling User-Defined Subprograms

An important capability of GDB is the ability to call user-defined subprograms while debugging. This is achieved simply by entering a subprogram call statement in the form:

```
call subprogram-name (parameters)
```

The keyword `call` can be omitted in the normal case where the `subprogram-name` does not
coincide with any of the predefined GDB commands.

The effect is to invoke the given subprogram, passing it the list of parameters that is
supplied. The parameters can be expressions and can include variables from the program
being debugged. The subprogram must be defined at the library level within your program,
and GDB will call the subprogram within the environment of your program execution (which
means that the subprogram is free to access or even modify variables within your program).

The most important use of this facility is in allowing the inclusion of debugging routines
that are tailored to particular data structures in your program. Such debugging routines
can be written to provide a suitably high-level description of an abstract type, rather than
a low-level dump of its physical layout. After all, the standard GDB `print` command only
knows the physical layout of your types, not their abstract meaning. Debugging routines
can provide information at the desired semantic level and are thus enormously useful.

For example, when debugging GNAT itself, it is crucial to have access to the contents
of the tree nodes used to represent the program internally. But tree nodes are represented
simply by an integer value (which in turn is an index into a table of nodes). Using the `print`
command on a tree node would simply print this integer value, which is not very useful. But
the PN routine (defined in file treepr.adb in the GNAT sources) takes a tree node as input,
and displays a useful high level representation of the tree node, which includes the syntactic
category of the node, its position in the source, the integers that denote descendant nodes
and parent node, as well as varied semantic information. To study this example in more
detail, you might want to look at the body of the PN procedure in the stated file.

26.6 Using the Next Command in a Function

When you use the `next` command in a function, the current source location will advance to the next statement as usual. A special case arises in the case of a `return` statement.

Part of the code for a return statement is the "epilog" of the function. This is the code that returns to the caller. There is only one copy of this epilog code, and it is typically associated with the last return statement in the function if there is more than one return. In some implementations, this epilog is associated with the first statement of the function.

The result is that if you use the `next` command from a return statement that is not the last return statement of the function you may see a strange apparent jump to the last return statement or to the start of the function. You should simply ignore this odd jump. The value returned is always that from the first return statement that was stepped through.

26.7 Breaking on Ada Exceptions

You can set breakpoints that trip when your program raises selected exceptions.

`break exception`
> Set a breakpoint that trips whenever (any task in the) program raises any exception.

`break exception` *name*
> Set a breakpoint that trips whenever (any task in the) program raises the exception *name*.

`break exception` `unhandled`
> Set a breakpoint that trips whenever (any task in the) program raises an exception for which there is no handler.

`info exceptions`
`info exceptions` *regexp*
> The `info exceptions` command permits the user to examine all defined exceptions within Ada programs. With a regular expression, *regexp*, as argument, prints out only those exceptions whose name matches *regexp*.

26.8 Ada Tasks

GDB allows the following task-related commands:

`info tasks`
> This command shows a list of current Ada tasks, as in the following example:

```
(gdb) info tasks
  ID       TID P-ID   Thread Pri State                Name
   1   8088000   0   807e000  15 Child Activation Wait main_task
   2   80a4000   1   80ae000  15 Accept/Select Wait    b
   3   809a800   1   80a4800  15 Child Activation Wait a
*  4   80ae800   3   80b8000  15 Running               c
```

> In this listing, the asterisk before the first task indicates it to be the currently running task. The first column lists the task ID that is used to refer to tasks in the following commands.

```
break linespec task taskid
break linespec task taskid if ...
```

> These commands are like the `break ... thread ....` *linespec* specifies source lines.
>
> Use the qualifier 'task *taskid*' with a breakpoint command to specify that you only want GDB to stop the program when a particular Ada task reaches this breakpoint. *taskid* is one of the numeric task identifiers assigned by GDB, shown in the first column of the 'info tasks' display.
>
> If you do not specify 'task *taskid*' when you set a breakpoint, the breakpoint applies to *all* tasks of your program.
>
> You can use the `task` qualifier on conditional breakpoints as well; in this case, place 'task *taskid*' before the breakpoint condition (before the `if`).

```
task taskno
```

> This command allows to switch to the task referred by *taskno*. In particular, This allows to browse the backtrace of the specified task. It is advised to switch back to the original task before continuing execution otherwise the scheduling of the program may be perturbed.

For more detailed information on the tasking support, see *Debugging with GDB*.

26.9 Debugging Generic Units

GNAT always uses code expansion for generic instantiation. This means that each time an instantiation occurs, a complete copy of the original code is made, with appropriate substitutions of formals by actuals.

It is not possible to refer to the original generic entities in GDB, but it is always possible to debug a particular instance of a generic, by using the appropriate expanded names. For example, if we have

```
procedure g is

   generic package k is
      procedure kp (v1 : in out integer);
   end k;

   package body k is
      procedure kp (v1 : in out integer) is
      begin
         v1 := v1 + 1;
      end kp;
   end k;

   package k1 is new k;
   package k2 is new k;

   var : integer := 1;

begin
   k1.kp (var);
   k2.kp (var);
   k1.kp (var);
   k2.kp (var);
end;
```

Then to break on a call to procedure kp in the k2 instance, simply use the command:

```
(gdb) break g.k2.kp
```

When the breakpoint occurs, you can step through the code of the instance in the normal manner and examine the values of local variables, as for other units.

26.10 GNAT Abnormal Termination or Failure to Terminate

When presented with programs that contain serious errors in syntax or semantics, GNAT may on rare occasions experience problems in operation, such as aborting with a segmentation fault or illegal memory access, raising an internal exception, terminating abnormally, or failing to terminate at all. In such cases, you can activate various features of GNAT that can help you pinpoint the construct in your program that is the likely source of the problem.

The following strategies are presented in increasing order of difficulty, corresponding to your experience in using GNAT and your familiarity with compiler internals.

1. Run gcc with the '-gnatf'. This first switch causes all errors on a given line to be reported. In its absence, only the first error on a line is displayed.

   The '-gnatd0' switch causes errors to be displayed as soon as they are encountered, rather than after compilation is terminated. If GNAT terminates prematurely or goes into an infinite loop, the last error message displayed may help to pinpoint the culprit.

2. Run gcc with the '-v (verbose)' switch. In this mode, gcc produces ongoing information about the progress of the compilation and provides the name of each procedure as code is generated. This switch allows you to find which Ada procedure was being compiled when it encountered a code generation problem.

3. Run gcc with the '-gnatdc' switch. This is a GNAT specific switch that does for the front-end what '-v' does for the back end. The system prints the name of each unit, either a compilation unit or nested unit, as it is being analyzed.

4. Finally, you can start `gdb` directly on the `gnat1` executable. `gnat1` is the front-end of GNAT, and can be run independently (normally it is just called from `gcc`). You can use `gdb` on `gnat1` as you would on a C program (but see Section 26.1 [The GNAT Debugger GDB], page 257 for caveats). The `where` command is the first line of attack; the variable `lineno` (seen by `print lineno`), used by the second phase of `gnat1` and by the `gcc` backend, indicates the source line at which the execution stopped, and `input_file name` indicates the name of the source file.

26.11 Naming Conventions for GNAT Source Files

In order to examine the workings of the GNAT system, the following brief description of its organization may be helpful:

- Files with prefix '`sc`' contain the lexical scanner.
- All files prefixed with '`par`' are components of the parser. The numbers correspond to chapters of the Ada Reference Manual. For example, parsing of select statements can be found in '`par-ch9.adb`'.
- All files prefixed with '`sem`' perform semantic analysis. The numbers correspond to chapters of the Ada standard. For example, all issues involving context clauses can be found in '`sem_ch10.adb`'. In addition, some features of the language require sufficient special processing to justify their own semantic files: sem_aggr for aggregates, sem_disp for dynamic dispatching, etc.
- All files prefixed with '`exp`' perform normalization and expansion of the intermediate representation (abstract syntax tree, or AST). these files use the same numbering scheme as the parser and semantics files. For example, the construction of record initialization procedures is done in '`exp_ch3.adb`'.
- The files prefixed with '`bind`' implement the binder, which verifies the consistency of the compilation, determines an order of elaboration, and generates the bind file.
- The files '`atree.ads`' and '`atree.adb`' detail the low-level data structures used by the front-end.
- The files '`sinfo.ads`' and '`sinfo.adb`' detail the structure of the abstract syntax tree as produced by the parser.
- The files '`einfo.ads`' and '`einfo.adb`' detail the attributes of all entities, computed during semantic analysis.
- Library management issues are dealt with in files with prefix '`lib`'.
- Ada files with the prefix '`a-`' are children of `Ada`, as defined in Annex A.
- Files with prefix '`i-`' are children of `Interfaces`, as defined in Annex B.
- Files with prefix '`s-`' are children of `System`. This includes both language-defined children and GNAT run-time routines.
- Files with prefix '`g-`' are children of `GNAT`. These are useful general-purpose packages, fully documented in their specifications. All the other '`.c`' files are modifications of common `gcc` files.

26.12 Getting Internal Debugging Information

Most compilers have internal debugging switches and modes. GNAT does also, except GNAT internal debugging switches and modes are not secret. A summary and full description of all the compiler and binder debug flags are in the file 'debug.adb'. You must obtain the sources of the compiler to see the full detailed effects of these flags.

The switches that print the source of the program (reconstructed from the internal tree) are of general interest for user programs, as are the options to print the full internal tree, and the entity table (the symbol table information). The reconstructed source provides a readable version of the program after the front-end has completed analysis and expansion, and is useful when studying the performance of specific constructs. For example, constraint checks are indicated, complex aggregates are replaced with loops and assignments, and tasking primitives are replaced with run-time calls.

26.13 Stack Traceback

Traceback is a mechanism to display the sequence of subprogram calls that leads to a specified execution point in a program. Often (but not always) the execution point is an instruction at which an exception has been raised. This mechanism is also known as *stack unwinding* because it obtains its information by scanning the run-time stack and recovering the activation records of all active subprograms. Stack unwinding is one of the most important tools for program debugging.

The first entry stored in traceback corresponds to the deepest calling level, that is to say the subprogram currently executing the instruction from which we want to obtain the traceback.

Note that there is no runtime performance penalty when stack traceback is enabled, and no exception is raised during program execution.

26.13.1 Non-Symbolic Traceback

Note: this feature is not supported on all platforms. See 'GNAT.Traceback spec in g-traceb.ads' for a complete list of supported platforms.

26.13.1.1 Tracebacks From an Unhandled Exception

A runtime non-symbolic traceback is a list of addresses of call instructions. To enable this feature you must use the '-E' gnatbind's option. With this option a stack traceback is stored as part of exception information. You can retrieve this information using the addr2line tool.

Here is a simple example:

```
procedure STB is

   procedure P1 is
   begin
      raise Constraint_Error;
   end P1;

   procedure P2 is
   begin
      P1;
   end P2;

begin
   P2;
end STB;
```

```
$ gnatmake stb -bargs -E
$ stb

Execution terminated by unhandled exception
Exception name: CONSTRAINT_ERROR
Message: stb.adb:5
Call stack traceback locations:
0x401373 0x40138b 0x40139c 0x401335 0x4011c4 0x4011f1 0x77e892a4
```

As we see the traceback lists a sequence of addresses for the unhandled exception
CONSTRAINT_ERROR raised in procedure P1. It is easy to guess that this exception come
from procedure P1. To translate these addresses into the source lines where the calls
appear, the addr2line tool, described below, is invaluable. The use of this tool requires
the program to be compiled with debug information.

```
$ gnatmake -g stb -bargs -E
$ stb

Execution terminated by unhandled exception
Exception name: CONSTRAINT_ERROR
Message: stb.adb:5
Call stack traceback locations:
0x401373 0x40138b 0x40139c 0x401335 0x4011c4 0x4011f1 0x77e892a4

$ addr2line --exe=stb 0x401373 0x40138b 0x40139c 0x401335 0x4011c4
    0x4011f1 0x77e892a4

00401373 at d:/stb/stb.adb:5
0040138B at d:/stb/stb.adb:10
0040139C at d:/stb/stb.adb:14
00401335 at d:/stb/b~stb.adb:104
004011C4 at /build/.../crt1.c:200
004011F1 at /build/.../crt1.c:222
77E892A4 in ?? at ??:0
```

The addr2line tool has several other useful options:

--functions

> to get the function name corresponding to any location

--demangle=gnat

> to use the gnat decoding mode for the function names. Note that for binutils
> version 2.9.x the option is simply '--demangle'.

```
$ addr2line --exe=stb --functions --demangle=gnat 0x401373 0x40138b
   0x40139c 0x401335 0x4011c4 0x4011f1

00401373 in stb.p1 at d:/stb/stb.adb:5
0040138B in stb.p2 at d:/stb/stb.adb:10
0040139C in stb at d:/stb/stb.adb:14
00401335 in main at d:/stb/b~stb.adb:104
004011C4 in <__mingw_CRTStartup> at /build/.../crt1.c:200
004011F1 in <mainCRTStartup> at /build/.../crt1.c:222
```

From this traceback we can see that the exception was raised in 'stb.adb' at line 5, which was reached from a procedure call in 'stb.adb' at line 10, and so on. The 'b~std.adb' is the binder file, which contains the call to the main program. See Section 4.1 [Running gnatbind], page 79. The remaining entries are assorted runtime routines, and the output will vary from platform to platform.

It is also possible to use GDB with these traceback addresses to debug the program. For example, we can break at a given code location, as reported in the stack traceback:

```
$ gdb -nw stb

Furthermore, this feature is not implemented inside Windows DLL. Only
the non-symbolic traceback is reported in this case.

(gdb) break *0x401373
Breakpoint 1 at 0x401373: file stb.adb, line 5.
```

It is important to note that the stack traceback addresses do not change when debug information is included. This is particularly useful because it makes it possible to release software without debug information (to minimize object size), get a field report that includes a stack traceback whenever an internal bug occurs, and then be able to retrieve the sequence of calls with the same program compiled with debug information.

26.13.1.2 Tracebacks From Exception Occurrences

Non-symbolic tracebacks are obtained by using the '-E' binder argument. The stack traceback is attached to the exception information string, and can be retrieved in an exception handler within the Ada program, by means of the Ada facilities defined in Ada.Exceptions. Here is a simple example:

```
with Ada.Text_IO;
with Ada.Exceptions;

procedure STB is

   use Ada;
   use Ada.Exceptions;

   procedure P1 is
      K : Positive := 1;
   begin
      K := K - 1;
   exception
      when E : others =>
         Text_IO.Put_Line (Exception_Information (E));
   end P1;

   procedure P2 is
```

```
      begin
         P1;
      end P2;

   begin
      P2;
   end STB;
```

This program will output:

```
$ stb

Exception name: CONSTRAINT_ERROR
Message: stb.adb:12
Call stack traceback locations:
0x4015e4 0x401633 0x401644 0x401461 0x4011c4 0x4011f1 0x77e892a4
```

26.13.1.3 Tracebacks From Anywhere in a Program

It is also possible to retrieve a stack traceback from anywhere in a program. For this you need to use the GNAT.Traceback API. This package includes a procedure called Call_Chain that computes a complete stack traceback, as well as useful display procedures described below. It is not necessary to use the '-E gnatbind' option in this case, because the stack traceback mechanism is invoked explicitly.

In the following example we compute a traceback at a specific location in the program, and we display it using GNAT.Debug_Utilities.Image to convert addresses to strings:

```
with Ada.Text_IO;
with GNAT.Traceback;
with GNAT.Debug_Utilities;

procedure STB is

   use Ada;
   use GNAT;
   use GNAT.Traceback;

   procedure P1 is
      TB  : Tracebacks_Array (1 .. 10);
      --  We are asking for a maximum of 10 stack frames.
      Len : Natural;
      --  Len will receive the actual number of stack frames returned.
   begin
      Call_Chain (TB, Len);

      Text_IO.Put ("In STB.P1 : ");

      for K in 1 .. Len loop
         Text_IO.Put (Debug_Utilities.Image (TB (K)));
         Text_IO.Put (' ');
      end loop;

      Text_IO.New_Line;
   end P1;

   procedure P2 is
   begin
      P1;
   end P2;
```

```
begin
   P2;
end STB;
```
```
$ gnatmake -g stb
$ stb
```
```
In STB.P1 : 16#0040_F1E4# 16#0040_14F2# 16#0040_170B# 16#0040_171C#
16#0040_1461# 16#0040_11C4# 16#0040_11F1# 16#77E8_92A4#
```

You can then get further information by invoking the `addr2line` tool as described earlier (note that the hexadecimal addresses need to be specified in C format, with a leading "0x").

26.13.2 Symbolic Traceback

A symbolic traceback is a stack traceback in which procedure names are associated with each code location.

Note that this feature is not supported on all platforms. See 'GNAT.Traceback.Symbolic spec in g-trasym.ads' for a complete list of currently supported platforms.

Note that the symbolic traceback requires that the program be compiled with debug information. If it is not compiled with debug information only the non-symbolic information will be valid.

26.13.2.1 Tracebacks From Exception Occurrences

```
with Ada.Text_IO;
with GNAT.Traceback.Symbolic;

procedure STB is

   procedure P1 is
   begin
      raise Constraint_Error;
   end P1;

   procedure P2 is
   begin
      P1;
   end P2;

   procedure P3 is
   begin
      P2;
   end P3;

begin
   P3;
exception
   when E : others =>
      Ada.Text_IO.Put_Line (GNAT.Traceback.Symbolic.Symbolic_Traceback (E));
end STB;
```
```
$ gnatmake -g .\stb -bargs -E -largs -lgnat -laddr2line -lintl
$ stb
```
```
0040149F in stb.p1 at stb.adb:8
004014B7 in stb.p2 at stb.adb:13
004014CF in stb.p3 at stb.adb:18
```

```
004015DD in ada.stb at stb.adb:22
00401461 in main at b~stb.adb:168
004011C4 in __mingw_CRTStartup at crt1.c:200
004011F1 in mainCRTStartup at crt1.c:222
77E892A4 in ?? at ??:0
```

In the above example the ".\" syntax in the `gnatmake` command is currently required by `addr2line` for files that are in the current working directory. Moreover, the exact sequence of linker options may vary from platform to platform. The above '-largs' section is for Windows platforms. By contrast, under Unix there is no need for the '-largs' section. Differences across platforms are due to details of linker implementation.

26.13.2.2 Tracebacks From Anywhere in a Program

It is possible to get a symbolic stack traceback from anywhere in a program, just as for non-symbolic tracebacks. The first step is to obtain a non-symbolic traceback, and then call `Symbolic_Traceback` to compute the symbolic information. Here is an example:

```
with Ada.Text_IO;
with GNAT.Traceback;
with GNAT.Traceback.Symbolic;

procedure STB is

   use Ada;
   use GNAT.Traceback;
   use GNAT.Traceback.Symbolic;

   procedure P1 is
      TB  : Tracebacks_Array (1 .. 10);
      --  We are asking for a maximum of 10 stack frames.
      Len : Natural;
      --  Len will receive the actual number of stack frames returned.
   begin
      Call_Chain (TB, Len);
      Text_IO.Put_Line (Symbolic_Traceback (TB (1 .. Len)));
   end P1;

   procedure P2 is
   begin
      P1;
   end P2;

begin
   P2;
end STB;
```

Appendix A Platform-Specific Information for the Run-Time Libraries

The GNAT run-time implementation may vary with respect to both the underlying threads library and the exception handling scheme. For threads support, one or more of the following are supplied:

- **native threads library**, a binding to the thread package from the underlying operating system
- **pthreads library** (Sparc Solaris only), a binding to the Solaris POSIX thread package

For exception handling, either or both of two models are supplied:

- **Zero-Cost Exceptions** ("ZCX"),[1] which uses binder-generated tables that are interrogated at run time to locate a handler
- **setjmp / longjmp** ("SJLJ"), which uses dynamically-set data to establish the set of handlers

This appendix summarizes which combinations of threads and exception support are supplied on various GNAT platforms. It then shows how to select a particular library either permanently or temporarily, explains the properties of (and tradeoffs among) the various threads libraries, and provides some additional information about several specific platforms.

A.1 Summary of Run-Time Configurations

alpha-openvms

rts-native (default)

Tasking	native VMS threads
Exceptions	ZCX

alpha-tru64

rts-native (default)

Tasking	native TRU64 threads
Exceptions	ZCX

rts-sjlj

Tasking	native TRU64 threads
Exceptions	SJLJ

ia64-hp_linux

rts-native (default)

Tasking	pthread library
Exceptions	ZCX

ia64-hpux

rts-native (default)

Tasking	native HP-UX threads

---

[1] Most programs should experience a substantial speed improvement by being compiled with a ZCX run-time. This is especially true for tasking applications or applications with many exception handlers.

	Exceptions	SJLJ

ia64-openvms
rts-native (default)

	Tasking	native VMS threads
	Exceptions	ZCX

ia64-sgi_linux
rts-native (default)

	Tasking	pthread library
	Exceptions	ZCX

mips-irix
rts-native (default)

	Tasking	native IRIX threads
	Exceptions	ZCX

pa-hpux
rts-native (default)

	Tasking	native HP-UX threads
	Exceptions	ZCX

rts-sjlj

	Tasking	native HP-UX threads
	Exceptions	SJLJ

ppc-aix
rts-native (default)

	Tasking	native AIX threads
	Exceptions	SJLJ

ppc-darwin
rts-native (default)

	Tasking	native MacOS threads
	Exceptions	ZCX

sparc-solaris
rts-native (default)

	Tasking	native Solaris threads library
	Exceptions	ZCX

rts-pthread

	Tasking	pthread library
	Exceptions	ZCX

rts-sjlj

Tasking	native Solaris threads library
Exceptions	SJLJ

sparc64-solaris
rts-native (default)

Tasking	native Solaris threads library
Exceptions	ZCX

x86-linux
rts-native (default)

Tasking	pthread library
Exceptions	ZCX

rts-sjlj

Tasking	pthread library
Exceptions	SJLJ

x86-lynx
rts-native (default)

Tasking	native LynxOS threads
Exceptions	SJLJ

x86-solaris
rts-native (default)

Tasking	native Solaris threads
Exceptions	SJLJ

x86-windows
rts-native (default)

Tasking	native Win32 threads
Exceptions	ZCX

rts-sjlj (default)

Tasking	native Win32 threads
Exceptions	SJLJ

x86_64-linux
rts-native (default)

Tasking	pthread library
Exceptions	ZCX

rts-sjlj

Tasking	pthread library
Exceptions	SJLJ

A.2 Specifying a Run-Time Library

The 'adainclude' subdirectory containing the sources of the GNAT run-time library, and the 'adalib' subdirectory containing the 'ALI' files and the static and/or shared GNAT library, are located in the gcc target-dependent area:

```
target=$prefix/lib/gcc/gcc-dumpmachine/gcc-dumpversion/
```

As indicated above, on some platforms several run-time libraries are supplied. These libraries are installed in the target dependent area and contain a complete source and binary subdirectory. The detailed description below explains the differences between the different libraries in terms of their thread support.

The default run-time library (when GNAT is installed) is *rts-native*. This default run time is selected by the means of soft links. For example on x86-linux:

```
$(target-dir)
     |
     +--- adainclude----------+
     |                        |
     +--- adalib-----------+  |
     |                     |  |
     +--- rts-native       |  |
     |     |               |  |
     |     +--- adainclude <---+
     |     |                |
     |     +--- adalib <----+
     |
     +--- rts-sjlj
           |
           +--- adainclude
           |
           +--- adalib
```

If the *rts-sjlj* library is to be selected on a permanent basis, these soft links can be modified with the following commands:

```
$ cd $target
$ rm -f adainclude adalib
$ ln -s rts-sjlj/adainclude adainclude
$ ln -s rts-sjlj/adalib adalib
```

Alternatively, you can specify 'rts-sjlj/adainclude' in the file '$target/ada_source_path' and 'rts-sjlj/adalib' in '$target/ada_object_path'.

Selecting another run-time library temporarily can be achieved by using the '--RTS' switch, e.g., '--RTS=sjlj'

A.3 Choosing the Scheduling Policy

When using a POSIX threads implementation, you have a choice of several scheduling policies: SCHED_FIFO, SCHED_RR and SCHED_OTHER. Typically, the default is SCHED_OTHER, while using SCHED_FIFO or SCHED_RR requires special (e.g., root) privileges.

By default, GNAT uses the SCHED_OTHER policy. To specify SCHED_FIFO, you can use one of the following:

- pragma Time_Slice (0.0)
- the corresponding binder option '-T0'
- pragma Task_Dispatching_Policy (FIFO_Within_Priorities)

To specify `SCHED_RR`, you should use `pragma Time_Slice` with a value greater than `0.0`, or else use the corresponding '`-T`' binder option.

A.4 Solaris-Specific Considerations

This section addresses some topics related to the various threads libraries on Sparc Solaris.

A.4.1 Solaris Threads Issues

GNAT under Solaris/Sparc 32 bits comes with an alternate tasking run-time library based on POSIX threads — *rts-pthread*. This run-time library has the advantage of being mostly shared across all POSIX-compliant thread implementations, and it also provides under Solaris 8 the `PTHREAD_PRIO_INHERIT` and `PTHREAD_PRIO_PROTECT` semantics that can be selected using the predefined pragma `Locking_Policy` with respectively `Inheritance_Locking` and `Ceiling_Locking` as the policy.

As explained above, the native run-time library is based on the Solaris thread library (`libthread`) and is the default library.

When the Solaris threads library is used (this is the default), programs compiled with GNAT can automatically take advantage of and can thus execute on multiple processors. The user can alternatively specify a processor on which the program should run to emulate a single-processor system. The multiprocessor / uniprocessor choice is made by setting the environment variable `GNAT_PROCESSOR` to one of the following:

`-2` Use the default configuration (run the program on all available processors) - this is the same as having `GNAT_PROCESSOR` unset

`-1` Let the run-time implementation choose one processor and run the program on that processor

`0 .. Last_Proc` Run the program on the specified processor. `Last_Proc` is equal to `_SC_NPROCESSORS_CONF - 1` (where `_SC_NPROCESSORS_CONF` is a system variable).

A.5 Linux-Specific Considerations

On GNU/Linux without NPTL support (usually system with GNU C Library older than 2.3), the signal model is not POSIX compliant, which means that to send a signal to the process, you need to send the signal to all threads, e.g. by using `killpg()`.

A.6 AIX-Specific Considerations

On AIX, the resolver library initializes some internal structure on the first call to `get*by*` functions, which are used to implement `GNAT.Sockets.Get_Host_By_Name` and `GNAT.Sockets.Get_Host_By_Address`. If such initialization occurs within an Ada task, and the stack size for the task is the default size, a stack overflow may occur.

To avoid this overflow, the user should either ensure that the first call to `GNAT.Sockets.Get_Host_By_Name` or `GNAT.Sockets.Get_Host_By_Addrss` occurs in the environment task, or use `pragma Storage_Size` to specify a sufficiently large size for the stack of the task that contains this call.

Appendix B Example of Binder Output File

This Appendix displays the source code for **gnatbind**'s output file generated for a simple "Hello World" program. Comments have been added for clarification purposes.

```
--  The package is called Ada_Main unless this name is actually used
--  as a unit name in the partition, in which case some other unique
--  name is used.

with System;
package ada_main is

   Elab_Final_Code : Integer;
   pragma Import (C, Elab_Final_Code, "__gnat_inside_elab_final_code");

   --  The main program saves the parameters (argument count,
   --  argument values, environment pointer) in global variables
   --  for later access by other units including
   --  Ada.Command_Line.

   gnat_argc : Integer;
   gnat_argv : System.Address;
   gnat_envp : System.Address;

   --  The actual variables are stored in a library routine. This
   --  is useful for some shared library situations, where there
   --  are problems if variables are not in the library.

   pragma Import (C, gnat_argc);
   pragma Import (C, gnat_argv);
   pragma Import (C, gnat_envp);

   --  The exit status is similarly an external location

   gnat_exit_status : Integer;
   pragma Import (C, gnat_exit_status);

   GNAT_Version : constant String :=
                    "GNAT Version: 6.0.0w (20061115)";
   pragma Export (C, GNAT_Version, "__gnat_version");

   --  This is the generated adafinal routine that performs
   --  finalization at the end of execution. In the case where
   --  Ada is the main program, this main program makes a call
   --  to adafinal at program termination.

   procedure adafinal;
   pragma Export (C, adafinal, "adafinal");

   --  This is the generated adainit routine that performs
   --  initialization at the start of execution. In the case
   --  where Ada is the main program, this main program makes
   --  a call to adainit at program startup.

   procedure adainit;
   pragma Export (C, adainit, "adainit");
```

```
--  This routine is called at the start of execution. It is
--  a dummy routine that is used by the debugger to breakpoint
--  at the start of execution.

procedure Break_Start;
pragma Import (C, Break_Start, "__gnat_break_start");

--  This is the actual generated main program (it would be
--  suppressed if the no main program switch were used). As
--  required by standard system conventions, this program has
--  the external name main.

function main
  (argc : Integer;
   argv : System.Address;
   envp : System.Address)
   return Integer;
pragma Export (C, main, "main");

--  The following set of constants give the version
--  identification values for every unit in the bound
--  partition. This identification is computed from all
--  dependent semantic units, and corresponds to the
--  string that would be returned by use of the
--  Body_Version or Version attributes.

type Version_32 is mod 2 ** 32;
u00001 : constant Version_32 := 16#7880BEB3#;
u00002 : constant Version_32 := 16#0D24CBD0#;
u00003 : constant Version_32 := 16#3283DBEB#;
u00004 : constant Version_32 := 16#2359F9ED#;
u00005 : constant Version_32 := 16#664FB847#;
u00006 : constant Version_32 := 16#68E803DF#;
u00007 : constant Version_32 := 16#5572E604#;
u00008 : constant Version_32 := 16#46B173D8#;
u00009 : constant Version_32 := 16#156A40CF#;
u00010 : constant Version_32 := 16#033DABE0#;
u00011 : constant Version_32 := 16#6AB38FEA#;
u00012 : constant Version_32 := 16#22B6217D#;
u00013 : constant Version_32 := 16#68A22947#;
u00014 : constant Version_32 := 16#18CC4A56#;
u00015 : constant Version_32 := 16#08258E1B#;
u00016 : constant Version_32 := 16#367D5222#;
u00017 : constant Version_32 := 16#20C9ECA4#;
u00018 : constant Version_32 := 16#50D32CB6#;
u00019 : constant Version_32 := 16#39A8BB77#;
u00020 : constant Version_32 := 16#5CF8FA2B#;
u00021 : constant Version_32 := 16#2F1EB794#;
u00022 : constant Version_32 := 16#31AB6444#;
u00023 : constant Version_32 := 16#1574B6E9#;
u00024 : constant Version_32 := 16#5109C189#;
u00025 : constant Version_32 := 16#56D770CD#;
u00026 : constant Version_32 := 16#02F9DE3D#;
u00027 : constant Version_32 := 16#08AB6B2C#;
u00028 : constant Version_32 := 16#3FA37670#;
u00029 : constant Version_32 := 16#476457A0#;
u00030 : constant Version_32 := 16#731E1B6E#;
u00031 : constant Version_32 := 16#23C2E789#;
```

```
u00032 : constant Version_32 := 16#0F1BD6A1#;
u00033 : constant Version_32 := 16#7C25DE96#;
u00034 : constant Version_32 := 16#39ADFFA2#;
u00035 : constant Version_32 := 16#571DE3E7#;
u00036 : constant Version_32 := 16#5EB646AB#;
u00037 : constant Version_32 := 16#4249379B#;
u00038 : constant Version_32 := 16#0357E00A#;
u00039 : constant Version_32 := 16#3784FB72#;
u00040 : constant Version_32 := 16#2E723019#;
u00041 : constant Version_32 := 16#623358EA#;
u00042 : constant Version_32 := 16#107F9465#;
u00043 : constant Version_32 := 16#6843F68A#;
u00044 : constant Version_32 := 16#63305874#;
u00045 : constant Version_32 := 16#31E56CE1#;
u00046 : constant Version_32 := 16#02917970#;
u00047 : constant Version_32 := 16#6CCBA70E#;
u00048 : constant Version_32 := 16#41CD4204#;
u00049 : constant Version_32 := 16#572E3F58#;
u00050 : constant Version_32 := 16#20729FF5#;
u00051 : constant Version_32 := 16#1D4F93E8#;
u00052 : constant Version_32 := 16#30B2EC3D#;
u00053 : constant Version_32 := 16#34054F96#;
u00054 : constant Version_32 := 16#5A199860#;
u00055 : constant Version_32 := 16#0E7F912B#;
u00056 : constant Version_32 := 16#5760634A#;
u00057 : constant Version_32 := 16#5D851835#;


--  The following Export pragmas export the version numbers
--  with symbolic names ending in B (for body) or S
--  (for spec) so that they can be located in a link. The
--  information provided here is sufficient to track down
--  the exact versions of units used in a given build.

pragma Export (C, u00001, "helloB");
pragma Export (C, u00002, "system__standard_libraryB");
pragma Export (C, u00003, "system__standard_libraryS");
pragma Export (C, u00004, "adaS");
pragma Export (C, u00005, "ada__text_ioB");
pragma Export (C, u00006, "ada__text_ioS");
pragma Export (C, u00007, "ada__exceptionsB");
pragma Export (C, u00008, "ada__exceptionsS");
pragma Export (C, u00009, "gnatS");
pragma Export (C, u00010, "gnat__heap_sort_aB");
pragma Export (C, u00011, "gnat__heap_sort_aS");
pragma Export (C, u00012, "systemS");
pragma Export (C, u00013, "system__exception_tableB");
pragma Export (C, u00014, "system__exception_tableS");
pragma Export (C, u00015, "gnat__htableB");
pragma Export (C, u00016, "gnat__htableS");
pragma Export (C, u00017, "system__exceptionsS");
pragma Export (C, u00018, "system__machine_state_operationsB");
pragma Export (C, u00019, "system__machine_state_operationsS");
pragma Export (C, u00020, "system__machine_codeS");
pragma Export (C, u00021, "system__storage_elementsB");
pragma Export (C, u00022, "system__storage_elementsS");
pragma Export (C, u00023, "system__secondary_stackB");
pragma Export (C, u00024, "system__secondary_stackS");
pragma Export (C, u00025, "system__parametersB");
```

```
pragma Export (C, u00026, "system__parametersS");
pragma Export (C, u00027, "system__soft_linksB");
pragma Export (C, u00028, "system__soft_linksS");
pragma Export (C, u00029, "system__stack_checkingB");
pragma Export (C, u00030, "system__stack_checkingS");
pragma Export (C, u00031, "system__tracebackB");
pragma Export (C, u00032, "system__tracebackS");
pragma Export (C, u00033, "ada__streamsS");
pragma Export (C, u00034, "ada__tagsB");
pragma Export (C, u00035, "ada__tagsS");
pragma Export (C, u00036, "system__string_opsB");
pragma Export (C, u00037, "system__string_opsS");
pragma Export (C, u00038, "interfacesS");
pragma Export (C, u00039, "interfaces__c_streamsB");
pragma Export (C, u00040, "interfaces__c_streamsS");
pragma Export (C, u00041, "system__file_ioB");
pragma Export (C, u00042, "system__file_ioS");
pragma Export (C, u00043, "ada__finalizationB");
pragma Export (C, u00044, "ada__finalizationS");
pragma Export (C, u00045, "system__finalization_rootB");
pragma Export (C, u00046, "system__finalization_rootS");
pragma Export (C, u00047, "system__finalization_implementationB");
pragma Export (C, u00048, "system__finalization_implementationS");
pragma Export (C, u00049, "system__string_ops_concat_3B");
pragma Export (C, u00050, "system__string_ops_concat_3S");
pragma Export (C, u00051, "system__stream_attributesB");
pragma Export (C, u00052, "system__stream_attributesS");
pragma Export (C, u00053, "ada__io_exceptionsS");
pragma Export (C, u00054, "system__unsigned_typesS");
pragma Export (C, u00055, "system__file_control_blockS");
pragma Export (C, u00056, "ada__finalization__list_controllerB");
pragma Export (C, u00057, "ada__finalization__list_controllerS");

-- BEGIN ELABORATION ORDER
-- ada (spec)
-- gnat (spec)
-- gnat.heap_sort_a (spec)
-- gnat.heap_sort_a (body)
-- gnat.htable (spec)
-- gnat.htable (body)
-- interfaces (spec)
-- system (spec)
-- system.machine_code (spec)
-- system.parameters (spec)
-- system.parameters (body)
-- interfaces.c_streams (spec)
-- interfaces.c_streams (body)
-- system.standard_library (spec)
-- ada.exceptions (spec)
-- system.exception_table (spec)
-- system.exception_table (body)
-- ada.io_exceptions (spec)
-- system.exceptions (spec)
-- system.storage_elements (spec)
-- system.storage_elements (body)
-- system.machine_state_operations (spec)
-- system.machine_state_operations (body)
-- system.secondary_stack (spec)
```

```
-- system.stack_checking (spec)
-- system.soft_links (spec)
-- system.soft_links (body)
-- system.stack_checking (body)
-- system.secondary_stack (body)
-- system.standard_library (body)
-- system.string_ops (spec)
-- system.string_ops (body)
-- ada.tags (spec)
-- ada.tags (body)
-- ada.streams (spec)
-- system.finalization_root (spec)
-- system.finalization_root (body)
-- system.string_ops_concat_3 (spec)
-- system.string_ops_concat_3 (body)
-- system.traceback (spec)
-- system.traceback (body)
-- ada.exceptions (body)
-- system.unsigned_types (spec)
-- system.stream_attributes (spec)
-- system.stream_attributes (body)
-- system.finalization_implementation (spec)
-- system.finalization_implementation (body)
-- ada.finalization (spec)
-- ada.finalization (body)
-- ada.finalization.list_controller (spec)
-- ada.finalization.list_controller (body)
-- system.file_control_block (spec)
-- system.file_io (spec)
-- system.file_io (body)
-- ada.text_io (spec)
-- ada.text_io (body)
-- hello (body)
-- END ELABORATION ORDER

end ada_main;

--   The following source file name pragmas allow the generated file
--   names to be unique for different main programs. They are needed
--   since the package name will always be Ada_Main.

pragma Source_File_Name (ada_main, Spec_File_Name => "b~hello.ads");
pragma Source_File_Name (ada_main, Body_File_Name => "b~hello.adb");

--   Generated package body for Ada_Main starts here

package body ada_main is

   --   The actual finalization is performed by calling the
   --   library routine in System.Standard_Library.Adafinal

   procedure Do_Finalize;
   pragma Import (C, Do_Finalize, "system__standard_library__adafinal");

   -------------
   -- adainit --
   -------------
```

```
procedure adainit is

    --  These booleans are set to True once the associated unit has
    --  been elaborated. It is also used to avoid elaborating the
    --  same unit twice.

    E040 : Boolean;
    pragma Import (Ada, E040, "interfaces__c_streams_E");

    E008 : Boolean;
    pragma Import (Ada, E008, "ada__exceptions_E");

    E014 : Boolean;
    pragma Import (Ada, E014, "system__exception_table_E");

    E053 : Boolean;
    pragma Import (Ada, E053, "ada__io_exceptions_E");

    E017 : Boolean;
    pragma Import (Ada, E017, "system__exceptions_E");

    E024 : Boolean;
    pragma Import (Ada, E024, "system__secondary_stack_E");

    E030 : Boolean;
    pragma Import (Ada, E030, "system__stack_checking_E");

    E028 : Boolean;
    pragma Import (Ada, E028, "system__soft_links_E");

    E035 : Boolean;
    pragma Import (Ada, E035, "ada__tags_E");

    E033 : Boolean;
    pragma Import (Ada, E033, "ada__streams_E");

    E046 : Boolean;
    pragma Import (Ada, E046, "system__finalization_root_E");

    E048 : Boolean;
    pragma Import (Ada, E048, "system__finalization_implementation_E");

    E044 : Boolean;
    pragma Import (Ada, E044, "ada__finalization_E");

    E057 : Boolean;
    pragma Import (Ada, E057, "ada__finalization__list_controller_E");

    E055 : Boolean;
    pragma Import (Ada, E055, "system__file_control_block_E");

    E042 : Boolean;
    pragma Import (Ada, E042, "system__file_io_E");

    E006 : Boolean;
    pragma Import (Ada, E006, "ada__text_io_E");

    --  Set_Globals is a library routine that stores away the
```

```
--  value of the indicated set of global values in global
--  variables within the library.

procedure Set_Globals
  (Main_Priority          : Integer;
   Time_Slice_Value       : Integer;
   WC_Encoding            : Character;
   Locking_Policy         : Character;
   Queuing_Policy         : Character;
   Task_Dispatching_Policy : Character;
   Adafinal               : System.Address;
   Unreserve_All_Interrupts : Integer;
   Exception_Tracebacks   : Integer);
pragma Import (C, Set_Globals, "__gnat_set_globals");

--  SDP_Table_Build is a library routine used to build the
--  exception tables. See unit Ada.Exceptions in files
--  a-except.ads/adb for full details of how zero cost
--  exception handling works. This procedure, the call to
--  it, and the two following tables are all omitted if the
--  build is in longjmp/setjump exception mode.

procedure SDP_Table_Build
  (SDP_Addresses   : System.Address;
   SDP_Count       : Natural;
   Elab_Addresses  : System.Address;
   Elab_Addr_Count : Natural);
pragma Import (C, SDP_Table_Build, "__gnat_SDP_Table_Build");

--  Table of Unit_Exception_Table addresses. Used for zero
--  cost exception handling to build the top level table.

ST : aliased constant array (1 .. 23) of System.Address := (
  Hello'UET_Address,
  Ada.Text_Io'UET_Address,
  Ada.Exceptions'UET_Address,
  Gnat.Heap_Sort_A'UET_Address,
  System.Exception_Table'UET_Address,
  System.Machine_State_Operations'UET_Address,
  System.Secondary_Stack'UET_Address,
  System.Parameters'UET_Address,
  System.Soft_Links'UET_Address,
  System.Stack_Checking'UET_Address,
  System.Traceback'UET_Address,
  Ada.Streams'UET_Address,
  Ada.Tags'UET_Address,
  System.String_Ops'UET_Address,
  Interfaces.C_Streams'UET_Address,
  System.File_Io'UET_Address,
  Ada.Finalization'UET_Address,
  System.Finalization_Root'UET_Address,
  System.Finalization_Implementation'UET_Address,
  System.String_Ops_Concat_3'UET_Address,
  System.Stream_Attributes'UET_Address,
  System.File_Control_Block'UET_Address,
  Ada.Finalization.List_Controller'UET_Address);

--  Table of addresses of elaboration routines. Used for
```

```
      --  zero cost exception handling to make sure these
      --  addresses are included in the top level procedure
      --  address table.

      EA : aliased constant array (1 .. 23) of System.Address := (
        adainit'Code_Address,
        Do_Finalize'Code_Address,
        Ada.Exceptions'Elab_Spec'Address,
        System.Exceptions'Elab_Spec'Address,
        Interfaces.C_Streams'Elab_Spec'Address,
        System.Exception_Table'Elab_Body'Address,
        Ada.Io_Exceptions'Elab_Spec'Address,
        System.Stack_Checking'Elab_Spec'Address,
        System.Soft_Links'Elab_Body'Address,
        System.Secondary_Stack'Elab_Body'Address,
        Ada.Tags'Elab_Spec'Address,
        Ada.Tags'Elab_Body'Address,
        Ada.Streams'Elab_Spec'Address,
        System.Finalization_Root'Elab_Spec'Address,
        Ada.Exceptions'Elab_Body'Address,
        System.Finalization_Implementation'Elab_Spec'Address,
        System.Finalization_Implementation'Elab_Body'Address,
        Ada.Finalization'Elab_Spec'Address,
        Ada.Finalization.List_Controller'Elab_Spec'Address,
        System.File_Control_Block'Elab_Spec'Address,
        System.File_Io'Elab_Body'Address,
        Ada.Text_Io'Elab_Spec'Address,
        Ada.Text_Io'Elab_Body'Address);

   --  Start of processing for adainit

   begin

      --  Call SDP_Table_Build to build the top level procedure
      --  table for zero cost exception handling (omitted in
      --  longjmp/setjump mode).

      SDP_Table_Build (ST'Address, 23, EA'Address, 23);

      --  Call Set_Globals to record various information for
      --  this partition.  The values are derived by the binder
      --  from information stored in the ali files by the compiler.

      Set_Globals
        (Main_Priority          => -1,
         --  Priority of main program, -1 if no pragma Priority used

         Time_Slice_Value       => -1,
         --  Time slice from Time_Slice pragma, -1 if none used

         WC_Encoding            => 'b',
         --  Wide_Character encoding used, default is brackets

         Locking_Policy         => ' ',
         --  Locking_Policy used, default of space means not
         --  specified, otherwise it is the first character of
         --  the policy name.
```

```
       Queuing_Policy            => ' ',
       --  Queuing_Policy used, default of space means not
       --  specified, otherwise it is the first character of
       --  the policy name.

       Task_Dispatching_Policy  => ' ',
       --  Task_Dispatching_Policy used, default of space means
       --  not specified, otherwise first character of the
       --  policy name.

       Adafinal                 => System.Null_Address,
       --  Address of Adafinal routine, not used anymore

       Unreserve_All_Interrupts => 0,
       --  Set true if pragma Unreserve_All_Interrupts was used

       Exception_Tracebacks     => 0);
       --  Indicates if exception tracebacks are enabled

   Elab_Final_Code := 1;

   --  Now we have the elaboration calls for all units in the partition.
   --  The Elab_Spec and Elab_Body attributes generate references to the
   --  implicit elaboration procedures generated by the compiler for
   --  each unit that requires elaboration.

   if not E040 then
      Interfaces.C_Streams'Elab_Spec;
   end if;
   E040 := True;
   if not E008 then
      Ada.Exceptions'Elab_Spec;
   end if;
   if not E014 then
      System.Exception_Table'Elab_Body;
      E014 := True;
   end if;
   if not E053 then
      Ada.Io_Exceptions'Elab_Spec;
      E053 := True;
   end if;
   if not E017 then
      System.Exceptions'Elab_Spec;
      E017 := True;
   end if;
   if not E030 then
      System.Stack_Checking'Elab_Spec;
   end if;
   if not E028 then
      System.Soft_Links'Elab_Body;
      E028 := True;
   end if;
   E030 := True;
   if not E024 then
      System.Secondary_Stack'Elab_Body;
      E024 := True;
   end if;
   if not E035 then
```

```
         Ada.Tags'Elab_Spec;
      end if;
      if not E035 then
         Ada.Tags'Elab_Body;
         E035 := True;
      end if;
      if not E033 then
         Ada.Streams'Elab_Spec;
         E033 := True;
      end if;
      if not E046 then
         System.Finalization_Root'Elab_Spec;
      end if;
      E046 := True;
      if not E008 then
         Ada.Exceptions'Elab_Body;
         E008 := True;
      end if;
      if not E048 then
         System.Finalization_Implementation'Elab_Spec;
      end if;
      if not E048 then
         System.Finalization_Implementation'Elab_Body;
         E048 := True;
      end if;
      if not E044 then
         Ada.Finalization'Elab_Spec;
      end if;
      E044 := True;
      if not E057 then
         Ada.Finalization.List_Controller'Elab_Spec;
      end if;
      E057 := True;
      if not E055 then
         System.File_Control_Block'Elab_Spec;
         E055 := True;
      end if;
      if not E042 then
         System.File_Io'Elab_Body;
         E042 := True;
      end if;
      if not E006 then
         Ada.Text_Io'Elab_Spec;
      end if;
      if not E006 then
         Ada.Text_Io'Elab_Body;
         E006 := True;
      end if;

   Elab_Final_Code := 0;
end adainit;

--------------
-- adafinal --
--------------

procedure adafinal is
begin
```

```
    Do_Finalize;
end adafinal;

----------
-- main --
----------

--  main is actually a function, as in the ANSI C standard,
--  defined to return the exit status. The three parameters
--  are the argument count, argument values and environment
--  pointer.

function main
  (argc : Integer;
   argv : System.Address;
   envp : System.Address)
   return Integer
is
    --  The initialize routine performs low level system
    --  initialization using a standard library routine which
    --  sets up signal handling and performs any other
    --  required setup. The routine can be found in file
    --  a-init.c.

    procedure initialize;
    pragma Import (C, initialize, "__gnat_initialize");

    --  The finalize routine performs low level system
    --  finalization using a standard library routine. The
    --  routine is found in file a-final.c and in the standard
    --  distribution is a dummy routine that does nothing, so
    --  really this is a hook for special user finalization.

    procedure finalize;
    pragma Import (C, finalize, "__gnat_finalize");

    --  We get to the main program of the partition by using
    --  pragma Import because if we try to with the unit and
    --  call it Ada style, then not only do we waste time
    --  recompiling it, but also, we don't really know the right
    --  switches (e.g. identifier character set) to be used
    --  to compile it.

    procedure Ada_Main_Program;
    pragma Import (Ada, Ada_Main_Program, "_ada_hello");

--  Start of processing for main

begin
    --  Save global variables

    gnat_argc := argc;
    gnat_argv := argv;
    gnat_envp := envp;

    --  Call low level system initialization

    Initialize;
```

```
      -- Call our generated Ada initialization routine

   adainit;

      -- This is the point at which we want the debugger to get
      -- control

   Break_Start;

      -- Now we call the main program of the partition

   Ada_Main_Program;

      -- Perform Ada finalization

   adafinal;

      -- Perform low level system finalization

   Finalize;

      -- Return the proper exit status
   return (gnat_exit_status);
end;

-- This section is entirely comments, so it has no effect on the
-- compilation of the Ada_Main package. It provides the list of
-- object files and linker options, as well as some standard
-- libraries needed for the link. The gnatlink utility parses
-- this b~hello.adb file to read these comment lines to generate
-- the appropriate command line arguments for the call to the
-- system linker. The BEGIN/END lines are used for sentinels for
-- this parsing operation.

-- The exact file names will of course depend on the environment,
-- host/target and location of files on the host system.

-- BEGIN Object file/option list
--    ./hello.o
--    -L./
--    -L/usr/local/gnat/lib/gcc-lib/i686-pc-linux-gnu/2.8.1/adalib/
--    /usr/local/gnat/lib/gcc-lib/i686-pc-linux-gnu/2.8.1/adalib/libgnat.a
-- END Object file/option list

end ada_main;
```

The Ada code in the above example is exactly what is generated by the binder. We have added comments to more clearly indicate the function of each part of the generated **Ada_Main** package.

The code is standard Ada in all respects, and can be processed by any tools that handle Ada. In particular, it is possible to use the debugger in Ada mode to debug the generated **Ada_Main** package. For example, suppose that for reasons that you do not understand, your program is crashing during elaboration of the body of **Ada.Text_IO**. To locate this bug, you can place a breakpoint on the call:

```
      Ada.Text_Io'Elab_Body;
```

and trace the elaboration routine for this package to find out where the problem might be (more usually of course you would be debugging elaboration code in your own application).

Appendix C Elaboration Order Handling in GNAT

This chapter describes the handling of elaboration code in Ada and in GNAT, and discusses how the order of elaboration of program units can be controlled in GNAT, either automatically or with explicit programming features.

C.1 Elaboration Code

Ada provides rather general mechanisms for executing code at elaboration time, that is to say before the main program starts executing. Such code arises in three contexts:

Initializers for variables.

> Variables declared at the library level, in package specs or bodies, can require initialization that is performed at elaboration time, as in:

```
Sqrt_Half : Float := Sqrt (0.5);
```

Package initialization code

> Code in a BEGIN-END section at the outer level of a package body is executed as part of the package body elaboration code.

Library level task allocators

> Tasks that are declared using task allocators at the library level start executing immediately and hence can execute at elaboration time.

Subprogram calls are possible in any of these contexts, which means that any arbitrary part of the program may be executed as part of the elaboration code. It is even possible to write a program which does all its work at elaboration time, with a null main program, although stylistically this would usually be considered an inappropriate way to structure a program.

An important concern arises in the context of elaboration code: we have to be sure that it is executed in an appropriate order. What we have is a series of elaboration code sections, potentially one section for each unit in the program. It is important that these execute in the correct order. Correctness here means that, taking the above example of the declaration of Sqrt_Half, if some other piece of elaboration code references Sqrt_Half, then it must run after the section of elaboration code that contains the declaration of Sqrt_Half.

There would never be any order of elaboration problem if we made a rule that whenever you with a unit, you must elaborate both the spec and body of that unit before elaborating the unit doing the with'ing:

```
with Unit_1;
package Unit_2 is ...
```

would require that both the body and spec of Unit_1 be elaborated before the spec of Unit_2. However, a rule like that would be far too restrictive. In particular, it would make it impossible to have routines in separate packages that were mutually recursive.

You might think that a clever enough compiler could look at the actual elaboration code and determine an appropriate correct order of elaboration, but in the general case, this is not possible. Consider the following example.

In the body of `Unit_1`, we have a procedure `Func_1` that references the variable `Sqrt_1`, which is declared in the elaboration code of the body of `Unit_1`:

```
Sqrt_1 : Float := Sqrt (0.1);
```

The elaboration code of the body of `Unit_1` also contains:

```
if expression_1 = 1 then
   Q := Unit_2.Func_2;
end if;
```

`Unit_2` is exactly parallel, it has a procedure `Func_2` that references the variable `Sqrt_2`, which is declared in the elaboration code of the body `Unit_2`:

```
Sqrt_2 : Float := Sqrt (0.1);
```

The elaboration code of the body of `Unit_2` also contains:

```
if expression_2 = 2 then
   Q := Unit_1.Func_1;
end if;
```

Now the question is, which of the following orders of elaboration is acceptable:

```
Spec of Unit_1
Spec of Unit_2
Body of Unit_1
Body of Unit_2
```

or

```
Spec of Unit_2
Spec of Unit_1
Body of Unit_2
Body of Unit_1
```

If you carefully analyze the flow here, you will see that you cannot tell at compile time the answer to this question. If `expression_1` is not equal to 1, and `expression_2` is not equal to 2, then either order is acceptable, because neither of the function calls is executed. If both tests evaluate to true, then neither order is acceptable and in fact there is no correct order.

If one of the two expressions is true, and the other is false, then one of the above orders is correct, and the other is incorrect. For example, if `expression_1` $/= 1$ and `expression_2` $= 2$, then the call to `Func_1` will occur, but not the call to `Func_2`. This means that it is essential to elaborate the body of `Unit_1` before the body of `Unit_2`, so the first order of elaboration is correct and the second is wrong.

By making `expression_1` and `expression_2` depend on input data, or perhaps the time of day, we can make it impossible for the compiler or binder to figure out which of these expressions will be true, and hence it is impossible to guarantee a safe order of elaboration at run time.

C.2 Checking the Elaboration Order

In some languages that involve the same kind of elaboration problems, e.g. Java and C++, the programmer is expected to worry about these ordering problems himself, and it is common to write a program in which an incorrect elaboration order gives surprising results, because it references variables before they are initialized. Ada is designed to be a safe language, and a programmer-beware approach is clearly not sufficient. Consequently, the language provides three lines of defense:

Standard rules

> Some standard rules restrict the possible choice of elaboration order. In particular, if you `with` a unit, then its spec is always elaborated before the unit doing the `with`. Similarly, a parent spec is always elaborated before the child spec, and finally a spec is always elaborated before its corresponding body.

Dynamic elaboration checks

> Dynamic checks are made at run time, so that if some entity is accessed before it is elaborated (typically by means of a subprogram call) then the exception (`Program_Error`) is raised.

Elaboration control

> Facilities are provided for the programmer to specify the desired order of elaboration.

Let's look at these facilities in more detail. First, the rules for dynamic checking. One possible rule would be simply to say that the exception is raised if you access a variable which has not yet been elaborated. The trouble with this approach is that it could require expensive checks on every variable reference. Instead Ada has two rules which are a little more restrictive, but easier to check, and easier to state:

Restrictions on calls

> A subprogram can only be called at elaboration time if its body has been elaborated. The rules for elaboration given above guarantee that the spec of the subprogram has been elaborated before the call, but not the body. If this rule is violated, then the exception `Program_Error` is raised.

Restrictions on instantiations

> A generic unit can only be instantiated if the body of the generic unit has been elaborated. Again, the rules for elaboration given above guarantee that the spec of the generic unit has been elaborated before the instantiation, but not the body. If this rule is violated, then the exception `Program_Error` is raised.

The idea is that if the body has been elaborated, then any variables it references must have been elaborated; by checking for the body being elaborated we guarantee that none of its references causes any trouble. As we noted above, this is a little too restrictive, because a subprogram that has no non-local references in its body may in fact be safe to call. However, it really would be unsafe to rely on this, because it would mean that the caller was aware of details of the implementation in the body. This goes against the basic tenets of Ada.

A plausible implementation can be described as follows. A Boolean variable is associated with each subprogram and each generic unit. This variable is initialized to False, and is set to True at the point body is elaborated. Every call or instantiation checks the variable, and raises `Program_Error` if the variable is False.

Note that one might think that it would be good enough to have one Boolean variable for each package, but that would not deal with cases of trying to call a body in the same package as the call that has not been elaborated yet. Of course a compiler may be able to do enough analysis to optimize away some of the Boolean variables as unnecessary, and `GNAT` indeed does such optimizations, but still the easiest conceptual model is to think of there being one variable per subprogram.

C.3 Controlling the Elaboration Order

In the previous section we discussed the rules in Ada which ensure that `Program_Error` is raised if an incorrect elaboration order is chosen. This prevents erroneous executions, but we need mechanisms to specify a correct execution and avoid the exception altogether. To achieve this, Ada provides a number of features for controlling the order of elaboration. We discuss these features in this section.

First, there are several ways of indicating to the compiler that a given unit has no elaboration problems:

packages that do not require a body

A library package that does not require a body does not permit a body (this rule was introduced in Ada 95). Thus if we have a such a package, as in:

```
package Definitions is
   generic
      type m is new integer;
   package Subp is
      type a is array (1 .. 10) of m;
      type b is array (1 .. 20) of m;
   end Subp;
end Definitions;
```

A package that `with`'s `Definitions` may safely instantiate `Definitions.Subp` because the compiler can determine that there definitely is no package body to worry about in this case

pragma Pure

Places sufficient restrictions on a unit to guarantee that no call to any subprogram in the unit can result in an elaboration problem. This means that the compiler does not need to worry about the point of elaboration of such units, and in particular, does not need to check any calls to any subprograms in this unit.

pragma Preelaborate

This pragma places slightly less stringent restrictions on a unit than does pragma Pure, but these restrictions are still sufficient to ensure that there are no elaboration problems with any calls to the unit.

pragma Elaborate_Body

This pragma requires that the body of a unit be elaborated immediately after its spec. Suppose a unit A has such a pragma, and unit B does a `with` of unit

A. Recall that the standard rules require the spec of unit `A` to be elaborated before the `with`'ing unit; given the pragma in `A`, we also know that the body of `A` will be elaborated before `B`, so that calls to `A` are safe and do not need a check.

Note that, unlike pragma `Pure` and pragma `Preelaborate`, the use of `Elaborate_Body` does not guarantee that the program is free of elaboration problems, because it may not be possible to satisfy the requested elaboration order. Let's go back to the example with `Unit_1` and `Unit_2`. If a programmer marks `Unit_1` as `Elaborate_Body`, and not `Unit_2`, then the order of elaboration will be:

```
Spec of Unit_2
Spec of Unit_1
Body of Unit_1
Body of Unit_2
```

Now that means that the call to `Func_1` in `Unit_2` need not be checked, it must be safe. But the call to `Func_2` in `Unit_1` may still fail if `Expression_1` is equal to 1, and the programmer must still take responsibility for this not being the case.

If all units carry a pragma `Elaborate_Body`, then all problems are eliminated, except for calls entirely within a body, which are in any case fully under programmer control. However, using the pragma everywhere is not always possible. In particular, for our `Unit_1/Unit_2` example, if we marked both of them as having pragma `Elaborate_Body`, then clearly there would be no possible elaboration order.

The above pragmas allow a server to guarantee safe use by clients, and clearly this is the preferable approach. Consequently a good rule is to mark units as `Pure` or `Preelaborate` if possible, and if this is not possible, mark them as `Elaborate_Body` if possible. As we have seen, there are situations where neither of these three pragmas can be used. So we also provide methods for clients to control the order of elaboration of the servers on which they depend:

pragma Elaborate (unit)

> This pragma is placed in the context clause, after a `with` clause, and it requires that the body of the named unit be elaborated before the unit in which the pragma occurs. The idea is to use this pragma if the current unit calls at elaboration time, directly or indirectly, some subprogram in the named unit.

pragma Elaborate_All (unit)

> This is a stronger version of the Elaborate pragma. Consider the following example:
>
> ```
> Unit A with's unit B and calls B.Func in elab code
> Unit B with's unit C, and B.Func calls C.Func
> ```

Now if we put a pragma `Elaborate (B)` in unit `A`, this ensures that the body of `B` is elaborated before the call, but not the body of `C`, so the call to `C.Func` could still cause `Program_Error` to be raised.

The effect of a pragma `Elaborate_All` is stronger, it requires not only that the body of the named unit be elaborated before the unit doing the `with`, but also the bodies of all units that the named unit uses, following `with` links transitively. For example, if we put a pragma `Elaborate_All (B)` in unit `A`, then it requires not only that the body of `B` be elaborated before `A`, but also the body of `C`, because `B` `with`'s `C`.

We are now in a position to give a usage rule in Ada for avoiding elaboration problems, at least if dynamic dispatching and access to subprogram values are not used. We will handle these cases separately later.

The rule is simple. If a unit has elaboration code that can directly or indirectly make a call to a subprogram in a `with`'ed unit, or instantiate a generic package in a `with`'ed unit, then if the `with`'ed unit does not have pragma `Pure` or `Preelaborate`, then the client should have a pragma `Elaborate_All` for the `with`'ed unit. By following this rule a client is assured that calls can be made without risk of an exception.

For generic subprogram instantiations, the rule can be relaxed to require only a pragma `Elaborate` since elaborating the body of a subprogram cannot cause any transitive elaboration (we are not calling the subprogram in this case, just elaborating its declaration).

If this rule is not followed, then a program may be in one of four states:

No order exists

> No order of elaboration exists which follows the rules, taking into account any `Elaborate`, `Elaborate_All`, or `Elaborate_Body` pragmas. In this case, an Ada compiler must diagnose the situation at bind time, and refuse to build an executable program.

One or more orders exist, all incorrect

> One or more acceptable elaboration orders exist, and all of them generate an elaboration order problem. In this case, the binder can build an executable program, but `Program_Error` will be raised when the program is run.

Several orders exist, some right, some incorrect

> One or more acceptable elaboration orders exists, and some of them work, and some do not. The programmer has not controlled the order of elaboration, so the binder may or may not pick one of the correct orders, and the program may or may not raise an exception when it is run. This is the worst case, because it means that the program may fail when moved to another compiler, or even another version of the same compiler.

One or more orders exists, all correct

> One ore more acceptable elaboration orders exist, and all of them work. In this case the program runs successfully. This state of affairs can be guaranteed by following the rule we gave above, but may be true even if the rule is not followed.

Note that one additional advantage of following our rules on the use of `Elaborate` and `Elaborate_All` is that the program continues to stay in the ideal (all orders OK) state even if maintenance changes some bodies of some units. Conversely, if a program that does not follow this rule happens to be safe at some point, this state of affairs may deteriorate silently as a result of maintenance changes.

You may have noticed that the above discussion did not mention the use of `Elaborate_Body`. This was a deliberate omission. If you `with` an `Elaborate_Body` unit, it still may be the case that code in the body makes calls to some other unit, so it is still necessary to use `Elaborate_All` on such units.

C.4 Controlling Elaboration in GNAT - Internal Calls

In the case of internal calls, i.e. calls within a single package, the programmer has full control over the order of elaboration, and it is up to the programmer to elaborate declarations in an appropriate order. For example writing:

```
function One return Float;

Q : Float := One;

function One return Float is
begin
     return 1.0;
end One;
```

will obviously raise `Program_Error` at run time, because function One will be called before its body is elaborated. In this case GNAT will generate a warning that the call will raise `Program_Error`:

```
1. procedure y is
2.    function One return Float;
3.
4.    Q : Float := One;
                   |
   >>> warning: cannot call "One" before body is elaborated
   >>> warning: Program_Error will be raised at run time

5.
6.    function One return Float is
7.    begin
8.         return 1.0;
9.    end One;
10.
11. begin
12.    null;
13. end;
```

Note that in this particular case, it is likely that the call is safe, because the function One does not access any global variables. Nevertheless in Ada, we do not want the validity of the check to depend on the contents of the body (think about the separate compilation case), so this is still wrong, as we discussed in the previous sections.

The error is easily corrected by rearranging the declarations so that the body of One appears before the declaration containing the call (note that in Ada 95 and Ada 2005, declarations can appear in any order, so there is no restriction that would prevent this reordering, and if we write:

```
function One return Float;

function One return Float is
begin
     return 1.0;
end One;

Q : Float := One;
```

then all is well, no warning is generated, and no `Program_Error` exception will be raised. Things are more complicated when a chain of subprograms is executed:

```
function A return Integer;
function B return Integer;
function C return Integer;

function B return Integer is begin return A; end;
function C return Integer is begin return B; end;

X : Integer := C;

function A return Integer is begin return 1; end;
```

Now the call to `C` at elaboration time in the declaration of `X` is correct, because the body of `C` is already elaborated, and the call to `B` within the body of `C` is correct, but the call to `A` within the body of `B` is incorrect, because the body of `A` has not been elaborated, so `Program_Error` will be raised on the call to `A`. In this case GNAT will generate a warning that `Program_Error` may be raised at the point of the call. Let's look at the warning:

```
 1. procedure x is
 2.     function A return Integer;
 3.     function B return Integer;
 4.     function C return Integer;
 5.
 6.     function B return Integer is begin return A; end;
                                                  |
    >>> warning: call to "A" before body is elaborated may
                  raise Program_Error
    >>> warning: "B" called at line 7
    >>> warning: "C" called at line 9

 7.     function C return Integer is begin return B; end;
 8.
 9.     X : Integer := C;
10.
11.     function A return Integer is begin return 1; end;
12.
13. begin
14.     null;
15. end;
```

Note that the message here says "may raise", instead of the direct case, where the message says "will be raised". That's because whether `A` is actually called depends in general on run-time flow of control. For example, if the body of `B` said

```
function B return Integer is
begin
   if some-condition-depending-on-input-data then
      return A;
   else
      return 1;
   end if;
end B;
```

then we could not know until run time whether the incorrect call to A would actually occur, so `Program_Error` might or might not be raised. It is possible for a compiler to do a better job of analyzing bodies, to determine whether or not `Program_Error` might be raised, but it certainly couldn't do a perfect job (that would require solving the halting problem and is provably impossible), and because this is a warning anyway, it does not seem worth the effort to do the analysis. Cases in which it would be relevant are rare.

In practice, warnings of either of the forms given above will usually correspond to real errors, and should be examined carefully and eliminated. In the rare case where a warning is bogus, it can be suppressed by any of the following methods:

- Compile with the '`-gnatws`' switch set

- Suppress `Elaboration_Check` for the called subprogram

- Use pragma `Warnings_Off` to turn warnings off for the call

For the internal elaboration check case, GNAT by default generates the necessary run-time checks to ensure that `Program_Error` is raised if any call fails an elaboration check. Of course this can only happen if a warning has been issued as described above. The use of pragma `Suppress (Elaboration_Check)` may (but is not guaranteed to) suppress some of these checks, meaning that it may be possible (but is not guaranteed) for a program to be able to call a subprogram whose body is not yet elaborated, without raising a `Program_Error` exception.

C.5 Controlling Elaboration in GNAT - External Calls

The previous section discussed the case in which the execution of a particular thread of elaboration code occurred entirely within a single unit. This is the easy case to handle, because a programmer has direct and total control over the order of elaboration, and furthermore, checks need only be generated in cases which are rare and which the compiler can easily detect. The situation is more complex when separate compilation is taken into account. Consider the following:

```
package Math is
   function Sqrt (Arg : Float) return Float;
end Math;

package body Math is
   function Sqrt (Arg : Float) return Float is
   begin

      ...
   end Sqrt;
end Math;
with Math;
package Stuff is
   X : Float := Math.Sqrt (0.5);
end Stuff;

with Stuff;
procedure Main is
begin

   ...
end Main;
```

where `Main` is the main program. When this program is executed, the elaboration code must first be executed, and one of the jobs of the binder is to determine the order in which the units of a program are to be elaborated. In this case we have four units: the spec and body of `Math`, the spec of `Stuff` and the body of `Main`). In what order should the four separate sections of elaboration code be executed?

There are some restrictions in the order of elaboration that the binder can choose. In particular, if unit U has a `with` for a package `X`, then you are assured that the spec of `X` is elaborated before U , but you are not assured that the body of `X` is elaborated before U. This means that in the above case, the binder is allowed to choose the order:

```
spec of Math
spec of Stuff
body of Math
body of Main
```

but that's not good, because now the call to `Math.Sqrt` that happens during the elaboration of the `Stuff` spec happens before the body of `Math.Sqrt` is elaborated, and hence causes `Program_Error` exception to be raised. At first glance, one might say that the binder is misbehaving, because obviously you want to elaborate the body of something you `with` first, but that is not a general rule that can be followed in all cases. Consider

```
package X is ...

package Y is ...

with X;
package body Y is ...

with Y;
package body X is ...
```

This is a common arrangement, and, apart from the order of elaboration problems that might arise in connection with elaboration code, this works fine. A rule that says that you must first elaborate the body of anything you `with` cannot work in this case: the body of

X with's Y, which means you would have to elaborate the body of Y first, but that with's X, which means you have to elaborate the body of X first, but ... and we have a loop that cannot be broken.

It is true that the binder can in many cases guess an order of elaboration that is unlikely to cause a `Program_Error` exception to be raised, and it tries to do so (in the above example of `Math/Stuff/Spec`, the GNAT binder will by default elaborate the body of `Math` right after its spec, so all will be well).

However, a program that blindly relies on the binder to be helpful can get into trouble, as we discussed in the previous sections, so GNAT provides a number of facilities for assisting the programmer in developing programs that are robust with respect to elaboration order.

C.6 Default Behavior in GNAT - Ensuring Safety

The default behavior in GNAT ensures elaboration safety. In its default mode GNAT implements the rule we previously described as the right approach. Let's restate it:

- *If a unit has elaboration code that can directly or indirectly make a call to a subprogram in a* with*'ed unit, or instantiate a generic package in a* with*'ed unit, then if the* with*'ed unit does not have pragma* Pure *or* Preelaborate*, then the client should have an* Elaborate_All *pragma for the* with*'ed unit.*

  In the case of instantiating a generic subprogram, it is always sufficient to have only an Elaborate *pragma for the* with*'ed unit.*

By following this rule a client is assured that calls and instantiations can be made without risk of an exception.

In this mode GNAT traces all calls that are potentially made from elaboration code, and puts in any missing implicit `Elaborate` and `Elaborate_All` pragmas. The advantage of this approach is that no elaboration problems are possible if the binder can find an elaboration order that is consistent with these implicit `Elaborate` and `Elaborate_All` pragmas. The disadvantage of this approach is that no such order may exist.

If the binder does not generate any diagnostics, then it means that it has found an elaboration order that is guaranteed to be safe. However, the binder may still be relying on implicitly generated `Elaborate` and `Elaborate_All` pragmas so portability to other compilers than GNAT is not guaranteed.

If it is important to guarantee portability, then the compilations should use the '-gnatwl' (warn on elaboration problems) switch. This will cause warning messages to be generated indicating the missing `Elaborate` and `Elaborate_All` pragmas. Consider the following source program:

```
with k;
package j is
  m : integer := k.r;
end;
```

where it is clear that there should be a pragma `Elaborate_All` for unit k. An implicit pragma will be generated, and it is likely that the binder will be able to honor it. However, if you want to port this program to some other Ada compiler than GNAT, it is safer to

include the pragma explicitly in the source. If this unit is compiled with the '-gnatwl'
switch, then the compiler outputs a warning:

```
1. with k;
2. package j is
3.    m : integer := k.r;
                      |
   >>> warning: call to "r" may raise Program_Error
   >>> warning: missing pragma Elaborate_All for "k"

4. end;
```

and these warnings can be used as a guide for supplying manually the missing pragmas. It
is usually a bad idea to use this warning option during development. That's because it will
warn you when you need to put in a pragma, but cannot warn you when it is time to take
it out. So the use of pragma `Elaborate_All` may lead to unnecessary dependencies and
even false circularities.

This default mode is more restrictive than the Ada Reference Manual, and it is possible
to construct programs which will compile using the dynamic model described there, but
will run into a circularity using the safer static model we have described.

Of course any Ada compiler must be able to operate in a mode consistent with the
requirements of the Ada Reference Manual, and in particular must have the capability of
implementing the standard dynamic model of elaboration with run-time checks.

In GNAT, this standard mode can be achieved either by the use of the '-gnatE' switch
on the compiler (`gcc` or `gnatmake`) command, or by the use of the configuration pragma:

    pragma Elaboration_Checks (RM);

Either approach will cause the unit affected to be compiled using the standard dynamic
run-time elaboration checks described in the Ada Reference Manual. The static model is
generally preferable, since it is clearly safer to rely on compile and link time checks rather
than run-time checks. However, in the case of legacy code, it may be difficult to meet the
requirements of the static model. This issue is further discussed in Section C.10 [What to
Do If the Default Elaboration Behavior Fails], page 309.

Note that the static model provides a strict subset of the allowed behavior and programs
of the Ada Reference Manual, so if you do adhere to the static model and no circularities
exist, then you are assured that your program will work using the dynamic model, providing
that you remove any pragma Elaborate statements from the source.

C.7 Treatment of Pragma Elaborate

The use of `pragma Elaborate` should generally be avoided in Ada 95 and Ada 2005 programs, since there is no guarantee that transitive calls will be properly handled. Indeed at
one point, this pragma was placed in Annex J (Obsolescent Features), on the grounds that
it is never useful.

Now that's a bit restrictive. In practice, the case in which `pragma Elaborate` is useful
is when the caller knows that there are no transitive calls, or that the called unit contains
all necessary transitive `pragma Elaborate` statements, and legacy code often contains such
uses.

Strictly speaking the static mode in GNAT should ignore such pragmas, since there is no assurance at compile time that the necessary safety conditions are met. In practice, this would cause GNAT to be incompatible with correctly written Ada 83 code that had all necessary `pragma Elaborate` statements in place. Consequently, we made the decision that GNAT in its default mode will believe that if it encounters a `pragma Elaborate` then the programmer knows what they are doing, and it will trust that no elaboration errors can occur.

The result of this decision is two-fold. First to be safe using the static mode, you should remove all `pragma Elaborate` statements. Second, when fixing circularities in existing code, you can selectively use `pragma Elaborate` statements to convince the static mode of GNAT that it need not generate an implicit `pragma Elaborate_All` statement.

When using the static mode with '`-gnatwl`', any use of `pragma Elaborate` will generate a warning about possible problems.

C.8 Elaboration Issues for Library Tasks

In this section we examine special elaboration issues that arise for programs that declare library level tasks.

Generally the model of execution of an Ada program is that all units are elaborated, and then execution of the program starts. However, the declaration of library tasks definitely does not fit this model. The reason for this is that library tasks start as soon as they are declared (more precisely, as soon as the statement part of the enclosing package body is reached), that is to say before elaboration of the program is complete. This means that if such a task calls a subprogram, or an entry in another task, the callee may or may not be elaborated yet, and in the standard Reference Manual model of dynamic elaboration checks, you can even get timing dependent Program_Error exceptions, since there can be a race between the elaboration code and the task code.

The static model of elaboration in GNAT seeks to avoid all such dynamic behavior, by being conservative, and the conservative approach in this particular case is to assume that all the code in a task body is potentially executed at elaboration time if a task is declared at the library level.

This can definitely result in unexpected circularities. Consider the following example

```
package Decls is
   task Lib_Task is
      entry Start;
   end Lib_Task;

   type My_Int is new Integer;

   function Ident (M : My_Int) return My_Int;
end Decls;

with Utils;
package body Decls is
   task body Lib_Task is
   begin
      accept Start;
      Utils.Put_Val (2);
   end Lib_Task;
```

```
      function Ident (M : My_Int) return My_Int is
      begin
         return M;
      end Ident;
   end Decls;

   with Decls;
   package Utils is
      procedure Put_Val (Arg : Decls.My_Int);
   end Utils;

   with Text_IO;
   package body Utils is
      procedure Put_Val (Arg : Decls.My_Int) is
      begin
         Text_IO.Put_Line (Decls.My_Int'Image (Decls.Ident (Arg)));
      end Put_Val;
   end Utils;

   with Decls;
   procedure Main is
   begin
      Decls.Lib_Task.Start;
   end;
```

If the above example is compiled in the default static elaboration mode, then a circularity occurs. The circularity comes from the call `Utils.Put_Val` in the task body of `Decls.Lib_Task`. Since this call occurs in elaboration code, we need an implicit pragma `Elaborate_All` for `Utils`. This means that not only must the spec and body of `Utils` be elaborated before the body of `Decls`, but also the spec and body of any unit that is `with`'ed by the body of `Utils` must also be elaborated before the body of `Decls`. This is the transitive implication of pragma `Elaborate_All` and it makes sense, because in general the body of `Put_Val` might have a call to something in a `with`'ed unit.

In this case, the body of Utils (actually its spec) `with`'s Decls. Unfortunately this means that the body of `Decls` must be elaborated before itself, in case there is a call from the body of `Utils`.

Here is the exact chain of events we are worrying about:

1. In the body of `Decls` a call is made from within the body of a library task to a subprogram in the package `Utils`. Since this call may occur at elaboration time (given that the task is activated at elaboration time), we have to assume the worst, i.e. that the call does happen at elaboration time.

2. This means that the body and spec of `Util` must be elaborated before the body of `Decls` so that this call does not cause an access before elaboration.

3. Within the body of `Util`, specifically within the body of `Util.Put_Val` there may be calls to any unit `with`'ed by this package.

4. One such `with`'ed package is package `Decls`, so there might be a call to a subprogram in `Decls` in `Put_Val`. In fact there is such a call in this example, but we would have to assume that there was such a call even if it were not there, since we are not supposed to write the body of `Decls` knowing what is in the body of `Utils`; certainly in the case of the static elaboration model, the compiler does not know what is in other bodies and must assume the worst.

5. This means that the spec and body of `Decls` must also be elaborated before we elaborate the unit containing the call, but that unit is `Decls`! This means that the body of `Decls` must be elaborated before itself, and that's a circularity.

Indeed, if you add an explicit pragma `Elaborate_All` for `Utils` in the body of `Decls` you will get a true Ada Reference Manual circularity that makes the program illegal.

In practice, we have found that problems with the static model of elaboration in existing code often arise from library tasks, so we must address this particular situation.

Note that if we compile and run the program above, using the dynamic model of elaboration (that is to say use the '-gnatE' switch), then it compiles, binds, links, and runs, printing the expected result of 2. Therefore in some sense the circularity here is only apparent, and we need to capture the properties of this program that distinguish it from other library-level tasks that have real elaboration problems.

We have four possible answers to this question:

- Use the dynamic model of elaboration.

  If we use the '-gnatE' switch, then as noted above, the program works. Why is this? If we examine the task body, it is apparent that the task cannot proceed past the `accept` statement until after elaboration has been completed, because the corresponding entry call comes from the main program, not earlier. This is why the dynamic model works here. But that's really giving up on a precise analysis, and we prefer to take this approach only if we cannot solve the problem in any other manner. So let us examine two ways to reorganize the program to avoid the potential elaboration problem.

- Split library tasks into separate packages.

  Write separate packages, so that library tasks are isolated from other declarations as much as possible. Let us look at a variation on the above program.

```
package Decls1 is
  task Lib_Task is
     entry Start;
  end Lib_Task;
end Decls1;

with Utils;
package body Decls1 is
  task body Lib_Task is
  begin
     accept Start;
     Utils.Put_Val (2);
  end Lib_Task;
end Decls1;

package Decls2 is
  type My_Int is new Integer;
  function Ident (M : My_Int) return My_Int;
end Decls2;

with Utils;
package body Decls2 is
  function Ident (M : My_Int) return My_Int is
  begin
     return M;
  end Ident;
```

```
end Decls2;

with Decls2;
package Utils is
  procedure Put_Val (Arg : Decls2.My_Int);
end Utils;

with Text_IO;
package body Utils is
  procedure Put_Val (Arg : Decls2.My_Int) is
  begin
     Text_IO.Put_Line (Decls2.My_Int'Image (Decls2.Ident (Arg)));
  end Put_Val;
end Utils;

with Decls1;
procedure Main is
begin
   Decls1.Lib_Task.Start;
end;
```

All we have done is to split `Decls` into two packages, one containing the library task, and one containing everything else. Now there is no cycle, and the program compiles, binds, links and executes using the default static model of elaboration.

- Declare separate task types.

  A significant part of the problem arises because of the use of the single task declaration form. This means that the elaboration of the task type, and the elaboration of the task itself (i.e. the creation of the task) happen at the same time. A good rule of style in Ada is to always create explicit task types. By following the additional step of placing task objects in separate packages from the task type declaration, many elaboration problems are avoided. Here is another modified example of the example program:

```
package Decls is
  task type Lib_Task_Type is
     entry Start;
  end Lib_Task_Type;

  type My_Int is new Integer;

  function Ident (M : My_Int) return My_Int;
end Decls;

with Utils;
package body Decls is
  task body Lib_Task_Type is
  begin
     accept Start;
     Utils.Put_Val (2);
  end Lib_Task_Type;

  function Ident (M : My_Int) return My_Int is
  begin
     return M;
  end Ident;
end Decls;

with Decls;
```

```
package Utils is
  procedure Put_Val (Arg : Decls.My_Int);
end Utils;

with Text_IO;
package body Utils is
  procedure Put_Val (Arg : Decls.My_Int) is
  begin
     Text_IO.Put_Line (Decls.My_Int'Image (Decls.Ident (Arg)));
  end Put_Val;
end Utils;

with Decls;
package Declst is
   Lib_Task : Decls.Lib_Task_Type;
end Declst;

with Declst;
procedure Main is
begin
   Declst.Lib_Task.Start;
end;
```

What we have done here is to replace the `task` declaration in package `Decls` with a `task type` declaration. Then we introduce a separate package `Declst` to contain the actual task object. This separates the elaboration issues for the `task type` declaration, which causes no trouble, from the elaboration issues of the task object, which is also unproblematic, since it is now independent of the elaboration of `Utils`. This separation of concerns also corresponds to a generally sound engineering principle of separating declarations from instances. This version of the program also compiles, binds, links, and executes, generating the expected output.

• Use No_Entry_Calls_In_Elaboration_Code restriction.

The previous two approaches described how a program can be restructured to avoid the special problems caused by library task bodies. in practice, however, such restructuring may be difficult to apply to existing legacy code, so we must consider solutions that do not require massive rewriting.

Let us consider more carefully why our original sample program works under the dynamic model of elaboration. The reason is that the code in the task body blocks immediately on the `accept` statement. Now of course there is nothing to prohibit elaboration code from making entry calls (for example from another library level task), so we cannot tell in isolation that the task will not execute the accept statement during elaboration.

However, in practice it is very unusual to see elaboration code make any entry calls, and the pattern of tasks starting at elaboration time and then immediately blocking on `accept` or `select` statements is very common. What this means is that the compiler is being too pessimistic when it analyzes the whole package body as though it might be executed at elaboration time.

If we know that the elaboration code contains no entry calls, (a very safe assumption most of the time, that could almost be made the default behavior), then we can compile all units of the program under control of the following configuration pragma:

```
pragma Restrictions (No_Entry_Calls_In_Elaboration_Code);
```

This pragma can be placed in the 'gnat.adc' file in the usual manner. If we take our original unmodified program and compile it in the presence of a 'gnat.adc' containing the above pragma, then once again, we can compile, bind, link, and execute, obtaining the expected result. In the presence of this pragma, the compiler does not trace calls in a task body, that appear after the first `accept` or `select` statement, and therefore does not report a potential circularity in the original program.

The compiler will check to the extent it can that the above restriction is not violated, but it is not always possible to do a complete check at compile time, so it is important to use this pragma only if the stated restriction is in fact met, that is to say no task receives an entry call before elaboration of all units is completed.

C.9 Mixing Elaboration Models

So far, we have assumed that the entire program is either compiled using the dynamic model or static model, ensuring consistency. It is possible to mix the two models, but rules have to be followed if this mixing is done to ensure that elaboration checks are not omitted.

The basic rule is that *a unit compiled with the static model cannot be* `with`'ed *by a unit compiled with the dynamic model.* The reason for this is that in the static model, a unit assumes that its clients guarantee to use (the equivalent of) pragma `Elaborate_All` so that no elaboration checks are required in inner subprograms, and this assumption is violated if the client is compiled with dynamic checks.

The precise rule is as follows. A unit that is compiled with dynamic checks can only `with` a unit that meets at least one of the following criteria:

- The `with`'ed unit is itself compiled with dynamic elaboration checks (that is with the '-gnatE' switch.

- The `with`'ed unit is an internal GNAT implementation unit from the System, Interfaces, Ada, or GNAT hierarchies.

- The `with`'ed unit has pragma Preelaborate or pragma Pure.

- The `with`'ing unit (that is the client) has an explicit pragma `Elaborate_All` for the `with`'ed unit.

If this rule is violated, that is if a unit with dynamic elaboration checks `with`'s a unit that does not meet one of the above four criteria, then the binder (**gnatbind**) will issue a warning similar to that in the following example:

```
warning: "x.ads" has dynamic elaboration checks and with's
warning:   "y.ads" which has static elaboration checks
```

These warnings indicate that the rule has been violated, and that as a result elaboration checks may be missed in the resulting executable file. This warning may be suppressed using the '-ws' binder switch in the usual manner.

One useful application of this mixing rule is in the case of a subsystem which does not itself `with` units from the remainder of the application. In this case, the entire subsystem can be compiled with dynamic checks to resolve a circularity in the subsystem, while allowing the main application that uses this subsystem to be compiled using the more reliable default static model.

C.10 What to Do If the Default Elaboration Behavior Fails

If the binder cannot find an acceptable order, it outputs detailed diagnostics. For example:

```
error: elaboration circularity detected
info:    "proc (body)" must be elaborated before "pack (body)"
info:      reason: Elaborate_All probably needed in unit "pack (body)"
info:      recompile "pack (body)" with -gnatwl
info:                             for full details
info:          "proc (body)"
info:            is needed by its spec:
info:          "proc (spec)"
info:            which is withed by:
info:          "pack (body)"
info:    "pack (body)" must be elaborated before "proc (body)"
info:      reason: pragma Elaborate in unit "proc (body)"
```

In this case we have a cycle that the binder cannot break. On the one hand, there is an explicit pragma Elaborate in proc for pack. This means that the body of pack must be elaborated before the body of proc. On the other hand, there is elaboration code in pack that calls a subprogram in proc. This means that for maximum safety, there should really be a pragma Elaborate_All in pack for proc which would require that the body of proc be elaborated before the body of pack. Clearly both requirements cannot be satisfied. Faced with a circularity of this kind, you have three different options.

Fix the program
> The most desirable option from the point of view of long-term maintenance is to rearrange the program so that the elaboration problems are avoided. One useful technique is to place the elaboration code into separate child packages. Another is to move some of the initialization code to explicitly called subprograms, where the program controls the order of initialization explicitly. Although this is the most desirable option, it may be impractical and involve too much modification, especially in the case of complex legacy code.

Perform dynamic checks
> If the compilations are done using the '-gnatE' (dynamic elaboration check) switch, then GNAT behaves in a quite different manner. Dynamic checks are generated for all calls that could possibly result in raising an exception. With this switch, the compiler does not generate implicit Elaborate or Elaborate_All pragmas. The behavior then is exactly as specified in the Ada Reference Manual. The binder will generate an executable program that may or may not raise Program_Error, and then it is the programmer's job to ensure that it does not raise an exception. Note that it is important to compile all units with the switch, it cannot be used selectively.

Suppress checks
> The drawback of dynamic checks is that they generate a significant overhead at run time, both in space and time. If you are absolutely sure that your program cannot raise any elaboration exceptions, and you still want to use the dynamic elaboration model, then you can use the configuration pragma

`Suppress (Elaboration_Check)` to suppress all such checks. For example this pragma could be placed in the 'gnat.adc' file.

Suppress checks selectively

When you know that certain calls or instantiations in elaboration code cannot possibly lead to an elaboration error, and the binder nevertheless complains about implicit `Elaborate` and `Elaborate_All` pragmas that lead to elaboration circularities, it is possible to remove those warnings locally and obtain a program that will bind. Clearly this can be unsafe, and it is the responsibility of the programmer to make sure that the resulting program has no elaboration anomalies. The pragma `Suppress (Elaboration_Check)` can be used with different granularity to suppress warnings and break elaboration circularities:

- Place the pragma that names the called subprogram in the declarative part that contains the call.

- Place the pragma in the declarative part, without naming an entity. This disables warnings on all calls in the corresponding declarative region.

- Place the pragma in the package spec that declares the called subprogram, and name the subprogram. This disables warnings on all elaboration calls to that subprogram.

- Place the pragma in the package spec that declares the called subprogram, without naming any entity. This disables warnings on all elaboration calls to all subprograms declared in this spec.

- Use Pragma Elaborate As previously described in section See Section C.7 [Treatment of Pragma Elaborate], page 302, GNAT in static mode assumes that a `pragma` Elaborate indicates correctly that no elaboration checks are required on calls to the designated unit. There may be cases in which the caller knows that no transitive calls can occur, so that a `pragma Elaborate` will be sufficient in a case where `pragma Elaborate_All` would cause a circularity.

These five cases are listed in order of decreasing safety, and therefore require increasing programmer care in their application. Consider the following program:

```
package Pack1 is
  function F1 return Integer;
  X1 : Integer;
end Pack1;

package Pack2 is
  function F2 return Integer;
  function Pure (x : integer) return integer;
  --   pragma Suppress (Elaboration_Check, On => Pure);  -- (3)
  --   pragma Suppress (Elaboration_Check);              -- (4)
end Pack2;

with Pack2;
package body Pack1 is
  function F1 return Integer is
  begin
    return 100;
```

```
        end F1;
        Val : integer := Pack2.Pure (11);      -- Elab. call (1)
   begin
     declare
        -- pragma Suppress(Elaboration_Check, Pack2.F2);    -- (1)
        -- pragma Suppress(Elaboration_Check);              -- (2)
     begin
        X1 := Pack2.F2 + 1;                     -- Elab. call (2)
     end;
   end Pack1;

   with Pack1;
   package body Pack2 is
     function F2 return Integer is
     begin
        return Pack1.F1;
     end F2;
     function Pure (x : integer) return integer is
     begin
        return x ** 3 - 3 * x;
     end;
   end Pack2;

   with Pack1, Ada.Text_IO;
   procedure Proc3 is
   begin
      Ada.Text_IO.Put_Line(Pack1.X1'Img); -- 101
   end Proc3;
```

In the absence of any pragmas, an attempt to bind this program produces the following diagnostics:

```
error: elaboration circularity detected
info:     "pack1 (body)" must be elaborated before "pack1 (body)"
info:       reason: Elaborate_All probably needed in unit "pack1 (body)"
info:       recompile "pack1 (body)" with -gnatwl for full details
info:       "pack1 (body)"
info:          must be elaborated along with its spec:
info:       "pack1 (spec)"
info:          which is withed by:
info:       "pack2 (body)"
info:          which must be elaborated along with its spec:
info:       "pack2 (spec)"
info:          which is withed by:
info:       "pack1 (body)"
```

The sources of the circularity are the two calls to Pack2.Pure and Pack2.F2 in the body of Pack1. We can see that the call to F2 is safe, even though F2 calls F1, because the call appears after the elaboration of the body of F1. Therefore the pragma (1) is safe, and will remove the warning on the call. It is also possible to use pragma (2) because there are no other potentially unsafe calls in the block.

The call to Pure is safe because this function does not depend on the state of Pack2. Therefore any call to this function is safe, and it is correct to place pragma (3) in the corresponding package spec.

Finally, we could place pragma (4) in the spec of `Pack2` to disable warnings on all calls to functions declared therein. Note that this is not necessarily safe, and requires more detailed examination of the subprogram bodies involved. In particular, a call to `F2` requires that `F1` be already elaborated.

It is hard to generalize on which of these four approaches should be taken. Obviously if it is possible to fix the program so that the default treatment works, this is preferable, but this may not always be practical. It is certainly simple enough to use '`-gnatE`' but the danger in this case is that, even if the GNAT binder finds a correct elaboration order, it may not always do so, and certainly a binder from another Ada compiler might not. A combination of testing and analysis (for which the warnings generated with the '`-gnatwl`' switch can be useful) must be used to ensure that the program is free of errors. One switch that is useful in this testing is the '`-p (pessimistic elaboration order)`' switch for `gnatbind`. Normally the binder tries to find an order that has the best chance of avoiding elaboration problems. However, if this switch is used, the binder plays a devil's advocate role, and tries to choose the order that has the best chance of failing. If your program works even with this switch, then it has a better chance of being error free, but this is still not a guarantee.

For an example of this approach in action, consider the C-tests (executable tests) from the ACVC suite. If these are compiled and run with the default treatment, then all but one of them succeed without generating any error diagnostics from the binder. However, there is one test that fails, and this is not surprising, because the whole point of this test is to ensure that the compiler can handle cases where it is impossible to determine a correct order statically, and it checks that an exception is indeed raised at run time.

This one test must be compiled and run using the '`-gnatE`' switch, and then it passes. Alternatively, the entire suite can be run using this switch. It is never wrong to run with the dynamic elaboration switch if your code is correct, and we assume that the C-tests are indeed correct (it is less efficient, but efficiency is not a factor in running the ACVC tests.)

C.11 Elaboration for Access-to-Subprogram Values

Access-to-subprogram types (introduced in Ada 95) complicate the handling of elaboration. The trouble is that it becomes impossible to tell at compile time which procedure is being called. This means that it is not possible for the binder to analyze the elaboration requirements in this case.

If at the point at which the access value is created (i.e., the evaluation of `P'Access` for a subprogram `P`), the body of the subprogram is known to have been elaborated, then the access value is safe, and its use does not require a check. This may be achieved by appropriate arrangement of the order of declarations if the subprogram is in the current unit, or, if the subprogram is in another unit, by using pragma `Pure`, `Preelaborate`, or `Elaborate_Body` on the referenced unit.

If the referenced body is not known to have been elaborated at the point the access value is created, then any use of the access value must do a dynamic check, and this dynamic check will fail and raise a `Program_Error` exception if the body has not been elaborated yet. GNAT will generate the necessary checks, and in addition, if the '`-gnatwl`' switch is set, will generate warnings that such checks are required.

The use of dynamic dispatching for tagged types similarly generates a requirement for dynamic checks, and premature calls to any primitive operation of a tagged type before the body of the operation has been elaborated, will result in the raising of `Program_Error`.

C.12 Summary of Procedures for Elaboration Control

First, compile your program with the default options, using none of the special elaboration control switches. If the binder successfully binds your program, then you can be confident that, apart from issues raised by the use of access-to-subprogram types and dynamic dispatching, the program is free of elaboration errors. If it is important that the program be portable, then use the '-gnatwl' switch to generate warnings about missing `Elaborate` or `Elaborate_All` pragmas, and supply the missing pragmas.

If the program fails to bind using the default static elaboration handling, then you can fix the program to eliminate the binder message, or recompile the entire program with the '-gnatE' switch to generate dynamic elaboration checks, and, if you are sure there really are no elaboration problems, use a global pragma `Suppress (Elaboration_Check)`.

C.13 Other Elaboration Order Considerations

This section has been entirely concerned with the issue of finding a valid elaboration order, as defined by the Ada Reference Manual. In a case where several elaboration orders are valid, the task is to find one of the possible valid elaboration orders (and the static model in GNAT will ensure that this is achieved).

The purpose of the elaboration rules in the Ada Reference Manual is to make sure that no entity is accessed before it has been elaborated. For a subprogram, this means that the spec and body must have been elaborated before the subprogram is called. For an object, this means that the object must have been elaborated before its value is read or written. A violation of either of these two requirements is an access before elaboration order, and this section has been all about avoiding such errors.

In the case where more than one order of elaboration is possible, in the sense that access before elaboration errors are avoided, then any one of the orders is "correct" in the sense that it meets the requirements of the Ada Reference Manual, and no such error occurs.

However, it may be the case for a given program, that there are constraints on the order of elaboration that come not from consideration of avoiding elaboration errors, but rather from extra-lingual logic requirements. Consider this example:

```
with Init_Constants;
package Constants is
   X : Integer := 0;
   Y : Integer := 0;
end Constants;

package Init_Constants is
   procedure P; -- require a body
end Init_Constants;

with Constants;
package body Init_Constants is
   procedure P is begin null; end;
begin
   Constants.X := 3;
```

```
      Constants.Y := 4;
   end Init_Constants;

   with Constants;
   package Calc is
      Z : Integer := Constants.X + Constants.Y;
   end Calc;

   with Calc;
   with Text_IO; use Text_IO;
   procedure Main is
   begin
      Put_Line (Calc.Z'Img);
   end Main;
```

In this example, there is more than one valid order of elaboration. For example both the following are correct orders:

```
Init_Constants spec
Constants spec
Calc spec
Init_Constants body
Main body

   and

Init_Constants spec
Init_Constants body
Constants spec
Calc spec
Main body
```

There is no language rule to prefer one or the other, both are correct from an order of elaboration point of view. But the programmatic effects of the two orders are very different. In the first, the elaboration routine of `Calc` initializes Z to zero, and then the main program runs with this value of zero. But in the second order, the elaboration routine of `Calc` runs after the body of Init_Constants has set X and Y and thus Z is set to 7 before `Main` runs.

One could perhaps by applying pretty clever non-artificial intelligence to the situation guess that it is more likely that the second order of elaboration is the one desired, but there is no formal linguistic reason to prefer one over the other. In fact in this particular case, GNAT will prefer the second order, because of the rule that bodies are elaborated as soon as possible, but it's just luck that this is what was wanted (if indeed the second order was preferred).

If the program cares about the order of elaboration routines in a case like this, it is important to specify the order required. In this particular case, that could have been achieved by adding to the spec of Calc:

```
pragma Elaborate_All (Constants);
```

which requires that the body (if any) and spec of `Constants`, as well as the body and spec of any unit `with`'ed by `Constants` be elaborated before `Calc` is elaborated.

Clearly no automatic method can always guess which alternative you require, and if you are working with legacy code that had constraints of this kind which were not properly specified by adding `Elaborate` or `Elaborate_All` pragmas, then indeed it is possible that two different compilers can choose different orders.

However, GNAT does attempt to diagnose the common situation where there are uninitialized variables in the visible part of a package spec, and the corresponding package body has an elaboration block that directly or indirectly initialized one or more of these variables. This is the situation in which a pragma Elaborate_Body is usually desirable, and GNAT will generate a warning that suggests this addition if it detects this situation.

The `gnatbind` '`-p`' switch may be useful in smoking out problems. This switch causes bodies to be elaborated as late as possible instead of as early as possible. In the example above, it would have forced the choice of the first elaboration order. If you get different results when using this switch, and particularly if one set of results is right, and one is wrong as far as you are concerned, it shows that you have some missing `Elaborate` pragmas. For the example above, we have the following output:

```
gnatmake -f -q main
main
 7
gnatmake -f -q main -bargs -p
main
 0
```

It is of course quite unlikely that both these results are correct, so it is up to you in a case like this to investigate the source of the difference, by looking at the two elaboration orders that are chosen, and figuring out which is correct, and then adding the necessary `Elaborate` or `Elaborate_All` pragmas to ensure the desired order.

Appendix D Conditional Compilation

It is often necessary to arrange for a single source program to serve multiple purposes, where it is compiled in different ways to achieve these different goals. Some examples of the need for this feature are

- Adapting a program to a different hardware environment
- Adapting a program to a different target architecture
- Turning debugging features on and off
- Arranging for a program to compile with different compilers

In C, or C++, the typical approach would be to use the preprocessor that is defined as part of the language. The Ada language does not contain such a feature. This is not an oversight, but rather a very deliberate design decision, based on the experience that overuse of the preprocessing features in C and C++ can result in programs that are extremely difficult to maintain. For example, if we have ten switches that can be on or off, this means that there are a thousand separate programs, any one of which might not even be syntactically correct, and even if syntactically correct, the resulting program might not work correctly. Testing all combinations can quickly become impossible.

Nevertheless, the need to tailor programs certainly exists, and in this Appendix we will discuss how this can be achieved using Ada in general, and GNAT in particular.

D.1 Use of Boolean Constants

In the case where the difference is simply which code sequence is executed, the cleanest solution is to use Boolean constants to control which code is executed.

```
FP_Initialize_Required : constant Boolean := True;
...
if FP_Initialize_Required then
...
end if;
```

Not only will the code inside the `if` statement not be executed if the constant Boolean is `False`, but it will also be completely deleted from the program. However, the code is only deleted after the `if` statement has been checked for syntactic and semantic correctness. (In contrast, with preprocessors the code is deleted before the compiler ever gets to see it, so it is not checked until the switch is turned on.)

Typically the Boolean constants will be in a separate package, something like:

```
package Config is
   FP_Initialize_Required : constant Boolean := True;
   Reset_Available        : constant Boolean := False;
   ...
end Config;
```

The `Config` package exists in multiple forms for the various targets, with an appropriate script selecting the version of `Config` needed. Then any other unit requiring conditional compilation can do a `with` of `Config` to make the constants visible.

D.2 Debugging - A Special Case

A common use of conditional code is to execute statements (for example dynamic checks, or output of intermediate results) under control of a debug switch, so that the debugging behavior can be turned on and off. This can be done using a Boolean constant to control whether the code is active:

```
if Debugging then
   Put_Line ("got to the first stage!");
end if;
```

or

```
if Debugging and then Temperature > 999.0 then
   raise Temperature_Crazy;
end if;
```

Since this is a common case, there are special features to deal with this in a convenient manner. For the case of tests, Ada 2005 has added a pragma `Assert` that can be used for such tests. This pragma is modeled on the `Assert` pragma that has always been available in GNAT, so this feature may be used with GNAT even if you are not using Ada 2005 features. The use of pragma `Assert` is described in the *GNAT Reference Manual*, but as an example, the last test could be written:

```
pragma Assert (Temperature <= 999.0, "Temperature Crazy");
```

or simply

```
pragma Assert (Temperature <= 999.0);
```

In both cases, if assertions are active and the temperature is excessive, the exception `Assert_Failure` will be raised, with the given string in the first case or a string indicating the location of the pragma in the second case used as the exception message.

You can turn assertions on and off by using the `Assertion_Policy` pragma. This is an Ada 2005 pragma which is implemented in all modes by GNAT, but only in the latest versions of GNAT which include Ada 2005 capability. Alternatively, you can use the '-gnata' switch to enable assertions from the command line (this is recognized by all versions of GNAT).

For the example above with the `Put_Line`, the GNAT-specific pragma `Debug` can be used:

```
pragma Debug (Put_Line ("got to the first stage!"));
```

If debug pragmas are enabled, the argument, which must be of the form of a procedure call, is executed (in this case, `Put_Line` will be called). Only one call can be present, but of course a special debugging procedure containing any code you like can be included in the program and then called in a pragma `Debug` argument as needed.

One advantage of pragma `Debug` over the `if Debugging then` construct is that pragma `Debug` can appear in declarative contexts, such as at the very beginning of a procedure, before local declarations have been elaborated.

Debug pragmas are enabled using either the '-gnata' switch that also controls assertions, or with a separate Debug_Policy pragma. The latter pragma is new in the Ada 2005 versions of GNAT (but it can be used in Ada 95 and Ada 83 programs as well), and is analogous to pragma `Assertion_Policy` to control assertions.

`Assertion_Policy` and `Debug_Policy` are configuration pragmas, and thus they can appear in 'gnat.adc' if you are not using a project file, or in the file designated to contain configuration pragmas in a project file. They then apply to all subsequent compilations. In practice the use of the '-gnata' switch is often the most convenient method of controlling the status of these pragmas.

Note that a pragma is not a statement, so in contexts where a statement sequence is required, you can't just write a pragma on its own. You have to add a `null` statement.

```
if ... then
   ... -- some statements
else
   pragma Assert (Num_Cases < 10);
   null;
end if;
```

D.3 Conditionalizing Declarations

In some cases, it may be necessary to conditionalize declarations to meet different requirements. For example we might want a bit string whose length is set to meet some hardware message requirement.

In some cases, it may be possible to do this using declare blocks controlled by conditional constants:

```
if Small_Machine then
   declare
      X : Bit_String (1 .. 10);
   begin
      ...
   end;
else
   declare
      X : Large_Bit_String (1 .. 1000);
   begin
      ...
   end;
end if;
```

Note that in this approach, both declarations are analyzed by the compiler so this can only be used where both declarations are legal, even though one of them will not be used.

Another approach is to define integer constants, e.g. `Bits_Per_Word`, or Boolean constants, e.g. `Little_Endian`, and then write declarations that are parameterized by these constants. For example

```
for Rec use
   Field1 at 0 range Boolean'Pos (Little_Endian) * 10 .. Bits_Per_Word;
end record;
```

If `Bits_Per_Word` is set to 32, this generates either

```
for Rec use
   Field1 at 0 range 0 .. 32;
end record;
```

for the big endian case, or

```
for Rec use record
   Field1 at 0 range 10 .. 32;
end record;
```

for the little endian case. Since a powerful subset of Ada expression notation is usable for creating static constants, clever use of this feature can often solve quite difficult problems in conditionalizing compilation (note incidentally that in Ada 95, the little endian constant was introduced as `System.Default_Bit_Order`, so you do not need to define this one yourself).

D.4 Use of Alternative Implementations

In some cases, none of the approaches described above are adequate. This can occur for example if the set of declarations required is radically different for two different configurations.

In this situation, the official Ada way of dealing with conditionalizing such code is to write separate units for the different cases. As long as this does not result in excessive duplication of code, this can be done without creating maintenance problems. The approach is to share common code as far as possible, and then isolate the code and declarations that are different. Subunits are often a convenient method for breaking out a piece of a unit that is to be conditionalized, with separate files for different versions of the subunit for different targets, where the build script selects the right one to give to the compiler.

As an example, consider a situation where a new feature in Ada 2005 allows something to be done in a really nice way. But your code must be able to compile with an Ada 95 compiler. Conceptually you want to say:

```
if Ada_2005 then
    ... neat Ada 2005 code
else
    ... not quite as neat Ada 95 code
end if;
```

where `Ada_2005` is a Boolean constant.

But this won't work when `Ada_2005` is set to `False`, since the `then` clause will be illegal for an Ada 95 compiler. (Recall that although such unreachable code would eventually be deleted by the compiler, it still needs to be legal. If it uses features introduced in Ada 2005, it will be illegal in Ada 95.)

So instead we write

```
procedure Insert is separate;
```

Then we have two files for the subunit `Insert`, with the two sets of code. If the package containing this is called `File_Queries`, then we might have two files

- `file_queries-insert-2005.adb`
- `file_queries-insert-95.adb`

and the build script renames the appropriate file to

```
file_queries-insert.adb
```

and then carries out the compilation.

This can also be done with project files' naming schemes. For example:

```
For Body ("File_Queries.Insert") use "file_queries-insert-2005.ada";
```

Note also that with project files it is desirable to use a different extension than 'ads' / 'adb' for alternative versions. Otherwise a naming conflict may arise through another commonly used feature: to declare as part of the project a set of directories containing all the sources obeying the default naming scheme.

The use of alternative units is certainly feasible in all situations, and for example the Ada part of the GNAT run-time is conditionalized based on the target architecture using this approach. As a specific example, consider the implementation of the AST feature in VMS. There is one spec:

```
s-asthan.ads
```

which is the same for all architectures, and three bodies:

's-asthan.adb'
> used for all non-VMS operating systems

's-asthan-vms-alpha.adb'
> used for VMS on the Alpha

's-asthan-vms-ia64.adb'
> used for VMS on the ia64

The dummy version 's-asthan.adb' simply raises exceptions noting that this operating system feature is not available, and the two remaining versions interface with the corresponding versions of VMS to provide VMS-compatible AST handling. The GNAT build script knows the architecture and operating system, and automatically selects the right version, renaming it if necessary to 's-asthan.adb' before the run-time build.

Another style for arranging alternative implementations is through Ada's access-to-subprogram facility. In case some functionality is to be conditionally included, you can declare an access-to-procedure variable `Ref` that is initialized to designate a "do nothing" procedure, and then invoke `Ref.all` when appropriate. In some library package, set `Ref` to `Proc'Access` for some procedure `Proc` that performs the relevant processing. The initialization only occurs if the library package is included in the program. The same idea can also be implemented using tagged types and dispatching calls.

D.5 Preprocessing

Although it is quite possible to conditionalize code without the use of C-style preprocessing, as described earlier in this section, it is nevertheless convenient in some cases to use the C approach. Moreover, older Ada compilers have often provided some preprocessing capability, so legacy code may depend on this approach, even though it is not standard.

To accommodate such use, GNAT provides a preprocessor (modeled to a large extent on the various preprocessors that have been used with legacy code on other compilers, to enable easier transition).

The preprocessor may be used in two separate modes. It can be used quite separately from the compiler, to generate a separate output source file that is then fed to the compiler as a separate step. This is the **gnatprep** utility, whose use is fully described in Chapter 16 [Preprocessing Using gnatprep], page 199.

The preprocessing language allows such constructs as

```
#if DEBUG or PRIORITY > 4 then
   bunch of declarations
#else
   completely different bunch of declarations
#end if;
```

The values of the symbols `DEBUG` and `PRIORITY` can be defined either on the command line or in a separate file.

The other way of running the preprocessor is even closer to the C style and often more convenient. In this approach the preprocessing is integrated into the compilation process. The compiler is fed the preprocessor input which includes `#if` lines etc, and then the compiler carries out the preprocessing internally and processes the resulting output. For more details on this approach, see Section 3.2.17 [Integrated Preprocessing], page 74.

Appendix E Inline Assembler

If you need to write low-level software that interacts directly with the hardware, Ada provides two ways to incorporate assembly language code into your program. First, you can import and invoke external routines written in assembly language, an Ada feature fully supported by GNAT. However, for small sections of code it may be simpler or more efficient to include assembly language statements directly in your Ada source program, using the facilities of the implementation-defined package `System.Machine_Code`, which incorporates the gcc Inline Assembler. The Inline Assembler approach offers a number of advantages, including the following:

- No need to use non-Ada tools
- Consistent interface over different targets
- Automatic usage of the proper calling conventions
- Access to Ada constants and variables
- Definition of intrinsic routines
- Possibility of inlining a subprogram comprising assembler code
- Code optimizer can take Inline Assembler code into account

This chapter presents a series of examples to show you how to use the Inline Assembler. Although it focuses on the Intel x86, the general approach applies also to other processors. It is assumed that you are familiar with Ada and with assembly language programming.

E.1 Basic Assembler Syntax

The assembler used by GNAT and gcc is based not on the Intel assembly language, but rather on a language that descends from the AT&T Unix assembler *as* (and which is often referred to as "AT&T syntax"). The following table summarizes the main features of *as* syntax and points out the differences from the Intel conventions. See the gcc *as* and *gas* (an *as* macro pre-processor) documentation for further information.

Register names
> gcc / *as*: Prefix with "%"; for example `%eax`
> Intel: No extra punctuation; for example `eax`

Immediate operand
> gcc / *as*: Prefix with "$"; for example `$4`
> Intel: No extra punctuation; for example `4`

Address
> gcc / *as*: Prefix with "$"; for example `$loc`
> Intel: No extra punctuation; for example `loc`

Memory contents
> gcc / *as*: No extra punctuation; for example `loc`
> Intel: Square brackets; for example `[loc]`

Register contents
> gcc / *as*: Parentheses; for example `(%eax)`
> Intel: Square brackets; for example `[eax]`

Hexadecimal numbers

> gcc / *as*: Leading "0x" (C language syntax); for example `0xA0`
> Intel: Trailing "h"; for example `A0h`

Operand size

> gcc / *as*: Explicit in op code; for example `movw` to move a 16-bit word
> Intel: Implicit, deduced by assembler; for example `mov`

Instruction repetition

> gcc / *as*: Split into two lines; for example
> ```
> rep
> stosl
> ```
> Intel: Keep on one line; for example `rep stosl`

Order of operands

> gcc / *as*: Source first; for example `movw $4, %eax`
> Intel: Destination first; for example `mov eax, 4`

E.2 A Simple Example of Inline Assembler

The following example will generate a single assembly language statement, `nop`, which does nothing. Despite its lack of run-time effect, the example will be useful in illustrating the basics of the Inline Assembler facility.

```
with System.Machine_Code; use System.Machine_Code;
procedure Nothing is
begin
   Asm ("nop");
end Nothing;
```

`Asm` is a procedure declared in package `System.Machine_Code`; here it takes one parameter, a *template string* that must be a static expression and that will form the generated instruction. `Asm` may be regarded as a compile-time procedure that parses the template string and additional parameters (none here), from which it generates a sequence of assembly language instructions.

The examples in this chapter will illustrate several of the forms for invoking `Asm`; a complete specification of the syntax is found in the *GNAT Reference Manual*.

Under the standard GNAT conventions, the `Nothing` procedure should be in a file named 'nothing.adb'. You can build the executable in the usual way:

```
gnatmake nothing
```

However, the interesting aspect of this example is not its run-time behavior but rather the generated assembly code. To see this output, invoke the compiler as follows:

```
gcc -c -S -fomit-frame-pointer -gnatp 'nothing.adb'
```

where the options are:

-c   compile only (no bind or link)

-S   generate assembler listing

-fomit-frame-pointer
            do not set up separate stack frames

-gnatp   do not add runtime checks

This gives a human-readable assembler version of the code. The resulting file will have the same name as the Ada source file, but with a .s extension. In our example, the file 'nothing.s' has the following contents:

```
.file "nothing.adb"
gcc2_compiled.:
___gnu_compiled_ada:
.text
    .align 4
.globl __ada_nothing
__ada_nothing:
#APP
    nop
#NO_APP
    jmp L1
    .align 2,0x90
L1:
    ret
```

The assembly code you included is clearly indicated by the compiler, between the #APP and #NO_APP delimiters. The character before the 'APP' and 'NOAPP' can differ on different targets. For example, GNU/Linux uses '#APP' while on NT you will see '/APP'.

If you make a mistake in your assembler code (such as using the wrong size modifier, or using a wrong operand for the instruction) GNAT will report this error in a temporary file, which will be deleted when the compilation is finished. Generating an assembler file will help in such cases, since you can assemble this file separately using the *as* assembler that comes with gcc.

Assembling the file using the command

```
as 'nothing.s'
```

will give you error messages whose lines correspond to the assembler input file, so you can easily find and correct any mistakes you made. If there are no errors, *as* will generate an object file 'nothing.out'.

E.3 Output Variables in Inline Assembler

The examples in this section, showing how to access the processor flags, illustrate how to specify the destination operands for assembly language statements.

```
with Interfaces; use Interfaces;
with Ada.Text_IO; use Ada.Text_IO;
with System.Machine_Code; use System.Machine_Code;
procedure Get_Flags is
   Flags : Unsigned_32;
   use ASCII;
begin
   Asm ("pushfl"          & LF & HT & -- push flags on stack
        "popl %%eax"       & LF & HT & -- load eax with flags
        "movl %%eax, %0",             -- store flags in variable
        Outputs => Unsigned_32'Asm_Output ("=g", Flags));
   Put_Line ("Flags register:" & Flags'Img);
end Get_Flags;
```

In order to have a nicely aligned assembly listing, we have separated multiple assembler statements in the Asm template string with linefeed (ASCII.LF) and horizontal tab (ASCII.HT) characters. The resulting section of the assembly output file is:

```
#APP
    pushfl
    popl %eax
    movl %eax, -40(%ebp)
#NO_APP
```

It would have been legal to write the Asm invocation as:

```
Asm ("pushfl popl %%eax movl %%eax, %0")
```

but in the generated assembler file, this would come out as:

```
#APP
    pushfl popl %eax movl %eax, -40(%ebp)
#NO_APP
```

which is not so convenient for the human reader.

We use Ada comments at the end of each line to explain what the assembler instructions actually do. This is a useful convention.

When writing Inline Assembler instructions, you need to precede each register and variable name with a percent sign. Since the assembler already requires a percent sign at the beginning of a register name, you need two consecutive percent signs for such names in the Asm template string, thus %%eax. In the generated assembly code, one of the percent signs will be stripped off.

Names such as %0, %1, %2, etc., denote input or output variables: operands you later define using Input or Output parameters to Asm. An output variable is illustrated in the third statement in the Asm template string:

```
movl %%eax, %0
```

The intent is to store the contents of the eax register in a variable that can be accessed in Ada. Simply writing movl %%eax, Flags would not necessarily work, since the compiler might optimize by using a register to hold Flags, and the expansion of the movl instruction would not be aware of this optimization. The solution is not to store the result directly but rather to advise the compiler to choose the correct operand form; that is the purpose of the %0 output variable.

Information about the output variable is supplied in the Outputs parameter to Asm:

```
Outputs => Unsigned_32'Asm_Output ("=g", Flags));
```

The output is defined by the Asm_Output attribute of the target type; the general format is

```
Type'Asm_Output (constraint_string, variable_name)
```

The constraint string directs the compiler how to store/access the associated variable. In the example

```
Unsigned_32'Asm_Output ("=m", Flags);
```

the "m" (memory) constraint tells the compiler that the variable Flags should be stored in a memory variable, thus preventing the optimizer from keeping it in a register. In contrast,

```
Unsigned_32'Asm_Output ("=r", Flags);
```

uses the "r" (register) constraint, telling the compiler to store the variable in a register.

If the constraint is preceded by the equal character (=), it tells the compiler that the variable will be used to store data into it.

In the `Get_Flags` example, we used the `"g"` (global) constraint, allowing the optimizer to choose whatever it deems best.

There are a fairly large number of constraints, but the ones that are most useful (for the Intel x86 processor) are the following:

=	output constraint
g	global (i.e. can be stored anywhere)
m	in memory
I	a constant
a	use eax
b	use ebx
c	use ecx
d	use edx
S	use esi
D	use edi
r	use one of eax, ebx, ecx or edx
q	use one of eax, ebx, ecx, edx, esi or edi

The full set of constraints is described in the gcc and *as* documentation; note that it is possible to combine certain constraints in one constraint string.

You specify the association of an output variable with an assembler operand through the `%n` notation, where n is a non-negative integer. Thus in

```
Asm ("pushfl"           & LF & HT & -- push flags on stack
     "popl %%eax"       & LF & HT & -- load eax with flags
     "movl %%eax, %0",              -- store flags in variable
     Outputs => Unsigned_32'Asm_Output ("=g", Flags));
```

`%0` will be replaced in the expanded code by the appropriate operand, whatever the compiler decided for the `Flags` variable.

In general, you may have any number of output variables:

- Count the operands starting at 0; thus `%0`, `%1`, etc.
- Specify the `Outputs` parameter as a parenthesized comma-separated list of `Asm_Output` attributes

For example:

```
Asm ("movl %%eax, %0" & LF & HT &
     "movl %%ebx, %1" & LF & HT &
     "movl %%ecx, %2",
     Outputs => (Unsigned_32'Asm_Output ("=g", Var_A),    -- %0 = Var_A
                 Unsigned_32'Asm_Output ("=g", Var_B),    -- %1 = Var_B
                 Unsigned_32'Asm_Output ("=g", Var_C)));  -- %2 = Var_C
```

where `Var_A`, `Var_B`, and `Var_C` are variables in the Ada program.

As a variation on the `Get_Flags` example, we can use the constraints string to direct the compiler to store the eax register into the `Flags` variable, instead of including the store instruction explicitly in the `Asm` template string:

```
with Interfaces; use Interfaces;
with Ada.Text_IO; use Ada.Text_IO;
with System.Machine_Code; use System.Machine_Code;
procedure Get_Flags_2 is
   Flags : Unsigned_32;
   use ASCII;
begin
   Asm ("pushfl"        & LF & HT & -- push flags on stack
        "popl %%eax",              -- save flags in eax
        Outputs => Unsigned_32'Asm_Output ("=a", Flags));
   Put_Line ("Flags register:" & Flags'Img);
end Get_Flags_2;
```

The "a" constraint tells the compiler that the Flags variable will come from the eax register. Here is the resulting code:

```
#APP
   pushfl
   popl %eax
#NO_APP
   movl %eax,-40(%ebp)
```

The compiler generated the store of eax into Flags after expanding the assembler code.

Actually, there was no need to pop the flags into the eax register; more simply, we could just pop the flags directly into the program variable:

```
with Interfaces; use Interfaces;
with Ada.Text_IO; use Ada.Text_IO;
with System.Machine_Code; use System.Machine_Code;
procedure Get_Flags_3 is
   Flags : Unsigned_32;
   use ASCII;
begin
   Asm ("pushfl"  & LF & HT & -- push flags on stack
        "pop %0",            -- save flags in Flags
        Outputs => Unsigned_32'Asm_Output ("=g", Flags));
   Put_Line ("Flags register:" & Flags'Img);
end Get_Flags_3;
```

E.4 Input Variables in Inline Assembler

The example in this section illustrates how to specify the source operands for assembly language statements. The program simply increments its input value by 1:

```
with Interfaces; use Interfaces;
with Ada.Text_IO; use Ada.Text_IO;
with System.Machine_Code; use System.Machine_Code;
procedure Increment is

   function Incr (Value : Unsigned_32) return Unsigned_32 is
      Result : Unsigned_32;
   begin
      Asm ("incl %0",
           Inputs  => Unsigned_32'Asm_Input ("a", Value),
           Outputs => Unsigned_32'Asm_Output ("=a", Result));
      return Result;
   end Incr;

   Value : Unsigned_32;

begin
   Value := 5;
   Put_Line ("Value before is" & Value'Img);
   Value := Incr (Value);
   Put_Line ("Value after is" & Value'Img);
end Increment;
```

The `Outputs` parameter to `Asm` specifies that the result will be in the eax register and that it is to be stored in the `Result` variable.

The `Inputs` parameter looks much like the `Outputs` parameter, but with an `Asm_Input` attribute. The `"="` constraint, indicating an output value, is not present.

You can have multiple input variables, in the same way that you can have more than one output variable.

The parameter count (%0, %1) etc, now starts at the first input statement, and continues with the output statements. When both parameters use the same variable, the compiler will treat them as the same %n operand, which is the case here.

Just as the `Outputs` parameter causes the register to be stored into the target variable after execution of the assembler statements, so does the `Inputs` parameter cause its variable to be loaded into the register before execution of the assembler statements.

Thus the effect of the `Asm` invocation is:

1. load the 32-bit value of `Value` into eax

2. execute the `incl %eax` instruction

3. store the contents of eax into the `Result` variable

The resulting assembler file (with '-O2' optimization) contains:

```
_increment__incr.1:
   subl $4,%esp
   movl 8(%esp),%eax
#APP
   incl %eax
#NO_APP
   movl %eax,%edx
   movl %ecx,(%esp)
   addl $4,%esp
   ret
```

E.5 Inlining Inline Assembler Code

For a short subprogram such as the `Incr` function in the previous section, the overhead of the call and return (creating / deleting the stack frame) can be significant, compared to the amount of code in the subprogram body. A solution is to apply Ada's `Inline` pragma to the subprogram, which directs the compiler to expand invocations of the subprogram at the point(s) of call, instead of setting up a stack frame for out-of-line calls. Here is the resulting program:

```
with Interfaces; use Interfaces;
with Ada.Text_IO; use Ada.Text_IO;
with System.Machine_Code; use System.Machine_Code;
procedure Increment_2 is

   function Incr (Value : Unsigned_32) return Unsigned_32 is
      Result : Unsigned_32;
   begin
      Asm ("incl %0",
           Inputs  => Unsigned_32'Asm_Input ("a", Value),
           Outputs => Unsigned_32'Asm_Output ("=a", Result));
      return Result;
   end Incr;
   pragma Inline (Increment);

   Value : Unsigned_32;

begin
   Value := 5;
   Put_Line ("Value before is" & Value'Img);
   Value := Increment (Value);
   Put_Line ("Value after is" & Value'Img);
end Increment_2;
```

Compile the program with both optimization ('-O2') and inlining enabled ('-gnatpn' instead of '-gnatp').

The `Incr` function is still compiled as usual, but at the point in `Increment` where our function used to be called:

```
pushl %edi
call _increment__incr.1
```

the code for the function body directly appears:

```
movl %esi,%eax
#APP
   incl %eax
#NO_APP
   movl %eax,%edx
```

thus saving the overhead of stack frame setup and an out-of-line call.

E.6 Other Asm Functionality

This section describes two important parameters to the `Asm` procedure: `Clobber`, which identifies register usage; and `Volatile`, which inhibits unwanted optimizations.

E.6.1 The Clobber Parameter

One of the dangers of intermixing assembly language and a compiled language such as Ada is that the compiler needs to be aware of which registers are being used by the assembly code.

In some cases, such as the earlier examples, the constraint string is sufficient to indicate register usage (e.g., `"a"` for the eax register). But more generally, the compiler needs an explicit identification of the registers that are used by the Inline Assembly statements.

Using a register that the compiler doesn't know about could be a side effect of an instruction (like `mull` storing its result in both eax and edx). It can also arise from explicit register usage in your assembly code; for example:

```
Asm ("movl %0, %%ebx" & LF & HT &
     "movl %%ebx, %1",
     Inputs  => Unsigned_32'Asm_Input  ("g", Var_In),
     Outputs => Unsigned_32'Asm_Output ("=g", Var_Out));
```

where the compiler (since it does not analyze the `Asm` template string) does not know you are using the ebx register.

In such cases you need to supply the `Clobber` parameter to `Asm`, to identify the registers that will be used by your assembly code:

```
Asm ("movl %0, %%ebx" & LF & HT &
     "movl %%ebx, %1",
     Inputs  => Unsigned_32'Asm_Input  ("g", Var_In),
     Outputs => Unsigned_32'Asm_Output ("=g", Var_Out),
     Clobber => "ebx");
```

The `Clobber` parameter is a static string expression specifying the register(s) you are using. Note that register names are *not* prefixed by a percent sign. Also, if more than one register is used then their names are separated by commas; e.g., `"eax, ebx"`

The `Clobber` parameter has several additional uses:

1. Use "register" name `cc` to indicate that flags might have changed
2. Use "register" name `memory` if you changed a memory location

E.6.2 The `Volatile` Parameter

Compiler optimizations in the presence of Inline Assembler may sometimes have unwanted effects. For example, when an `Asm` invocation with an input variable is inside a loop, the compiler might move the loading of the input variable outside the loop, regarding it as a one-time initialization.

If this effect is not desired, you can disable such optimizations by setting the `Volatile` parameter to `True`; for example:

```
Asm ("movl %0, %%ebx" & LF & HT &
     "movl %%ebx, %1",
     Inputs   => Unsigned_32'Asm_Input  ("g", Var_In),
     Outputs  => Unsigned_32'Asm_Output ("=g", Var_Out),
     Clobber  => "ebx",
     Volatile => True);
```

By default, `Volatile` is set to `False` unless there is no `Outputs` parameter.

Although setting `Volatile` to `True` prevents unwanted optimizations, it will also disable other optimizations that might be important for efficiency. In general, you should set `Volatile` to `True` only if the compiler's optimizations have created problems.

Appendix F Compatibility and Porting Guide

This chapter describes the compatibility issues that may arise between GNAT and other Ada compilation systems (including those for Ada 83), and shows how GNAT can expedite porting applications developed in other Ada environments.

F.1 Compatibility with Ada 83

Ada 95 and Ada 2005 are highly upwards compatible with Ada 83. In particular, the design intention was that the difficulties associated with moving from Ada 83 to Ada 95 or Ada 2005 should be no greater than those that occur when moving from one Ada 83 system to another.

However, there are a number of points at which there are minor incompatibilities. The *Ada 95 Annotated Reference Manual* contains full details of these issues, and should be consulted for a complete treatment. In practice the following subsections treat the most likely issues to be encountered.

F.1.1 Legal Ada 83 programs that are illegal in Ada 95

Some legal Ada 83 programs are illegal (i.e. they will fail to compile) in Ada 95 and thus also in Ada 2005:

Character literals

> Some uses of character literals are ambiguous. Since Ada 95 has introduced `Wide_Character` as a new predefined character type, some uses of character literals that were legal in Ada 83 are illegal in Ada 95. For example:
>
> ```
> for Char in 'A' .. 'Z' loop ... end loop;
> ```
>
> The problem is that 'A' and 'Z' could be from either `Character` or `Wide_Character`. The simplest correction is to make the type explicit; e.g.:
>
> ```
> for Char in Character range 'A' .. 'Z' loop ... end loop;
> ```

New reserved words

> The identifiers `abstract`, `aliased`, `protected`, `requeue`, `tagged`, and `until` are reserved in Ada 95. Existing Ada 83 code using any of these identifiers must be edited to use some alternative name.

Freezing rules

> The rules in Ada 95 are slightly different with regard to the point at which entities are frozen, and representation pragmas and clauses are not permitted past the freeze point. This shows up most typically in the form of an error message complaining that a representation item appears too late, and the appropriate corrective action is to move the item nearer to the declaration of the entity to which it refers.
>
> A particular case is that representation pragmas cannot be applied to a subprogram body. If necessary, a separate subprogram declaration must be introduced to which the pragma can be applied.

Optional bodies for library packages

> In Ada 83, a package that did not require a package body was nevertheless allowed to have one. This lead to certain surprises in compiling large systems

(situations in which the body could be unexpectedly ignored by the binder). In Ada 95, if a package does not require a body then it is not permitted to have a body. To fix this problem, simply remove a redundant body if it is empty, or, if it is non-empty, introduce a dummy declaration into the spec that makes the body required. One approach is to add a private part to the package declaration (if necessary), and define a parameterless procedure called `Requires_Body`, which must then be given a dummy procedure body in the package body, which then becomes required. Another approach (assuming that this does not introduce elaboration circularities) is to add an `Elaborate_Body` pragma to the package spec, since one effect of this pragma is to require the presence of a package body.

`Numeric_Error` *is now the same as* `Constraint_Error`

In Ada 95, the exception `Numeric_Error` is a renaming of `Constraint_Error`. This means that it is illegal to have separate exception handlers for the two exceptions. The fix is simply to remove the handler for the `Numeric_Error` case (since even in Ada 83, a compiler was free to raise `Constraint_Error` in place of `Numeric_Error` in all cases).

Indefinite subtypes in generics

In Ada 83, it was permissible to pass an indefinite type (e.g. `String`) as the actual for a generic formal private type, but then the instantiation would be illegal if there were any instances of declarations of variables of this type in the generic body. In Ada 95, to avoid this clear violation of the methodological principle known as the "contract model", the generic declaration explicitly indicates whether or not such instantiations are permitted. If a generic formal parameter has explicit unknown discriminants, indicated by using (<>) after the type name, then it can be instantiated with indefinite types, but no stand-alone variables can be declared of this type. Any attempt to declare such a variable will result in an illegality at the time the generic is declared. If the (<>) notation is not used, then it is illegal to instantiate the generic with an indefinite type. This is the potential incompatibility issue when porting Ada 83 code to Ada 95. It will show up as a compile time error, and the fix is usually simply to add the (<>) to the generic declaration.

F.1.2 More deterministic semantics

Conversions

Conversions from real types to integer types round away from 0. In Ada 83 the conversion Integer(2.5) could deliver either 2 or 3 as its value. This implementation freedom was intended to support unbiased rounding in statistical applications, but in practice it interfered with portability. In Ada 95 the conversion semantics are unambiguous, and rounding away from 0 is required. Numeric code may be affected by this change in semantics. Note, though, that this issue is no worse than already existed in Ada 83 when porting code from one vendor to another.

Tasking   The Real-Time Annex introduces a set of policies that define the behavior of features that were implementation dependent in Ada 83, such as the order in which open select branches are executed.

F.1.3 Changed semantics

The worst kind of incompatibility is one where a program that is legal in Ada 83 is also legal in Ada 95 but can have an effect in Ada 95 that was not possible in Ada 83. Fortunately this is extremely rare, but the one situation that you should be alert to is the change in the predefined type `Character` from 7-bit ASCII to 8-bit Latin-1.

Range of type `Character`

    The range of `Standard.Character` is now the full 256 characters of Latin-1, whereas in most Ada 83 implementations it was restricted to 128 characters. Although some of the effects of this change will be manifest in compile-time rejection of legal Ada 83 programs it is possible for a working Ada 83 program to have a different effect in Ada 95, one that was not permitted in Ada 83. As an example, the expression `Character'Pos(Character'Last)` returned 127 in Ada 83 and now delivers 255 as its value. In general, you should look at the logic of any character-processing Ada 83 program and see whether it needs to be adapted to work correctly with Latin-1. Note that the predefined Ada 95 API has a character handling package that may be relevant if code needs to be adapted to account for the additional Latin-1 elements. The desirable fix is to modify the program to accommodate the full character set, but in some cases it may be convenient to define a subtype or derived type of Character that covers only the restricted range.

F.1.4 Other language compatibility issues

'-gnat83' switch

    All implementations of GNAT provide a switch that causes GNAT to operate in Ada 83 mode. In this mode, some but not all compatibility problems of the type described above are handled automatically. For example, the new reserved words introduced in Ada 95 and Ada 2005 are treated simply as identifiers as in Ada 83. However, in practice, it is usually advisable to make the necessary modifications to the program to remove the need for using this switch. See Section 3.2.9 [Compiling Different Versions of Ada], page 66.

Support for removed Ada 83 pragmas and attributes

    A number of pragmas and attributes from Ada 83 were removed from Ada 95, generally because they were replaced by other mechanisms. Ada 95 and Ada 2005 compilers are allowed, but not required, to implement these missing elements. In contrast with some other compilers, GNAT implements all such pragmas and attributes, eliminating this compatibility concern. These include `pragma Interface` and the floating point type attributes (`Emax`, `Mantissa`, etc.), among other items.

F.2 Compatibility between Ada 95 and Ada 2005

Although Ada 2005 was designed to be upwards compatible with Ada 95, there are a number
of incompatibilities. Several are enumerated below; for a complete description please see
the Annotated Ada 2005 Reference Manual, or section 9.1.1 in *Rationale for Ada 2005*.

New reserved words.

> The words `interface`, `overriding` and `synchronized` are reserved in Ada
> 2005. A pre-Ada 2005 program that uses any of these as an identifier will be
> illegal.

New declarations in predefined packages.

> A number of packages in the predefined environment contain new declarations:
> `Ada.Exceptions`, `Ada.Real_Time`, `Ada.Strings`, `Ada.Strings.Fixed`,
> `Ada.Strings.Bounded`, `Ada.Strings.Unbounded`, `Ada.Strings.Wide_Fixed`,
> `Ada.Strings.Wide_Bounded`, `Ada.Strings.Wide_Unbounded`, `Ada.Tags`,
> `Ada.Text_IO`, and `Interfaces.C`. If an Ada 95 program does a `with` and `use`
> of any of these packages, the new declarations may cause name clashes.

Access parameters.

> A nondispatching subprogram with an access parameter cannot be renamed as
> a dispatching operation. This was permitted in Ada 95.

Access types, discriminants, and constraints.

> Rule changes in this area have led to some incompatibilities; for example, con-
> strained subtypes of some access types are not permitted in Ada 2005.

Aggregates for limited types.

> The allowance of aggregates for limited types in Ada 2005 raises the possibility
> of ambiguities in legal Ada 95 programs, since additional types now need to be
> considered in expression resolution.

Fixed-point multiplication and division.

> Certain expressions involving "*" or "/" for a fixed-point type, which were le-
> gal in Ada 95 and invoked the predefined versions of these operations, are now
> ambiguous. The ambiguity may be resolved either by applying a type conver-
> sion to the expression, or by explicitly invoking the operation from package
> `Standard`.

Return-by-reference types.

> The Ada 95 return-by-reference mechanism has been removed. Instead, the
> user can declare a function returning a value from an anonymous access type.

F.3 Implementation-dependent characteristics

Although the Ada language defines the semantics of each construct as precisely as practical,
in some situations (for example for reasons of efficiency, or where the effect is heavily
dependent on the host or target platform) the implementation is allowed some freedom.
In porting Ada 83 code to GNAT, you need to be aware of whether / how the existing
code exercised such implementation dependencies. Such characteristics fall into several
categories, and GNAT offers specific support in assisting the transition from certain Ada
83 compilers.

F.3.1 Implementation-defined pragmas

Ada compilers are allowed to supplement the language-defined pragmas, and these are a potential source of non-portability. All GNAT-defined pragmas are described in the GNAT Reference Manual, and these include several that are specifically intended to correspond to other vendors' Ada 83 pragmas. For migrating from VADS, the pragma Use_VADS_Size may be useful. For compatibility with HP Ada 83, GNAT supplies the pragmas Extend_System, Ident, Inline_Generic, Interface_Name, Passive, Suppress_All, and Volatile. Other relevant pragmas include External and Link_With. Some vendor-specific Ada 83 pragmas (Share_Generic, Subtitle, and Title) are recognized, thus avoiding compiler rejection of units that contain such pragmas; they are not relevant in a GNAT context and hence are not otherwise implemented.

F.3.2 Implementation-defined attributes

Analogous to pragmas, the set of attributes may be extended by an implementation. All GNAT-defined attributes are described in the *GNAT Reference Manual*, and these include several that are specifically intended to correspond to other vendors' Ada 83 attributes. For migrating from VADS, the attribute VADS_Size may be useful. For compatibility with HP Ada 83, GNAT supplies the attributes Bit, Machine_Size and Type_Class.

F.3.3 Libraries

Vendors may supply libraries to supplement the standard Ada API. If Ada 83 code uses vendor-specific libraries then there are several ways to manage this in Ada 95 or Ada 2005:

1. If the source code for the libraries (specifications and bodies) are available, then the libraries can be migrated in the same way as the application.

2. If the source code for the specifications but not the bodies are available, then you can reimplement the bodies.

3. Some features introduced by Ada 95 obviate the need for library support. For example most Ada 83 vendors supplied a package for unsigned integers. The Ada 95 modular type feature is the preferred way to handle this need, so instead of migrating or reimplementing the unsigned integer package it may be preferable to retrofit the application using modular types.

F.3.4 Elaboration order

The implementation can choose any elaboration order consistent with the unit dependency relationship. This freedom means that some orders can result in Program_Error being raised due to an "Access Before Elaboration": an attempt to invoke a subprogram its body has been elaborated, or to instantiate a generic before the generic body has been elaborated. By default GNAT attempts to choose a safe order (one that will not encounter access before elaboration problems) by implicitly inserting Elaborate or Elaborate_All pragmas where needed. However, this can lead to the creation of elaboration circularities and a resulting rejection of the program by gnatbind. This issue is thoroughly described in Appendix C [Elaboration Order Handling in GNAT], page 291. In brief, there are several ways to deal with this situation:

- Modify the program to eliminate the circularities, e.g. by moving elaboration-time code into explicitly-invoked procedures

- Constrain the elaboration order by including explicit `Elaborate_Body` or `Elaborate` pragmas, and then inhibit the generation of implicit `Elaborate_All` pragmas either globally (as an effect of the '`-gnatE`' switch) or locally (by selectively suppressing elaboration checks via pragma `Suppress(Elaboration_Check)` when it is safe to do so).

F.3.5 Target-specific aspects

Low-level applications need to deal with machine addresses, data representations, interfacing with assembler code, and similar issues. If such an Ada 83 application is being ported to different target hardware (for example where the byte endianness has changed) then you will need to carefully examine the program logic; the porting effort will heavily depend on the robustness of the original design. Moreover, Ada 95 (and thus Ada 2005) are sometimes incompatible with typical Ada 83 compiler practices regarding implicit packing, the meaning of the Size attribute, and the size of access values. GNAT's approach to these issues is described in Section F.5 [Representation Clauses], page 338.

F.4 Compatibility with Other Ada Systems

If programs avoid the use of implementation dependent and implementation defined features, as documented in the *Ada Reference Manual*, there should be a high degree of portability between GNAT and other Ada systems. The following are specific items which have proved troublesome in moving Ada 95 programs from GNAT to other Ada 95 compilers, but do not affect porting code to GNAT. (As of January 2007, GNAT is the only compiler available for Ada 2005; the following issues may or may not arise for Ada 2005 programs when other compilers appear.)

Ada 83 Pragmas and Attributes
> Ada 95 compilers are allowed, but not required, to implement the missing Ada 83 pragmas and attributes that are no longer defined in Ada 95. GNAT implements all such pragmas and attributes, eliminating this as a compatibility concern, but some other Ada 95 compilers reject these pragmas and attributes.

Specialized Needs Annexes
> GNAT implements the full set of special needs annexes. At the current time, it is the only Ada 95 compiler to do so. This means that programs making use of these features may not be portable to other Ada 95 compilation systems.

Representation Clauses
> Some other Ada 95 compilers implement only the minimal set of representation clauses required by the Ada 95 reference manual. GNAT goes far beyond this minimal set, as described in the next section.

F.5 Representation Clauses

The Ada 83 reference manual was quite vague in describing both the minimal required implementation of representation clauses, and also their precise effects. Ada 95 (and thus also Ada 2005) are much more explicit, but the minimal set of capabilities required is still quite limited.

GNAT implements the full required set of capabilities in Ada 95 and Ada 2005, but also goes much further, and in particular an effort has been made to be compatible with existing Ada 83 usage to the greatest extent possible.

A few cases exist in which Ada 83 compiler behavior is incompatible with the requirements in Ada 95 (and thus also Ada 2005). These are instances of intentional or accidental dependence on specific implementation dependent characteristics of these Ada 83 compilers. The following is a list of the cases most likely to arise in existing Ada 83 code.

Implicit Packing

Some Ada 83 compilers allowed a Size specification to cause implicit packing of an array or record. This could cause expensive implicit conversions for change of representation in the presence of derived types, and the Ada design intends to avoid this possibility. Subsequent AI's were issued to make it clear that such implicit change of representation in response to a Size clause is inadvisable, and this recommendation is represented explicitly in the Ada 95 (and Ada 2005) Reference Manuals as implementation advice that is followed by GNAT. The problem will show up as an error message rejecting the size clause. The fix is simply to provide the explicit pragma `Pack`, or for more fine tuned control, provide a Component_Size clause.

Meaning of Size Attribute

The Size attribute in Ada 95 (and Ada 2005) for discrete types is defined as the minimal number of bits required to hold values of the type. For example, on a 32-bit machine, the size of `Natural` will typically be 31 and not 32 (since no sign bit is required). Some Ada 83 compilers gave 31, and some 32 in this situation. This problem will usually show up as a compile time error, but not always. It is a good idea to check all uses of the 'Size attribute when porting Ada 83 code. The GNAT specific attribute Object_Size can provide a useful way of duplicating the behavior of some Ada 83 compiler systems.

Size of Access Types

A common assumption in Ada 83 code is that an access type is in fact a pointer, and that therefore it will be the same size as a System.Address value. This assumption is true for GNAT in most cases with one exception. For the case of a pointer to an unconstrained array type (where the bounds may vary from one value of the access type to another), the default is to use a "fat pointer", which is represented as two separate pointers, one to the bounds, and one to the array. This representation has a number of advantages, including improved efficiency. However, it may cause some difficulties in porting existing Ada 83 code which makes the assumption that, for example, pointers fit in 32 bits on a machine with 32-bit addressing.

To get around this problem, GNAT also permits the use of "thin pointers" for access types in this case (where the designated type is an unconstrained array type). These thin pointers are indeed the same size as a System.Address value. To specify a thin pointer, use a size clause for the type, for example:

```
type X is access all String;
for X'Size use Standard'Address_Size;
```

which will cause the type X to be represented using a single pointer. When using this representation, the bounds are right behind the array. This representation is slightly less efficient, and does not allow quite such flexibility in the use of foreign pointers or in using the Unrestricted_Access attribute to create pointers to non-aliased objects. But for any standard portable use of the access type it will work in a functionally correct manner and allow porting of existing code. Note that another way of forcing a thin pointer representation is to use a component size clause for the element size in an array, or a record representation clause for an access field in a record.

F.6 Compatibility with HP Ada 83

The VMS version of GNAT fully implements all the pragmas and attributes provided by HP Ada 83, as well as providing the standard HP Ada 83 libraries, including Starlet. In addition, data layouts and parameter passing conventions are highly compatible. This means that porting existing HP Ada 83 code to GNAT in VMS systems should be easier than most other porting efforts. The following are some of the most significant differences between GNAT and HP Ada 83.

Default floating-point representation

> In GNAT, the default floating-point format is IEEE, whereas in HP Ada 83, it is VMS format. GNAT does implement the necessary pragmas (Long_Float, Float_Representation) for changing this default.

System   The package System in GNAT exactly corresponds to the definition in the Ada 95 reference manual, which means that it excludes many of the HP Ada 83 extensions. However, a separate package Aux_DEC is provided that contains the additional definitions, and a special pragma, Extend_System allows this package to be treated transparently as an extension of package System.

To_Address

> The definitions provided by Aux_DEC are exactly compatible with those in the HP Ada 83 version of System, with one exception. HP Ada provides the following declarations:
>
> ```
> TO_ADDRESS (INTEGER)
> TO_ADDRESS (UNSIGNED_LONGWORD)
> TO_ADDRESS (universal_integer)
> ```
>
> The version of TO_ADDRESS taking a *universal integer* argument is in fact an extension to Ada 83 not strictly compatible with the reference manual. In GNAT, we are constrained to be exactly compatible with the standard, and this means we cannot provide this capability. In HP Ada 83, the point of this definition is to deal with a call like:
>
> ```
> TO_ADDRESS (16#12777#);
> ```
>
> Normally, according to the Ada 83 standard, one would expect this to be ambiguous, since it matches both the INTEGER and UNSIGNED_LONGWORD forms of TO_ADDRESS. However, in HP Ada 83, there is no ambiguity, since the definition using *universal_integer* takes precedence.
>
> In GNAT, since the version with *universal_integer* cannot be supplied, it is not possible to be 100% compatible. Since there are many programs using numeric

constants for the argument to TO_ADDRESS, the decision in GNAT was to change the name of the function in the UNSIGNED_LONGWORD case, so the declarations provided in the GNAT version of AUX_Dec are:

```
function To_Address (X : Integer) return Address;
pragma Pure_Function (To_Address);

function To_Address_Long (X : Unsigned_Longword)
  return Address;
pragma Pure_Function (To_Address_Long);
```

This means that programs using TO_ADDRESS for UNSIGNED_LONGWORD must change the name to TO_ADDRESS_LONG.

Task_Id values

The Task_Id values assigned will be different in the two systems, and GNAT does not provide a specified value for the Task_Id of the environment task, which in GNAT is treated like any other declared task.

For full details on these and other less significant compatibility issues, see appendix E of the HP publication entitled *HP Ada, Technical Overview and Comparison on HP Platforms*.

For GNAT running on other than VMS systems, all the HP Ada 83 pragmas and attributes are recognized, although only a subset of them can sensibly be implemented. The description of pragmas in the *GNAT Reference Manual* indicates whether or not they are applicable to non-VMS systems.

Appendix G Microsoft Windows Topics

This chapter describes topics that are specific to the Microsoft Windows platforms (NT, 2000, and XP Professional).

G.1 Using GNAT on Windows

One of the strengths of the GNAT technology is that its tool set (gcc, gnatbind, gnatlink, gnatmake, the gdb debugger, etc.) is used in the same way regardless of the platform.

On Windows this tool set is complemented by a number of Microsoft-specific tools that have been provided to facilitate interoperability with Windows when this is required. With these tools:

- You can build applications using the CONSOLE or WINDOWS subsystems.

- You can use any Dynamically Linked Library (DLL) in your Ada code (both relocatable and non-relocatable DLLs are supported).

- You can build Ada DLLs for use in other applications. These applications can be written in a language other than Ada (e.g., C, C++, etc). Again both relocatable and non-relocatable Ada DLLs are supported.

- You can include Windows resources in your Ada application.

- You can use or create COM/DCOM objects.

Immediately below are listed all known general GNAT-for-Windows restrictions. Other restrictions about specific features like Windows Resources and DLLs are listed in separate sections below.

- It is not possible to use GetLastError and SetLastError when tasking, protected records, or exceptions are used. In these cases, in order to implement Ada semantics, the GNAT run-time system calls certain Win32 routines that set the last error variable to 0 upon success. It should be possible to use GetLastError and SetLastError when tasking, protected record, and exception features are not used, but it is not guaranteed to work.

- It is not possible to link against Microsoft libraries except for import libraries. The library must be built to be compatible with 'MSVCRT.LIB' (/MD Microsoft compiler option), 'LIBC.LIB' and 'LIBCMT.LIB' (/ML or /MT Microsoft compiler options) are known to not be compatible with the GNAT runtime. Even if the library is compatible with 'MSVCRT.LIB' it is not guaranteed to work.

- When the compilation environment is located on FAT32 drives, users may experience recompilations of the source files that have not changed if Daylight Saving Time (DST) state has changed since the last time files were compiled. NTFS drives do not have this problem.

- No components of the GNAT toolset use any entries in the Windows registry. The only entries that can be created are file associations and PATH settings, provided the user has chosen to create them at installation time, as well as some minimal book-keeping information needed to correctly uninstall or integrate different GNAT products.

G.2 Using a network installation of GNAT

Make sure the system on which GNAT is installed is accessible from the current machine, i.e. the install location is shared over the network. Shared resources are accessed on Windows by means of UNC paths, which have the format \\server\sharename\path

In order to use such a network installation, simply add the UNC path of the 'bin' directory of your GNAT installation in front of your PATH. For example, if GNAT is installed in '\GNAT' directory of a share location called 'c-drive' on a machine 'LOKI', the following command will make it available:

```
path \\loki\c-drive\gnat\bin;%path%
```

Be aware that every compilation using the network installation results in the transfer of large amounts of data across the network and will likely cause serious performance penalty.

G.3 CONSOLE and WINDOWS subsystems

There are two main subsystems under Windows. The CONSOLE subsystem (which is the default subsystem) will always create a console when launching the application. This is not something desirable when the application has a Windows GUI. To get rid of this console the application must be using the WINDOWS subsystem. To do so the '-mwindows' linker option must be specified.

```
$ gnatmake winprog -largs -mwindows
```

G.4 Temporary Files

It is possible to control where temporary files gets created by setting the TMP environment variable. The file will be created:

- Under the directory pointed to by the TMP environment variable if this directory exists.
- Under c:\temp, if the TMP environment variable is not set (or not pointing to a directory) and if this directory exists.
- Under the current working directory otherwise.

This allows you to determine exactly where the temporary file will be created. This is particularly useful in networked environments where you may not have write access to some directories.

G.5 Mixed-Language Programming on Windows

Developing pure Ada applications on Windows is no different than on other GNAT-supported platforms. However, when developing or porting an application that contains a mix of Ada and C/C++, the choice of your Windows C/C++ development environment conditions your overall interoperability strategy.

If you use gcc to compile the non-Ada part of your application, there are no Windows-specific restrictions that affect the overall interoperability with your Ada code. If you plan to use Microsoft tools (e.g. Microsoft Visual C/C++), you should be aware of the following limitations:

- You cannot link your Ada code with an object or library generated with Microsoft tools if these use the `.tls` section (Thread Local Storage section) since the GNAT linker does not yet support this section.

- You cannot link your Ada code with an object or library generated with Microsoft tools if these use I/O routines other than those provided in the Microsoft DLL: `msvcrt.dll`. This is because the GNAT run time uses the services of `msvcrt.dll` for its I/Os. Use of other I/O libraries can cause a conflict with `msvcrt.dll` services. For instance Visual C++ I/O stream routines conflict with those in `msvcrt.dll`.

If you do want to use the Microsoft tools for your non-Ada code and hit one of the above limitations, you have two choices:

1. Encapsulate your non Ada code in a DLL to be linked with your Ada application. In this case, use the Microsoft or whatever environment to build the DLL and use GNAT to build your executable (see Section G.8 [Using DLLs with GNAT], page 348).

2. Or you can encapsulate your Ada code in a DLL to be linked with the other part of your application. In this case, use GNAT to build the DLL (see Section G.9 [Building DLLs with GNAT], page 351) and use the Microsoft or whatever environment to build your executable.

G.6 Windows Calling Conventions

When a subprogram F (caller) calls a subprogram G (callee), there are several ways to push G's parameters on the stack and there are several possible scenarios to clean up the stack upon G's return. A calling convention is an agreed upon software protocol whereby the responsibilities between the caller (F) and the callee (G) are clearly defined. Several calling conventions are available for Windows:

- C (Microsoft defined)
- Stdcall (Microsoft defined)
- Win32 (GNAT specific)
- DLL (GNAT specific)

G.6.1 C Calling Convention

This is the default calling convention used when interfacing to C/C++ routines compiled with either gcc or Microsoft Visual C++.

In the C calling convention subprogram parameters are pushed on the stack by the caller from right to left. The caller itself is in charge of cleaning up the stack after the call. In addition, the name of a routine with C calling convention is mangled by adding a leading underscore.

The name to use on the Ada side when importing (or exporting) a routine with C calling convention is the name of the routine. For instance the C function:

```
int get_val (long);
```

should be imported from Ada as follows:

```
function Get_Val (V : Interfaces.C.long) return Interfaces.C.int;
pragma Import (C, Get_Val, External_Name => "get_val");
```

Note that in this particular case the `External_Name` parameter could have been omitted since, when missing, this parameter is taken to be the name of the Ada entity in lower case.

When the `Link_Name` parameter is missing, as in the above example, this parameter is set to be the `External_Name` with a leading underscore.

When importing a variable defined in C, you should always use the `C` calling convention unless the object containing the variable is part of a DLL (in which case you should use the `Stdcall` calling convention, see Section G.6.2 [Stdcall Calling Convention], page 346).

G.6.2 `Stdcall` Calling Convention

This convention, which was the calling convention used for Pascal programs, is used by Microsoft for all the routines in the Win32 API for efficiency reasons. It must be used to import any routine for which this convention was specified.

In the `Stdcall` calling convention subprogram parameters are pushed on the stack by the caller from right to left. The callee (and not the caller) is in charge of cleaning the stack on routine exit. In addition, the name of a routine with `Stdcall` calling convention is mangled by adding a leading underscore (as for the `C` calling convention) and a trailing `@nn`, where *nn* is the overall size (in bytes) of the parameters passed to the routine.

The name to use on the Ada side when importing a C routine with a `Stdcall` calling convention is the name of the C routine. The leading underscore and trailing `@nn` are added automatically by the compiler. For instance the Win32 function:

```
APIENTRY int get_val (long);
```

should be imported from Ada as follows:

```
function Get_Val (V : Interfaces.C.long) return Interfaces.C.int;
pragma Import (Stdcall, Get_Val);
-- On the x86 a long is 4 bytes, so the Link_Name is "_get_val@4"
```

As for the `C` calling convention, when the `External_Name` parameter is missing, it is taken to be the name of the Ada entity in lower case. If instead of writing the above import pragma you write:

```
function Get_Val (V : Interfaces.C.long) return Interfaces.C.int;
pragma Import (Stdcall, Get_Val, External_Name => "retrieve_val");
```

then the imported routine is `_retrieve_val@4`. However, if instead of specifying the `External_Name` parameter you specify the `Link_Name` as in the following example:

```
function Get_Val (V : Interfaces.C.long) return Interfaces.C.int;
pragma Import (Stdcall, Get_Val, Link_Name => "retrieve_val");
```

then the imported routine is `retrieve_val`, that is, there is no decoration at all. No leading underscore and no Stdcall suffix `@nn`.

This is especially important as in some special cases a DLL's entry point name lacks a trailing `@nn` while the exported name generated for a call has it.

It is also possible to import variables defined in a DLL by using an import pragma for a variable. As an example, if a DLL contains a variable defined as:

```
int my_var;
```

then, to access this variable from Ada you should write:

```
My_Var : Interfaces.C.int;
pragma Import (Stdcall, My_Var);
```

Note that to ease building cross-platform bindings this convention will be handled as a `C` calling convention on non Windows platforms.

G.6.3 `Win32` Calling Convention

This convention, which is GNAT-specific is fully equivalent to the `Stdcall` calling convention described above.

G.6.4 `DLL` Calling Convention

This convention, which is GNAT-specific is fully equivalent to the `Stdcall` calling convention described above.

G.7 Introduction to Dynamic Link Libraries (DLLs)

A Dynamically Linked Library (DLL) is a library that can be shared by several applications running under Windows. A DLL can contain any number of routines and variables.

One advantage of DLLs is that you can change and enhance them without forcing all the applications that depend on them to be relinked or recompiled. However, you should be aware than all calls to DLL routines are slower since, as you will understand below, such calls are indirect.

To illustrate the remainder of this section, suppose that an application wants to use the services of a DLL 'API.dll'. To use the services provided by 'API.dll' you must statically link against the DLL or an import library which contains a jump table with an entry for each routine and variable exported by the DLL. In the Microsoft world this import library is called 'API.lib'. When using GNAT this import library is called either 'libAPI.dll.a', 'libapi.dll.a', 'libAPI.a' or 'libapi.a' (names are case insensitive).

After you have linked your application with the DLL or the import library and you run your application, here is what happens:

1. Your application is loaded into memory.

2. The DLL 'API.dll' is mapped into the address space of your application. This means that:

   - The DLL will use the stack of the calling thread.
   - The DLL will use the virtual address space of the calling process.
   - The DLL will allocate memory from the virtual address space of the calling process.
   - Handles (pointers) can be safely exchanged between routines in the DLL routines and routines in the application using the DLL.

3. The entries in the jump table (from the import library 'libAPI.dll.a' or 'API.lib' or automatically created when linking against a DLL) which is part of your application are initialized with the addresses of the routines and variables in 'API.dll'.

4. If present in 'API.dll', routines `DllMain` or `DllMainCRTStartup` are invoked. These routines typically contain the initialization code needed for the well-being of the routines and variables exported by the DLL.

There is an additional point which is worth mentioning. In the Windows world there are two kind of DLLs: relocatable and non-relocatable DLLs. Non-relocatable DLLs can only be loaded at a very specific address in the target application address space. If the addresses of two non-relocatable DLLs overlap and these happen to be used by the same application, a conflict will occur and the application will run incorrectly. Hence, when possible, it is always preferable to use and build relocatable DLLs. Both relocatable and non-relocatable

DLLs are supported by GNAT. Note that the '-s' linker option (see GNU Linker User's Guide) removes the debugging symbols from the DLL but the DLL can still be relocated.

As a side note, an interesting difference between Microsoft DLLs and Unix shared libraries, is the fact that on most Unix systems all public routines are exported by default in a Unix shared library, while under Windows it is possible (but not required) to list exported routines in a definition file (see Section G.8.2.1 [The Definition File], page 349).

G.8 Using DLLs with GNAT

To use the services of a DLL, say 'API.dll', in your Ada application you must have:

1. The Ada spec for the routines and/or variables you want to access in 'API.dll'. If not available this Ada spec must be built from the C/C++ header files provided with the DLL.

2. The import library ('libAPI.dll.a' or 'API.lib'). As previously mentioned an import library is a statically linked library containing the import table which will be filled at load time to point to the actual 'API.dll' routines. Sometimes you don't have an import library for the DLL you want to use. The following sections will explain how to build one. Note that this is optional.

3. The actual DLL, 'API.dll'.

Once you have all the above, to compile an Ada application that uses the services of 'API.dll' and whose main subprogram is My_Ada_App, you simply issue the command

```
$ gnatmake my_ada_app -largs -lAPI
```

The argument '-largs -lAPI' at the end of the gnatmake command tells the GNAT linker to look first for a library named 'API.lib' (Microsoft-style name) and if not found for a libraries named 'libAPI.dll.a', 'API.dll.a' or 'libAPI.a'. (GNAT-style name). Note that if the Ada package spec for 'API.dll' contains the following pragma

```
pragma Linker_Options ("-lAPI");
```

you do not have to add '-largs -lAPI' at the end of the gnatmake command.

If any one of the items above is missing you will have to create it yourself. The following sections explain how to do so using as an example a fictitious DLL called 'API.dll'.

G.8.1 Creating an Ada Spec for the DLL Services

A DLL typically comes with a C/C++ header file which provides the definitions of the routines and variables exported by the DLL. The Ada equivalent of this header file is a package spec that contains definitions for the imported entities. If the DLL you intend to use does not come with an Ada spec you have to generate one such spec yourself. For example if the header file of 'API.dll' is a file 'api.h' containing the following two definitions:

```
int some_var;
int get (char *);
```

then the equivalent Ada spec could be:

```
with Interfaces.C.Strings;
package API is
   use Interfaces;

   Some_Var : C.int;
   function Get (Str : C.Strings.Chars_Ptr) return C.int;

private
   pragma Import (C, Get);
   pragma Import (DLL, Some_Var);
end API;
```

Note that a variable is **always imported with a Stdcall convention**. A function can have C or Stdcall convention. (see Section G.6 [Windows Calling Conventions], page 345).

G.8.2 Creating an Import Library

If a Microsoft-style import library 'API.lib' or a GNAT-style import library 'libAPI.dll.a' or 'libAPI.a' is available with 'API.dll' you can skip this section. You can also skip this section if 'API.dll' or 'libAPI.dll' is built with GNU tools as in this case it is possible to link directly against the DLL. Otherwise read on.

G.8.2.1 The Definition File

As previously mentioned, and unlike Unix systems, the list of symbols that are exported from a DLL must be provided explicitly in Windows. The main goal of a definition file is precisely that: list the symbols exported by a DLL. A definition file (usually a file with a .def suffix) has the following structure:

```
[LIBRARY name]
[DESCRIPTION string]
EXPORTS
   symbol1
   symbol2
   ...
```

LIBRARY name
          This section, which is optional, gives the name of the DLL.

DESCRIPTION string
          This section, which is optional, gives a description string that will be embedded in the import library.

EXPORTS   This section gives the list of exported symbols (procedures, functions or variables). For instance in the case of 'API.dll' the EXPORTS section of 'API.def' looks like:

```
EXPORTS
   some_var
   get
```

Note that you must specify the correct suffix (@nn) (see Section G.6 [Windows Calling Conventions], page 345) for a Stdcall calling convention function in the exported symbols list.

There can actually be other sections in a definition file, but these sections are not relevant to the discussion at hand.

G.8.2.2 GNAT-Style Import Library

To create a static import library from 'API.dll' with the GNAT tools you should proceed as follows:

1. Create the definition file 'API.def' (see Section G.8.2.1 [The Definition File], page 349). For that use the dll2def tool as follows:

   ```
   $ dll2def API.dll > API.def
   ```

   dll2def is a very simple tool: it takes as input a DLL and prints to standard output the list of entry points in the DLL. Note that if some routines in the DLL have the **Stdcall** convention (see Section G.6 [Windows Calling Conventions], page 345) with stripped @*nn* suffix then you'll have to edit 'api.def' to add it, and specify -k to gnatdll when creating the import library.

   Here are some hints to find the right @*nn* suffix.

   1. If you have the Microsoft import library (.lib), it is possible to get the right symbols by using Microsoft **dumpbin** tool (see the corresponding Microsoft documentation for further details).

      ```
      $ dumpbin /exports api.lib
      ```

   2. If you have a message about a missing symbol at link time the compiler tells you what symbol is expected. You just have to go back to the definition file and add the right suffix.

2. Build the import library libAPI.dll.a, using gnatdll (see Section G.11.7 [Using gnatdll], page 356) as follows:

   ```
   $ gnatdll -e API.def -d API.dll
   ```

   gnatdll takes as input a definition file 'API.def' and the name of the DLL containing the services listed in the definition file 'API.dll'. The name of the static import library generated is computed from the name of the definition file as follows: if the definition file name is *xyz*.def, the import library name will be lib*xyz*.a. Note that in the previous example option '-e' could have been removed because the name of the definition file (before the ".def" suffix) is the same as the name of the DLL (see Section G.11.7 [Using gnatdll], page 356 for more information about gnatdll).

G.8.2.3 Microsoft-Style Import Library

With GNAT you can either use a GNAT-style or Microsoft-style import library. A Microsoft import library is needed only if you plan to make an Ada DLL available to applications developed with Microsoft tools (see Section G.5 [Mixed-Language Programming on Windows], page 344).

To create a Microsoft-style import library for 'API.dll' you should proceed as follows:

1. Create the definition file 'API.def' from the DLL. For this use either the dll2def tool as described above or the Microsoft dumpbin tool (see the corresponding Microsoft documentation for further details).

2. Build the actual import library using Microsoft's lib utility:

   ```
   $ lib -machine:IX86 -def:API.def -out:API.lib
   ```

If you use the above command the definition file 'API.def' must contain a line giving the name of the DLL:

```
LIBRARY     "API"
```

See the Microsoft documentation for further details about the usage of lib.

G.9 Building DLLs with GNAT

This section explain how to build DLLs using the GNAT built-in DLL support. With the following procedure it is straight forward to build and use DLLs with GNAT.

1. building object files

   The first step is to build all objects files that are to be included into the DLL. This is done by using the standard gnatmake tool.

2. building the DLL

   To build the DLL you must use gcc's -shared option. It is quite simple to use this method:

   ```
   $ gcc -shared -o api.dll obj1.o obj2.o ...
   ```

   It is important to note that in this case all symbols found in the object files are automatically exported. It is possible to restrict the set of symbols to export by passing to gcc a definition file, see Section G.8.2.1 [The Definition File], page 349. For example:

   ```
   $ gcc -shared -o api.dll api.def obj1.o obj2.o ...
   ```

   If you use a definition file you must export the elaboration procedures for every package that required one. Elaboration procedures are named using the package name followed by "_E".

3. preparing DLL to be used

   For the DLL to be used by client programs the bodies must be hidden from it and the .ali set with read-only attribute. This is very important otherwise GNAT will recompile all packages and will not actually use the code in the DLL. For example:

   ```
   $ mkdir apilib
   $ copy *.ads *.ali api.dll apilib
   $ attrib +R apilib\*.ali
   ```

At this point it is possible to use the DLL by directly linking against it. Note that you must use the GNAT shared runtime when using GNAT shared libraries. This is achieved by using -shared binder's option.

```
$ gnatmake main -Iapilib -bargs -shared -largs -Lapilib -lAPI
```

G.10 Building DLLs with GNAT Project files

There is nothing specific to Windows in the build process. see Section 11.12 [Library Projects], page 149.

Due to a system limitation, it is not possible under Windows to create threads when inside the DllMain routine which is used for auto-initialization of shared libraries, so it is not possible to have library level tasks in SALs.

G.11 Building DLLs with gnatdll

Note that it is preferred to use the built-in GNAT DLL support (see Section G.9 [Building DLLs with GNAT], page 351) or GNAT Project files (see Section G.10 [Building DLLs with GNAT Project files], page 351) to build DLLs.

This section explains how to build DLLs containing Ada code using gnatdll. These DLLs will be referred to as Ada DLLs in the remainder of this section.

The steps required to build an Ada DLL that is to be used by Ada as well as non-Ada applications are as follows:

1. You need to mark each Ada *entity* exported by the DLL with a C or Stdcall calling convention to avoid any Ada name mangling for the entities exported by the DLL (see Section G.11.2 [Exporting Ada Entities], page 353). You can skip this step if you plan to use the Ada DLL only from Ada applications.

2. Your Ada code must export an initialization routine which calls the routine adainit generated by gnatbind to perform the elaboration of the Ada code in the DLL (see Section G.11.3 [Ada DLLs and Elaboration], page 354). The initialization routine exported by the Ada DLL must be invoked by the clients of the DLL to initialize the DLL.

3. When useful, the DLL should also export a finalization routine which calls routine adafinal generated by gnatbind to perform the finalization of the Ada code in the DLL (see Section G.11.4 [Ada DLLs and Finalization], page 354). The finalization routine exported by the Ada DLL must be invoked by the clients of the DLL when the DLL services are no further needed.

4. You must provide a spec for the services exported by the Ada DLL in each of the programming languages to which you plan to make the DLL available.

5. You must provide a definition file listing the exported entities (see Section G.8.2.1 [The Definition File], page 349).

6. Finally you must use gnatdll to produce the DLL and the import library (see Section G.11.7 [Using gnatdll], page 356).

Note that a relocatable DLL stripped using the strip binutils tool will not be relocatable anymore. To build a DLL without debug information pass -largs -s to gnatdll. This restriction does not apply to a DLL built using a Library Project. see Section 11.12 [Library Projects], page 149.

G.11.1 Limitations When Using Ada DLLs from Ada

When using Ada DLLs from Ada applications there is a limitation users should be aware of. Because on Windows the GNAT run time is not in a DLL of its own, each Ada DLL includes a part of the GNAT run time. Specifically, each Ada DLL includes the services of the GNAT run time that are necessary to the Ada code inside the DLL. As a result, when an Ada program uses an Ada DLL there are two independent GNAT run times: one in the Ada DLL and one in the main program.

It is therefore not possible to exchange GNAT run-time objects between the Ada DLL and the main Ada program. Example of GNAT run-time objects are file handles (e.g. Text_IO.File_Type), tasks types, protected objects types, etc.

It is completely safe to exchange plain elementary, array or record types, Windows object handles, etc.

G.11.2 Exporting Ada Entities

Building a DLL is a way to encapsulate a set of services usable from any application. As a result, the Ada entities exported by a DLL should be exported with the C or Stdcall calling conventions to avoid any Ada name mangling. As an example here is an Ada package API, spec and body, exporting two procedures, a function, and a variable:

```
with Interfaces.C; use Interfaces;
package API is
   Count : C.int := 0;
   function Factorial (Val : C.int) return C.int;

   procedure Initialize_API;
   procedure Finalize_API;
   --   Initialization & Finalization routines. More in the next section.
private
   pragma Export (C, Initialize_API);
   pragma Export (C, Finalize_API);
   pragma Export (C, Count);
   pragma Export (C, Factorial);
end API;
```

```
package body API is
   function Factorial (Val : C.int) return C.int is
      Fact : C.int := 1;
   begin
      Count := Count + 1;
      for K in 1 .. Val loop
         Fact := Fact * K;
      end loop;
      return Fact;
   end Factorial;

   procedure Initialize_API is
      procedure Adainit;
      pragma Import (C, Adainit);
   begin
      Adainit;
   end Initialize_API;

   procedure Finalize_API is
      procedure Adafinal;
      pragma Import (C, Adafinal);
   begin
      Adafinal;
   end Finalize_API;
end API;
```

If the Ada DLL you are building will only be used by Ada applications you do not have to export Ada entities with a C or Stdcall convention. As an example, the previous package could be written as follows:

```
package API is
   Count : Integer := 0;
   function Factorial (Val : Integer) return Integer;

   procedure Initialize_API;
   procedure Finalize_API;
   --  Initialization and Finalization routines.
end API;
```

```
package body API is
   function Factorial (Val : Integer) return Integer is
      Fact : Integer := 1;
   begin
      Count := Count + 1;
      for K in 1 .. Val loop
         Fact := Fact * K;
      end loop;
      return Fact;
   end Factorial;

   ...
   --  The remainder of this package body is unchanged.
end API;
```

Note that if you do not export the Ada entities with a C or Stdcall convention you will have to provide the mangled Ada names in the definition file of the Ada DLL (see Section G.11.6 [Creating the Definition File], page 355).

G.11.3 Ada DLLs and Elaboration

The DLL that you are building contains your Ada code as well as all the routines in the Ada library that are needed by it. The first thing a user of your DLL must do is elaborate the Ada code (see Appendix C [Elaboration Order Handling in GNAT], page 291).

To achieve this you must export an initialization routine (Initialize_API in the previous example), which must be invoked before using any of the DLL services. This elaboration routine must call the Ada elaboration routine adainit generated by the GNAT binder (see Section 4.2.5 [Binding with Non-Ada Main Programs], page 86). See the body of Initialize_Api for an example. Note that the GNAT binder is automatically invoked during the DLL build process by the gnatdll tool (see Section G.11.7 [Using gnatdll], page 356).

When a DLL is loaded, Windows systematically invokes a routine called DllMain. It would therefore be possible to call adainit directly from DllMain without having to provide an explicit initialization routine. Unfortunately, it is not possible to call adainit from the DllMain if your program has library level tasks because access to the DllMain entry point is serialized by the system (that is, only a single thread can execute "through" it at a time), which means that the GNAT run time will deadlock waiting for the newly created task to complete its initialization.

G.11.4 Ada DLLs and Finalization

When the services of an Ada DLL are no longer needed, the client code should invoke the DLL finalization routine, if available. The DLL finalization routine is in charge of releasing all resources acquired by the DLL. In the case of the Ada code contained in the DLL, this is achieved by calling routine `adafinal` generated by the GNAT binder (see Section 4.2.5 [Binding with Non-Ada Main Programs], page 86). See the body of `Finalize_Api` for an example. As already pointed out the GNAT binder is automatically invoked during the DLL build process by the `gnatdll` tool (see Section G.11.7 [Using gnatdll], page 356).

G.11.5 Creating a Spec for Ada DLLs

To use the services exported by the Ada DLL from another programming language (e.g. C), you have to translate the specs of the exported Ada entities in that language. For instance in the case of `API.dll`, the corresponding C header file could look like:

```
extern int *_imp__count;
#define count (*_imp__count)
int factorial (int);
```

It is important to understand that when building an Ada DLL to be used by other Ada applications, you need two different specs for the packages contained in the DLL: one for building the DLL and the other for using the DLL. This is because the `DLL` calling convention is needed to use a variable defined in a DLL, but when building the DLL, the variable must have either the `Ada` or `C` calling convention. As an example consider a DLL comprising the following package `API`:

```
package API is
   Count : Integer := 0;
   ...
   --  Remainder of the package omitted.
end API;
```

After producing a DLL containing package `API`, the spec that must be used to import `API.Count` from Ada code outside of the DLL is:

```
package API is
   Count : Integer;
   pragma Import (DLL, Count);
end API;
```

G.11.6 Creating the Definition File

The definition file is the last file needed to build the DLL. It lists the exported symbols. As an example, the definition file for a DLL containing only package `API` (where all the entities are exported with a `C` calling convention) is:

```
EXPORTS
   count
   factorial
   finalize_api
   initialize_api
```

If the `C` calling convention is missing from package `API`, then the definition file contains the mangled Ada names of the above entities, which in this case are:

```
EXPORTS
    api__count
    api__factorial
    api__finalize_api
    api__initialize_api
```

G.11.7 Using gnatdll

gnatdll is a tool to automate the DLL build process once all the Ada and non-Ada sources that make up your DLL have been compiled. gnatdll is actually in charge of two distinct tasks: build the static import library for the DLL and the actual DLL. The form of the gnatdll command is

```
$ gnatdll [switches] list-of-files [-largs opts]
```

where *list-of-files* is a list of ALI and object files. The object file list must be the exact list of objects corresponding to the non-Ada sources whose services are to be included in the DLL. The ALI file list must be the exact list of ALI files for the corresponding Ada sources whose services are to be included in the DLL. If *list-of-files* is missing, only the static import library is generated.

You may specify any of the following switches to gnatdll:

-a[*address*]

Build a non-relocatable DLL at *address*. If *address* is not specified the default address *0x11000000* will be used. By default, when this switch is missing, gnatdll builds relocatable DLL. We advise the reader to build relocatable DLL.

-b *address*

Set the relocatable DLL base address. By default the address is *0x11000000*.

-bargs *opts*

Binder options. Pass *opts* to the binder.

-d *dllfile*

dllfile is the name of the DLL. This switch must be present for gnatdll to do anything. The name of the generated import library is obtained algorithmically from *dllfile* as shown in the following example: if *dllfile* is xyz.dll, the import library name is libxyz.dll.a. The name of the definition file to use (if not specified by option '-e') is obtained algorithmically from *dllfile* as shown in the following example: if *dllfile* is xyz.dll, the definition file used is xyz.def.

-e *deffile*

deffile is the name of the definition file.

-g

Generate debugging information. This information is stored in the object file and copied from there to the final DLL file by the linker, where it can be read by the debugger. You must use the '-g' switch if you plan on using the debugger or the symbolic stack traceback.

-h

Help mode. Displays gnatdll switch usage information.

-Idir   Direct **gnatdll** to search the *dir* directory for source and object files needed to build the DLL. (see Section 3.3 [Search Paths and the Run-Time Library (RTL)], page 76).

-k   Removes the @*nn* suffix from the import library's exported names, but keeps them for the link names. You must specify this option if you want to use a **Stdcall** function in a DLL for which the @*nn* suffix has been removed. This is the case for most of the Windows NT DLL for example. This option has no effect when '-n' option is specified.

-l *file*   The list of ALI and object files used to build the DLL are listed in *file*, instead of being given in the command line. Each line in *file* contains the name of an ALI or object file.

-n   No Import. Do not create the import library.

-q   Quiet mode. Do not display unnecessary messages.

-v   Verbose mode. Display extra information.

-largs *opts*
       Linker options. Pass *opts* to the linker.

G.11.7.1 gnatdll Example

As an example the command to build a relocatable DLL from 'api.adb' once 'api.adb' has been compiled and 'api.def' created is

```
$ gnatdll -d api.dll api.ali
```

The above command creates two files: 'libapi.dll.a' (the import library) and 'api.dll' (the actual DLL). If you want to create only the DLL, just type:

```
$ gnatdll -d api.dll -n api.ali
```

Alternatively if you want to create just the import library, type:

```
$ gnatdll -d api.dll
```

G.11.7.2 gnatdll behind the Scenes

This section details the steps involved in creating a DLL. **gnatdll** does these steps for you. Unless you are interested in understanding what goes on behind the scenes, you should skip this section.

We use the previous example of a DLL containing the Ada package **API**, to illustrate the steps necessary to build a DLL. The starting point is a set of objects that will make up the DLL and the corresponding ALI files. In the case of this example this means that 'api.o' and 'api.ali' are available. To build a relocatable DLL, **gnatdll** does the following:

1. **gnatdll** builds the base file ('api.base'). A base file gives the information necessary to generate relocation information for the DLL.

```
$ gnatbind -n api
$ gnatlink api -o api.jnk -mdll -Wl,--base-file,api.base
```

In addition to the base file, the **gnatlink** command generates an output file 'api.jnk' which can be discarded. The '-mdll' switch asks **gnatlink** to generate the routines **DllMain** and **DllMainCRTStartup** that are called by the Windows loader when the DLL is loaded into memory.

2. gnatdll uses dlltool (see Section G.11.7.3 [Using dlltool], page 358) to build the export table ('api.exp'). The export table contains the relocation information in a form which can be used during the final link to ensure that the Windows loader is able to place the DLL anywhere in memory.

```
$ dlltool --dllname api.dll --def api.def --base-file api.base \
          --output-exp api.exp
```

3. gnatdll builds the base file using the new export table. Note that gnatbind must be called once again since the binder generated file has been deleted during the previous call to gnatlink.

```
$ gnatbind -n api
$ gnatlink api -o api.jnk api.exp -mdll
      -Wl,--base-file,api.base
```

4. gnatdll builds the new export table using the new base file and generates the DLL import library 'libAPI.dll.a'.

```
$ dlltool --dllname api.dll --def api.def --base-file api.base \
          --output-exp api.exp --output-lib libAPI.a
```

5. Finally gnatdll builds the relocatable DLL using the final export table.

```
$ gnatbind -n api
$ gnatlink api api.exp -o api.dll -mdll
```

G.11.7.3 Using dlltool

dlltool is the low-level tool used by gnatdll to build DLLs and static import libraries. This section summarizes the most common dlltool switches. The form of the dlltool command is

```
$ dlltool [switches]
```

dlltool switches include:

'--base-file *basefile*'

>   Read the base file *basefile* generated by the linker. This switch is used to create a relocatable DLL.

'--def *deffile*'

>   Read the definition file.

'--dllname *name*'

>   Gives the name of the DLL. This switch is used to embed the name of the DLL in the static import library generated by dlltool with switch '--output-lib'.

'-k'   Kill @*nn* from exported names (see Section G.6 [Windows Calling Conventions], page 345 for a discussion about Stdcall-style symbols.

'--help'   Prints the dlltool switches with a concise description.

'--output-exp *exportfile*'

>   Generate an export file *exportfile*. The export file contains the export table (list of symbols in the DLL) and is used to create the DLL.

'--output-lib *libfile*'

>   Generate a static import library *libfile*.

'-v'   Verbose mode.

'--as *assembler-name*'

> Use *assembler-name* as the assembler. The default is as.

G.12 GNAT and Windows Resources

Resources are an easy way to add Windows specific objects to your application. The objects that can be added as resources include:

- menus
- accelerators
- dialog boxes
- string tables
- bitmaps
- cursors
- icons
- fonts

This section explains how to build, compile and use resources.

G.12.1 Building Resources

A resource file is an ASCII file. By convention resource files have an '.rc' extension. The easiest way to build a resource file is to use Microsoft tools such as imagedit.exe to build bitmaps, icons and cursors and dlgedit.exe to build dialogs. It is always possible to build an '.rc' file yourself by writing a resource script.

It is not our objective to explain how to write a resource file. A complete description of the resource script language can be found in the Microsoft documentation.

G.12.2 Compiling Resources

This section describes how to build a GNAT-compatible (COFF) object file containing the resources. This is done using the Resource Compiler windres as follows:

```
$ windres -i myres.rc -o myres.o
```

By default windres will run gcc to preprocess the '.rc' file. You can specify an alternate preprocessor (usually named 'cpp.exe') using the windres '--preprocessor' parameter. A list of all possible options may be obtained by entering the command windres '--help'.

It is also possible to use the Microsoft resource compiler rc.exe to produce a '.res' file (binary resource file). See the corresponding Microsoft documentation for further details. In this case you need to use windres to translate the '.res' file to a GNAT-compatible object file as follows:

```
$ windres -i myres.res -o myres.o
```

G.12.3 Using Resources

To include the resource file in your program just add the GNAT-compatible object file for the resource(s) to the linker arguments. With gnatmake this is done by using the '-largs' option:

```
$ gnatmake myprog -largs myres.o
```

G.13 Debugging a DLL

Debugging a DLL is similar to debugging a standard program. But we have to deal with two different executable parts: the DLL and the program that uses it. We have the following four possibilities:

1. The program and the DLL are built with GCC/GNAT.

2. The program is built with foreign tools and the DLL is built with GCC/GNAT.

3. The program is built with GCC/GNAT and the DLL is built with foreign tools.

4.

In this section we address only cases one and two above. There is no point in trying to debug a DLL with GNU/GDB, if there is no GDB-compatible debugging information in it. To do so you must use a debugger compatible with the tools suite used to build the DLL.

G.13.1 Program and DLL Both Built with GCC/GNAT

This is the simplest case. Both the DLL and the program have GDB compatible debugging information. It is then possible to break anywhere in the process. Let's suppose here that the main procedure is named ada_main and that in the DLL there is an entry point named ada_dll.

The DLL (see Section G.7 [Introduction to Dynamic Link Libraries (DLLs)], page 347) and program must have been built with the debugging information (see GNAT -g switch). Here are the step-by-step instructions for debugging it:

1. Launch GDB on the main program.

        $ gdb -nw ada_main

2. Start the program and stop at the beginning of the main procedure

        (gdb) start

   This step is required to be able to set a breakpoint inside the DLL. As long as the program is not run, the DLL is not loaded. This has the consequence that the DLL debugging information is also not loaded, so it is not possible to set a breakpoint in the DLL.

3. Set a breakpoint inside the DLL

        (gdb) break ada_dll
        (gdb) cont

At this stage a breakpoint is set inside the DLL. From there on you can use the standard approach to debug the whole program (see Chapter 26 [Running and Debugging Ada Programs], page 257).

G.13.2 Program Built with Foreign Tools and DLL Built with GCC/GNAT

In this case things are slightly more complex because it is not possible to start the main program and then break at the beginning to load the DLL and the associated DLL debugging information. It is not possible to break at the beginning of the program because there is no GDB debugging information, and therefore there is no direct way of getting initial control. This section addresses this issue by describing some methods that can be used to break somewhere in the DLL to debug it.

First suppose that the main procedure is named `main` (this is for example some C code built with Microsoft Visual C) and that there is a DLL named `test.dll` containing an Ada entry point named `ada_dll`.

The DLL (see Section G.7 [Introduction to Dynamic Link Libraries (DLLs)], page 347) must have been built with debugging information (see GNAT -g option).

G.13.2.1 Debugging the DLL Directly

1. Find out the executable starting address

   ```
   $ objdump --file-header main.exe
   ```

   The starting address is reported on the last line. For example:

   ```
   main.exe:     file format pei-i386
   architecture: i386, flags 0x0000010a:
   EXEC_P, HAS_DEBUG, D_PAGED
   start address 0x00401010
   ```

2. Launch the debugger on the executable.

   ```
   $ gdb main.exe
   ```

3. Set a breakpoint at the starting address, and launch the program.

   ```
   $ (gdb) break *0x00401010
   $ (gdb) run
   ```

   The program will stop at the given address.

4. Set a breakpoint on a DLL subroutine.

   ```
   (gdb) break ada_dll.adb:45
   ```

   Or if you want to break using a symbol on the DLL, you need first to select the Ada language (language used by the DLL).

   ```
   (gdb) set language ada
   (gdb) break ada_dll
   ```

5. Continue the program.

   ```
   (gdb) cont
   ```

   This will run the program until it reaches the breakpoint that has been set. From that point you can use the standard way to debug a program as described in (see Chapter 26 [Running and Debugging Ada Programs], page 257).

It is also possible to debug the DLL by attaching to a running process.

G.13.2.2 Attaching to a Running Process

With `GDB` it is always possible to debug a running process by attaching to it. It is possible to debug a DLL this way. The limitation of this approach is that the DLL must run long enough to perform the attach operation. It may be useful for instance to insert a time wasting loop in the code of the DLL to meet this criterion.

1. Launch the main program 'main.exe'.

   ```
   $ main
   ```

2. Use the Windows *Task Manager* to find the process ID. Let's say that the process PID for 'main.exe' is 208.

3. Launch gdb.

   ```
   $ gdb
   ```

4. Attach to the running process to be debugged.

      (gdb) `attach 208`

5. Load the process debugging information.

      (gdb) `symbol-file main.exe`

6. Break somewhere in the DLL.

      (gdb) `break ada_dll`

7. Continue process execution.

      (gdb) `cont`

This last step will resume the process execution, and stop at the breakpoint we have set. From there you can use the standard approach to debug a program as described in (see Chapter 26 [Running and Debugging Ada Programs], page 257).

G.14 Setting Stack Size from `gnatlink`

It is possible to specify the program stack size at link time. On modern versions of Windows, starting with XP, this is mostly useful to set the size of the main stack (environment task). The other task stacks are set with pragma Storage_Size or with the `gnatbind -d` command.

Since older versions of Windows (2000, NT4, etc.) do not allow setting the reserve size of individual tasks, the link-time stack size applies to all tasks, and pragma Storage_Size has no effect. In particular, Stack Overflow checks are made against this link-time specified size.

This setting can be done with `gnatlink` using either:

* using '`-Xlinker`' linker option

      $ `gnatlink hello -Xlinker --stack=0x10000,0x1000`

  This sets the stack reserve size to 0x10000 bytes and the stack commit size to 0x1000 bytes.

* using '`-Wl`' linker option

      $ `gnatlink hello -Wl,--stack=0x1000000`

  This sets the stack reserve size to 0x1000000 bytes. Note that with '`-Wl`' option it is not possible to set the stack commit size because the coma is a separator for this option.

G.15 Setting Heap Size from `gnatlink`

Under Windows systems, it is possible to specify the program heap size from `gnatlink` using either:

* using '`-Xlinker`' linker option

      $ `gnatlink hello -Xlinker --heap=0x10000,0x1000`

  This sets the heap reserve size to 0x10000 bytes and the heap commit size to 0x1000 bytes.

* using '`-Wl`' linker option

      $ `gnatlink hello -Wl,--heap=0x1000000`

  This sets the heap reserve size to 0x1000000 bytes. Note that with '`-Wl`' option it is not possible to set the heap commit size because the coma is a separator for this option.

GNU Free Documentation License

Version 1.2, November 2002

Copyright © 2000,2001,2002 Free Software Foundation, Inc.

51 Franklin Street, Fifth Floor, Boston, MA 02110-1301, USA

0. PREAMBLE

The purpose of this License is to make a manual, textbook, or other functional and useful document *free* in the sense of freedom: to assure everyone the effective freedom to copy and redistribute it, with or without modifying it, either commercially or non-commercially. Secondarily, this License preserves for the author and publisher a way to get credit for their work, while not being considered responsible for modifications made by others.

This License is a kind of "copyleft", which means that derivative works of the document must themselves be free in the same sense. It complements the GNU General Public License, which is a copyleft license designed for free software.

We have designed this License in order to use it for manuals for free software, because free software needs free documentation: a free program should come with manuals providing the same freedoms that the software does. But this License is not limited to software manuals; it can be used for any textual work, regardless of subject matter or whether it is published as a printed book. We recommend this License principally for works whose purpose is instruction or reference.

1. APPLICABILITY AND DEFINITIONS

This License applies to any manual or other work, in any medium, that contains a notice placed by the copyright holder saying it can be distributed under the terms of this License. Such a notice grants a world-wide, royalty-free license, unlimited in duration, to use that work under the conditions stated herein. The "Document", below, refers to any such manual or work. Any member of the public is a licensee, and is addressed as "you". You accept the license if you copy, modify or distribute the work in a way requiring permission under copyright law.

A "Modified Version" of the Document means any work containing the Document or a portion of it, either copied verbatim, or with modifications and/or translated into another language.

A "Secondary Section" is a named appendix or a front-matter section of the Document that deals exclusively with the relationship of the publishers or authors of the Document to the Document's overall subject (or to related matters) and contains nothing that could fall directly within that overall subject. (Thus, if the Document is in part a textbook of mathematics, a Secondary Section may not explain any mathematics.) The relationship could be a matter of historical connection with the subject or with related matters, or of legal, commercial, philosophical, ethical or political position regarding them.

The "Invariant Sections" are certain Secondary Sections whose titles are designated, as being those of Invariant Sections, in the notice that says that the Document is released under this License. If a section does not fit the above definition of Secondary then it is not allowed to be designated as Invariant. The Document may contain zero Invariant Sections. If the Document does not identify any Invariant Sections then there are none.

The "Cover Texts" are certain short passages of text that are listed, as Front-Cover Texts or Back-Cover Texts, in the notice that says that the Document is released under this License. A Front-Cover Text may be at most 5 words, and a Back-Cover Text may be at most 25 words.

A "Transparent" copy of the Document means a machine-readable copy, represented in a format whose specification is available to the general public, that is suitable for revising the document straightforwardly with generic text editors or (for images composed of pixels) generic paint programs or (for drawings) some widely available drawing editor, and that is suitable for input to text formatters or for automatic translation to a variety of formats suitable for input to text formatters. A copy made in an otherwise Transparent file format whose markup, or absence of markup, has been arranged to thwart or discourage subsequent modification by readers is not Transparent. An image format is not Transparent if used for any substantial amount of text. A copy that is not "Transparent" is called "Opaque".

Examples of suitable formats for Transparent copies include plain ASCII without markup, Texinfo input format, LaTeX input format, SGML or XML using a publicly available DTD, and standard-conforming simple HTML, PostScript or PDF designed for human modification. Examples of transparent image formats include PNG, XCF and JPG. Opaque formats include proprietary formats that can be read and edited only by proprietary word processors, SGML or XML for which the DTD and/or processing tools are not generally available, and the machine-generated HTML, PostScript or PDF produced by some word processors for output purposes only.

The "Title Page" means, for a printed book, the title page itself, plus such following pages as are needed to hold, legibly, the material this License requires to appear in the title page. For works in formats which do not have any title page as such, "Title Page" means the text near the most prominent appearance of the work's title, preceding the beginning of the body of the text.

A section "Entitled XYZ" means a named subunit of the Document whose title either is precisely XYZ or contains XYZ in parentheses following text that translates XYZ in another language. (Here XYZ stands for a specific section name mentioned below, such as "Acknowledgements", "Dedications", "Endorsements", or "History".) To "Preserve the Title" of such a section when you modify the Document means that it remains a section "Entitled XYZ" according to this definition.

The Document may include Warranty Disclaimers next to the notice which states that this License applies to the Document. These Warranty Disclaimers are considered to be included by reference in this License, but only as regards disclaiming warranties: any other implication that these Warranty Disclaimers may have is void and has no effect on the meaning of this License.

2. VERBATIM COPYING

You may copy and distribute the Document in any medium, either commercially or noncommercially, provided that this License, the copyright notices, and the license notice saying this License applies to the Document are reproduced in all copies, and that you add no other conditions whatsoever to those of this License. You may not use technical measures to obstruct or control the reading or further copying of the copies you make or distribute. However, you may accept compensation in exchange for copies. If you distribute a large enough number of copies you must also follow the conditions in section 3.

You may also lend copies, under the same conditions stated above, and you may publicly display copies.

3. COPYING IN QUANTITY

If you publish printed copies (or copies in media that commonly have printed covers) of the Document, numbering more than 100, and the Document's license notice requires Cover Texts, you must enclose the copies in covers that carry, clearly and legibly, all these Cover Texts: Front-Cover Texts on the front cover, and Back-Cover Texts on the back cover. Both covers must also clearly and legibly identify you as the publisher of these copies. The front cover must present the full title with all words of the title equally prominent and visible. You may add other material on the covers in addition. Copying with changes limited to the covers, as long as they preserve the title of the Document and satisfy these conditions, can be treated as verbatim copying in other respects.

If the required texts for either cover are too voluminous to fit legibly, you should put the first ones listed (as many as fit reasonably) on the actual cover, and continue the rest onto adjacent pages.

If you publish or distribute Opaque copies of the Document numbering more than 100, you must either include a machine-readable Transparent copy along with each Opaque copy, or state in or with each Opaque copy a computer-network location from which the general network-using public has access to download using public-standard network protocols a complete Transparent copy of the Document, free of added material. If you use the latter option, you must take reasonably prudent steps, when you begin distribution of Opaque copies in quantity, to ensure that this Transparent copy will remain thus accessible at the stated location until at least one year after the last time you distribute an Opaque copy (directly or through your agents or retailers) of that edition to the public.

It is requested, but not required, that you contact the authors of the Document well before redistributing any large number of copies, to give them a chance to provide you with an updated version of the Document.

4. MODIFICATIONS

You may copy and distribute a Modified Version of the Document under the conditions of sections 2 and 3 above, provided that you release the Modified Version under precisely this License, with the Modified Version filling the role of the Document, thus licensing distribution and modification of the Modified Version to whoever possesses a copy of it. In addition, you must do these things in the Modified Version:

A. Use in the Title Page (and on the covers, if any) a title distinct from that of the Document, and from those of previous versions (which should, if there were any, be listed in the History section of the Document). You may use the same title as a previous version if the original publisher of that version gives permission.

B. List on the Title Page, as authors, one or more persons or entities responsible for authorship of the modifications in the Modified Version, together with at least five of the principal authors of the Document (all of its principal authors, if it has fewer than five), unless they release you from this requirement.

C. State on the Title page the name of the publisher of the Modified Version, as the publisher.

D. Preserve all the copyright notices of the Document.

E. Add an appropriate copyright notice for your modifications adjacent to the other copyright notices.

F. Include, immediately after the copyright notices, a license notice giving the public permission to use the Modified Version under the terms of this License, in the form shown in the Addendum below.

G. Preserve in that license notice the full lists of Invariant Sections and required Cover Texts given in the Document's license notice.

H. Include an unaltered copy of this License.

I. Preserve the section Entitled "History", Preserve its Title, and add to it an item stating at least the title, year, new authors, and publisher of the Modified Version as given on the Title Page. If there is no section Entitled "History" in the Document, create one stating the title, year, authors, and publisher of the Document as given on its Title Page, then add an item describing the Modified Version as stated in the previous sentence.

J. Preserve the network location, if any, given in the Document for public access to a Transparent copy of the Document, and likewise the network locations given in the Document for previous versions it was based on. These may be placed in the "History" section. You may omit a network location for a work that was published at least four years before the Document itself, or if the original publisher of the version it refers to gives permission.

K. For any section Entitled "Acknowledgements" or "Dedications", Preserve the Title of the section, and preserve in the section all the substance and tone of each of the contributor acknowledgements and/or dedications given therein.

L. Preserve all the Invariant Sections of the Document, unaltered in their text and in their titles. Section numbers or the equivalent are not considered part of the section titles.

M. Delete any section Entitled "Endorsements". Such a section may not be included in the Modified Version.

N. Do not retitle any existing section to be Entitled "Endorsements" or to conflict in title with any Invariant Section.

O. Preserve any Warranty Disclaimers.

If the Modified Version includes new front-matter sections or appendices that qualify as Secondary Sections and contain no material copied from the Document, you may at your option designate some or all of these sections as invariant. To do this, add their titles to the list of Invariant Sections in the Modified Version's license notice. These titles must be distinct from any other section titles.

You may add a section Entitled "Endorsements", provided it contains nothing but endorsements of your Modified Version by various parties—for example, statements of peer review or that the text has been approved by an organization as the authoritative definition of a standard.

You may add a passage of up to five words as a Front-Cover Text, and a passage of up to 25 words as a Back-Cover Text, to the end of the list of Cover Texts in the Modified Version. Only one passage of Front-Cover Text and one of Back-Cover Text may be added by (or through arrangements made by) any one entity. If the Document already includes a cover text for the same cover, previously added by you or by arrangement made by the same entity you are acting on behalf of, you may not add another; but you may replace the old one, on explicit permission from the previous publisher that added the old one.

The author(s) and publisher(s) of the Document do not by this License give permission to use their names for publicity for or to assert or imply endorsement of any Modified Version.

5. COMBINING DOCUMENTS

You may combine the Document with other documents released under this License, under the terms defined in section 4 above for modified versions, provided that you include in the combination all of the Invariant Sections of all of the original documents, unmodified, and list them all as Invariant Sections of your combined work in its license notice, and that you preserve all their Warranty Disclaimers.

The combined work need only contain one copy of this License, and multiple identical Invariant Sections may be replaced with a single copy. If there are multiple Invariant Sections with the same name but different contents, make the title of each such section unique by adding at the end of it, in parentheses, the name of the original author or publisher of that section if known, or else a unique number. Make the same adjustment to the section titles in the list of Invariant Sections in the license notice of the combined work.

In the combination, you must combine any sections Entitled "History" in the various original documents, forming one section Entitled "History"; likewise combine any sections Entitled "Acknowledgements", and any sections Entitled "Dedications". You must delete all sections Entitled "Endorsements."

6. COLLECTIONS OF DOCUMENTS

You may make a collection consisting of the Document and other documents released under this License, and replace the individual copies of this License in the various documents with a single copy that is included in the collection, provided that you follow the rules of this License for verbatim copying of each of the documents in all other respects.

You may extract a single document from such a collection, and distribute it individually under this License, provided you insert a copy of this License into the extracted document, and follow this License in all other respects regarding verbatim copying of that document.

7. AGGREGATION WITH INDEPENDENT WORKS

A compilation of the Document or its derivatives with other separate and independent documents or works, in or on a volume of a storage or distribution medium, is called an "aggregate" if the copyright resulting from the compilation is not used to limit the legal rights of the compilation's users beyond what the individual works permit. When the Document is included in an aggregate, this License does not apply to the other works in the aggregate which are not themselves derivative works of the Document.

If the Cover Text requirement of section 3 is applicable to these copies of the Document, then if the Document is less than one half of the entire aggregate, the Document's Cover Texts may be placed on covers that bracket the Document within the aggregate, or the electronic equivalent of covers if the Document is in electronic form. Otherwise they must appear on printed covers that bracket the whole aggregate.

8. TRANSLATION

Translation is considered a kind of modification, so you may distribute translations of the Document under the terms of section 4. Replacing Invariant Sections with translations requires special permission from their copyright holders, but you may include translations of some or all Invariant Sections in addition to the original versions of these Invariant Sections. You may include a translation of this License, and all the license notices in the Document, and any Warranty Disclaimers, provided that you also include the original English version of this License and the original versions of those notices and disclaimers. In case of a disagreement between the translation and the original version of this License or a notice or disclaimer, the original version will prevail.

If a section in the Document is Entitled "Acknowledgements", "Dedications", or "History", the requirement (section 4) to Preserve its Title (section 1) will typically require changing the actual title.

9. TERMINATION

You may not copy, modify, sublicense, or distribute the Document except as expressly provided for under this License. Any other attempt to copy, modify, sublicense or distribute the Document is void, and will automatically terminate your rights under this License. However, parties who have received copies, or rights, from you under this License will not have their licenses terminated so long as such parties remain in full compliance.

10. FUTURE REVISIONS OF THIS LICENSE

The Free Software Foundation may publish new, revised versions of the GNU Free Documentation License from time to time. Such new versions will be similar in spirit to the present version, but may differ in detail to address new problems or concerns. See http://www.gnu.org/copyleft/.

Each version of the License is given a distinguishing version number. If the Document specifies that a particular numbered version of this License "or any later version" applies to it, you have the option of following the terms and conditions either of that specified version or of any later version that has been published (not as a draft) by the Free Software Foundation. If the Document does not specify a version number of this License, you may choose any version ever published (not as a draft) by the Free Software Foundation.

ADDENDUM: How to use this License for your documents

To use this License in a document you have written, include a copy of the License in the document and put the following copyright and license notices just after the title page:

```
Copyright (C)  year  your name.
Permission is granted to copy, distribute and/or modify this document
under the terms of the GNU Free Documentation License, Version 1.2
or any later version published by the Free Software Foundation;
with no Invariant Sections, no Front-Cover Texts, and no Back-Cover
Texts.  A copy of the license is included in the section entitled ''GNU
Free Documentation License''.
```

If you have Invariant Sections, Front-Cover Texts and Back-Cover Texts, replace the "with...Texts." line with this:

```
with the Invariant Sections being list their titles, with
the Front-Cover Texts being list, and with the Back-Cover Texts
being list.
```

If you have Invariant Sections without Cover Texts, or some other combination of the three, merge those two alternatives to suit the situation.

If your document contains nontrivial examples of program code, we recommend releasing these examples in parallel under your choice of free software license, such as the GNU General Public License, to permit their use in free software.

Index

A

B

C

D

E

Table of Contents

24831316R00212

Made in the USA
Lexington, KY
02 August 2013